CUMBRIAN DISCOVERY

BY THE SAME AUTHOR:

CUMBERLAND HERITAGE

SAMUEL TAYLOR COLERIDGE: A BONDAGE OF OPIUM

CUMBRIAN DISCOVERY

by

MOLLY LEFEBURE

LONDON
VICTOR GOLLANCZ LTD
1977

ISBN 0 575 02235 3

Printed in Great Britain by
The Camelot Press Ltd, Southampton

FOR A. W.,
the last person on earth
to need a guide to
this part of
the world!

CONTENTS

Part Four Furness

ILLUSTRATIONS

Following page 128

Following page 256

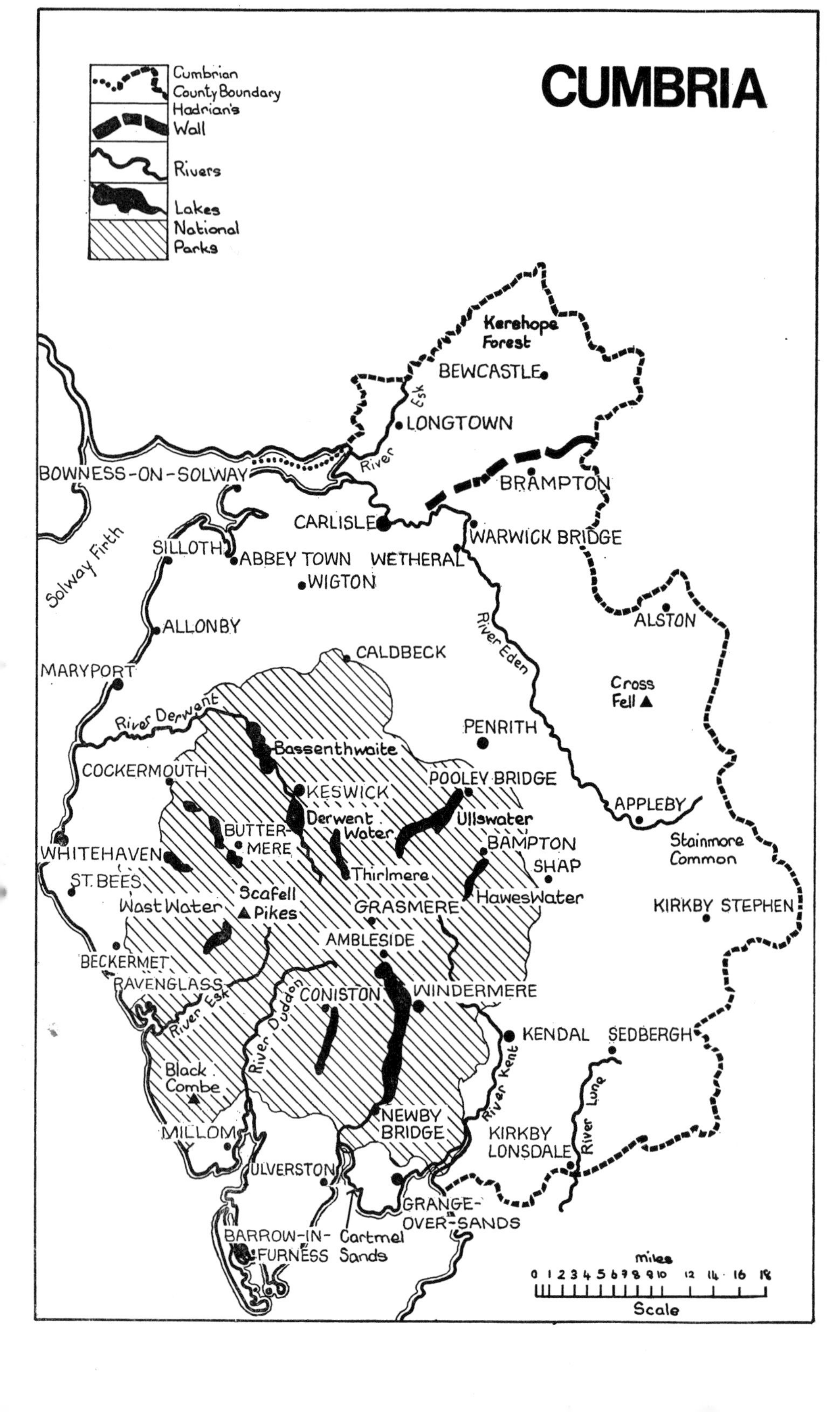
CUMBRIA
Cumbrian County Boundary
Hadrian's Wall
Rivers
Lakes
National Parks
Kershope Forest
BEWCASTLE
Esk
LONGTOWN
River
BOWNESS-ON-SOLWAY
BRAMPTON
CARLISLE
WARWICK BRIDGE
SILLOTH
ABBEY TOWN
WETHERAL
WIGTON
Solway Firth
ALLONBY
ALSTON
River Eden
CALDBECK
MARYPORT
Cross Fell
River Derwent
PENRITH
Bassenthwaite
COCKERMOUTH
KESWICK
POOLEY BRIDGE
Ullswater
Derwent Water
APPLEBY
BUTTER-MERE
WHITEHAVEN
BAMPTON
Stainmore Common
SHAP
Thirlmere
ST. BEES
Scafell Pikes
Hawes Water
Wast Water
GRASMERE
KIRKBY STEPHEN
AMBLESIDE
BECKERMET
RAVENGLASS
CONISTON
WINDERMERE
River Esk
River Duddon
KENDAL
SEDBERGH
Black Combe
River Kent
River Lune
NEWBY BRIDGE
MILLOM
KIRKBY LONSDALE
ULVERSTON
GRANGE-OVER-SANDS
BARROW-IN-FURNESS
Cartmel Sands
miles
0 1 2 3 4 5 6 7 8 9 10 12 14 16 18
Scale

ACKNOWLEDGEMENTS

IT WOULD BE impossible to acknowledge, here in cold print, all the help that I have received with this book: I can do no more than express my sincere thanks to those many, many people who have so generously placed at my disposal their valuable time and knowledge.

I am particularly indebted to Mr Warren Elsby and his assistants, County Library, Keswick; the City Library, Tullie House, Carlisle; the Records Office, Carlisle; the British Museum; the Victoria and Albert Museum; Miss Phyllis Mayson; Mr George Hartop; the Charles Lamb Society; David Wright and Hodder & Stoughton Ltd., for permission to use Mr Wright's poem "Storm".

The inclusion of maps in this book has posed a problem: Cumbria is such a very large region that any attempt to provide a detailed map would necessitate the reduction of it in size to an extent which would render it virtually useless. The map shown opposite is intended purely as a means whereby newcomers to Cumbria may obtain a quick, basic idea of the general topography, and the situation of the salient towns and villages mentioned in the text.

INTRODUCTION

ROLL THE GREAT WHEEL

. . . for I would walk alone
Under the quiet stars . . .
and I would stand,
If the night blackened with a coming storm,
Beneath some rock, listening to notes that are
The ghostly language of the ancient earth,
Or make their dim abode in distant winds.

William Wordsworth, *The Prelude*, II

Not Man's hills but all for themselves the sky and the clouds and a few wild creatures.

Dorothy Wordsworth, *Grasmere Journal*: Friday 23 April 1802

WILL IT RAIN?

Yes, it will rain. Every kind of rain that Heaven has invented falls upon Cumbria.

Indeed it is to rain that Cumbria is indebted for so much of its beauty: its clouds and cataracts, its magical changes of mood and light, its everlasting music of waters.

In counterpoint to the mysterious, loud-singing element which we call water, is the stone of Cumbria. Stone jutting and thrusting in peaks and pinnacles; stone quivering in a myriad fragments on the shilly-beds, running like water itself when stirred; stone gouged and chiselled by the glaciers of the Ice Ages to rival the Gothic majesty of cathedrals; stone weathered down the centuries to assume the grotesque fantasy of Aztec monuments. Wherever the eye travels, behold, stone.

Stone reverently placed in sacred circles by Bronze Age man; stone used by Romans to build time-defying walls and roads; stone crosses carved by early Christians who intertwined ancient pagan symbols with those of the new faith; stone for Norman abbeys and castles; stone handled by generations of dalesmen for sheepfolds and farmsteads, churches and cottages, bridges and mills; the very stuff of Cumbrian lives.

Stones in the tranquil dale bottoms; stones clustered in precarious colonies on ledges and in gulleys; stones crouched in their millions on the storm-swept summits of the central fells, or sitting out the long white nights of midsummer in rapt silence under a sky that never grows truly dark. Stones by the multitude; a vast concourse of stones.

Gradually, irresistibly, stone fills us with a sense of awe. We feel tempted, obliged almost, to succumb to the conviction that, dormant and silent as it is, each stone nonetheless has an invisible yet steady pulse throbbing at its centre. And we find ourselves repeating the lines of Henry Vaughan,[1]

> So hills and valleys into singing break,
> And though poor stones have neither speech nor tong,
> While active winds and streams both run and speak,
> Yet stones are deep in admiration.

Intermingling with this flowing music of streams, with the speaking of upland breezes and the plaintive cries of the sheep which roam both high and low, sound the voices of poets: of wild Celtic bards, whose haunting harp-strings vibrate in the random flurries of rain that fly out from crags and gulleys half hidden in mist; of Viking sagas chanted by every beck and force; of keening laments and ballads which blood-scented Border winds still intone on wild nights; and of the Lake Poets themselves. Above all, the voice of one who stands in the valley in the rain, an imperishable spirit transfixed under his umbrella, rejoicing in the showers that "darkening, or brightening, as they fly from hill to hill, are not less grateful to the eye than finely interwoven passages of gay and sad music are touching to the ear".[2] Thus we see Wordsworth, and hear him too, composing aloud, as was his habit,

> Army of Clouds! ye wingèd host in troops
> Ascending from behind the motionless brow
> Of that tall rock, as from a hidden world,
> Oh whither with such eagerness of speed?
> What seek ye, or what shun ye? of the gale
> Companions, fear ye to be left behind,
> Or racing o'er your blue ethereal field
> Contend ye with each other? of the sea
> Children, thus post ye over vale and height
> To sink upon your mother's lap—and rest?
> Or were ye rightlier hailed, when first
> mine eyes
> Beheld in your impetuous march the likeness
> Of a wide army pressing on to meet
> Or overtake some unknown enemy? . . .
> Whence, whence, ye Clouds? this eagerness
> of speed?
> Speak, silent creatures.—They are gone,
> are fled,
> Buried together in yon gloomy mass
> That loads the middle heaven; and clear
> and bright
> And vacant doth the region which they
> thronged
> Appear; a calm descent of sky conducting

Down to the unapproachable abyss,
Down to that hidden gulf from which they
rose
To vanish—fleet as days and months and
years,
Fleet as the generations of mankind . . .[3]

For many enthusiasts Wordsworth means the Lake Country, and the Lake Country means Wordsworth. There is much truth in this. Region and poet have indeed become inextricably part of one another. Wordsworth is rooted in the very rock of the region, like one of those trees that you sometimes find miraculously growing from a huge boulder in an ancient Cumbrian wood; the tree rooted in a cleft of the rock so that, over the course of time, the living roots have penetrated the very core of the rock. Rock and tree have become as one; the tree seeming to be a living expression of the primeval philosophy of the rock. The rock reposes motionless and voiceless and eternal; the ephemeral tree stirs and moves and sings and sighs and voices aloud all that the rock holds at its heart.

However, the vast majority of visitors, let it be confessed, come to Cumbria and the Lake Country knowing and caring next to nothing about Wordsworth and blithely supposing that they are going to get through their visit without having to bother themselves with *him.*

"Wordsworth? Dead as a dodo. I've come here to relax; sit by a lake; have a good time. No ruddy Wordsworth for me, thank you. All I want is . . ."

"We are upon the outset of several days' journey of pleasure, from which, by the majority of those who undertake it, pleasure and amusement alone are desired."

The voice booms forth; coming very loud and strong apparently from the other side of an old wall; so that for one wild moment we think that a bull, in a field, is bellowing at us. Before we have recovered from being boomed at so loudly and fiercely, the voice is booming again; until it dawns upon us that we are being spoken to, or, more correctly, boomed at by somebody. And sure enough, there now rises up into view, from behind the wall, a tall, thin old man, with the longest legs in the world, a big beaky nose and a face red from being endlessly exposed to wind and rain. He furthermore has this tremendously powerful, resonant voice:

"After all, it is upon the *mind* which a traveller brings along with him that his acquisitions, whether of pleasure or profit, must principally depend—— May I be allowed a few words on this subject?"

Under the circumstances we can scarcely say, "No"! So he carries on talking.

This is William Wordsworth; not come back from the dead, for he has never died; he lives eternally here in Cumbria, and not exclusively among the Lakes, either; he stalks with those enormously long striding legs of his across all of his native Cumbria, from the Border down to the Duddon estuary. It is pointless to try to ignore him; he will not be ignored. Fatuous to accuse him of being out-of-date; what he says may sound old fashioned on the surface, but basically he is always right when he talks about his native country. No use repeating that you aren't interested in poets; he will merely draw closer, to boom directly into your ear; a voice that you can't escape, however much you may try.

When he is reciting his poetry, his voice is great music; at other times, at this present moment for instance, he tends to become more than a trifle pompous (what Coleridge once irreverently called Wordsworth's "my-brother-the-Dean-and-I voice"). But whichever voice he is using, you find yourself listening; you *have* to listen. The speaker is so magnificently convinced that he is absolutely right in everything that he says. Moreover he takes it completely for granted that you will listen, respectfully, until he has finished what he is saying, to the bitter end. "Mr Wordsworth is *never* interrupted," as Mrs Wordsworth warned young Mr Keats.

Thus, on booms the Master (as the ladies of his family-circle adoringly called him); propounding to us how we should approach his native Lakes and mountains and how to extract the utmost appreciation from our visit.

By approach, Wordsworth does not mean anything so mundane as a given route into Cumbria. He is referring to the pilgrim's spiritual preparation for an advance upon the Promised Land; the essential purifications and self-chastisements that must be endured before the Supreme Moment of entry is experienced. The flesh must be well subjugated; the mind brought under control; the sensibilities refined to a degree of perceptivity and receptivity unknown to those whose holiday ambitions stop at sunny diversions upon the beaches of Torquay or St Tropez.

Not that the Master is so impossibly high-minded that he dismisses entirely the notion that people who come to Cumbria for a holiday do so with the basic intention of enjoying themselves. Pleasure, amusement, these things are looked for; well enough; such human indulgences must be taken into account, even by a poet who himself resembles a

Peak so high
Above us, and so distant in its height . . .
The loneliest place we have among the clouds . . .[4]

"But," continues the master, bearing our frailties in mind, "But . . . I will venture to say . . . that Nature will be far more bountiful in granting to tourists what they look for if they aspire at something beyond a superficial entertainment. . . . The Soul of objects must be communicated with."[5]

How to communicate thus? By doing things the hard way, of course. Above all, by walking. Again and again the tourist is strictly ordered to walk; especially where the scenery is at its most delectable.

Yet even Wordsworth had to face the fact that there were some shameless persons who simply refused to get down from their carriages. At these a weary Wordsworthian sarcasm was directed. All very well for these insensitive trippers to be "contented with what they can collect with their eyes from the barouch box or from the seat of the open Landau . . . as the several vehicles whirl along at the rate of 7 miles an hour—But if the Author is to proceed at this rate what must become of the Book which he has undertaken to write——?"[6] (Ah, what indeed? murmurs Lefebure, massaging her weary feet.)

Nevertheless, Wordsworth was perfectly correct. Those who merely see this marvellous part of the world from a vehicle (be it a landau at seven miles an hour, or a motor car at thirty) will never see it properly. This is a country where the pedestrian is the rich aristocrat revelling in limitless wealth, while the motorist is the poor beggar who must make-do with pathetically little.

The famous meres of the Lake Country lie deep within the rocky recesses of Cumbria, like a hoard of jewels within the heart of an ancient fortress. Every visitor to Cumbria has these waters and mountains of the region's interior as a prime goal, but to see only the Lake Country while leaving the rest of Cumbria unexplored is to have enjoyed but a fraction of one of the most visually and historically exciting regions in the western world.

This mistake was certainly not made by the Master. When at last he came to apply himself, in his rôle of Guide to the Lakes, to the "tedious task of supplying the Tourist" with factual routes of approach, Wordsworth produced a variety of suggestions, which would introduce the visitor, by way of preamble, to the manifold beauties and fascinations of north-eastern Westmorland; of the River Lune and pretty Kirkby Lonsdale; of the great and ancient highway over Stanemoor; of Carlisle and the West Cumberland coastal plain; of the valleys of the Irthing and the Eden; of Wetherby and Nunnery and Corby and Croglin; of the Sands, Ulverston, Cartmel and Furness.

Wordsworth sagely urged his disciples to discover the outer reaches of Cumbria before penetrating the lake-gleaming centre, "For, by this way of approach, the traveller faces the grander features of the scene, and is gradually conducted into its most sublime recesses."

Thus a carefully prepared, progressive crescendo of effect, ritualistic almost, is achieved; Cumbria opens up, stage by stage and step by step; a succession of marvels, one after another unfolding themselves before us as we travel: "from the circumference to the centre . . . from the sea or plain country to the . . . grand mountains".

"But," most daringly interrupts a reader who, in preparation for his intended exploration of this wonderland has taken the trouble to procure and inspect a map, "how can anyone speak of mountains in this part of the world when there isn't a single summit in the whole area that is much over 3,000 feet! Even Scafell Pike, the highest of the lot, is no more than a mere 3,210 feet!"

There is no denying that, in terms of the Himalaya or the Rockies, the Sierra Nevada or the Alps, these Cumbrian heights are not within laughing distance of being mountains. Yet mountains are not measured by cold statistics alone. Climbers with world-wide experience confirm that the excitement and awe (not to mention the danger) of being among and upon mountains is experienced in the Lake District as fully as among any of the giant ranges. This is because the Lake District is a great mountainous region reduced to miniature; the reduction in size carried out so perfectly to scale that every peak, pass, lake and valley is in exactly related proportion, thereby achieving a miraculous *trompe d'œil* effect. Visitors who come here anticipating mere mole-hills are confounded.

The master's retort to disparagement of his native mountains was lofty. "In magnitude and grandeur they are individually inferior to the most celebrated of those in some other parts . . . but, in the combinations which they make, towering above each other, or lifting themselves in ridges like the waves of a tumultuous sea, and in the beauty and variety of their surfaces and colours, they are surpassed by none."[7]

Buttressed thus, we will speak, therefore, with total confidence of these mountains which, cradling deep and narrow lakes in their glacier-carved valley basins, leap abruptly upward from the Duddon estuary in the south, the Solway Firth coastal strip in the west, the Carlisle-guarded plain to the north and the gentle lowlands of Burneside, Kendal and Levens in the south-east.

Strictly, there are no lakes in the Lake District. Meres and waters and tarns abound, but nobody spoke of lakes, in this part of the world, until the tourists began to arrive in the late eighteenth century. They dubbed these northern waters "lakes" and the region rapidly became known to the outside world as the Lake Country. Today, when we have all become less poetic than formerly, it is usually spoken of as the Lake District.

Three counties have hitherto contributed to the Lake District: Cumberland, Westmorland and Lancashire North-of-the-Sands (that part of Lancashire historically known as Furness). The three counties met at the Three Shire Stone, some 50 yards short of the summit of the Wrynose Pass (the stone itself is an unimpressive upright pillar inscribed, "Lancashire, W. F. 1818". The name, Wrynose, is of greater significance: *wrey*, or *rey*, a boundary; *ness* [old local pronunciation, *neese*], a long snout of fellside: The Wrey Neese). In the recent reorganization of counties the three former so-called Lake Counties have been amalgamated to form Cumbria; an ancient name for the region now revived.

Yet Cumbria is not synonymous with the Lake District, although the Lake District lies within Cumbria.

It is fascinating, and perhaps also bewildering, to note that the actual boundaries of the famous Lake District have never been categorically defined. Each person who knows and loves the district has his own idea of where it begins and ends: no two people can be found to agree on this vexed subject.

When all is said and done, as good a definition of the Lake District as any, in our era, is the boundary of the National Park (the Lake District National Park came into being in 1951). The definition of a national park, in England and Wales, is an area of scenically significant country which is conserved with special care for the enjoyment and benefit of all. A national park, however, is not nationally owned: thus, while the Park Authority, the National Trust, Forestry Commission and Nature Conservancy all hold land in the Lake District National Park, most of the Park is owned by farmers and other private individuals, and public access rights are no different from those prevailing outside the Park.

It was Wordsworth who first popularized the image of the Lake Country as a great wheel with the mountain ridges radiating, spoke-like, from a central hub.[8] Wordsworth, when he escorted Samuel Taylor Coleridge on a tour of the Lakes in 1799, in effect conducted Coleridge on an inspection of this wheel; first stalking along the rim, by the eastern confines of Ullswater and Haweswater; from thence skirting the foot of Windermere by Cartmel into Furness; then, abandoning the rim, and making use of the valleys rather than the fell spokes, exploring the inside of the wheel; arriving at last at the very heart of the hub, the central massif, then moving back towards the rim again, returning to Ullswater and Eusemere at a point very close to where the two poets had first stepped on to the wheel's rim.

How did the Lake Country originally come into being? First, some 500 million years ago, came the Skiddaw Slate, which started as the sludgy mud-rock bed of a warm, shallow, silting sea. Fossilized, this mud-rock now forms most of the District's northern mountains, with Black Combe as an unexpected outcrop in the south. Bassenthwaite, Crummock and Loweswater are all enfolded by Skiddaw Slate, Derwent Water and Buttermere almost entirely so, Ennerdale and Ullswater partly so, too. Skiddaw and Saddleback, Grisedale Pike, the Newlands Fells, Grasmoor and Whinlatter Fells are all of this fossilized fabric; they are among the oldest mountains in the world.

After the mud-rock of the shallow silting sea came volcanoes, discharging vast showers of lava, ashes and débris, which now form the so-called Borrowdale Volcanic Rock of the central massif. Scafell and the Pikes, Gable, Honister, the Langdales, Helvellyn and High Street, Borrowdale, Upper Eskdale, Wasdale, Dunnerdale, Upper Patterdale and Mardale are all Borrowdale Volcanic.

The actual volcanoes from which the Borrowdale Volcanic erupted are perceptible only to the eyes of experts. We are told, however, that the craggy crown of Castle Head, Keswick, may well be a plug which solidified inside a volcano vent.

This volcanic débris formed a hard crust over the original mud-rock, which bent into folds and tented up into a dome, then sank under a warm sea again.

Next developed what is now the Coniston Limestone, composed of volcanic waste and a mixture of pebbles and coral from the shallow, all-embracing sea (Coniston Limestone runs in a narrow belt from the Duddon Estuary across the district to Shap).

The sea deepened, then silted up again; thus the Silurian slates and grits were formed. These are found almost entirely in Westmorland, providing the scenery round Windermere and the greater part of Coniston; a tender, pretty, happy landscape. This Silurian group is the youngest of the four major rock groups of the Lake District; 360 million years old, or thereabouts.

Earthquakes now tented these four rock groups into a vast pyramid. Molten rock masses boiled and seethed, forming those pockets of granite, granophyte, gabbro and the rest, which appear unexpectedly in various parts of the district. This was one of the great mountain-building epochs of the earth's history.

The future Lake District lay hoisted up in the air and for 50 or 60 million years the elements gnawed at it and peeled it, as Herdwick sheep in a hard winter gnaw bark from trees. Then everything sank under water again.

The new sea in its turn silted up; steamy tropical forests of giant ferns and feathery-foliaged trees grew, crashing with old age into the mud from which they had sprung, fossilizing to form the Maryport–Whitehaven coalfields. The ever-rising ground dried out, becoming bare and hard; a desiccated land which we now greet as Old Red Sandstone. Fresh earth upheavals raised the Old Red Sandstone and the rest into a new and enormous dome. Once again the elements with tireless hands and teeth massaged and gnawed the dome's surface: back to light came the Silurian rocks, the Coniston Limestone, the Volcanic rocks and the Skiddaw slate, now with an irregular band of Carboniferous rock round the edges. Débris from the centre of the dome dispersed on to the outer rim to form new Red Sandstone.

The dome, eroded over the ages, sank lower; lagoons spread, at last everything was under water once more. This new ocean, in due course, silted up exactly as the earlier oceans had done. For the next 100 million years the future Lake District was a steamy swampland. Then, perhaps some 60 million years ago, there was a period (known as the Tertiary) of fresh and violent earth convulsions and up from the sea heaved land again, in basic form more like the Lake District we know today; a huge, tilted rock wheel with an outward drainage movement of valleys and spurs. By the close of the Tertiary period, perhaps two million years ago, the Lakeland giants, Scafell, Helvellyn, and Skiddaw, must have stood at virtually their present height.

The true sculpting of the Lake District, as we know it, was the labour of a succession of Ice Ages; at least three, perhaps five of them, each separated one from the other by long, warmer periods. At the zenith of each Ice Age the District lay submerged under a giant ice-cap.

From time to time a sculptor has to stop work to sweep away the detritus which has collected on his studio floor. Similarly, the rock débris of each Ice Age was swept, or scoured away, by the glaciers of the next. The general movement of the ice was outward, in the direction of the lowlands; thus the alluvia of the Lake District was carried off to be dumped on distant plains.

So thorough was the sweeping and scraping process of the last Ice Age (which ended about 15,000 years ago) that no trace remains of the débris of previous glacifications. Only the residue of the final glaciers remains: those humps, ridges and mounds which geologists call "moraines"; incessantly eroded by subsequent winds and waters, and therefore greatly diminished in size since the ice deposited them.

Also left behind by the ever-moving ice (a movement so slow that to the eye it would have seemed motionless) are those huge, isolated rocks which never cease to fascinate; petrified pre-historic monsters:

> As a huge stone is sometimes seen to lie
> Crouched on the bald tip of some eminence;
> Wonder to all who do the same espy:
> By what means it could thither come, and whence;
> So that it seems a thing endued with sense:
> Like a sea-beast crawled forth, that on a shelf
> Of rock or sand reposeth, there to sun itself...[9]

You will find these stone sea-beasts sunning themselves, or patiently enduring the rain, throughout the District.

Thus to the ice, then, we owe this marvellously sculptured landscape: the deep, narrow, U-shaped dales; the small, high, tributary, or "hanging" valleys; the magical tarns which so often lie in them; the echo-filled corries, the waterfalls, the soaring Gothic of the crags of Scafell, Great End, Great Gable and Pillar, to mention but a few of those famous façades which in grandeur, nobility and sheer exciting beauty rival anything that Chartres, Durham or Toledo offer.

And, of course, there are the lakes; rock basins gouged out by the successive Ice Ages and dammed by the moraine of the last of these.

Yet ice should not be named as sole artist-craftsman of the Lake

Country. The winds and the rain have also worked here endlessly; modelling, perhaps, rather than carving. The resultant masterpieces are to be seen everywhere among the mountains.

These wonders and beauties have been created by natural forces, over millions of years. The landscape of the Lake Country has been, from the first, ever changing. Even as we look at the mountains today natural changes are imperceptibly continuing: the wind, the rain, in winter the frost, ice and snow; in summer the heat of the sun, all work ceaselessly on the fell-faces. The weather works at the mountains incessantly, like an obsessive artist who is never satisfied; but we ourselves, transient creatures, do not live long enough to grasp the full significance of the natural changes that are going on, so that, like Coleridge, we say, "Blessings to the mountains! To the eye and ear they are always faithful."

PART ONE

WEST CUMBERLAND, THE SOLWAY & THE BORDER

An axe age, a sword age,
shields shall be cloven,
a wind age, a wolf age . . .
Poetic Edda: Völuspá

I

AN AXE AGE

The West Cumberland Plain—Early Man in Cumbria—Famous Henge Sites and Stone Circles of the Region

PRIMEVAL CONVULSIONS AND cataclysms. Then the ice: a millennial Michelangelo, carving and scraping, and the elements working ceaselessly like a team of artist-craftsmen in some Florentine workshop of the Renaissance. How humbling to reflect that all these miracles were performed without a single specimen of *homo-sapiens* around! He was a late arrival; particularly so in Cumbria, which, during so much of the Palaeolithic (Early Stone Age) still lay buried under the ice. Man's story here begins with Mesolithic (Middle Stone Age) nomads; and it would seem chiefly to begin in the region of the West Cumberland coastal plain.

But first a word about today's West Cumberland. The visitor who comes to this history-soaked coastal strip in quest of Stone Age nomads, Romans, Saxons, Vikings and Normans, finds himself in an almost treeless, highly industrial region with a long record of recurrent boom and slump that has resulted in a landscape of optimistic new plant and housing estates set down among acres upon decaying acres of abandoned and derelict pits, foundries, spoil-heaps, wharves, works, warehouses, silted ports and crumbling human habitations; a paradise for the industrial archaeologist. Nowhere is the story of a region, in all its dramatic *chiaroscuro* of success and tragedy, more plainly and poignantly apparent to the eye than upon West Cumberland's coastal plain.

Yet this industrial plain, dramatically positioned between mountains and sea, is not without a certain unique beauty. Much of the coastline, although no longer set with salt-pans, is ancient salt-pan country and is highly reminiscent of the salt-pan flats of Brittany. The Cumbrian salt-pans, that started when the Romans were in occupation, prospered over the centuries; medieval West Cumberland was famed for its saline industry. Thriving fishing fleets, based upon the small ports dotting this coast, were too a feature of the region's prosperity from Roman times until the close of the nineteenth-century, when rapid decline of this industry set in. The coalfields of today's Whitehaven region were being worked by 1272 at the latest; the iron industry of Egremont dates to at least the twelfth-century.

The mid-seventeenth century saw West Cumberland's spectacular emergence as a leading industrial region. Textiles, sail-cloth, ropes, pottery, clay-pipes and tobacco were all manufactured here. Over the ensuing 100 years ports expanded, the coalfields extended their workings further and further under the sea, the slagheaps of the mines grew larger and larger, foundries lit the skies at night. Workers flocked to the region. Important workmen's benefit and compensation schemes were pioneered here.

This era of expansion and prosperity was virtually over by the close of the nineteenth-century. The working population became depleted as people left to seek employment and better conditions elsewhere; often overseas. Between the two World Wars West Cumberland's unemployment figures were among the highest in the country.

The second World War revived the region's industry and restored some of its prosperity. But pits and plant alike proved unsuitable for economic survival far into the post-war decades. Mines, coalfields and foundries are today closed down. Energetic efforts have been made, and are being made, to replace these defunct industries with new; but the recently introduced industry is all of the lighter kind and does not satisfy the instincts of men descended from generations of colliers and miners.

Meantime the Atomic Energy Plant, built at Seascale shortly after the last war, broods monstrously over everyone and everything; a beautiful giant whom not everyone trusts, despite all protestations of harmless amiability made on its behalf by officialdom.

The three major towns of the industrial coastal belt developed as Maryport, Workington and Whitehaven. These (together with Millom and Silloth) all possess (or possessed) grid-pattern street planning and delightful, cobbled, tree-lined squares.

Maryport, named after Mrs Humphrey Senhouse, was developed as a coal-port by the Senhouses in the eighteenth century. Over the past year or two the greater part of this beautiful and unique little port has been demolished; a marina complex is planned.

Workington, associated with the Curwen family, is not a handsome town, but it is a place of continuing industrial vivacity, despite many hard blows in the past. It boasts as chief visual attraction two fine and solid churches, a neglected but impressive sprinkling of handsome old houses, and the beautiful Portland Square area. The great Curwen mansion was Workington Hall, while at Schoose Farm John Curwen ran his famous eighteenth-century experiment in model progressive farming.

For the wholly delightful town of Whitehaven we are indebted to the Lowthers. Sir John Lowther built Whitehaven as a coal-port in the late seventeenth century and thereafter it rapidly developed into one of the major ports in the north.

It was at Whitehaven that John Paul Jones, a naval hero of the American Revolutionary War, made one of the most daring raids recorded against the English (there is little doubt that Jones was aided by the fact that he knew the Solway Firth well, for he was Kirkcudbright born). In 1778 he was cruising in European waters, where he took prizes in the English Channel and the Irish Sea. Encouraged by these successes Jones, leading a party of 31 volunteers, on 23 April 1778 went ashore at Whitehaven, before daylight, and spiked the cannon in two forts guarding the harbour, though he was unable to carry out his intended burning of the shipping therein. He and his men made good their escape back to his ship, *Ranger*, and next day, off the Irish coast, Jones climaxed his cruise with a victorious engagement against the British man-o'-war, *Drake*.

The very situation of Whitehaven is in itself thrilling; tucked down within the embracement of steep cliffs. Pevsner[1] calls Whitehaven "the earliest post-medieval planned town in England": it is a straightforward grid of streets with one entire block left for the church. The layout of Whitehaven has survived virtually intact; it is a wonderful place, full of architectural delights.

The old port and surrounding streets reward sauntering exploration. Part of the Old Quay of 1687 still remains; its round lighthouse dates to 1730. The Old New Quay is of 1741 and was lengthened in 1769; the West Pier, by Rennie, dates from 1824–39. The old market square is hard-by the port; market days are worth attending. There are also many excellent shops in Whitehaven.

The Friends Meeting House in Sandhills Lane dates to 1722. Whitehaven Hospital was built in 1769 by Sir John Lowther. The finest house in Whitehaven is Number 14, Scotch Street, dating to mid-eighteenth century; but Scotch Street is altogether full of fine things, and so are Irish Street and Howgill Street. Here the Assembly Rooms of 1736 should not be missed. In Catherine Street, at the bottom of Howgill

Street, you will see the old militia barracks, probably built in the early nineteenth century as a linen mill, and today a factory. In Roper Street is the former theatre, built in 1769. Duke Street and Lowther Street also reward exploration for those with the time to spare.

One of the greatest glories in all Whitehaven (and we keep it to the last as a heavenly *bonne bouche*) is the superb Georgian interior of the church of St James, built in 1752–3 on high ground at the far end of Queen Street. This interior has galleries round two sides; these are supported on simple Tuscan columns and carry graceful, unfluted Ionic ones. The pulpit (in the manner of a ship's crow's-nest) is perched aloft on a tremendously tall column; a dizzy eyrie permitting the preacher to keep a look-out for slumberers in the galleries, as well as in the pews below him. "Sleepers awake!" The ceiling has two enchanting stucco roundels; one depicting the Ascension, the other the Virgin with angels, all portrayed with an exquisite lightness and total lack of pomposity. It is hoped that their mood similarly infected the style of the preacher, who was considerably closer to them than he was to the rows of listeners in the depths of the aisles!

At the east end of the church is an apse with a fine arch supported on Ionic pilasters; the altarpiece is also flanked by Ionic pilasters carrying a pediment. The entire effect of apse and pediment builds up to an exceptionally impressive, indeed dramatic, framing of the altarpiece itself, a Transfiguration, in the tradition of Correggio, by Giulio Cesare Procaccini (1548?–1626), one of a family of Italian painters of the Bolognese school. This altarpiece is said to come from the Escorial and was presented to the church by the third Earl of Lonsdale.

How different was the landscape of Middle Stone Age Cumbria! Following the retreat of the ice came warmer, drier weather and in due course forest grew, covering the region as ice had once covered it. Only the highest summits of the mountains remained treeless. The valley bottoms were dense with scrubby woodland. Man, who with his tree-felling, sheep grazing and farming was at last to change the face of Cumbria to the open terrain upon which we gaze today, first arrived in nomad groups of hardy hunting, fishing, foraging people, who had travelled here on foot from the Baltic (at this time Britain was not yet an island).

These nomads made their camps on the Cumbrian coastal plain and hunted the abundant game in the less impenetrable forests of the foothills. It is possible that man began to explore, and hunt, in the central mountains of the Lake Country some time during 4000 BC. Tiny, chipped flint tools have been found, made of tuff from Borrowdale Volcanic rock, suggesting that there was at least some discovery of the high country.

Implements for hunting and fishing have been found at coastal sites in an area ranging from St Bees (West Cumberland) to Walney Island (Furness), and in the park of Levens Hall (Westmorland). Traces of settlements and of burial mounds and cairns also have been found; outstandingly, about a century ago, when Ehenside Tarn, Beckermet (West Cumberland), was drained, to reveal tools of all kinds, a hand-mill and pottery (most of this equipment and pottery is now at the British Museum, London). A dug-out canoe is said also to have been found at Ehenside. Recent radio-carbon datings applied to these finds cover a period ranging from 3014–1570 BC.

Modern methods of scientific archaeological investigation, particularly radio-carbon dating and pollen analysis, today provide us with information which helps us to reconstruct the way of life of these early Cumbrians.

As every sufferer from hay-fever knows, large quantities of pollen are shed annually into the atmosphere by local plants and trees, to fall as "pollen rain" on land and water. This pollen rain is preserved intact wherever the environment is free of oxygen; as, for instance, in the sediments of lakes or growing peat. Furthermore, most pollen grains are identifiable. Thus, the kinds of pollen found and the proportions in which the various types are discovered provide a picture of the vegetation of successive periods (Pennington).

In Cumbria (an area especially well provided with suitable sediments and peat tracts) it is possible to reconstruct a close portrait of vegetation changes. Thus, we now know that the Cumbria of Middle Stone Age man was covered with heavy deciduous forest, and that at Ehenside Tarn there was clearance of trees and undergrowth, probably for a camp site, round about 4000 BC. Similar camp-site clearance is probable, too, at Barfield Tarn, near Bootle.

These earliest settlers were the pioneer farmers of Cumbria. Unable to pasture their small flocks and herds in the dense forests, they fed them on leaves from the trees, particularly elm (if we accept the evidence of a sudden decrease in the proportion of elm pollen in the pollen rain for that period).

The Lake District is famous for its Neolithic (Late Stone Age) axe factories. These have been found where outcrops of the fine-grained tuff of the Borrowdale Volcanic rock occur. In these factories were made tools designed to cut down trees with astonishing efficiency: as a result there was widespread clearance of the coastal and foothill forests, with the spread of grassland for grazing, and the cultivation of cereal crops in small, enclosed plots. There was some clearance of the high-country forests, too, particularly in the neighbourhood of the Langdale axe factories. Burning, as well as felling, was used to clear the ground. These vanquished forests never sprang up again: soil erosion set in and resultant increasing soil acidity transformed the old forest soils into peat.

The activity of the axe factories was seasonal. Their output was amazing. Implements from these factories were widely distributed by trading; by about 2500 BC axes were being exported to Scotland, the Isle of Man, and even Ireland. Radio-carbon dates of 2730 and 2550 BC have been obtained for one axe factory site below Thunacar Knott.

So-called "Beaker people" reached Britain from Iberia, Maritime France, the Low Countries and the north-European plain about 2000 BC, (their culture extended until at least 1500 BC, when it merged with the "Food vessel" culture of the early Bronze Age). To this late Neolithic period of around 2000 BC belong the henge sites; used, it seems, for seasonal gatherings and feasts, but whether of secular or ritual significance, or both, is not known.

In Cumbria the most celebrated of these sites is Mayburgh, at Little Salkeld, Eamont Bridge (near Penrith): a great ring of cobbles enclosing an area of well over an acre. A single entrance, or gateway, faces east. Within this enclosure stands one vast stone. We know that, as late as the eighteenth century, at least seven other stones stood with it; three in the centre, and two pairs flanking the entrance. Alas, these have now gone; to be broken up for building purposes, or road surfacing. Possibly there were other stones on this site which earlier underwent a similar fate (according to West,[2] quoting local tradition, the principal stones for Penrith Castle were taken from Mayburgh).

Close to Mayburgh (upon the opposite side of the Pooley Bridge road) is another, smaller henge site, known locally to countless generations as King Arthur's Round Table; this being the only interpretation that could be found for such a perplexing circle. It provided a splendid small-scale arena for cock fights, bull baiting, wrestling bouts and the like. A third, even smaller ring, Little Round Table, has since disappeared.

In northern England the gradual replacement of stone implements by bronze began about the seventeenth century BC. Little is known about the manufacture of bronze tools in Cumbria. This region, which had so successfully exported stone axes, now imported metal tools from Ireland, where, in the early Bronze Age, there flourished a fine bronze industry.

Equipped, thus, with bronze implements vastly superior to the former stone ones, man attained increasing mastery over his environment. This, in turn, resulted in an increase in population, which resulted in an expansion in grazing and, in due course, cereal cultivation.

A fragment of woollen cloth, found adhering to burnt matter in a cremation-urn discovered on Banniside Moor, Coniston, reveals that there were sheep on these fells by the mid-second millennium BC.

These small flocks would have required careful guarding against wolves. Perhaps they went hobbled in pairs, to prevent them from roaming, like the rope-hobbled sheep that I saw among the cairns of Barnscar not long since, stumbling together through vagrant mist across the wastes of tummocky grass. Immensely ancient customs have incredible powers of survival in this part of the world.

Another urn, found at Papcastle, near Cockermouth, gives clear evidence of having contained barley grains.

From such finds as these, we know that there was mixed farming in Cumbria by 1500 BC at the latest.

The region at that time enjoyed a drier, warmer climate than it does today. For this reason there was increasing pastoral activity on the higher ground. Actual settlements for this period have not yet been discovered, but together with evidence of pasturings are found presumed burial mounds. Yet even these so-called cairn-fields may well be no more than heaps of stones cleared from a now vanished agricultural system, rather than the burial circles we at present tend to suppose them to be.

Some time between 800 and 500 BC the climate changed, becoming much colder and wetter. Pastoral occupation of the uplands dwindled to a close. Man became more active in the low country again. Late Bronze Age "corduroy" roads, built of logs laid side to side, were made across the bogs of the Morecambe Bay estuaries to keep communications open in this increasingly populated part of the region.

For the average visitor the most exciting legacy of early man in Cumbria must be his mysterious circles of great stones. That these were the scene of important and impressive ceremonies we need not doubt; though we know nothing of the religious beliefs of these people who gathered in these marvellous temples.

As aforesaid, many stone circles and pre-historic sites in this part of the world have been destroyed in fairly recent times, including the once famous Shap Stones (or Karl Lofts); a stupendous monument, we are told, with two stone circles and a double mile-long avenue of single stones (megaliths), rivalling the celebrated alignments of Carnac, in Morbihan, Brittany. The enthusiastic traveller may still visit Carnac, but, alas, the marvel that was Karl Lofts has been lost for ever.

The three most celebrated circles left standing in Cumbria today are Long Meg and her Daughters, near Little Salkeld; the Castlerigg stone circle, just outside Keswick, in the Lake Country proper; and Swinside stone circle on Black Combe, near Millom, at the southern extremity of the West Cumberland plain.

Let us, therefore, start our epic of Cumbrian discovery by climbing together up to the Swinside circle where it stands in solemn grandeur upon the sweeping flank of Black Combe; that magic mountain of Skiddaw slate which somehow escaped from the rest of the school of whale-like monsters shaped from that most ancient fossilized mud of the western central fells, to appear, in solitary might, between the Duddon estuary and the Irish Sea.

The Black Combe from which the mountain takes its name lies on the south-east side of the fell, near the top; a deep and mysterious gill, with the stone circle lying below it. This circle, nearly 100 yards in circumference, has been known locally, down the ages, as the Sunkenkirk.

It is said (though it is always difficult to assess the truth of such sayings) that Black Combe commands a more extensive view than any other point in Britain. From its summit on a clear day you may see the mountains of Wales to the south and, to the north, the Scottish mountains. Out to sea stands the Isle of Man, and beyond it are Ireland's Mountains of Mourne.

The Black Combe district, in old local lore, has always been particularly associated with the Little People. Time-honoured superstitions and customs lingered hereabouts long after they had been lost elsewhere in Cumbria. Here the bees sang and four-footed creatures conversed and the labouring ox knelt in adoration at twelve o'clock at night on Christmas Eve; and here it was believed that "what quarter so ever a bull lies facing, on Allhalloween, thence will blow the prevailing winter wind". Here was one of the final strongholds of Hob Thross, "a body all ower rough" (the Cumbrian variant of "Jack o' the Hob" of beyond the Border), who came in the midnight hours to favoured homesteads, there to perform humble household chores and for whom a saucer of porritch, or milk, would always be left on the hearth.

Even as late as the mid-nineteenth century newly-married couples about Black Combe did not buy corn for their first sowing, but instead went "cornlaiting" (*lait* being Cumberland dialect for seeking, or looking for); the newly-weds went through their neighbouring countryside, begging a handful of corn here and a handful there, until friends and neighbours had filled the "laitin' sack" with grain, with which to start a future crop. Were the young pair to purchase their corn for sowing, never a loaf of bread would they produce.

Other customs, too, persisted here when they had been abandoned in other parts, including waking the dead.

Of such things, more later. At present we stand in the Swinside stone circle, gazing now at the stones themselves and now at the marvellous view spread before us; while we wonder about the men who built the circle (small, dark folk, progenitors of the Little People themselves, perhaps), and of the many time-muffled tales and half-smothered legends to which they gave rise: tales handed down through countless generations, until no one knew for certain what was the kernel of truth, and what had been invented on the way.

Much of the obscurity of late Bronze Age man's activity in this region is due to the deterioration of the Cumbrian climate during that period, whereby many important clues were lost for posterity. Therefore it is not known when the iron-using Celts arrived in Cumbria, but by the third and second centuries BC they had crossed the Pennines and were moving westward; hardy pioneers bringing their ponies, carts and chariots, their advanced mixed-farming economy, their cattle ranching, their beautiful jewelry and armoury, their bardic legends, their reverence for the spirits of trees and rocks, springs and fountains: a people of vast creative energy, of poetry and imagination.

Where had they come from originally? The Greeks referred to all peoples living north of the Alps as *Keltoi*. Physically the *Keltoi* fell into two groups, each shading off into the other. The first of these groups, the Nordic, was restricted to north-western Europe, having its chief seat in Scandinavia; its characteristics were a long head, a narrow aquiline nose, blue eyes, blond hair, long limbs and exceptional height. The second group was round-headed, with a broad face and blunt features, hazel eyes and brown hair, in build being thick-set and of medium height. From the early Stone Age times people of this second group had lived all along the great Alpine chain from south-west France to the Danube. But during the period of the so-called *La Tène* culture (500 BC to the first century AD), they expanded dramatically across Europe, penetrating eastwards into Asia Minor, invading Italy in a southward thrust (even occupying Rome itself for a short period of the late fourth-century BC) and, in that same century, moving westward too. One tribe, the Brythons, established themselves in England and Wales. Another, the Goidels, passed directly from the Loire to Ireland.

Much of the power of these people of the *La Tène* culture seems to have been attributable to their great skill as metallurgists, especially their exploitation of iron. But, energetic and successfully aggressive as they were, expert opinion considers it unlikely that these Celtic invaders arrived in Britain in large migrating hordes which displaced the native population. It is believed that the new Celtic strain became amalgamated comparatively quickly with the indigenous residents; imposing upon these, however, the Celtic language and a predominantly Celtic ruling class, or, perhaps more correctly, aristocracy.

The fascinating mixed race of natives and Celts thus formed the ethnic basis of the early British. Traces of the settlements of these people are to be found all over Cumbria, yet very little is so far actually known about the pre-Roman Iron Age in this region. We know that the settlements were first of wooden, then stone-based, circular huts within stone-walled enclosures, flanked by small rectangular fields. Cattle, sheep and pigs, and the breeding of ponies, formed the main basis of the economy: it is highly possible, too, that these people worked the haematite ores of the region. We have only to examine the surviving examples of their art to appreciate that theirs was an advanced and, in many respects, highly sophisticated culture. But it was their destiny to face the full military might of the greatest imperial power known to the entire history of man. The Romans came; a race of ruthless supermen, marching relentlessly northward.

2

A SWORD AGE

Hadrian's Wall—A Progress along the Line of the Western Wall from Gilsland to Bowness-on-Solway

ROMAN OCCUPATION OF Britain lasted for almost three and a half centuries and for the greater part of that time the hill tribesmen of the north, the Brigantes, remained intractable.

Cumbria formed part of the kingdom of Brigantia (the most populous kingdom in Britain, according to Tacitus). The Roman troops first thrust northward over Stanemoor, from their legionary headquarters in York, some time between AD 71 and 74, following the suppression of an open revolt by the Brigantes in Yorkshire, led by their king Venutius. It was clear that the northern tribesmen were not to be easily subdued and an expanded and ruthlessly tightened grip was taken by the Roman military, under the governorship of Agricola (78–84), who established a most formidably efficient road-communication system to serve and subject this northern territory.

The road from York ran over Stanemoor to Brough and from thence to Kirkby Thore and Brougham, near Penrith. The road from the legionary stronghold at Chester entered Westmorland up the River Lune, passing through Tebay gorge to Brougham, where it joined the road from York. At Brougham was built the fort of Brocavum. The road from Brougham to Carlisle (Luguvallium) had a marching-camp at Plumpton Head and a fort at Old Penrith (Voreda). Carlisle was linked to Corbridge in Northumberland by a fortified road, the Stanegate (a stoned, or metalled, road). Another road ran from Carlisle, down the west coast, to Maryport.

The marching-camps at Rey Cross, Crackenthorpe, Plumpton Head and Troutbeck were intended purely for troops on the move: they could garrison 500 men, either infantry or cavalry. The large, permanent forts garrisoned 1,000; they were manned by auxiliary units, both infantry and cavalry, drawn from all parts of the Roman Empire. It was a strict rule, for obvious reasons, that these auxiliary soldiers never served in the country of their origin (thus, men from Thrace, Dalmatia and Spain manned the forts along the Solway and we know that a cohort of Dalmatians were garrisoned at Hardknott in the second century). The right of full Roman citizenship was accorded to all veteran soldiers and some of them, at least, never returned to their native countries, but married Brigante lasses, raised families in the civil settlements near the forts, acquired a little land of their own and enjoyed honourable retirement as Roman citizens and men of property and proved worth.

The crack troops of the Imperial Army were based at York and Chester. Here were found Roman officers who were true Romans; who carried in their mind's eye a picture of the toga-clad crowds of the Forum, the gilded temples, the magnificent baths and splendid villas of Rome. To these men the road home was along the Appian Way.

Despite their victory in the Grampians, the Romans became convinced that it would be senseless to press further northward into the enfilades of mist shrouded hills. A period of uneasy peace followed this decision, lasting until the reign of the Emperor Trajan (AD 98–117). Then the tribesmen, their energy revived and their hatred for the occupiers in no way abated, once again attacked, destroying the famous Ninth Legion.

As a result Trajan's successor, Hadrian, after a tour of inspection of North Britain in the year 122, personally initiated the construction of the great fortified barrier (known to posterity as "Hadrian's Wall") which was "to separate the Romans from the Barbarians". The construction of this barrier was under the control of the governor of the province, Aulus Platorius Nepos.

This massive artificial frontier (one of the world's outstanding Roman relics) was erected on the line of Agricola's forts from Bowness-on-Solway to Wallsend-on-Tyne. (Agricola had an unrivalled eye for ground, as we are told by Tacitus, his biographer and son-in-law. This strategical eye was subsequently confirmed by the way in which the Normans chose to build their castles on the sites of Roman forts: both Brough and Brougham being cases in point.)

The Wall was planned as a twenty foot high, ten foot thick curtain-wall; 79 Roman miles in length (about 73 English miles). In front of it (that is, on the northern side) was to be a *vallum* (earthwork). The Wall was interspaced at every Roman mile (1,620 yards) by a gate, each gate defended by a fortlet (milecastle) built into the Wall. Between each pair of milecastles (and thus 540 yards apart) were two turrets, used as look-out signal posts.

In the event certain modifications were made. The barbarians, in their opposition to the frontier, launched a sustained succession of attacks which forced the Romans to bring up their main fighting forces that hitherto had been stationed in forts along the Stanegate. These troops were now rehoused in seventeen massive forts sited at five-mile intervals along the Wall. Each of these forts accommodated either an infantry cohort 800 strong, or a cavalry *ala* 500 strong.

The proposed *vallum* was placed at the rear (that is, south) of the Wall; not before it, as had originally been planned. This *vallum* was a vast, flat-bottomed ditch, with twenty foot wide, six foot high mounds on either side; these mounds being set well back, to leave 30 foot wide berms. The *vallum* ditch was ten feet deep and eight feet wide at the bottom. The total width of the *vallum* was 120 feet. It was not a defence, in the strict military sense, but rather a boundary-line of the military zone; it also served both as a fortified supply route and a frontier customs barrier. It could only be crossed by the causeways opposite the forts; these causeways were manned by customs posts and officials.

Between *vallum* and Wall ran a military way; not to be confused with General Wade's eighteenth-century military road (B6318). This road was largely constructed with stones taken from the eastern half of the Wall and indeed for much of its way was built upon the very line of the Wall itself. The Roman military way is to be seen *between* the *vallum* and the Wall; it remains clearly visible in many places along the line of the Wall.

The fighting ditch ran in front of the Wall (that is, to the north of the Wall); save where steep crag or water rendered this defence unnecessary. This ditch was 27 feet wide and twelve feet deep. Both fighting ditch in front of the Wall and *vallum* behind it are plain to see, for extensive stretches.

In the north-west sector of the Wall strongly fortified outposts were built; these were at Bewcastle, Netherby and Birrens.

This immense military project took some twelve years to complete in all. The western part posed especially difficult problems of defence (at first, probably for this very reason, the Wall and milecastles of this sector were built of turf-work; later, when this part of the line had been better secured, the turf-work was replaced with stone). The rear of the Wall, here in the west, was constantly threatened by tribesmen from the mountains; the Solway Firth placed the Wall in equal perpetual danger of being outflanked from the sea; while the Cumberland coastal plain provided the barbarians with an area wherein to mass for attempted revolt.

The rear was secured, therefore, by a formidable system of roads and forts carried across the southern face of Brigantia's central massif. The mountain route from Brougham, running over Barton Fell and along the ridge between Martindale and Bampton commons (most aptly known to posterity as High Street) descended to Windermere where, at the fort of Galava (Borrans* Field, Waterhead, Ambleside), it connected with the northern part of the road which ran from Ravenglass, via Ambleside and Watercrook, to the south. The Ambleside–Ravenglass stretch of this road travelled up Little Langdale and over the Wrynose and Hardknott passes (at Hardknott stood another fort, Mediobogdun) and thence down Eskdale to the fort of Glennaventa guarding the port of today's Ravenglass.

At Borrans Field a small timber-built fort was replaced in the second century AD by a larger, stone-built fort, erected on an artificial gravel platform overlying two-thirds of the earlier fort. The garrison headquarters, the commandant's house and the granaries were also built of stone, but the barrack blocks were of timber. Some of these wooden buildings were destroyed by fire, in all likelihood during attacks by tribesmen. A recently discovered tombstone outside the fort tells us that Julius Romanus, a records clerk, was killed in the fort by the enemy. This fort, it seems, remained garrisoned until the final withdrawal of Roman troops from the Wall. But, well before then, the local tribesmen in the Galava area had become considerably less hostile and a civil settlement (the forerunner of today's Ambleside) had sprung up on the eastern side of the fort; industrial activities, including leatherwork, being carried out there.

Mediobogdun (Hardknott Castle, as it subsequently became known) was first begun in the time of Hadrian. A building inscription suggests that it was constructed by the IVth Cohort of Dalmatians, between AD 117 and 138. It seems that the fort did not carry a regular garrison after the end of the second century.

* A *borran* is a pile of stones. It is obvious enough why this lakeside meadow at Waterhead was given its name by a later generation of men.

The fort was built on the usual plan of barrack blocks, headquarters, regimental chapel, commanding-officer's house, offices, store-rooms and granaries. To the south-east of the fort were the soldiers' baths with cold, warm and hot rooms. Two hundred and fifty yards to the north-east of the fort lay the parade ground. It is interesting to know that throughout the centuries, before excavation and scientific archaeological activity were even thought of, local legend of Eskdale had it that Hardknott Castle was of Roman origin and that the flat, platformed area north-east of it was "the parade ground". What many people supposed to be mere legend, or myth, has now been substantiated as historical fact. There may be a lesson here, somewhere.

The hill tribes of central Brigantia were thus contained within a system of military roads along which troops might be moved at speed to crush any outbreak of tribal revolt. The main areas of native settlement were, in fact, cut across by the roads and this strategy, together with the careful siting of the forts, made it almost impossible for mass tribal assaults to be organized and assembled without discovery.

Of these native settlements we know, as yet, very little. Of native defences we know even less, though knowledge of the sites of some of the hillforts of these Celtic warriors have been handed down in local lore: Carrock, above Mungrisedale; Croglam Castle, near Kirkby Stephen; Castlehead, above Natland, and Castle Crag, in Mardale, are among the larger sites known to us.

The Solway Firth was secured for the Romans by a system of forts, milecastles and turrets extended from Bowness-on-Solway southwards along the coast to beyond Beckfoot, three miles south of Silloth. Here is a site of a fort some three acres in extent, with six foot thick walls backed by internally placed rectangular towers. Traces of a civil settlement lie to the south-east of this fort. Beyond this fort was a further chain of strategically placed, isolated, auxiliary forts. The port of Uxelodunum (Maryport) was defended by a fort on elevated ground to the north: this fort had a double ditch and a wall. The positions of the four entrance gates are still discernible. To the south of the fort was a levelled parade ground and immediately adjacent to this the tribunal (Pudding Pie Hill). Attached to this fort and the post was an extensive civil-settlement.

Further forts were at Burrow Walls (near Workington) and Moresby. At Ravenglass (a harbour now silted up but in Roman times a most useful port) stood the fortress of Glennaventa. Little remains today of the actual fort, but the walls of the bath-house (Walls Castle) are excellently preserved, in one place standing to a height of over twelve feet. Two doorways of this building survive likewise and there are traces of five windows.

Further to control this treacherous coastal plain a crack regiment of 1,000 cavalry, the *ala Petriana*, was stationed at Stanwyx, Carlisle; a mobile unit able to dash at speed to any potential trouble spot.

Supplies for this great fortified frontier-zone came by sea to South Shields in the east and, on the western seaboard, to Maryport and Ravenglass.

During the early reign of Antoninus Pius, Hadrian's successor, the Romans advanced beyond Hadrian's Wall and built a new, if less mighty, barrier from Tyne to Forth. Hadrian's frontier was temporarily abandoned. But barbarian uprisings in 155–8, 162, 181 and finally in 197 (when the Hadrianic Wall itself was overrun and Roman strongholds as far south as Chester were devastated) rendered the Tyne–Forth line untenable. The Emperor Severus eventually ordered a return to Hadrian's Wall, which henceforth became the permanent northern limit of the Province. The Wall, despite its massive fortification, suffered serious attack on at least two subsequent occasions, in 296 and 367, the latter date being that of the uprising known as the "Barbarian conspiracy".

Contrary to what historians have previously believed, there was some garrisoning of the Wall until early in the fifth century. Then the Romans departed, their empire crumbling about them.

The people of the Celtic strongholds of the north-west and Wales, that is to say, the peoples who had preserved their national integrity throughout the Roman occupation, were lauded by the early Welsh bards as the *Cymry*: the compatriots. It is from this word that the Welsh Cambria and the northern Cumbria were to evolve.

The finest section of the Wall is undoubtedly in Northumberland, where the great fortification marches dramatically along the crest of Whinsill, high above the waters of Crag Lough. The Cumbrian remains of the Wall, though visually less sensational, nonetheless deserve far more attention than they receive.

That this Wall country is frontier country is abundantly clear: everywhere is evidence of Border unrest, both of Roman times and much later. It is a region not only of the Wall, but of mottes-and-baileys, pele-towers and bastle-houses, as well as an abundancy of castles. In effect, the line of Roman fortifications became replaced by a line of castles and peles stretching from east coast to west; strongholds erected by the great barons and more influential landowners of the Middle Ages. Much of the fabric of these castles, towers, fortified churches and farmhouses that we see in this frontier country is of obvious Roman origin. Post-Roman generations demolished the Imperial fortifications to use the stone as building materials for themselves.

The Romans initially quarried the stone locally: inscriptions carved by their quarrymen on the faces of quarries such as Pigeon Crag and the celebrated Written Rock, on the Gelt, south of Brampton, and at Coombe Crag quarry near Nether Denton, kept generations of men wondering and gaping.

The Wall and its forts required great quantities of stone. There were six wall forts in the western (Cumbrian) sector of the Wall: these were at Birdoswald (the best preserved), Castlesteads (levelled in the eighteenth century), Stanwix, Burgh-by-Sands, Drumburgh and Bowness-on-Solway.

The best base from which to visit the surviving sectors of Cumbrian Wall is Brampton; a delightful little market town some ten miles north-east of Carlisle and a mere two or three miles south of the Wall. In the centuries of rampant Border unrest it must have taken nerve to dwell in Brampton, yet the town's market charter dates from the thirteenth century; indication that some stalwart folk were prepared to live under decidedly harrowing conditions.

Until the early thirteenth century Cumberland and Westmorland lay within Scots territory; tradition holding that the Border between Scotland and England was marked by the Rey Cross of Stanemore. In 1327 these two countries finally became annexed to England, but even so the Border remained a region of dispute; and remained so for centuries to come, never knowing 50 consecutive years of quiet until after the defeat of the 1745 Jacobite Rising. With that Rising, Brampton was much involved, for it was here that Bonnie Prince Charlie, on 17 November 1745, received the keys of Carlisle from the mayor and corporation of that capitulated city, prior to the Prince's triumphant entry into Carlisle on the following morning.

Brampton, even today, remains virtually unspoiled; retaining much of its old market town character. Nevertheless, the town's most interesting and important building is, properly speaking, modern. This is the parish church of St Martin, designed in 1874 by Philip Webb; a building which, to quote Pevsner, "suddenly threw Cumberland into the centre of architectural events in England".

Webb, the friend and disciple of William Morris, was architect of Morris's famous Red House, at Walthamstow, near London. The Earl of Carlisle, a great admirer of Webb's work, obtained for him the commission for Brampton's church. Interesting and impressive as this building is, its glory lies in the stained glass; all designed by Morris & Co. (chiefly Morris and Burne-Jones) and made in the Morris workshop in 1878–80. These windows are deservedly renowned and should not be missed.

In Brampton, therefore, we find little to remind us of Romans, apart from the basic fact that much of the original building fabric of the town was of Roman origin. But once in the surrounding countryside we find evidence of the Romans everywhere.

For instance, at Old Church Brampton, a mile west of today's Brampton, is the site of one of the early Stanegate forts, where troops were stationed from Flavian until Hadrianic times. Old Church Brampton fort now lies under the church, which itself was built with stones from it. Little is known of the actual layout of the fort, though excavation has revealed the foundations of inner buildings of masonry. The Norman church of nearby Upper Denton is also built with Roman stone and the craggy little chancel arch is said to be a reconstructed Roman arch brought here from the Hadrianic fort of Camboglanna (Birdoswald). While at this church don't miss the typically Anglo-Saxon quoins on the (east) exterior wall; it is rare indeed to find any evidence of Anglo-Saxon stone-church building in Cumbria (Chapter Four). The ruined barn at this eastern end of the church should also be noted; in all likelihood it was the vicar's pele.

Nether Denton is the site of a fort occupied by Roman troops before transfer to the Wall and, again, a church has been built on the site of the fort. The vicarage stands on the site of the former fort bath-house. The church is famous for a unique twelfth-century cross depicting Christ in Majesty upon the Tree.

Before tracing the Wall itself, a sortie of a mere extra nine miles must be made to Bewcastle, one of the three major Hadrianic outposts and, moreover, the possible birth-place of St Patrick, who is thought to have been the son of a Roman official. The great and famous Bewcastle Cross

(Chapter Four) stands here in the churchyard of the twelfth-century church of St Cuthbert. The north side of this church, it should be noticed, is windowless; a defence against the attacks of wind and raiding Scots alike.

At Bewcastle, church, rectory, a neighbouring farm and a thirteenth-century castle all stand within, or rather upon, the site of the Roman fort, Severan; a large one, covering a natural plateau of six acres. Excavation in 1937 revealed the foundations of several buildings. One, the head-quarters, was of immense interest, for it bore evidence of having been violently destroyed soon after the year 297. A basement storeroom of the HQ, filled with rubbish, contained amongst this débris an altar, a statue base and several silver plaques which must have fallen into this basement from a sanctuary chamber above, when the building was destroyed by the enemy. Evidence was found, too, of rebuilding, following this destruction.

Bewcastle Fort was linked to the Wall by a road to the Wall-fort of Camboglanna (Birdoswald).

The Wall enters Cumbria at Gilsland (the actual village of this name is in Northumberland). At Gilsland there are interesting stretches of Wall exposed in the former vicarage garden, while west of Gilsland railway station is a well-preserved Milecastle, no. 48: Poltross Burn. A good length of curtain-wall leads from here to Willowford, on the River Irthing; the *vallum* running very close to the Wall at this point. In this curtain-wall survive the foundations of two turrets, nos. 48a and 48b; the latter standing up clearly to the left of Willowfield Farm yard. Traces of a temporary camp may be seen on Willowfield Hill. At Willowford the Romans had a bridge, to carry the Wall across the river (remains of bridge and the Roman mill may still be discerned in the flood plain). From the ford the Wall ascended the incline up to Harrow Scar (Milecastle 49).

From Harrow Scar to Birdoswald there is such a splendidly preserved section of Wall that true *aficianados* will find themselves stopping occasionally to pat the stones. Nor is the fort of Camboglanna a disappointment when it is reached. It has been much excavated and there are some rewarding things to see. Particularly exciting are the double-portalled main east and south gates, and the western postern-gate, its threshold deeply rutted by the wheels of the chariots and carts which rattled and jolted over it almost 2,000 years ago.

A short distance from the south gate lies the Irthing gorge, at the foot of a steep escarpment. It was from this winding gorge that the fort got its name of Camboglanna: the "Crooked Glen".

Westward beyond Birdoswald the Wall has been uncovered and consolidated and is easy to follow. For a considerable distance it runs parallel with the modern highway. The *vallum* is clearly visible, too. The turf Wall is also discernible for much of this stretch; particularly in Wall Brook valley, along the old cart-track to Lanerton. It is also discernible at Turret 49b, Milecastle 50 TW and Turret 51a. Turf and stone Walls merge at Wall Bowers, the site of Milecastle 51: this Milecastle housed two barracks and was surrounded by an unfinished ditch.

On Pike Hill stood a tower, probably used for long-distance signalling; the view from this point being very extensive. This signal-tower is incorporated in the Wall; 150 yards to the west is Turret 52a.

The site of Milecastle 53 is at Banks Burn, just under a mile to the north-east of Lanercost Priory, reached by a winding downhill road. The Wall here formed the boundary of the Priory deer-park. At Banks Turret (celebrated for its truly magnificent view) the Wall survives to the height of ten feet (with some help from a face-lift in the last century). Embedded in the northern façade of this section of Wall is a centurial stone, found at nearby Moneyholes.

With this section the visible Wall ends to all intent and purpose. Most visitors will probably abandon Wall detection at this point, therefore, and return to Carlisle; noticing, nonetheless, how the Wall thrusts up its head in the place-names hereabouts, Walton, Old Wall, Wallhead, Walby.

The city of Carlisle (Chapter 6) originated as Roman Luguvalium; a wooden bridge-head fort of the Flavian period, which was demolished following the construction of Hadrian's Wall. Its garrison, a 1,000-strong cavalry unit, was transferred to the new fort of Petriana, on the opposite bank of the Eden at Stanwix (today covered by modern buildings and the parish church and churchyard).

Luguvalium was completely replanned as an administrative headquarters and civil settlement. Its fine streets and handsome buildings made it the north's most impressive city, and such it remained, for several centuries after the Romans had departed, until it was ferociously sacked by Hafdan and his Danes in 875.

Luguvalium may best be recaptured today in the Carlisle City Museum, Tullie House. Here, on the ground floor, is a remarkable collection of Roman antiquities which have been discovered in and about Carlisle.

Particularly fine are the sculptured memorial stones from the Roman cemeteries in Botchergate and Harraby.

Westwards beyond Carlisle the Wall, for reasons of strategy, turned northwards to the very shoreline of the Solway estuary. Here the eye no longer sees any actual Wall standing; its stones have all gone into churches, farms and, indeed, whole villages. The village of Beaumont, for instance, stands virtually on the Wall and much, if not all, of its early fabric must have come from the Wall.

At Burgh-by-Sands, the village beyond Beaumont, history is indeed in every stone. This was the site of a five-acre cavalry fort, Aballava, built astride the Wall; the fort is now underneath Burgh. The church of St Michael, constructed with great grey stones taken direct from the Wall, stands in what was once the centre of the fort.

St Michael's, with enormously thick walls and squat pele-tower, itself seems more fortress than church. The building is the work of the fourteenth-century, when Scots raiding was at its height. Everything is designed in terms of stronghold; the tower (originally one of two) has minute look-out windows and its ground floor is a small tunnel-vaulted chamber, the very essence of the impregnable. This chamber has no doorway giving direct to the outside world, but is gained, through a low archway, from the nave of the church; this archway is still guarded by its original iron yatt (very rare, only three have survived). Above this tunnel-vaulted chamber was a look-out platform (replaced, probably in Georgian times, by the present second storey).

The Romans have bequeathed a strain of paganism which lingers visibly, not only in the very stones of the walls, but even more so in the form of two fragments of bas-relief sculpture; one of some exotic, Moorish-seeming deity; the second (this in the tunnel-vaulted chamber) of a beast which may be either a horse or an elephant, according to the eye and inclination of the beholder.

The atmosphere of the building is in every respect one of conflict; piety and prayer overlaid by the echoes of sword-clash and the oaths of struggling men; the clang of the yatt being slammed to. Indeed, St Michael's of Burgh-on-Sands is an expression of the most basic and lasting instincts of all mankind: the need for worship and prayer, and the terrible urge for warfare.

Just over a mile from the village, on Burgh Marsh, stands a monument to that most war-dedicated of English monarchs; "long-time-a-dying" Edward I, the "Hammer of the Scots", who finally rendered up his ghost here, on 7 July 1307, while journeying with his retinue from Lanercost Priory to Holme Cultram Abbey. Edward had come north to subdue Robert Bruce of Scotland, but the 68-year-old king succumbed to chronic illness before reaching Skinburness, where he had intended embarking for Scotland in a ship of the Royal Navy (Chapter 6).

The final Wall fort but one, Drumburgh (Congavata) lies out on the marsh and is reached by Dykesfield. Two-acre Congavata was dismantled in the early sixteenth century by Thomas, Lord Dacre, who used the stones to build a fortified manorhouse, Drumborough Castle.

So to Bowness-on-Solway, the lowest point at which the Solway could be forded, where, with the fort of Maia, Hadrian's Wall ended. This fort was a large one of seven acres, facing westward across the Solway; there was probably a small port attached to the fort. To the west of Bowness, at Cardurnock, began the chain of mile-fortlets and signal-towers which, together with four more forts, carried the Roman defences a further 40 miles down the Cumberland coast. Today's village of Bowness stands on the site of Maia and, it almost goes without saying, is built of Roman stones.

Here, then, on the shore of the Solway estuary, a farewell is said to the Wall, or rather to its shades. Gratitude should be expressed to this astounding bulwark if only because it has led us to the Solway; one of the most beautiful estuaries imaginable. At low tide sand and sea stretch in sable and silver bars to Scotland, where Cryffel raises himself into the sky; a light and airy mountain, with almost always a twist of cloud riding at his brow. To the right of the estuary stand a group of water-towers; majestic figures, with huge plumes of vapour billowing and streaming from their heads: how Turner would have loved these water-towers! Everywhere there is light, lightness and movement; shadows and shining water; and birds, an unbelievable wealth of birds; flocks of oyster-catchers with their aspen-trembling flight and curiously quavering cry; gulls of every kind—slate-and-white, black-headed, or great black-backed—all screaming, yapping, crooning, a cacophony of voices. Dunlin, plover, lapwing, all are here; and, as we watch, one huge heron flaps in, descending on a slow, curved flight with steeply tented wings, lowering and flexing his long legs for a landing strike: then pacing, jerkily, to a standstill, folding his wings in the methodical manner of one who puts away a valuable piece of apparatus. Finally, subsiding into utter immobility, he surveys the shoreline with a long, long glance down his stiletto beak, and if we did not know that he was there we should never discover him.

Arched over the vastness of estuary, plain and mountains, is a gigantic sky. At all times these Solway skies are marvellous, but the sunsets are especially famous; those of winter being immeasurably grander and more dramatic, even, than those of summer. Across these burning immensities of northern winter's nightfall fly the geese: long skeins of birds, the living symbol of time, every stroke of their wings immutably beating the here and now into the past and gone.

3

A WIND AGE, A WOLF AGE

West Cumberland—Cumbrian Saints and Pagans—Northumbrian Conquest—Anglo-Saxon Cumbria—and Sculpture—Bewcastle Cross—Irton Cross—Dearham—Viking Invasion—Anglo-Viking Sculpture—Pagan-Christian Art—The Norse Thing—Burial of Chieftains—"Edith Little Maid"

CUMBRIA, LIKE ITS neighbour Northumbria, is a region renowned for saints and stone crosses. The lowlands of Cumbria give us a landscape thick with early stone crosses, dating from the seventh century to the early twelfth century; a few still standing upright, one or two intact, others lying fallen and fragmented. It is as though we wander in an ancient and sacred wood, much ravaged by storms and time, but still full of mystery and strange beauty,

> I say that I hung
> on a wind-rocked tree . . .
> on that tree,
> of which no one knows
> from what root it springs.[1]

The Christian faith became the official religion of the Roman Empire in the early fourth-century. However, it is not known to what extent Christianity took root among the British of the north-west during the Roman occupation. The fact that a number of missionaries thought it fruitful to visit the region during the fifth and sixth centuries suggests that the Brigantes had tended to remain heathen.

Cumbria is associated with three famous missionaries: St Ninian, St Patrick, and St Kentigern. St Ninian and St Patrick are both thought to have travelled in the region on evangelical missions during the early decades of the fifth century. These were troubled times; the Roman Empire was crumbling and all official Roman units had been withdrawn from the Cumbrian forts. Even the Wall had been evacuated; in 410 the Emperor Honorius, needing troops to defend the very gates of Rome itself, bleakly ordered the Romano-British to supervise and rely upon their own defences against barbarian attack.

Following withdrawal of the Romans an intense period of tribal strife ensued in the north-west. The British kingdom which subsequently emerged here was known as Rheged. It extended its territory on either side of the Solway and had Carlisle as its administrative centre and defensive headquarters. North of the Wall and south of the Forth–Clyde isthmus were other British kingdoms; the most powerful of these being Strathclyde, which had its stronghold at Dumbarton, near today's Glasgow.

Tradition has it that St Ninian was the first holy man to come to our region on an evangelical mission; probably sometime about the year 410. He was a native of Strathclyde who had been instructed in the Christian faith in Rome, subsequently returning to his native land where, as bishop of the kingdom of the Picts, he founded a monastic house and cathedral church at Whithorn (where he is thought to have died in 432).

The church of Ninekirk (Ninian's kirk) near Brougham (p. 148), in the neighbourhood of Penrith, is dedicated to this saint. Brougham (Brocavium) in St Ninian's time was still an important Roman road junction and centre, with an adjacent civil settlement that continued to thrive after the Romans had left. There is therefore valid historical reason to believe that St Ninian may well have made Brocavium the base for his mission work and that St Patrick, too, may also have come there. Brocavium would have been the logical starting point for Patrick's missionary expedition into the Ullswater region, served by the famous Roman mountain highway which we today call High Street, and which started from Brocavium.

Patrick, as we have already learned, was possibly born at Bewcastle in, or about, the year 389. He was reared in the Christian faith. At the age of sixteen or so he was captured by a band of marauding pirates from Ireland; it is suggested that this happened somewhere along the coast between Skinburness and Maryport. Patrick was held captive in Ireland for some six years; during this time he experienced powerful visions and heard angelic voices telling him that he had been chosen to spread the message of Christ.

Following his escape back to his own country Patrick obeyed this call and travelled into the mountains of the interior to convert the natives thereof. The dale which we today call Patterdale (St Patrick's Dale) is named after him; it is known to have been an area of well-established, albeit scattered, British settlement (see p. 176). At Bampton, not far distant from Patterdale, is another church dedicated to St Patrick. Barton church, the mother church of the greater part of this region, is merely some ten miles from Bampton and gives every indication of being a very early foundation of both pagan and Celtic Christian significance. The church stands in a circular churchyard, perched upon an artificially raised knoll, or small mount, close to a spring which here wells up to feed the River Eamont. It is believed that, upon this prehistoric sacred site, some early Christian holy man (St Patrick at once comes to mind) set up his cross, to preach, convert, and baptize in the nearby sacred spring.

Between the evangelical missions in Cumbria of St Ninian and St Kentigern the Cumbrian lowlands were invaded by Anglicans from Jutland. The heights of the Cumbrian interior held no attraction for these agricultural people from flat lands and soon most of them moved on, eastwards and southwards. Elsewhere in Britain the impact of these Anglo-Saxon invaders was more than considerable. It was they who filled the void left by the departed Romans.

The greatest king of Rheged was Urien; the mighty warrior of whom Taliesin, the Welsh bard, sang with such fervour. Urien lived at Lywyfenedd; which is thought by some to have been the river Lyvennet in Westmorland. He led his British troops against the encroaching forces of the Anglo-Saxons and, in 574, besieged Anglian-held Lindisfarne and, together with the King of Strathclyde and two Welsh princes, attacked the Anglian king, Hussa of Bernicia.

With the death of Urien, at the close of the sixth century, the kingdom of Rheged became absorbed in that of Strathclyde. The Anglian kingdoms of Deira (based on York) and Bernicia (centred on Bamburgh) were united into one kingdom, Northumbria. This took place during the reign of Aethelfrith (593–617), of whom Bede said that he conquered more British territory than did any other English king. Certainly the main English conquest of the north occurred under him and his immediate successors; Aethelfrith's expansion into Strathclyde gained impetus following his defeat of the Welsh at Chester in 613.

It is scarcely surprising to learn that the Cumbrian tribesmen lapsed back into their original state of "ydolatrie" during these decades of disruption. Thus it was that the intrepid St Kentigern, or Kyentyern (popularly known as St Mungo: *mynghu*, dear one, dear friend) came striding among the Cumbrian mountains to convert the heathen therein, some time about the year 553.

According to his biographer and disciple, St Asaph,[2] Kentigern was the bastard son of King Euginius, or Ewen, of Strathclyde and an unbaptized Christian girl named Tenew. Kentigern entered monastic life early and by merit of his outstanding scholarship and personality became bishop of the kingdom of Cambrensis at the age of 25. Following his consecration as bishop (which at that time automatically brought canonization) St Kentigern, a man of prodigious strength and energy, travelled on foot about his extensive diocese, on a prolonged evangelical mission. Such a zealous and categorical priest was bound to make enemies: a heathen chieftain named Morken was aroused to intense animosity and St Kentigern was obliged to flee for his life. In 553 he left his diocese to seek refuge with St Dewi (St David), Bishop of Menœvia, in North Wales.

However, upon reaching Carlisle, on the first leg of his journey, St Kentigern learned "that many among the mountains were given to idolatry or ignorant of the divine law"; whereat, without further ado, the saint (who was then about 35 years of age) marched away into the mountains.

There are ten churches and several wells dedicated to him in Cumbria (either in the name of St Kentigern, or St Mungo). We find dedications at Caldbeck, Castle Sowerby, Greystoke (where is the locally famous Thanet Well, named after St Kentigern's mother, Thanew, or Tenew), at Mungrisedale (Mungo's Dale) and at Crosthwaite (p. 184) by the shores of Derwent Water.

We do not know how long St Kentigern remained at any of these places, setting up his cross, preaching, converting and baptizing. We can only quote his biographer, "Turning aside from thence [Crosthwaite] the saint directed his steps to the sea-shore, and through all his journey scattering the seed of divine word, gathered in a plentiful and fertile harvest unto the Lord. At length safe and sound he reached St Dewi."

The three churches dedicated to the saint on the route from Crosthwaite to the coast are Dearham, Aspatria and Bromfeld; all on the West Cumberland plain.

During his exile of some twenty years in Wales St Kentigern established his own monastic house on the banks of the Elwy. He returned to his original diocese following the great battle of Ardderyd (Arthuret, north of Carlisle), fought in 573. This battle placed a Christian king, Rederich Hael, on the throne of Strathclyde.

St Kentigern lived to extreme old age, dying at last in 603. His feast-day is 13 January and on that day the great Canon Rawnsley of Crosthwaite (he who helped found the National Trust) loved to preach a tremendous sermon commemorating not only St Kentigern, but also St Herbert, or Herebert, who lived as a hermit on an island of Derwent Water[3] and was the beloved friend and disciple of St Cuthbert of Lindisfarne; another saint to whom many churches and wells are dedicated in Cumbria.

The main conquest of British Cumbria by the Northumbrian English seems to date from the second half of the seventh-century. Symeon of Durham, in his *Historia Regum*, records that Ecgfrith, King of Northumbria (670–85), gave St Cuthbert, Bishop of Lindisfarne, "The land called Cartmel and all the Britons in it". This suggests that Cartmel, in Lancashire-North-of-the-Sands, came under English rule somewhat later than did Carlisle, which was in Ecgfrith's possession well before the gift of Cartmel to St Cuthbert.

St Cuthbert, who was probably Northumbrian by birth, had been a shepherd before entering the monastery of Melrose in 651. Here, ten years later, he became prior. In 664 he was transferred from Melrose to Lindisfarne (Holy Island), of which he became bishop in 685.

In that same year (according to Bede) St Cuthbert visited Ecgfrith's queen when she was staying at Carlisle with her sister-in-law, the Abbess of Carlisle, during the absence of Ecgfrith on his fatal campaign against the Picts. The citizens of Carlisle escorted St Cuthbert on a sightseeing tour of what remained of the Roman city; including a magnificent fountain at the city centre, the former Roman forum. By that period in time the art of the mason and stone-carver was lost in Britain; native British and Anglo-Saxons alike built exclusively in wood. The stone buildings and fortifications of the Romans were marvelled at as "the cunning work of giants". St Cuthbert again visited Carlisle the following year, consecrating priests and blessing the by now widowed queen.

We are told that St Cuthbert was visited annually by his beloved disciple, St Herbert and that, in return, a pilgrimage of monks from Lindisfarne journeyed each year to Derwent Water, to be blessed by St Herbert.[4] When St Herbert visited St Cuthbert in Carlisle in 686 he found the bishop an ailing man, speaking of approaching death. Legend has it that St Herbert begged the bishop to pray that they might die together. "I beseech you by the Lord not to leave me, but be mindful of your companion, and pray the Almighty goodness that, as we have served Him together on earth, we may at the same pass to heaven to see His light." St Cuthbert prayed accordingly. The friends then parted; on the night of 20 March 687, St Cuthbert died in retreat on Great Farne and St Herbert breathed his last on his island on Derwent Water.

For centuries to follow, the Vicar of Crosthwaite, attended by clergy and pilgrims from all over the northern region, including monks from Lindisfarne, went in solemn boat-borne procession up Derwent Water on each 13 April to celebrate upon St Herbert's Isle a mass in honour of the two friends, St Cuthbert and St Herbert. A 40-days' indulgence was granted to all persons who attended.

The finds of archaeologists over recent decades have revealed how extensive was the impact of Christianity upon Anglo-Saxon society, secular as well as ecclesiastical. The Christian Church, with its Mediterranean background, was like a warm wind blowing from the south; thawing the frosty north, stirring green shoots to spring up, buds to unfold and flowers to bloom. It was the Church, for example, that reintroduced the art of the mason and stone-carver to England when, in the seventh century, Benedict Biscop brought masons and glaziers from Gaul to Northumberland to work on the construction of Monkwearmouth and Jarrow. Anglo-Saxon England,[5] over the next two centuries, became the founthead of learning, literature and the arts in Europe. English illuminated manuscripts, jewelry, sculpture and metalwork became renowned. Anglo-Saxon scribes were asked for by the new monasteries of Germany and France; while the skill of the Anglo-Saxon metalworkers was such that, in Rome, Anglo-Saxon craftsmen of the *Schola Saxonum* made vessels for the altar of St Peter's.

Yet, although there were soon so many Anglo-Saxon visitors to Rome that an Anglo-Saxon quarter sprang up in that city, Northumbria's next-door neighbour, Cumbria, remained largely untouched by Anglo-Saxon influence, once away from the lowlands and the more easily accessible of the valleys. Anglian farming was arable farming; the pastoral way of life of the British in their mountain fastnesses did not attract the Anglian newcomers (indeed, it has been suggested that Cumbric continued to be spoken in the central Lake District, rather than English, until

Strathclyde finally merged in the kingdom of Scotland in the early eleventh-century).

Anglian farmsteads have not survived in Cumbria; they were built of wood, a perishable substance. The villages occupied by Anglian settlers remain living villages still; but centuries of occupation of these sites have obliterated all traces of the early buildings. No Cumbrian churches for this period have survived; though here and there we find traces of Anglo-Saxon stone fabric, as at Upper Denton (p. 46).

Instead the region abounds, gloriously, in sculptured stone crosses in Northumbrian style (it should be noted that these are never found in the central fells, for here the Anglians failed to penetrate).

These early stone crosses are invariably found in the vicinity of a holy well. The early Christian missionaries knew that every native settlement was established close by a spring, or fountain; not only for reasons of domestic water supply, but even more importantly because of the sacred associations that springs and fountains, and the trees and groves which grew by them, held for the pagan mind.

Therefore, having arrived in a suitably benighted district, the saintly evangelical would locate the sacred water source, set up his wooden cross (a symbolic Sacred Tree) and preach; baptizing his converts in the waters which they already revered and which they were thereby predisposed to accept as being inhabited by the Holy Ghost of which their impassioned visitor spoke, just as they accepted that the wooden cross stood for the Holy Tree upon which (their visitor assured them) Christ, the Son of God, who died to save them, was crucified in a country under Roman rule: a story not at all unlikely sounding to these people, who knew only too well, from their own not too distant experience of Roman rule, that the Romans never hesitated to capture and put to death any popular leader, priest, or agitating spokesman of native peoples under their domination.

In course of time these original wooden crosses were replaced by stone ones. The original pagan theme of the sacred tree (which underlies every Christian cross in mysterious counterpart) was not forgotten when these stone crosses were carved. Many of the stone crosses which survive today have been carved to resemble wooden crosses hewn from real trees; the shaft of the stone cross being round at the base and perhaps for as much as a third of the way up, like a natural tree trunk. Thereafter the rounded shaft is squared off, to present four flat façades upon which carved figures, scenes and inscriptions might be executed to the best possible visual advantage. It is perfectly possible that the original wooden crosses were squared off and decorated, or inscribed, similarly. These prototypes have not survived.

The stone crosses did not always stand alone; often there must have been several standing together; sacred groves of crosses, as it were; Christian descendants of pagan sacred groves of real trees. Whether these crosses stood in the company of small wooden chapels or if the chapels came later than the crosses, we do not know. What we do know is that today crosses and churches are found in neighbouring proximity, and that, furthermore, a holy well is often near at hand.

The earlier these stone crosses, the finer are they. The great cross of Bewcastle is not only the earliest known in Cumbria; it is also the finest. It is linked always with the cross at Ruthwell in Dumfriesshire (just over the Border and a mere 30 miles distant from Bewcastle). Both these crosses are late seventh century; Bewcastle possibly dates to the turn of the century; but it cannot be any later, its date is determined by its inscription. Ruthwell Cross, for reasons of style, is thought to pre-date Bewcastle Cross slightly. Over these two crosses Pevsner rightly becomes ecstatic, calling them "the greatest achievement of their date in the whole of Europe".

The quality of the Bewcastle Cross may perhaps not quite equal that of Ruthwell; it remains, none the less, a major work of art. The cross-head is missing (that of Ruthwell has survived) and the west face of the shaft alone bears figures. At the base of this face, in a shallow arched recess, is St John the Evangelist with the eagle. Above him is an inscription in runic; telling us that the cross commemorates Alcfrith one-time king, son of Oswi. Above this inscription, in another recess, is the figure of a youthful, touchingly human-looking Christ, stepping on a lion and an adder (a Coptic motif). Above him in a third, but this time rectangular, recess is John the Baptist with the *Agnus Dei*.

On the east face of the shaft is an inhabited vine-scroll; that is, a vine-scroll in the interstices of which perch and clamber a variety of birds and beasts. This vine-scrolling of Bewcastle Cross is of an extraordinary animation; you feel, as you look at it, that if you watch long enough the birds and animals must at last lose their shyness at your presence and begin to move.

Vine-scrolling is of eastern Mediterranean origin. Mediterranean, too, is the knotty interlace patterning on the south and north faces of the shaft. Furthermore, on the north face, is a panel of check-work design highly reminiscent of the illustrative work in the Coptic Book of Durrow. This is not surprising: Coptic inspiration has been proved for the inconography of the Bewcastle and Ruthwell crosses. Monasticism had its origin in Egypt; Irish monasticism derived from the Coptic (that is, Egyptian), via the south of France; from Ireland the Coptic influence reached Scotland and Northumbria.

Cumbria's other celebrated Anglian cross, at Irton (Lower Eskdale, West Cumberland), is ninth century and has great affinity with Irish crosses of the same date. The carving which covers every inch of it is an intricate ecstasy of pattern-work, the overall effect of which is powerful to the point of disturbing.

If the Irton Cross ranks, in quality, next to Bewcastle, the Kenneth Cross, at Dearham, must rank next to Irton. Dearham church stands just outside its village (which lies between Cockermouth and Maryport). The church is of only recent dedication to St Mungo and should possibly more correctly be dedicated to St Kenneth.

The greater part of the present building is Norman (the north aisle was restored in 1882); its most arresting external feature is the square and formidable thirteenth-century tower, built as a pele-tower defence against Scots raiders. The church has a notable Norman font (p. 92), but above all it is famous for its Anglo-Saxon and Anglo-Viking sculptures (p. 70). There is every indication that Dearham, from very early times, was a place of considerable Christian significance. A small Anglo-Saxon church stood here (built, it is thought, with Roman stone) before the present early twelfth-century Norman edifice.

The beautiful (albeit fragmented) ninth-century Anglo-Saxon cross, known as the Kenneth Cross, tells the story of St Kenneth, or Kennedus. A large fragment of its cross-shaft stands in the west window of the tower. Kennedus, a child of noble birth, having been born lame was considered to have been cursed by an evil eye and so the infant was set adrift in a coracle, from which he was rescued by a seagull, who reared him in its nest; the bird bringing the baby goat's milk, in a bell, from the nearby forest. When Kennedus grew older he wandered in the forest and there he was adopted by a shepherd, who reared him as a Christian. In manhood Kennedus became a missionary, travelling about the country on horseback. The carving of this cross-shaft is lively and touching; the fragment under discussion shows the seagull and, above the bird, the saint mounted on his horse in the mission field.

It must be borne in mind that (the effects of weathering apart) the contemporary appearance of all these stone crosses would have been vastly different from what we see today, for it seems that they were all brightly painted (as surviving traces of gesso reveal).

Mediterranean echoes reach us, however faintly, from all these Anglo-Saxon crosses. The wind from the south blew strongly indeed to reach thus far north, with such force and energy! But a new wind was now to blow; from a very different direction.

"In this year", says the *Anglo-Saxon Chronicle* under the year 793,

> dire portents appeared over Northumbria and sorely frightened the people. They consisted of immense whirlwinds and flashes of lightning, and fiery dragons were seen flying in the air. A great famine immediately followed these signs, and a little after that, on 8 June, the ravages of heathen men miserably destroyed God's church on Lindisfarne, with plunder and slaughter.

These heathen marauders were of Danish origin. At first they came in small bands, intent on plunder, but by the middle of the ninth century large, organized armies of them were ravaging the country. Those Lindisfarne monks who survived the first attack rebuilt the church of their sacked monastery but, in 875, Bishop Eardulph, fearful of fresh assault, fled with his monks before the impending gale force. The monks took with them the body of St Cuthbert in its carved oak coffin, together with the saint's pectoral cross of gold, shell and garnet; his ivory comb; his small portable altar (the latter of a type not infrequently used by priests of those days on their evangelical missions) and his chalice,[6] presumably a small travelling one that went with the altar. In addition to these relics Bishop Eardulph took with him the glorious illustrated manuscript known to posterity as the *Lindisfarne Gospels* (today in the British Museum).

For a brief period the body of St Cuthbert rested at Carlisle. But fear of the Danes forced the monks of Lindisfarne to move on, bearing their precious burden with them (their fear was not misplaced; Carlisle was attacked by the Danes shortly after the monks had departed).

There are sixteen churches dedicated to St Cuthbert in Cumbria, ranging from Bewcastle in the north-east to Seascale in the south-west. A number of routes have been surmised for the fleeing monks, but we may be fairly certain that they travelled down the coastal plain to Workington, thereafter taking an easterly line, via Dearham and Lorton, to the Salkelds, Edenhall and Dufton; a route well marked by dedications of churches and holy wells. It was a long and weary period of virtual wandering in the wilderness; at last the homeless Lindisfarne community came to rest at Chester-le-Street, near Durham, where they remained from 883 to 995. In this year they finally settled at Durham itself. Here a cathedral was raised in St Cuthbert's honour and herein his remains were enshrined.

Hafdan had sacked Carlisle with such brutality that the city lay derelict for the next 200 years. The actual stay of the Danish invaders in Cumbria was of comparatively brief duration; they confined themselves to desecration of the coastal low country and then moved on, east of the Pennines.

But the gale from the north was not to cease blowing; in 925 a fresh wave of invaders arrived. These were Norsemen, coming up the Solway in a steady infiltration, not directly from Scandinavia, having sojourned for a considerable time in Ireland, where the Gaelic language had to some extent affected their own and where, furthermore, they had learned something of Christianity. They were not predators like the Danes who had come before them, but were of much more peaceable disposition and looking for a place to settle. The mountains, troughed valleys and gleaming glacial lakes of Cumbria struck deep chords; this was a country much resembling their ancestral homeland. These Vikings adopted the place as their own and, integrating with the native Cwymry as the Anglo-Saxons had never done, gave to modern Cumbria its remarkable and inimitable ancestry.

Near Gosforth, in south-west Cumberland, the rivers Esk and Mitre meet in a sad estuary. The cries of sea birds agitate the ear continually, but the eye meets with utter stillness; a motionless and almost undefined expanse of sand, water and sky, each melting into the other, silver and amber; a coast lost in silt and time. And we gaze at the dunes, and the sere grass tummocks, and the long glisk of firth beyond, and for a moment we think we see the black ships coming up it; one behind the other, riding very low and flat-backed in the water, with the prows reared high, stiff and straight, so that, from a great distance, they exactly resemble cormorants among the waves.

In Gosforth churchyard the great Anglo-Viking cross rears over us; tall, upright and prow-like; its shaft extremely slender and its head very small in relation to the shaft's height. It is carved from sandstone; the shaft rounded, like a tree trunk, for a third of the way up from the ground and thereafter squared-off and four-sided. This towering cross (which is in fact fourteen and a half feet high) stands in a rectangular socket of three plain steps. It is late tenth century in date.

Gosforth Cross is not only the Tree of Christ's crucifixion; it stands also as the pagan World Axis. It is the Ash tree, Yggdrasil, of Norse mythology; the Tree of the Universe, of Time and of Life. Norse legend has it that Yggdrasil's roots were planted in the depths of the ocean and that round this underwater base of the world's axis was coiled the Midgardsworm, or Jormungandr, the giant sea serpent that girdled the Earth, biting his tail with his own teeth.[7] The sacred stag, or hart, Eikthyrnir, browsed upon the leaf-buds of Yggdrasil, close to the highest point of the Tree: this highest point being known as Lärad (Peace-giver). Lärad overshadowed Valhalla, where were the twelve halls of the twelve gods. Raised high in the centre of Idavollr (the vale of the combat of champions) was the throne of Odin.

The Gosforth Cross is the most famous of the many remarkable Anglo-Viking sculptures that survive in Cumbria. It affords truly striking testimony of the transitory state of religious belief of the Norse immigrants: tentatively embracing Christian faith, yet with their ancient pagan convictions still vividly in mind, intertwined with the new teaching. The remarkable resultant conception is plain to see on Gosforth Cross, though not always easy to follow.

The best guide to the carving on this cross is the Reverend W. S. Calverley, one time vicar of Dearham, who made the cross and its associated sculpture a virtual life-long study. Together with C. A. Parker and Professor Magnus Petersen of Copenhagen, he produced a detailed account of the Gosforth Cross which has never been bettered.[8]

According to Calverley the Gosforth cross-head, with its threefold divisions in the four arms around the central boss, symbolized, for the followers of Odin, the twelve halls of the gods in Valhalla. The central boss was the seat of Odin in Idavollr. To the Christian these threefold divisions were the sacred symbols of the Trinity; the Triquetra, beloved by the early Christian church.

The scenes portrayed on the four sides of the cross-shaft are drawn from Vala's prophecy in the *Völuspá* and they depict the Twilight of the Gods (the Æsir), and the Last Battle, Ragnarök. Into this world of Nordic saga is introduced, and interwoven, the Christian theme of the Saviour, the Crucifixion and the battle with the Last Enemy, Death, and the triumphant rising of Christ from the dead.

The monsters against whom the Æsir fought in the Last Battle were the Midsgardsworm, the Fenris Wolf, and the Daughter of Hel. These three monsters were the children of the Witch of Jotenheim (the Land of Giants) by Loki, the Wolf-Demon.

Examining the carvings on the upper parts of the east and west faces of the cross we see that the first figure immediately beneath the Triquetra, in each instance, is a monster with a wolf's head. These two monsters are Skiöll and Hati, progeny of the Fenris Wolf (owing their exceptional ferocity to the diet of marrow-bones and blood of murderers and felons on which they had been reared, during the final Age, The Age of the Wolf, when all laws were broken and the destruction of the world drew near).

For Christians these monsters symbolized the forces of evil rushing from either side to destroy the Triquetra on the cross-head; that is to say, Christianity itself. Their Icelandic symbolism was drawn from the legendary rôle of Skiöll and Hati; one of whom should swallow the sun, the other the moon (the eastern face of the cross-head, in this context, represents the sun and the western face the moon).

The scene at the foot of the carved panel of the west face of the cross-shaft shows Loki bound, with the adder round his neck, while Sigūn kneels before her lord and master and holds out the basin. Loki, with his dirty tricks and jibes, had at last so disgusted the gods that Skadi, the wife of Niord, had warned him,

> Thou art merry, Loki!
> Not for long wilt thou
> frisk with unbinded tail;
> Thee, on a rock's point,
> with the entrails of thy ice-cold son,
> the gods shall bind.

So it came to pass. Loki was bound, and thus he lay in Hel's dark home beneath the gratings of the dead until the time of Ragnarök. Skadi took a venomous serpent (an adder) and fastened it up over Loki's face. The venom from its fangs trickled down and Sigūn, Loki's wife, caught the venom in a basin and when the basin became full she carried it out, whereat the venom dribbled down on to Loki, who writhed so violently that the whole earth shook (which, said the Old Norse, was the explanation of earthquakes!).

(At Kirkby Stephen church (p. 156) there is a very fine carving of Loki bound. This stone is traditionally known as the Bound Devil. Loki stands chained; half man, half wolf-demon, with a bearded, trowel-shaped, slant-eyed face, strangely, though perhaps on reflection not so strangely, akin to the devil-faces above the south door of not so distant St Michael's church at Brough. In Loki we find, already established, the traditional northern-hemisphere concept of the Devil's appearance, save that there are no horns. Yet, to compensate as it were for the lack of these, this Loki-Devil at Kirkby Stephen has one or two other fascinating characteristics. His boots, for instance, deserve attention; they are real Wicked Uncle's boots. Moreover there is something about him which tells us that if we could turn him round, thereby obtaining a view of his rear, we should discover that he has a wolf's tail.)

Above the Gosforth carving of Loki and Sigūn and below the wolf who rushes to swallow the moon are two more horrid wolf-headed demons, with knotted serpent-like bodies. They hang suspended heads downward, lower jaw to lower jaw, eyes fiercely glaring, fangs bared, in the act of leaping to attack the figure of a man. Bearded, and wearing a belted tunic, he stands calmly athwart the cross-shaft; holding the monsters at bay with his staff, which he grips magnificently in his right hand, while in his left he holds a horn. He is Heimdall, the warder of Asgard, and he has just blown his Gaillahorn to warn the gods of the imminence of the Last Battle against the forces of evil. Meantime he holds back the twin monsters, who cannot wait to sink their fangs in him.

Next to Heimdall we see another belted and bearded man, riding on a pony, or small horse. This horseman, who grasps a short spear in his right hand, is Odin; he has armed himself and mounted his steed, Sleipnir, to ride down to Mimir's Well, there to consult the oracle (horse and rider are *upside down* because they travel downward);

> Further forward I see,
> much can I say
> of Ragnarök
> and the gods' conflict.
> An axe age, a sword age,
> shields shall be cloven,

a wind age, a wolf age,
ere the world sinks . . .
Loud blows Heimdall,
his horn is raised;
Odin speaks
with Mimir's head.

On the south face of the cross we find Odin still riding; but the right way up, now, for he is on his way back. Beneath this mounted Odin is the coiled body of a headless serpent (an adder, as we can see from the zig-zag pattern on its back). This is the serpent who separates the land of the living from Naströnd, the shore of the dead.

Meantime simultaneous action is going on elsewhere, and this the rest of the carving on the south face depicts. At the top is a wolf-headed serpent-monster knotted upon itself and under this is another wolf-monster, bound and gagged; Loki's *doppelgänger*, his symbolic second self. Beneath this gagged wolf-monster is Eikthyrnir, the sacred hart, founthead of living waters,

From his horns fall drops
into Hvergelmir,
whence all waters rise.

Below Eikthyrnir and immediately above Odin's head we see the bonds and the adder from which Loki has now broken free. From his bonds now bursts too, in a loping bound, the great wolf-monster, Loki's *doppelgänger*,

Trembles Yggdrasil's Ash
yet standing;
the ancient tree groans
and the *jotün* [Loki] is loosed . . .
His bonds he rends asunder
and the wolf runs.

The Last Battle, Ragnarök, is about to begin; or, in the sense of the Christian interpretation, the fight with the Last Enemy, Death.

We now turn to the east face. In a central panel we find a figure with arms outstretched in crucified posture; this figure is bearded and garbed in belted tunic. He has been wounded in the right side by a man who stands *below* the panel, gazing upward, and who holds a spear with which he seems to have pierced in the side the man suspended, or standing, above him in the position of crucifixion (Calverley maintains that this figure with the spear is decisively a Roman soldier, because he is the only beardless figure on the cross-shaft and it was the Roman custom to go clean-shaven). Next to this man with the spear stands a woman, her long hair worn in a thick straight plait. She is holding a vial-shaped object. The figure in the central panel is beyond doubt Odin-Christ,

> I say that I hung
> on a wind-rocked tree,
> nine whole nights,
> with a spear wounded,
> and to Odin offered
> myself to myself;
> on that tree,
> of which no one knows
> from what root it springs.

The woman standing beside the supposed Roman soldier is, it seems, Mary Magdalene and she is holding an alabaston; that is, a sealed long-necked alabaster vial containing perfumed oils. According to the Gospel of St Mark, Mary Magdalene broke an alabaster box of ointment with which she proposed to anoint the body of Christ. This "box" would in all probability have been an alabaston; the necks of which were broken off when the oil was to be used.

Below this representation of the crucifixion of Odin-Christ are two furious wolf-headed monsters, clasped in mortal combat. Odin, says the saga, was swallowed by Loki, the wolf-demon. No sooner had the wolf-demon swallowed Odin than Vidar (a son, or reincarnation, of Odin) confronted the wolf. On the cross-shaft we see Vidar standing, pinning down the wolf's lower jaw with his foot and with his left hand prising wide the creature's upper jaw, while with his right hand Vidar grips his spear, ready to deliver a death blow.

Immediately above the crucifixion are five vertebrae with double ribs; a headless spine. Calverley suggests that this headless spine is a symbol of the wolf-monster of death now destroyed by decapitation at the hands of Vidar; or, in Christian terms, death vanquished.

This theme of triumph over death is continued on the north face of the cross. Here the central portion shows two armed horsemen; one advancing and the other, it seems, riding away. Calverley thinks that this latter is Odin, while the advancing horseman is Baldr (the Beautiful One, the Peacegiver, the Bright Son of the Father); in short, Baldr-Christ. He is returning and riding up the rainbow at the moment of the glorious resurrection. Thus, the Final Battle has been fought and the monsters of evil overcome; the Last Enemy, Death, has been defeated.

Whatever the doubts of the detailed meaning of the various episodes carved on the Gosforth Cross, there can be no question at all that here the Nordic pagan and Christian faiths meet and that the pagan belief is re-interpreted according to Christian gospel.

It seems that this cross, together with others to be found in lowland Cumbria, was inspired by the eighth- and ninth-century high crosses of Ireland. The Norse immigrants from across the Irish Sea, on arrival in this new country, erected crosses similar to those that they had left behind them.

An article in the *Gentlemen's Magazine* for 1799 tells us that Gosforth Cross originally had a fellow cross at some seven feet or so distant, the intervening space being covered by a horizontal stone on which was carved a large sword. The second cross was taken down "within living memory" (said this article) and was converted into a sundial to be "put into the parson's garden". It is worth noting that Gosforth church was extensively restored in 1789;[9] it is probable that this desecration of the second cross occurred then.

The village stocks stood close by the Gosforth Cross in the old days and it is recorded that the last person to be confined in them was a man called Sewell, whose offence was that he had shinned up the cross and seated himself on the top of it one Sunday morning when "parson" was late for Divine Service, due to his having enjoyed too "murry a neet Satada'".

In addition to the great cross there are other important sculptures of the same period to be seen inside Gosforth church; two may well be part of the destroyed cross-shaft. On one fragment of cross-shaft a deer, or stag, is trampling upon a knotted serpent, or serpents. Below this, in a second panel of carving, is a knotted serpent of vast proportions, lying beneath a boat with a short, sturdy mast topped with a crow's-nest. To the left of the mast sits a man holding what appears to be a mallet, or hammer, in his right hand, while in his left is the end of a very thick fishing line. This line has been severed and the other part of it extends deep down into the sea, where enormous fish (which have every appearance of being whales) approach to circle round a large bait on the end of the line; this bait being, perhaps, the head of a horned animal (though it is not possible to be certain about this).

In one episode of Icelandic mythology the god Thor decided to catch and destroy the Midgardsworm lying on the ocean bed. Thor baited a line with the head of the largest possible ox, belonging to Hyme, a giant. Thor then put out to sea with Hyme. The baited line was cast overboard and the Midgardsworm rose from the sea bed and took the bait, whereat Thor hauled the Midgardsworm to the surface; but the monster struggled so violently that the bottom of the boat was staved in. Thor then stood with his feet on the sea bed and again hauled the Midgardsworm to the surface and commenced to strike it on the head with his hammer. At which,

> The icebergs resounded,
> the caverns howled,
> the old earth
> shrank together

and Hyme became so overwhelmed with terror that he fetched out his hatchet and cut the line, whereat the Midgardsworm sank back into the sea and escaped!

Also inside this church are two Viking-Christian hogback tombstones, one of which, known as the Saint's Tomb, has a figure of Christ carved on one of its short ends. The second hogback has, on one of its long sides, a remarkable battle scene with two armies facing each other: they stand enflanked, holding spears and shields. One man, as if in capitulation, kneels between the two armies; he is stripped to the waist and unarmed. He may be capitulating on behalf of the entire army at his back; the foremost man of this holds a flag, but whether it is our equivalent of a white flag, or a standard, who can say? On the other hand, the kneeling figure may be a captive, brought in by one chieftain and his men and presented now to another. The one thing that is abundantly clear from the carving is that the kneeling man is unarmed, defeated and apprehensive.

Whatever meaning is read into these sculptures they are indisputably works of art and, moreover, deeply moving ones. They speak most poignantly of the human condition and of those dark fears and uncertainties and eternal hopes and longings which are as much part of that condition today as they were 1,000 years ago.

An idea of what Gosforth Cross and its now missing fellow cross must have looked like in juxtaposition, one with the other, will be obtained when we visit the celebrated so-called Giant's Grave in the churchyard of St Andrew's, Penrith.

The Giant's Grave is situated north of the north wall of the church and consists of two tenth-century, high Anglo-Viking crosses with small, free-armed cross-heads. The taller of the two crosses, just over eleven feet in height, is decorated with abundant interlace. The shorter cross, just under eleven feet tall, has not only interlace pattern but also, on one side of the squared section of the cross-shaft, a bound male figure with a woman beside him and a serpent above his head. Above the serpent is the *Agnus Dei*. Interesting as these crosses are they cannot compare in beauty and importance with the Gosforth Cross. Nevertheless the two of them still stand *in situ* and the intervening space between them is still covered by four sides of red-sandstone hogback coffins, decorated with various interlace motifs; but one coffin has a snake, and a small figure standing on the snake's head.

North-west of the west tower of the church stands a third tenth-century cross; traditionally known as the Giant's Thumb. This cross is shorter than the other two and its head is wheel-type. Its sides are ornamented with interlace, and close scroll in the Anglian tradition.

Dearham church rejoices in a major collection of Anglo-Viking sculpture, including a wonderful wheel-head cross. On the east face of the cross-shaft we see the interlacing boughs of Yggdrasil; the ash-tree's roots strike into the earth at the base of the sculpture. Depicted, too, are the pair of ravens which were the divine messengers of Odin. This cross formerly stood in the churchyard, before it was brought inside the church for preservation. It now stands in a side aisle, near the vestry door.

At Dearham too is the famous Adam Stone (thought originally to have been a grave cover but now placed upright, in stele position, on the left-hand side of a window near the main church door). It is possibly somewhat earlier than the tenth-century cross. The Adam Stone, so-called because it is inscribed "Adam" (upside down) at its base, is thought to represent the Fall and Redemption of Man. The top of the stone has been damaged; it is inscribed, in runic, "May Christ his soul save". Seven rather puzzling round bodies are said to represent the seven days of the creation of Heaven and Earth; below these seven circles we see Adam and Eve walking hand-in-hand, with God, in the Garden of Eden. Each stands beneath an arch studded with eight studs, said to be the star-studded vaults of Heaven. Biting the foot of Adam is a serpent, which has next to it another serpent described, by some experts, as having "a bruised head" (*Genesis* 3: 15), though this is a detail very difficult for the inexpert eye to distinguish! Under these two serpents is a large quatrefoil with a design of crossed bones beneath it, while beneath these bones are some mysterious geometrical shapes, or symbols, which, as we gaze earnestly at them, may (or may not!) resolve into a (possibly winged) bearded face (upside down), staring back at us from under an (inverted) arch of Heaven: this is God the Father, supposedly. The symbol alongside, a circular body encircled within a not quite circular circle, represents (so says the small booklet on sale in the church) the warmth of the Father's love. Finally comes the Viking interlace which everyone seems to agree symbolizes eternal Life.

This stone was discovered serving as a lintel over the north door. It is thought that it was probably placed there in the late twelfth century, being then removed from its original situation as a grave stone. Nobody today knows whether the stone, in its rôle as door-lintel, had its carved face visible to the congregation or not.

At Cross Canonby, a mile or so from Dearham, there is a fine fragment of cross-shaft with dragon-like monsters alternately the right way up and upside down. They appear to be entwined in some way and perhaps biting into themselves. One narrow face of the cross-shaft has a carving of a large, serpent-like dragon; the two remaining faces are designed with interlace. There is also a fine hogback in the churchyard and, inside the church, a fascinating coffin lid that is late Anglo-Scandinavian merging into Norman.

At neighbouring Gilcrux are two pieces of interesting cross-shaft; at nearby Plumbland is a hogback tombstone now in three large fragments; a pity, for it is carved with some impressive monsters.

The church of St Kentigern, Aspatria, is fascinating because of its association with that saint, as well as possessing a good collection of Viking sculpture. Pilgrims of St Kentigern will find, in a niche in the external east wall of the chancel, an extremely weathered and time-worn bust of "Sanctus Kentigernus". The holy well was in the old glebe meadow near the church. Inside the church an original Norman arch, formerly part of the chancel arch, will be noticed to have been re-used in the vestry doorway. The early- or mid-thirteenth-century font is famous and is thought to have been carved by the same craftsman-artist who made the very similar, and equally fine, font in the church at Cross Canonby (for discussion of these fonts see Chapter 7). The best Anglo-Viking piece here at Aspatria is an exceptionally fine hogback coffin; there is also a long fragment of cross-shaft, with interlace. A modern copy of the Gosforth Cross stands in the churchyard.

Bromfeld church is dedicated to St Mungo (Kentigern); though like Aspatria's church the building was extensively restored in Victorian times. Some fragments of Norman frieze survive and the south doorway has a handsome zig-zagged, re-set Norman arch. St Kentigern is depicted in the modern glass of the church's west window; he is shown as a feeble old man with his jaw supported by a linen band tied round his head, as Joscelin's *Life* tells us was the case in the saint's final years (this portrait was copied from a seal in the British Museum). Viking sculpture at Bromfeld is a little disappointing; there remains but a fragmentary cross-shaft.

In a field adjoining the churchyard you will find St Mungo's Well, with a humble little stone building erected over it.

During our subsequent travelling around Cumbria we should remember that at Lowther (some eight miles south of Penrith) there is a remarkable hogback coffin in the porch of the church of St Michael. This hogback is carved with scenes of naval battle; two Viking ships are shown, with shielded warriors. Between the ships floats a deity rising out of the waves and making a gesture of peace.

At Dacre (five miles north-west of Lowther) we find, in addition to the ninth-century Anglian cross-shaft, a tenth-century cross-shaft which is highly reminiscent of Dearham's Adam Stone. Here are Adam and Eve, and the World Ash, Yggdrasil; this Icelandic Sacred Tree counterparting the Biblical Tree of Knowledge. Present too is Eikthynir, the Sacred Hart.

Travelling from Lowther ten miles to the east, to Long Marton, we discover more mythological mystery. Here, in the eleventh- and twelfth-century church of St Margaret and St James, are two tympani which are quite extraordinary. The first, above the eleventh-century south doorway, is monopolized by two large creatures: one (a portrait of the Loch Ness monster far more convincing than anything yet produced by modern zoologists plumbing the depths of Loch Ness) symbolizes Evil. It stands with long, knotted tail and turned head, directing a malevolent reptilian glare at a quadruped which is obviously intended to represent something rather glorious; it has a buck's body and neck, greatly suggestive of Eikthynir, but with the head transformed into an eagle with fully extended wings. Meanwhile, high in the sky above these two creatures, floats the Christian emblem of the sacred quatrefoil and next to it is a winged disk much akin to the winged disk of Dearham's Adam Stone (and also distantly akin to the round-faced deity making gestures of peace towards the Lowther hogback's Viking ships). However, this winged disk at Long Marton is rendered especially perplexing by what seems to be a long-handled dagger thrust into it at the juncture of the wings; stressing, perhaps, that Christ, the Son of God the Father, died to save mankind? The second tympanum, above the west door, depicts, rather more obscurely, another fantastic beast and a horrifying reptilian bird.

Again, when we get to St Bees, West Cumberland, we shall find yet another somewhat similar lintel; this depicts a winged monster with a terrifying array of teeth that is being attacked by an armed figure (traditionally said to be St Michael). There is balancing design of Viking interlace, and what appears to be a bird within a circle; but this might equally well be a winged head of God the Father within an arc, or glory.

At Fell Foot in Little Langdale, about a mile up the Wrynose road above Little Langdale Tarn, is an old farmhouse with the arms of Fletcher Fleming over the door. Behind it may be detected an odd terraced knoll; this H. Swainson Cowper claimed to be the site at which the Norse council, or *Thing*, assembled. W. G. Collingwood doubted this, however, pointing out that here had been an ancient orchard and that the artificial terraces may well have resulted from cultivation. More recent scholarship suggests that a field in Swindale, in the Shap region, might have been the assembly place; a thirteenth-century charter assigns to it the name *Thengeheved*. Perhaps it was here, then, that Anglo-Viking leaders, or chieftains, met?

We might not unreasonably expect that Cumbria would yield up some exciting Viking burial-places. So far such has not been the case, though there is a persistent popular legend that, somewhere along the West Cumberland coast, lies a chieftain encased in gold and surrounded by great treasure! This tale is almost certainly apocryphal, albeit immensely alluring.

In the eighteenth century a Viking burial mound was excavated at Round Barrow, Gilcrux; the mound contained a stone burial chamber in which a warrior had been laid to rest, together with his weapons and a fine gold brooch. Other similar burials have been found at West Seaton, near Workington, and at not far distant Eaglesfield.

Such discoveries excite the imagination, but the relic which is the most poignantly moving is a monument in the churchyard of Beckermet St Bridget, the old parish church of Beckermet, just outside the village of Beckermet St John (in the church of which there are some interesting fragments of sculpture). The church of St Bridget is the plainest and simplest little building possible; it is mainly early eighteenth century in date, but it stands upon a raised mound that is an immensely ancient sacred site; time-honoured even when Saxon, Viking and Norman Cumbria were blending and the monument which we have come to see was placed here, in what was by then a well-established Christian churchyard.

This churchyard today is lonely and neglected. We search, and at a little distance beyond the church we find, among the much later graves, two cross-shafts, each still standing, but each broken short. The first is so excessively weathered that nothing can be made of its detail. The second is better preserved: it bears a runic inscription which, translated, reads,

To Beloved
Offspring Edih
Little Maid In
Slumber Waned
Years XII Pray Ye For Her Soul
Year M.C. III

4

AN ESSAY IN ESSENCE

Lower Eskdale—Herdwycks and Herdwick Sheep—Ravenglass—Ratty—Boot—Dalegarth Force—Eskdale Church—Burn Moor—Coffin Roads—Superstitions, Ancient Ceremonies and Customs—Place-names and Dialect

ESKDALE WAS PROBABLY one of the first valleys to be penetrated by the Norse immigrants.

The economy of these immigrants was, it seems, based chiefly on cattle; these and swine being their principal livestock, though recent research seems to have established that the immigrants brought sheep with them. However, since wolves were rife in the Cumbrian high country (as innumerable surviving place-names confirm) hill sheep farming as we know it would have been an impossibility; small flocks of sheep were kept in enclosures near the settlements. There was no expansion of sheep farming until the early fifteenth century, when the wolf finally disappeared from the region.

Cattle, less easy prey for wolves, were grazed in the woodlands by day and driven back to the settlements at nightfall. As the countryside surrounding the original settlements became overgrazed fresh grazing grounds further afield were sought. These outlying pastures were guarded by herdsmen who built themselves small hut-settlements; at first simply as summer *sætrs*, or shielings, but in due course developing into established all-the-year-round homesteads. By this process of gradual, but steady, outward expansion Norse occupation extended further and further into previously unoccupied places. Inevitably this process involved destruction of woodlands, because grazing prevented regeneration and, equally inevitably, this development of the more remote, hitherto impenetrable regions meant that the wolf was doomed to gradual extinction. Following elimination of the wolf, hill sheep farming could at last flourish.

The traditional Cumbrian breed of sheep is the Herdwick. This name, in monastic times, stood for the sheep farm itself, the *herd-wyck*, and was not applied to the sheep. The origin of this unique breed has always been shrouded in mystery. Herdwicks, says one legend, reached the region from off a wrecked Spanish ship following the Armada; not a convincing theory. A second legend has it that the Norsemen brought the sheep with them. Recent genetical work with sheep goes far to confirm this latter suggestion. The Herdwick is small in size, stockily built, whitey-grey faced, strongly and coarsely fleeced, exceptionally hardy and endowed with amazing powers of endurance all the year round upon the high fells. It is astoundingly agile ("terrible lish", capable of leaping a six-foot wall from a standing jump, as I have witnessed myself!). The ewes are hornless. All this adds up to an animal that strongly resembles and is "possibly the sole survivor of a hairy Norse sheep" said to have existed in south-west Scotland 200 years ago (Ryder). This same authority has pointed out that the combination of a whitey-grey face with a high frequency of the gene controlling the presence of haemoglobin *A* is not found in any other breed of mountain sheep in Britain, but does occur in some Scandinavian breeds.

Certain features of Cumbrian farmstead architecture have their counterparts in Norway today: for example, wool-lofts over shippons, the loft gained from outside by a cart ramp; covered spinning or storage galleries; the habit of constructing the farmstead as a long, single range of dwelling-house and outbuildings (a Norse "long-house"). As these features are found in the Cumbrian high country in buildings not dating before the sixteenth-century at the earliest it is clear that the building habits of the Norse settlers have been handed down over many generations.

Handed down, too, is the tradition, still universal throughout Cumbria today, as in medieval times, that the flock goes with the farm and is an integral part of the property, taken over by each new owner, or incoming tenant. He may build up an additional flock, or flocks, of his own which he, when he moves away, may sell, or take with him, but when he leaves he must hand over to his successor a farm flock of the same stipulated number of sheep as that which originally came to him with the farm. Records reveal that these "farm flocks", over the centuries, have scarcely varied in size from the original flocks of monastic times. The size of a farm's flocks has always been dictated by the grazing capacity of the available sheep heafs (heaths), or grazing grounds; each flock having a heaf traditionally allotted to it, and each heaf being reached by a recognized drove, or drift, road.

Since earliest times it has been found necessary to mark the sheep of each flock with certain identifying marks, so that they may be easily identified if they roam beyond their own heaf and thus be returned to their rightful flock. The method of marking consists of smitting, with a paint-like substance, and notching or slitting the ears. An expert can tell by one glance which flock a sheep belongs to.

Female sheep are called gimmers, the males are wethers, or wedders. During their first winter, however, they are all hoggs, or hoggets, irrespective of their sex. They remain hoggs until the ensuing spring, when they become shearlings; a gimmer shearling, a wedder shearling. After a second winter they become gimmer, or wedder, twinters and thereafter they graduate to becoming staid ewes and tups.

The prevalent breed of sheep upon the Cumbrian fells today is Herdwick crossed with Swaledale, or Herdwick crossed with Blackface. Herdwick wool, being coarser, fetches less than Swaledale; on the other hand a Herdwick will have more wool on it. Fortunately for the pure Herdwick breed there has been revived interest in this traditional native of the fells and today you will find many Lake Country farms where great pride is taken in a flock of pure-bred Herdwicks.

What breed of sheep dog the earliest Cumbrian flock-masters used we do not know; we must suppose that dogs were used, for a dog is an integral part of a shepherd. The medieval system of counting sheep, however, survived in remoter Cumbria down to the opening years of the present century. It has now ceased to be used and is repeated only as a delightful curiosity,

"Yan, tan, tether, mether, pimp,
Teezar, leezar, catterah, horna, dick,
Yan-dick, tan-dick, tether-dick, mether-dick, bumpit,
Yan-a-bumpit, tan-a-bumpit, tedera-bumpit, medera-bumpit, gigot."

After which you start again, notching off the twenties on your fingers.

The pundits who have defined the boundaries of the Lake District (at least in theory) have agreed that Eskdale lies partly within the District and partly in West Cumberland. The magic boundary line, they say, passes through the little hamlet of Boot, in mid-Eskdale; all above is Lake District, below is not. This, though not the National Park definition, is the opinion of Messrs Baddeley, Symonds and Wainwright, the three most famous of modern guides to the District.[1]

Tempting as it is to dismiss this kind of talk as categorical nonsense, it is correct inasmuch as Eskdale (always locally pronounced Eshd'll) is undoubtedly divided into two: Upper, and Lower. Upper Eskdale, uninhabited save for a farm or two at its lower end (including the famous Brotherilkeld, pronounced Buttrikelt, possibly the earliest of all the great dalehead *herd-wycks*), is dramatically rough upland country, strictly the province of the serious walking fraternity; there are no roads. Lower Eskdale, on the other hand, is of much milder disposition, blending at its outlet into the West Cumberland coastal plain.

The journey up Eskdale, to Boot, should be made by La'al Ratty, the miniature railway that is Eskdale's best-known, best-loved feature: a fifteen-inch gauge line running from Ravenglass to Boot and originally built in 1875 to transport the Eskdale granite from which iron ore was obtained. In due course Ratty's industrial rôle changed; he no longer conveyed granite, but instead carried increasing numbers of tourists until, today, a trip on this little railway is one of the most notable jaunts in the region. Railway buffs take Ratty very seriously indeed. Everything about the railway is to scale; the platforms, turntable, level-crossings. The engines themselves are perfect small-scale reproductions of the famous engines which crossed the Rocky Mountains.

The rail's end is at Dalegarth Halt, just outside Boot. A good mile beyond Dalegarth Halt is the celebrated Woolpack Inn and a little further beyond the inn is the Youth Hostel. This present Woolpack was built towards the close of the great pack-trains; these came over from the Langdales by the Wrynose and Hardknott passes, and from Hawkshead and Coniston via Walna Scar and Birker Moor, bound for the ports of the West Cumberland coast. The older inn, now Penny Hill Farm, lies about a quarter of a mile from the main road (see also p. 310). As is so often the case, the traffic that prompted the building of a larger inn drew to a close shortly after it was built.

From Penny Hill, reached by crossing a lovely little pack-horse bridge, a pleasant path takes you back in the direction of Boot, past Low Birker, to bring you out close by Dalegarth Hall, a former fortified manorhouse with pele, the ancient home of the Stanley family. Above the Hall are the falls known either as Stanley Gill Force, or Dalegarth Force; they are among the best of Cumbrian waterfalls.

The little church of St Catherine lies about a half-mile from the village;

in the churchyard you will find the grave of Tommy Dobson, one of the most famous of all Lake Country huntsmen and Master of the Eskdale and Ennerdale fox hounds for 53 years. His gravestone is unusual, inasmuch as it has his portrait carved upon it. Tommy Dobson was not an Eskdale man by birth; he came from Stavely in Westmorland in 1827; he was a bobbin-turner by trade and it is said that pursuit of work brought him to Eskdale, though a legend persists in hunting circles that Tommy moved to Eskdale because he was wanted for poaching. He was 23 when, for whatever reason, he made his move to his new home, where he began hunting with his own two hounds, Cruiser and Charmer. In those days there were no large, established packs of hounds; instead each dale and hamlet had its small pack made up of hounds from individual farms and cottages, "trencher-fed packs" as they were called. The scattered, individually-owned local hounds one by one joined Dobson's kennels during the hunting season, so that, almost by accident rather than design, a first-rate fell-pack became established. In 1883 the Eskdale and Ennerdale was born officially, with Tommy as Master and Huntsman. He died in 1910, aged 83; his funeral was attended from all over Cumberland and Westmorland.

His successor was the almost equally legendary Willie Porter, formerly the pack's Whip. He, like Tommy Dobson, hunted the pack until he was into his 80s, dying at last on the occasion of a Salvers' Meet on Middle Fell, Wasdale. The spot where he died is marked with a memorial stone and an inscription, "He's away, lads; he's away!" His grandson is the present Master and Huntsman of the Eskdale and Ennerdale.[2]

Foxes are rife in Cumbria and, in defiance of all that popular zoologists say, they attack, kill and devour weak young lambs. Fox hunting in the fells continues well into May; hounds going out "on call", that is, at the request of any farmer who is losing lambs. These are early morning hunts, starting at four-thirty or five, before the sun comes up and the ground dries.

From Boot an ancient pack-road crosses Burn Moor to Wasdale Head; some seven miles of rough track across lonesome heathery wastes and peaty mires, where the ancient borrans lie, giving their name to this desolate place and to the large, plain-faced tarn that shines there.

Wasdale Head (Chapter 15) lies within the parish of St Catherine's, Eskdale. The road over Burn Moor is one of the so-called coffin-roads;

thus named because some of the more remote, outlying dales, being but chapelries of a parish, had no burial ground of their own, so that the dead had to be conveyed on horseback (or, occasionally, by sled) to the parish church, for burial in the graveyard there.

Burn Moor is traditionally haunted by a spectre horse. The popular tale goes that a horse, complete with corpse, bolted into the mists one night, on the way from Wasdale Head to Boot. The horse, with its burden, was never seen again, save in spectre form. Lonely benighted travellers on Burn Moor hear the horse galloping after them, snorting and whinnying, and a large white shape, rather than actual horse, is occasionally seen! There can be little doubt that this tale of a lost, coffin-laden horse is one of late date superimposed (possibly for the amusement of tourists) upon an original theme of a Burn Moor *bargheist*.

In Cumbria the terminology, as well as the themes, of the supernatural are largely of Nordic origin. Thus the well-known Cumbrian "boggle" derives from the Norse *böig*. I have written elsewhere[3] of boggles; weird apparitions of the troll or faëry sort. The *bargheist*, or *bargueest*, was a wailing, or otherwise noisy spirit, which, if heard, presaged a death; the equivalent of the Irish banshee, in fact. A *bargheist* might also, more rarely, be seen; usually in the form of an animal. We are assured, by a number of reliable sources, that there was prevalent rural Cumbrian belief in the *bargheist* until well into the nineteenth century. A *gheist* is a visitant from the realm of life-after-death; a spirit that has become separate and distinct from the corporeal self. The *gheist* of a dying person, or of one soon to die, was sometimes seen by that person himself, as well as by others. This apparition would be in the shape of a swaith, waft, or fetch; different names being used in different parts of the region. We find Wordsworth, as a Hawkshead schoolboy, using this idea in a ballad that he wrote in 1789. The ballad was based on Hawkshead gossip and described the fate of one Mary Rigge, a broken-hearted girl deserted by her lover. She had pined away and died in 1760 and Ann Tyson, Wordsworth's old "household dame", who had known poor Mary as a neighbour, supplied the budding poet with full details of the sad story, two verses of which ran as follows:

For now her hour of Death was nigh,
And oft her waft was seen
With wan light standing at a door
Or shooting o'er the green.

She saw—she cried—" 'tis all in vain
For broken is my heart
And well I know my hour is nigh,
I know that we must part" . . .

Mrs Lynn Linton, writing a century later, mentions this belief in the fetch as one still widely discoverable in the Lake Country of her day ("fetch" seems to have been the name in use on the Keswick side of the district). Almost another 100 years later the belief was still to be encountered, lingering among the really old. A doctor friend tells me that, when she was in practice in Ambleside during 1940–45, she attended the deathbed of an aged woman living near Elterwater. The patient was awaiting her end in perfect tranquillity, save for an anxiety lest her husband and the doctor should omit to open the "*gheist* door", as she called it, in readiness for the departure of her spirit. The doctor looked, and sure enough there was the "*gheist* door" in the north wall of the house; a door which was normally kept blocked up, but which now was opened as the dying woman requested.[4]

That the *gheist* door should have been in the north wall of the house is both interesting and important. In the ancient mythology of the northern races the North was universally believed to be the realm of happy departed spirits and the Aurora Borealis, or Northern Lights (not infrequently visible in Cumbria, p. 192) were believed to be these spirits dancing in that

. . . realm of Souls
Where live the Innocent . . .[5]

The medieval chapels, churches and monastic foundations of Cumbria testified to the apparent triumph of Christian faith over the Fenris-wolf, just as the medieval *herd-wycks* and deer parks gave evidence of the disappearance of grey terror from the countryside itself. But whereas the extermination of the actual wolf was an established certainty, the vanquishing of pagan myth and superstition was a matter about which the honest were less categorical.

Bishop Nicolson[6] of Carlisle, who knew his diocese well, was obliged to admit that Scandinavian influence persisted therein even to the time of his own bishopric. We find him ruminating, in 1685, upon the still-lingering influence of the Vikings, who "were anciently gross Idolaters and Sorcerers . . . and . . . brought their Paganism along with them into this Kingdom. And therefore . . . might for some time practise their Hocus tricks here in the North, where they were most numerous and least disturbed." Thus arose

> the natural superstition of our Borderers at this day, who are much better acquainted with, and do more firmly believe their old Legendary Stories of Fairies and Witches, than the Articles of their Creed. And to convince me yet further, that they are not utter strangers to the *Black Arts* of their forefathers, I accidentally met with a Gentleman in the neighbourhood who shew'd me a Book of Spells and Magical Receipts, taken (two or three days before) in the Pocket of one of our Moss-Troopers.

The traditional supernatural beliefs of Cumbria were far removed from common superstitions of the "ghoulies and ghosties and things that go bump in the night" school. The old woman in Little Langdale waiting for her *gheist* to be released to travel, unimpeded, to join the spirits of her fathers in the beautiful realm of the North is reminiscent of old Äse's death-scene in Ibsen's *Peer Gynt*, when Peer, Äse's son, pretends to drive his mother through the night, in the sleigh which her bed has now become in his vivid and unbalanced imagination and her dying confusion. Faster and faster he whirls Äse northward across the ice of the *fiörd*, towards the magic Soria-Moria Castle that lies west of the moon and east of the sun; where there are blazing lights and dancing, and St Peter waits to greet the new arrivals.

The *gheist* was treated, in old Cumbria, with profound, albeit simple, respect; including ceremonial feasting in its honour both upon its arrival on this earth and at its departure. A piece of rum butter (that Cumbrian speciality compounded of butter and sugar flavoured with rum) was always placed in a new-born baby's mouth as its first taste of earthly food; a gesture of favour and welcome to a newly arrived spirit. A particular kind of sweet wheaten biscuit was also brought, often by the midwife, as a token gift for the baby from its first visitor.

Another ritual connected with the newly born was the "sugar bowl laitin' " of christenings. A basin of rum butter was hidden in the house and after the christening the member of the christening party who found the basin had to take it to the local inn, beg a loaf of bread from the publican and consume the loaf and all the rum butter in the basin. He (it goes without saying that the individual concerned was male!) then carried the basin from person to person at the inn, collecting donations towards a nest-egg for the baby. In early times the laiter then walked from household to household in the neighbourhood, collecting further donations. This ritual survived well into the twentieth century; though as a bit of traditional christening-party fun, rather than as a serious ceremony.

The dead were always honoured with an *arval*; popularly the name for a funeral but, strictly speaking, the funeral feast. An *arval*, however humble, was marked with solemn traditional ritual. This commenced with a "bidding": that is, a member of the deceased person's household called upon all the neighbours living within a defined distance, to inform them of the death and to bid them to the *arval*. Usually two guests were invited from each house.

"Waiting", or "waking", the dead was always observed in Cumbria in the old days: a vigil kept over the corpse, so long as it remained unburied, to ensure that it was not entered by malignant spirits now that its rightful inhabitant had departed. Traditionally the body, with a plate of salt on its breast to ward off evil spirits and witches, was placed under the table. Upon the table was placed refreshment (usually of an alcoholic nature) for the benefit of the waking party, who sat close round the table, guarding the corpse. By the very nature of these arrangements wakes tended to become merry!

The mood of the funeral itself was in marked contrast to that of the wake. A basin of sprigs of box was placed at the doorway of the house, or cottage, in which the body lay. This basin of box stood on a clean white cloth spread on a table specially placed by the door and everyone who came to pay their last respects to the dead took one of these green sprigs as a gesture both of remembrance and an avowal of faith in the survival of the spirit. From this springs the saying of "keeping green" the memory of the dead (in other regions and countries rosemary-sprigs were traditionally used, thus "rosemary for remembrance").

After the burial came the *arval* itself. All who had been "bidden" were obliged to attend. The *arval* was *not* refreshment for the mourners, but a feast in honour of the spirit of the dead. An *arval* traditionally consisted of ale and *haver* (oat) bread; in later years wheat (white) bread, too, was served, sometimes with cheese. This, in turn, became the ham funeral-tea which has survived into our own time.

Every dead person, from a wealthy man to a pauper, received a "decent funeral"; provided either by the family or, in cases of want, or lack of relatives, by the parish.

The ancient customs and beliefs have virtually died out now in modern Cumbria; indeed, today, it is becoming increasingly difficult to find people who can remember anything of them at all. None the less, the spirit of the Old Norse can never wholly be lost to this region unless there is a complete re-naming of places and a radical departure from dialect usage.

We have only to look at a map of the region to appreciate how profound, and persistent, is Norse influence here. *Dalr*, a valley; *fjall*, a hill; *gil*, a ravine; *bekkr*, a stream; *tjörn*, a small lake; thus, virtually unchanged from the original Norse are our dales, fells, gills, becks and tarns. We are led from one valley to the next over a hause (Norse, *háls*, meaning a neck); we test our muscles up the Sty to Sty Head, up Manesty, Kidsty, Stythwaite Steps, and so on, each sty (or stee, as they say locally) a Norse *stigi*, a ladder.

The Brathay is the broad (*breidr*) river; the Greta is a rocky (*griót, á*) one. The Lisa, that winds down Ennerdale, is named from the Icelandic river Lysa, meaning "bright water". Brotherilkeld (locally pronounced Bootrilkelt) in Upper Eskdale, means the broad water from the *keld*, or spring. Lowes Water is *laufser vatn*, the leafy water (local pronunciation rhymes it with Cows Butter, making a sound closely akin to the original Norse).

The region abounds in names ending in the Norse thwaite (a clearing) and garth (an enclosure). The use of *sǽtr* (a shieling) is encountered throughout the Lake District; as in Seatoller, Satterthwaite, Seatallan, and so on. The Norse dialect word, *ergh*, deriving from the Irish *airghe* (shieling) occurs in names ending in "-er", such as Birker and Mosser.

Cumbrian dialect is rich in words of Norse origin, but as Nicolson commented in 1685, "Our Borderers . . . speak a leash of Languages (British, Saxon, and Danish) in one; and 'tis hard to determine which of those three Nations has the greatest share in the Motley Breed".[6] Today we would substitute "Norse" for "Danish". But Cumbrian dialect is indeed a "leash of Languages"; combining, as it does, words of Celtic, Saxon and Nordic origin.

The subject of Cumbrian dialect is far too extensive and complex a one to be more than merely touched upon here. Map-reading, however, becomes more explicit when we remember that *brant* means steep; that *scale* means not only to spread (so that farmers speak of "scaling muck") but it also means to pour, or to spill, lavishly, in which way Scale Force gets its name; that *flou* (pronounced *flew*) means shallow, or muddy, thus most appropriately describing a place such as Floutern; while *slack* indicates a small valley, hollow or depression; Aaron's Slack gets its name not, as is commonly supposed, from the quantity of loose shale lying in that horrible gully, but from the fact that it is a depression between Green Gable and Great Gable. Grain Gill (today often misnamed Grains Gill) is so-called because it is *grained*, meaning that other small becks run into it, the place of joining being the *grain*. Piers Gill (spelled in some early guide-books as Pierce Gill) does indeed pierce deep into the heart of the Scafells. These last are so named because they are *scar*, or *scaur*; that is, places of bare and serious rock.

A sheep (or hiker) who becomes *binked* has got crag-fast on a ledge. To be "*ower feag'd*" is to be over-loaded, as, for instance, some hapless wretch staggering along under an enormous rucksack. *Frahdle* means to talk nonsense. *Glouping* means foolish. A *gryke* is a cranny, or a chink; you post a letter through a *gryke*. *Hirple* is to limp; many a walker becomes "hirpled wi' blisters". *Kaaikin* is to look about in a stupid fashion and is a term not infrequently applied to tourists. To *keave* is to plunge, or struggle. *Lownd* is a quiet, lee place; to be "well lownded" is to be well sheltered. *Slape* is slippery, as when a rock is slape with ice. To be *starved* is not to be dying of hunger, but with cold. *Spang* is a shooting pain, as from tooth-ache, but it also means "to jump out suddenly", as when a sheep spangs from a bank down into the road; a hazard well known to Lake Country motorists. *Starken* is to tighten. A *taakin* is a temper; the warning, "She's in a fine taakin" suggests that the person under discussion is best avoided for a while. A *teeht* is a lock of wool, or hair. A *wol* is a hole and should not be confused with a wall. *Yell*, on the other hand, means whole, "Did it comm awa' yell?" And, as a final turn of speech, in this most cursory of lists, to *wraul* is to fault-find, or to grumble; "My last visitors were a miseral wraulin lot!"

5

NORMAN LANDSCAPE

Conquest in Cumbria—Monastic Houses—Castles and Peles—Deer Forests—St Bees—Famous Fonts—Holme Cultram Abbey—Torpenhow—Boltongate

As I was walking all alane,
I heard twa corbies making mane;
Tane unto tother say,
"Where sall we gang and dine today?"

"In behint yon auld fail-dyke,
I wot there lies a new slain knight;
And nae body kens that he lies there,
But his hawk, his hound, and his lady fair.

"His hound is to the hunting gane,
His hawk to fetch the wild fowl hame,
His lady's ta'en another mate,
So we may make our dinner sweet.

"Ye'll sit on his white hause bane,
And I'll pike out his bonny blue een:
Wi' ae lock o' his gowden hair,
We'll theek our nest when it grows bare.

"Mony a one for him makes mane,
But none sall ken whare he is gane;
O'er his white banes, when they are bare,
The wind sall blaw for evermair."[1]

ABOVE THE NORMAN north doorway of All Saints church, Bolton,[2] two Norman knights, on horseback, fight to the death in a carved relief which though but small, and weathered, remains incredibly vivid. The helmeted figures thrust at one another with long lances, their horses standing head to head. The knight on the right (of the onlooker) sits upright and concentrated; he has thrust his lance in the base of the neck of his opponent, who reels back, his left arm flung up, his right hand letting his lance drop. It is a moment of dire and bloody truth, of the year 1100 or thereabouts.

At the time of the Norman conquest of England, in 1066, the Solway region, on both sides of the Firth, belonged to Scotland. Carlisle had not yet recovered from being sacked by the Danes; the former proud city, together with the district round it, remained a desolate waste. In the tenth century the English (with typical Sassenach cynicism?) had granted this area to the Scots.

Following the Conquest William I divided England among his leading Norman supporters. Ranulph de Meschins was given those "Lands of the County of Cumberland" that had not gone to the Scots (says Camden,[3] quoting from an early MS. from the library of the Dean and Chapter of Carlisle). To William de Meschins, brother of Ranulph, was given "all the land of Coupland, between Duden and Darwent", and to Gilfrid, a third brother, was given the "Whole County of Chestre". Gilfrid de Meschins dying without issue, Ranulph took his brother's title of Earl of Chester and surrendered all his former lands in Cumberland to the Crown.

The great men to whom the Conqueror had granted large areas of land as reward for their services divided their respective districts into "baronies" and installed their own henchmen as barons thereof. Thus Ranulph de Meschins "infeoffed" Hubbertus de Vallibus (de Vaux) in the barony of Gillisland (or Gilsland), while Waldevus, son of Gospatrick, Earl of Dunbar in Scotland, was "infeoffed . . . in all the Barony of Allerdale between Wathenpole and Darwent". William de Meschins, Lord of Coupland, likewise enfeoffed the fortunate "Waldevus son of Gospatricius" in "all the Land that lyes between Cocar and Darwent, and also in these five Townships, Brigham, Eglysfeld, Dene, Brainthwaite, and Grisothen; and in the two Cliftons and Staneburne" and he also enfeoffed "Ordardus le Clerk in the fourth part of Crostwaite . . . for keeping his Goshawkes".[3]

In course of time these and other baronies were in turn subdivided. By this method of progressive division and allocation a complex network of authority was established and a graduated caste of rank, privilege and wealth was brought into being.

All this did not take place without protest from the leaders of the old pre-Conquest Cumbria. For example, Camden gives a fascinating account of how Hubert de Vallibus (de Vaux) found himself unable to wrest Gilsland from its original owner, Gill, son of Bueth. This stalwart character disputed Ranulph de Meschins' ownership of what hitherto had been ancestral territory. As a result, Gill was banished to Scotland. The dispute over Gilsland continued down the years, until the next generation became involved. At last a Meeting of Arbitration was arranged between Gillesbueth, son of Gill, and Robert de Vallibus (de Vaux), who barbarously slew Gillesbueth at this meeting: an outrageous murder, for the parties to a dispute who came to a Meeting of Arbitration did so in the understanding that they were perfectly secure, under terms of truce. It was to atone for this murder that Robert de Vallibus (de Vaux) built the Priory of Lanercost and endowed it with all the lands that had been the cause of the dispute.

The great monastic houses of Cumbria are among its chief glories and beauties. Close on a dozen abbeys and priories were founded in this region within 80 years of the capture of Carlisle from the Scots by William II (William Rufus) in 1092.

The foundation of a medieval monastery was a long and complicated process, involving not only the selection of the religious order to be patronized, and the provision of a site for the projected monastic house, but also entailing a series of detailed legal transactions to ensure that the new establishment would be adequately endowed: a process often involving a number of feudal lords and ecclesiastical dignitaries.

Wetheral Priory, some five miles east of Carlisle and lying in a sheltered position beside the river Eden, was the first monastic house to be founded in Cumbria, in or about 1100, by Benedictines from St Mary York: they also established a sister cell at St Bees in 1120, and had granges at Kirkby Stephen and Kirkby Lonsdale.[4] There were also Benedictine nunneries at Armathwaite and Seaton, near Bootle, both founded in 1190, and a third, in all likelihood, near Kirkoswald.

The Augustinians established a priory at Carlisle in 1122. Lanercost, also Augustinian, was founded in 1166, or thereabouts (some authorities give the date as 1169). A third important Augustinian house was established at Cartmel in 1190, while at Conishead a small priory was founded shortly after Cartmel. At Shap, in Cumberland, the strict order of Premonstratensian Canons had a monastery. The Gilbertines had a grange at Ravenstonedale in Westmorland.

The greatest foundations of the region were Cistercian: Furness Abbey in Lancashire-North-of-the-Sands, founded in 1123, and Holme Cultram Abbey, in Cumberland, founded in 1150. Calder Abbey, also Cistercian, was set up as a colony of Furness in 1134.

The friars, unlike the monastic orders, were not well represented in Cumbria. There were Dominicans and Fransciscans at Carlisle after 1233; Carmelites at Appleby after 1281 or thereabouts, and Austin Friars at Penrith in the late thirteenth century.

In addition to the creation of a wealth of monastic houses the Normans built a wonderful heritage of churches; some of which were extensive restorations of Anglo-Saxon buildings, while others were of new foundation.

In counterpoint to these sanctuaries of peace and piety were the castles and pele-towers with which the Normans fortified the region.

The favoured post-Roman and early Norman defence system was the motte-and-bailey. The motte, or mound, was topped by a wooden tower and surrounded by a deep ditch and palisade, with an outer court, or bailey; this bailey also being defended by a ditch and a palisade.

The major Cumbrian castles—Carlisle, Appleby, Brough and Brougham—are logical developments of this system, with outer and inner bailey and massive Norman keeps; the keep being an integral part of the overall system of defence.

Pele-towers were, in essence, keeps built in isolation; strong stone towers standing within protective wooden palisades (from which the peles took their name). These timber stockades were subsequently replaced by a stone curtain-wall with a formidable entrance gateway.

The ground floor of the pele was always tunnel-vaulted. It was used both as a provision chamber and a byre for cattle and horses (themselves doomed to become provisions under circumstances of prolonged siege). From the ground floor a spiral staircase led to a narrow-windowed room for look-out and defence, with living quarters for the women and children above that. Warning of approaching invaders was given by a system of beacon fires. The alerted villagers seized their scanty valuables, deserted their wattle-built cabins, drove their cattle into lonely concealed shippens, and hastened to the peles for protection.

Bastle-houses, of which numerous instances still survive in the region, were small fortified stone buildings where, in times of trouble, the cattle were kept on the ground floor while family living quarters were on the storey above. Thick walls and tiny grilled windows provided protection.

All able-bodied males between sixteen and sixty living in this region were obliged under the terms of "Border tenure" (by which they held their land) to bear arms against an invader, whenever called upon to do so. A complicated system existed, stipulating the amount and the nature of the assistance to be provided by each man, according to his social position and means.

The deer forests were another important feature of the Norman Cumbrian landscape. These "forests" were not necessarily covered with trees, but were forests in the legal sense; protected by Forest Law which in turn protected the interests of the owner and kept the forests strictly as hunting preserves. Some were privately owned, some belonged to the Crown and others belonged to monastic foundations.

Inglewood Forest was the great Royal Forest in the Cumbrian region: indeed, it was the largest Forest in all of medieval England. This Forest had been colonized by the English from Northumbria during the seventh and eighth centuries; its name, Inglewood, meant, of course, the Angle Wood, or English Wood. By the time of Henry II, Inglewood had become one of England's largest hunting preserves; extending from Eamont Bridge, by Greystoke to Caldbeck, and from thence to "the bridge over Caldewe outside the City of Carlisle along the great metalled way to Thurseby" (the Roman road). The eastern limit of the Forest followed the river Eden, from Carlisle down to its junction with the Eamont, below Penrith: thus the Forest boundary was complete. It is interesting to note that Ranulph Engain, chief forester of Inglewood, granted a licence to the Prior of Carlisle to build a hospice at Caldbeck, to shelter travellers.

Inglewood Forest has long since disappeared, except by name. As early as the fourteenth century farming had virtually become more important than hunting in Inglewood and this process of agricultural development continued, until the eighteenth century Enclosure Acts at last brought about the final disappearance of Inglewood's open "forest" lands; culminating in the Enclosure Act for Inglewood Forest of 1819.

Among the chief privately owned (as opposed to Crown held) Forests of the region was Copeland Forest (between the rivers Esk and Eden in West Cumberland); this was owned by William de Meschins. Other notable Forests were those of Skiddaw and Ennerdale. But gradually, as the interests of husbandry expanded, these deer forests underwent curtailment, as in the case of Inglewood. From the thirteenth century onwards deer were confined in recognized "parks". There were deer parks at Wasdale Head; in Upper Eskdale (where part of the medieval deer fence may still be traced); at Cockermouth; and in Ennerdale, where was the famous deer park known as the Fence, or Side (the south-east side of the dale). There was another famous deer park at Troutbeck (Westmorland), while in Furness was the renowned Dale Park, enclosed by Abbot Banks in 1516, as a hunting-chase.

Of Wetheral Priory, the earliest of Cumbria's monastic foundations, nothing now survives with the exception of a fifteenth-century gatehouse. Wetheral's sister foundation, the nunnery at St Bees (West Cumberland), has fared a little better. This house of Benedictine nuns, founded by William de Meschins in, or about, 1120, was on the site of a much earlier nunnery, also Benedictine, founded here in 650 in honour of St Bega, who is said to have landed on the beach below the headland now named after her and to have established a cell near her landing place. This first nunnery of St Bega was totally destroyed by raiding Danes and the inmates were ravished and put to the sword.

Of the later, Norman nunnery, all that stands today is the red sandstone church of St Mary and St Bega; the domestic buildings of the nunnery survived until the opening years of the twentieth century, when they were demolished in order that St Bees school might be enlarged.

The most ancient fragment of fabric at St Bees today will be found above a gateway west of the west end of the church; it is the sculpture already referred to on p. 73. Prior to 1868 it was inside the church, built into the wall of the south aisle. In 1868 its disconcerting pagan undertones prompted the clergy of that day to have it removed to its present position.

The date of this sculpture is a matter of some dispute among experts; one school maintaining that it is genuine Anglo-Viking work, while the opposing camp declares it to be early Norman in date, but retaining much Viking spirit. One thing is certain; even if genuinely Anglo-Viking it is still too late in time to have belonged to the original nunnery of St Bega that the Danes destroyed.

The church of St Mary and St Bega is a fine place. Its great glory is the west doorway, of about 1160; a truly splendid example of late Norman work, richly columned, recessed and decorated. Beautiful too is the chancel; of much the same date. But when we come to the nave we are no longer with Norman building (or, as they call it in other countries, the Romanesque), but instead find ourselves into Early Gothic (or, as it is usually called in England, Early English). This nave, with its six bays of alternating round and octagonal piers, is very early Gothic; transitional, almost.[5] Yet it is already revealing a lighter, more complex touch than the Norman work. It is interesting to compare chancel with nave, and then to go on to compare the nave with the north transept front and the aisle windows, which are imitation Early English; the work of William Butterfield who partly restored the church in 1855–8. This restoration included the tower.

Also by Butterfield is the wrought-iron screen between nave and transept; considered by many to be a masterpiece. This was erected in 1886.

The church contains a number of late Norman coffin slabs. In the north transept look for a delightful incised effigy of Lady Johanna Lucy, wearing a tight-fitting dress; she died in 1369. Within railings in the churchyard repose two mutilated thirteenth-century knights, one bearing a shield with the arms of Ireby. The gravestone of Prior Thomas de Cotyngham (who died in 1300) is to be seen in the New College hall of the school. This stone was discovered in a badly damaged and fragmented state, but it has been most skilfully restored; it bears an incised portrait of a tonsured figure in monkish garb.

St Bees School was founded by Archbishop Edmund Grindal of Canterbury in 1583, as a Free Grammar School, by virtue of a charter of Queen Elizabeth. The archbishop was himself a West Cumbrian, being a native of Hensingham. The school buildings surround a courtyard which faces, and opens towards, the chancel of the church. The building on the north side of the courtyard is the original school of 1578. The west range was built in 1842–4; the chapel, the headmaster's house and the school buildings north of the chapel were built in 1907–10 and stand on the site of the aforementioned domestic range of the Norman Benedictine nunnery.

Before leaving West Cumberland for Carlisle and the Border region we must look at some famous and exceedingly fine fonts. The first, at Dearham, has already been mentioned (p. 92). This Dearham font is late Norman, of about 1170, and of the utmost simplicity in design; beautiful, and upon close inspection highly intriguing. A breath of Viking paganism lurks in its decoration: two essentially Nordic dragons embellish two of the sides of the squared-off capital; they cavort, not without amiability, and perhaps are kindly guarding the font? The third side is scrolled; the fourth is even more remarkable than the dragons, being patterned first with a row of five arched, blind windows (or so they seem), then a row of six diamond shapes, then six oblongs. What this signifies (for the design must once have possessed significance) we cannot even guess; the key to understanding is lost in time.

At the neighbouring village of Bridekirk we find another font; a mid-twelfth-century marvel more Byzantine in mood than Romanesque. Indeed, there could not be a greater contrast than between this and the Dearham font. Dearham's is simplicity itself in design. This Bridekirk font is sheer glorious exuberance; though not without reverence and a strong sense of service to the glory of God. On the north side of the font we see Christ being baptized, while on the west side Adam and Eve are being expelled from the Garden of Eden. There are also dragons, birds, a centaur, a huntsman in a wood and a fearsome animal that may possibly be a wolf. There is much foliage and beaded interlace-style work and there are several extraordinary, convoluted bird-plant-animal extravaganzas that are so weird as to be nightmarish; a case in point being the creeping cockatrice-tailed horror with two long-necked writhing heads, that fills the panel above the Baptism of Christ. Perhaps this is Limbo? Who in the world today can say?

The artist who produced this energetic and astonishing work was one Rikart (Richard): this we know because he inscribed the font (in runic) to the effect that he, Rikart, had wrought it and brought it to this place of glory. Not only did he inscribe his masterpiece thus, but he accompanied the inscription with a portrait of himself, hammering and chiselling away with single-minded intensity; as, indeed, he must have hammered and chiselled for a great length of time to complete this breathtaking achievement.

The two noble fonts of Aspatria and Cross Canonby are both early thirteenth century and are thought to be the work of one artist. They are devoid of Rikart's inspired freneticism, being thoughtfully balanced and sparingly reposeful; nor is there any pagan undertone to them. They are not, however, without Byzantine influence and we would not assign them to West Cumberland if we were shown them out of context.

A fifth famous Norman font is to be found at Bowness-on-Solway (p. 50). It is late Norman, with stylized foliage and beaded interlace-like trellis that carries echoes of much earlier, Irish design.

Now we have reached the marshes and mosses of the Solway estuary, and here the totally unexpected strains of string quartet and voice ensemble lead us in the direction of Holme Cultram, Abbey Town. It is music that would have fallen strangely upon Cistercian ears.

The Cistercian Order was first created in 1098, when twenty monks of the Benedictine Abbey of Molesme in Burgundy left the Benedictine Order because they felt that it had become too lax. These twenty men settled in a remote, marshy valley, which they named Citeaux (from which subsequently derived the name Cistercian). Here, in Citeaux, they practised a strict and frugal Rule which, over the ensuing decades, became an immensely powerful and effective Order. The Order's prime movers were St Stephen Harding, who was responsible for drawing up the established Rule, and St Bernard, who joined the Order fifteen years after it was founded.

The Cistercians always founded their abbeys in lonely, not to say unprepossessing, places; hence Furness was built in a deep and dreary dell named after the Deadly Nightshade, while Holme Cultram was sited on marshland, of which Allen of Allendale had tenure for purposes of wildfowling and hunting. He granted this land to the monks and in 1150 this grant was confirmed by the Earl of Cumberland, Prince Henry, son of David I of Scotland (Holme Cultram at that date lying within Scots territory).

The Cistercians, though starting with a most strict and frugal Rule, developed into a rich and formidable Order, having, at the height of their influence, over 1,000 abbeys. Much of this was due to the Order's use of lay brothers, or *conversi*. These were recruited from the peasantry and were simple, uneducated men. They were never ordained, but they took life vows. They were not admitted to the cloister or the choir, and had separate living quarters and wore a different habit. They provided labour and skills of every possible kind: farmers, smiths, carpenters, joiners, stone-masons, wainwrights, shepherds, millers, bakers, weavers, fullers, tanners, mechanics, male nurses, grange-masters, fishermen, salesmen of the monastery produce. From the monks, however, were drawn the scholars, the scribes of manuscripts, artists, architects, painters of glass and teachers.

Everything used by the Cistercians was home produced; even the habits that the monks and lay brothers wore were spun from the wool of their own sheep (the undyed, white cloth of the monks' habits gave the Cistercians their popular name of White Monks). Not only were the Cistercian communities entirely self-supporting, but as time passed the monasteries became productive upon a broad commercial scale; in some instances contributing to the national economy, as for example in the case of the great Cistercian English woollen industry.

During the founding years of Holme Cultram the labour performed must have been of a most exacting kind. When the monks first arrived they erected wooden huts in which they lived while the abbey and its domestic ranges were being built. The abbey itself was built of stone quarried in Dumfriesshire and ferried across the Solway to a point near Moss Side, where it was dressed and then conveyed to the abbey site. Most of the building was completed by 1192. But before the building could be commenced the marsh had to be drained, the scrubland cleared, and sea dykes constructed.

The countryside around the abbey gradually became a landscape of crops and pastures, well-tended granges, farmsteads, orchards and gardens. The extent of the abbey precincts alone was some 5,260 acres; comprising grazing and arable land, three acres of inland water and two of tidal. Holme Cultram was most generously endowed: gifts included fisheries, saltpans, and a quarry at Aspatria from which stone was obtained not only for day-to-day building purposes, but for repairing damage caused by raiding Scots.

Although the full extent of the main buildings is not yet known, there would have been a cloister on the south side of the abbey church, with the abbot's house on the corner. The abbey outer gatehouse stood on the site of today's Wheatsheaf Inn. Evidence exists of other buildings on the north side of the church and extending westward.

Our knowledge of what Holme Cultram must have been like is greatly helped by the fact that all Cistercian establishments were built according to one plan, whenever possible. This plan was a highly rational and efficient one, based upon St Bernard's own abbey of Clairvaux.

The Cistercians surrounded their abbey precincts with a strong wall, fortified with watch towers and other defensive works. The precinct itself was divided into an outer and inner ward, with a gatehouse affording communication between the two. At Clairvaux the abbot's house was immediately upon the right of this entrance, and close by was the guest house. On the opposite side of the courtyard were the stables for the accommodation of the steeds of the guests and their attendants. The abbey church stood in the central position of the community; to the south was the great cloister, surrounded by the chief monastic buildings. Further to the east, at Clairvaux, was a smaller cloister, and opening out of this was the infirmary, the novices' lodgings and quarters for the aged monks. Still further to the east, and divided from the monastic buildings by a wall, were the kitchen gardens, apiaries, orchards and fish tanks. The large fish ponds lay outside the abbey-precinct walls. It should be added that the greatest attention was paid to sanitation.

It is possible that Holme Cultram, because of its dangerous position hard by the Border, was obliged to pay more attention to defensive building than was usual. We know that at near-by Wolsty the monks built a small stronghold that Camden describes as "a Fortress" for "the securing of their Books and Charters against the sudden incursions of the Scots". This may have been erected following a particularly savage Scots attack in 1216, when troops led by Alexander II of Scotland carried off books, vestments and altar vessels of great value.

Many small chapels were built throughout the area over which the abbey had jurisdiction. One chapel was attached to Wolsty; another, St Thomas' Chapel, was probably the infirmary chapel and stood on the south side of the property known today as Mill Grove. At Skinburness there was a chapel dedicated to St John. However, in 1301 Skinburness was swept into the sea, whereat the monks, in 1305, built Newtown (Newtown Arlosh) to replace the lost town. The present church of St John Baptist dates back to this foundation. Like the church at Brough-by-Sands it is built on strictly defensive lines, with a tunnel-vaulted pele-tower which could be gained only from inside the church at first-floor level, and other military features such as tiny look-out windows, and a squint in the west wall of the tower.

Other chapels were St Christian's, at Chapel Garth, Sanden House; St Cuthbert's at Chapel Hill, and, half a mile distant from this, the chapel of St Roche.

The abbey church, in its days of glory, was larger than Carlisle cathedral. Holme Cultram had a total length of 279 feet, 23 more than Carlisle. The nave of nine bays was 162 feet long, the arcade was 18 feet in height. The transept was 135 feet wide, with east aisles, or chapels. The chancel was 96 feet long. The tower was 38 feet square and 114 feet high. In 1507 Abbot Chamber added a magnificent porch to the west façade.

Such splendour of dimensions shows some departure from the style of building stipulated by St Bernard. In the building of a Cistercian abbey church the renunciation of the world was to be made evident in all that met the eye. The crosses were to be of wood; the candlesticks of iron; there must be no effigies, no stained glass, the windows must be plain and undivided. Only one tower was permitted, a central one, and that was supposed to be very low. Unnecessary pinnacles and turrets were prohibited. The great beauty of Cistercian building was its uncluttered austerity.

Against this background the Cistercians lived lives of matching austerity. Each day was divided, according to the Roman system, into twelve equal hours from sunrise to sunset; each night from sunset to sunrise (thus, in the summer, each hour of the day was longer than was the case in winter). The monks retired to bed at seven in the evening and rose at two in the morning for Matins and Lauds; then followed Offices and meditation until sunrise. With daylight, work was begun. No food was permitted until two in the afternoon, when the monks dined. After dinner there was an hour's rest; then the monks resumed their respective tasks. At dusk they assembled in the church to be read to and to recite Compline. At seven the twelve-hour dedication to devotion and labour was complete.

It would be difficult to envisage a more orderly and, theoretically, less disturbed way of life. Indeed, writing in the twelfth century, St Aelred, third abbot of Rievaulx, gave an inspiring description of Cistercian Rule:

> our food is scanty, our garments rough, our drink is from the stream, and our sleep is often upon our book. . . . When sleep is sweetest we rise at bell's bidding. . . . Self-will has no scope, there is no moment for idleness or dissipation. . . . Everywhere peace, everywhere serenity and a marvellous freedom from the tumult of the world. Such unity and concord is there among the brethren, that each seems to belong to all and all to each.

The splendours of Holme Cultram's abbey church tell us much of the story of the abbey. By the early thirteenth century Holme Cultram had fallen into the habit of enhancing its already enormous prestige by lavishly entertaining important people. Adam de Kendal, Abbot of Holme Cultram from 1215–1223, squandered the fortunes of the abbey upon hospitality, in the hope that he might thereby secure the bishopric of Carlisle. He was to set a precedent which other of his successors would follow with similar exuberance.

Edward I, so-called "Hammer of the Scots", together with his entourage and troops, made an extended stay at Holme Cultram in 1300, prior to invasion of Scotland. The cost of this Royal visit was borne entirely by the abbey and must have been prodigious. However, Royalty could not be gainsaid; moreover Holme Cultram had obligations to discharge under laws of Border defence, and accommodating the monarch, in his rôle of Commander-in-Chief, was one such obligation. Certainly, in return for this hospitality, Edward conferred notable distinctions upon Holme Cultram. For instance, he appointed the abbot, Robert de Keldesik, a member of the King's Council. Furthermore, following the King's death, the royal entrails were buried at Holme Cultram. The rest of the cadaver was buried at Westminster Abbey (as Edward was a sufferer from some form of severe chronic dysentery this gesture might be seen by the cynical to have been less of a mark of favour to Holme Cultram than it might have at first seemed).

From the thirteenth century onwards the abbey lived always within the shadow of raiding Scots. The first violent attack had occurred in 1216. In 1319 Robert the Bruce sacked the abbey, despite the fact that his father, the Earl of Carrick, was buried there. This sacking was of such severity that it was recorded that the value of the abbey, after the raid, was one fifth of what it had been three decades earlier. In the final decade of the fourteenth century the monks only saved themselves from yet another sacking by buying off the Earl of Douglas with £200 (a very much greater sum then than now).

The combined strains placed upon Holme Cultram by its lavish hospitality, the contributions that it was obliged to make in money towards wars on the Continent, not to mention against the Scots, and the inroads made upon its wealth by ravaging Border attacks, at length reduced the abbey to the position where, in the fifteenth century, it sought, and received, assistance from the Pope.

The abbey had been further greatly weakened by the Black Death, which had decimated the monks. Following this calamity the lay brothers were replaced by hired labour; a step which seriously impaired the spiritual significance of the community.

But it was not Holme Cultram alone that experienced this decline. Cistercianism everywhere had now lost sight of its original discipline of strictest austerity, frugality and renunciation of all things worldly. The Cistercians had become immensely rich, politically powerful; they were unrivalled in commerce and trade. Their abbots enjoyed the wealth and influence of the biggest of feudal overlords; they were constantly involved in matters of Court and State. The Abbot of Holme Cultram was often absent from the abbey; when there, he lived apart, remote in his own establishment. The Night Office was said by rota now and not by the whole choir; duties were relaxed; there were scandals. The Dissolution officially saw the end of Cistercian Holme Cultram, but in truth the Cistercian Order had dissolved both here and elsewhere decades earlier.

After the Dissolution the local people petitioned for the preservation of the abbey church as their parish church; this they were allowed. Holme Cultram became one of only four Cistercian abbeys to continue as places of worship. Queen Mary (Tudor) gave the living of Holme Cultram to Oxford University.

But the abbey buildings proved too large and expensive for the parishioners to keep in repair; moreover much of the lead had been stolen from the roofs and the local people had no qualms about taking stone from the abbey to use for their own building purposes. At last the inevitable occurred; at three in the afternoon of New Year's Day, 1600, the abbey tower collapsed, together with much of the chancel and the east end of the roof of the nave. The vicar and one of his parishioners were in the church at the time, "yet by ye good pleasure of God . . . escaped all perils". It was a miraculous escape.

The building was restored by the expedient of bringing forward the east end of the church to the end of the nave which, together with the aisles, was repaired in its damaged parts. Before the nave's new roof could be completed it was burned in a fire caused by a workman who, carrying a live coal and a lighted candle into the roof to look for a chisel, on a gusty night, accidentally dropped the live coal, which fell into a jackdaw's nest.

A fresh attempt at restoration was made, lead for the purpose being taken from the south aisle, but by 1703 the church was once again in a state of severe dilapidation. Bishop Nicolson inspected it and reported upon it dismally. It was not until 1727 that rebuilding could be undertaken. The western part of the choir, the aisles and clerestory were removed, the arcades were filled in and windows inserted, the east end of the nave was brought forward three bays to its present position. Galleries were built, the roof was lowered, and a ceiling inserted. Thus a parish church of reasonable size and efficiency was created.

In 1885 the church was further restored, including removal of the galleries. In 1913 the ceiling was removed to reveal the fine pre-Reformation timbers (some of them may be the original twelth-century beams). Stone corbels were inserted under the beams and stained glass was placed in the east window (Pevsner assesses this window as Early Jacobean revival of Perpendicular, but local expert opinion maintains that it is genuine late Perpendicular).

The parish church of St Mary as we see it today is in effect the foreshortened late twelfth-century nave of Holme Cultram abbey church, deprived of its aisles, with early eighteenth-century walls blocking the arcade openings. The soaring piers and lofty, pure, pointed arches[6] give the interior an impressive dignity, despite the tragic truncation of the building. None the less it is impossible to forget that this is but, so to speak, a limbless trunk; strangely reminiscent of some glorious classical torso that was once the embodiment, in stone, of a whole and beautiful man, or god, but is now no more than an evocative fragment, still hugely impressive, but radically mutilated. Our eye automatically reaches for limbs and head; to meet with amputation, decapitation. So it is with Holme Cultram.

The west portal stands intact; a marvel in stone. The porch contains architectural and sculptural fragments, of which the monument to Robert Chamber, Abbot of Holme Cultram from about 1489–1519, is particularly interesting. The abbot is shown enthroned, with a procession of people kneeling before him.

The east window should be looked at from outside, as well as from within the abbey.

Holme Cultram now rejoices in the rôle of full-time Arts Centre; recitals of music and drama are held all the year round, and exhibitions are staged. The abbey church makes an exciting background for music and plays. During June, annually, there is held a distinguished Festival of the Arts.[7]

The church also continues to serve the parishioners as a house of religious worship.

From Abbey Town we turn towards Carlisle; preferably by Wigton, a solid market town. The advantage of travelling to Carlisle by this route is that we shall be able to visit Torpenhow (always pronounced Trepennah, with the accent on the middle vowel). It lies some eight miles south-west of Wigton and the object of our visit is to see the church of St Michael, where we shall find some exciting, if rather primitive, twelfth-century building and some lovely Decorated; the tracery of the chancel east window being particularly beautiful. The Norman font doesn't in any way rival those that we have just been looking at; but it is a fine one, none the less. Lastly, there is a splendid Jacobean pulpit.

Three miles north-east of Torpenhow is All Saints, Boltongate. Pevsner assures us that this late fifteenth-century building is "one of the architectural sensations of Cumberland". As usual when we take his advice and travel out of our way to look at something, we end up by thanking him for bringing to our notice a pleasure that we would otherwise have missed. All Saints is truly most dramatic; built for defence, in a spectacular tunnel-vault style derived from southern France via late fourteenth-century Scotland. Sir Walter Scott would have revelled in it. Visions of proud ladies and gallant knights, stolen brides, duels to the death, noble palfreys, banners, pages, hawks and hounds present themselves to the imagination in a whirling pageant; but then you notice that the church interior is becoming increasingly claustrophobic; the people who built this church were full of fear, not of divine justice and the wrath of God, but of a human enemy, who at any time might strike across the Border, bringing terror, fire and death. And instead of knights and ladies we see a rustic population, with many terrified women and children, crowding into this church, and we notice that it is built in such a way that it could not easily be burned to the ground. And when we go outside and look at the rectory we notice that that too was built for defence; obvious traces remain of the pele-tower. These are the hard facts of Border life and Border fray, in the olden days that Sir Walter always made sound so glamorous. All Saints, Boltongate, survives as something of the harsh reality.

6

CARLISLE

Early Carlisle—A Walled City—Edward I, "Hammer of the Scots"—Lanercost Priory—Carlisle Cathedral—The Citadel—Carlisle Cross—Carlisle Bells—Tullie House—Carlisle Castle—Ghosts of the '45—Sir Andrew de Harcla

CARLISLE IS THE very nub and nucleus of Border history and Border strife. It assumed this rôle from the instant that the Romans took up their mattocks to build their first, wooden bridgehead-fort on the spot where Carlisle cathedral now stands.

When William Rufus captured Carlisle in 1092 he, too, commenced his fortifications with a palisaded wooden structure; the forerunner of Carlisle Castle, situated on the highest, most inaccessible, northerly point of the town. He also built the city walls; which, though they were to be heightened, strengthened, repaired and rebuilt many times during the following centuries, were to enclose Carlisle for 700 years. Over this great period of time Carlisle changed but little in size; not escaping from medieval confinement until 1810, when demolition of the walls began.

Part of the west wall of the city has survived until this day. This west wall originally ran from the Citadel (near today's railway station) to the castle and was about 1,000 yards in length. What remains of it should certainly be walked along, for it promotes a marvellous idea, and understanding, of the old city of Carlisle.

The English, when in possession of Carlisle, strengthened it against the Scots; when the Scots held Carlisle they strengthened it against the English. Henry I of England visited Carlisle in 1122 and ordered William II's castle to be improved "with towers". After Cumberland was ceded to Scotland in 1136 King David I of Scotland heightened the city walls and, it is thought, built the castle keep. He died in the castle in 1153. In 1157 Henry II of England claimed Carlisle and the city passed into English hands once more. The castle was now further enlarged and fortified. In 1174 it withstood a three months' siege by the Scots, led by William the

Lion. In 1216 both castle and city were captured by Alexander II of Scotland. The castle was extensively damaged.

Thus for the origins of the castle. Now for the cathedral. Walter the Norman (sometimes known as Walter the Priest), who had been entrusted by William Rufus to fortify Carlisle, had also started to build a church and is said to have set aside endowments for a religious house. The church of the Blessed Virgin Mary, built of stone from Roman Carlisle, was completed by 1123 and became a priory of Augustinian (or "Black") canons. With the foundation of the See of Carlisle in 1133 the priory church became the cathedral. Somewhat confusingly the cathedral nave was also used as the parish church of St Mary (which continued to be the case until 1870).

If we judge this Norman cathedral by that part which survives today, it must have been a remarkably beautiful building. The Norman cathedral had a nave of eight bays; the choir had two, and probably ended in an apse. There was an apse on each of the east transepts and perhaps at the end of the choir aisles. The building was of the utmost simplicity and strength; almost the sole decoration, within the cathedral, being the scalloped capitals and some zig-zag.

Roman stone and Norman building, united, have produced a special atmosphere; it might almost be called an emotion. This emotion, this sense of formidable and divine miracle in stone, that we experience among the piers of Carlisle's Norman cathedral, is encountered likewise upon some of the great crags of the Lake Country; above all on the mighty west face of Scafell, and at Pillar Rock, in Ennerdale.

With breathtaking daring the small but incurably irrepressible voice of *homo sapiens* chirps up perkily (it is the equivalent of a rock climber perched on Central Buttress) from some wholly unexpected Norse runes set into the wall of the south transept. These, translated, read, "Dolfin wrote these runes". The cathedral *Guide* suggests that Dolfin, of Norse descent, was Governor of Carlisle when William Rufus seized the city and that the dispossessed official, as a gesture of defiance, inscribed his name on one of the stones used in the building of the church. But Dolfin was a common name in those days. He might equally well have been an artist-craftsman who worked on the building; or even a very early tourist! We shall never know his true identity; but we salute Dolfin.

About 1225 the decision was taken to enlarge and improve the cathedral in order that it might be better lit and afford more altar space. The choir was extended from two to seven bays and a short aisle-less chancel was added.

The new choir extension was twelve feet broader than the old and had to be made to the north, as the priory domestic buildings lay to the south (this explains why the nave is not central to the choir; a point that puzzles many visitors). Roman stone was no longer used.

In 1292 a terrible fire swept through the city of Carlisle, gutting a great part of it, including the cathedral: a symbolic disaster, presaging the flames that were to leap along the Border for the next 250 years.

1292 was the year in which Edward I commenced to set his bloody seal upon Scotland. The self-satisfied, mocking face of this royal psychopath surveys us today from the south-east corner of the south choir aisle in the cathedral. This carved stone portrait is almost certainly a contemporary likeness. With its vicious, smug nose, sadistic, greedy mouth, cold eyes and elegantly curled and trimmed whiskers this head is so repulsive that polite Victorian writers insisted that it must be a gargoyle. But we may rest assured that this is the face (albeit doubtless a cruelly handsome one in youth) of Edward Longshanks, "Hammer of the Scots", portrayed from life. No artist could invent anything so subtly nasty.

Edward I, before capturing Scotland, had already crushed the Welsh. He had first invaded Wales in 1277 and by 1295 had reduced that country to a condition of almost complete prostration (among Edward's targets for annihilation had been the Bards, those survivors of pre-Anglo-Saxon Britain, whose voices stirred ancient undercurrents dangerous to an England personified by Edward).

The Scotland that Edward I coveted was, at that time, far from being a weak and impoverished country. It was not a country which any sound military strategist would have wished to have as a potential threat at his back; nor was it a country which any prudent monarch would have chosen to provoke into violent and lasting animosity against his kingdom. In short, amicable compromise would have been of immense mutual benefit to both England and Scotland. But Edward's temperament seems to have been one that was utterly opposed to compromise. Employing a policy of diplomacy and threat, combined with crafty manipulation of the Scots nobles so that they were soon at loggerheads among themselves, Edward, by 1292, had manœuvred the Scots into recognition of his overall suzerainty and had adjudged John Balliol King of Scotland. Balliol, however, was seen as little more than a puppet by Edward, whose cynical juggling with Scots affairs to his own advantage stimulated Balliol to repudiate Edward's claims and to ally with France (thus did the famous "Auld Alliance" come into being).

Edward now attacked Scotland. He had conquered it by 1296. As a gesture of triumph he removed the Scots coronation stone from Scone and transported it to Westminster. The defeated Scots were obliged to swear allegiance to the cause of Edward I (Robert the Bruce himself took the oath on the sword of St Thomas à Becket). Notwithstanding this a Scots revolt against England was led by Wallace, a year later. The English, understandably, saw this as treachery. Despite the fact that Edward scored a victory over the Scots at Falkirk in 1298, he could not succeed in subduing them entirely. For the next five years he campaigned against the Scots; who not unsuccessfully employed what we today would call guerrilla tactics. In 1303 Edward, from Holme Cultram, launched a new, concentrated attack upon the Scots, capturing Stirling in 1304. Wallace was taken prisoner and executed as a traitor to the Crown in 1305. On 10 February of the following year Bruce murdered Sir John Comyn, third Earl of Buchan, co-claimant to the Scots throne, and was himself crowned King of Scotland.

Edward summoned his troops once again and marched north. Bruce, defeated by Edward, fled into Galloway.

Edward I was by now, however, a dying man. To be fair to him, it must be said that he was a man of prodigious determination, energy, and personal courage. He could now only travel by litter, so chronically sick was he. In September 1306, he had himself conveyed to Lanercost Priory. Here, together with his customarily large retinue, he wintered. It became increasingly evident to those about him that he had not much longer to live; in spite of this the pretence was maintained that, with the spring, he would lead his troops into Scotland.

Edward I had paid his first visit to Lanercost in 1280, together with his queen, Eleanor. The royal couple had then been greeted with immense pomp and ceremony; the prior and his canons receiving them at the gatehouse entry (of this now only the inner arch stands). It is amusing, and a little saddening, to learn that when Ralph de Ireton, Bishop of Carlisle, visited Lanercost in the year following this first royal visit he, not to be outdone, insisted upon being given a similar reception, with prior and canons awaiting him at the gatehouse!

The King's patronage had proved to be the reverse of real benefit to Lanercost; the Scots, as a result of Edward's visiting there, had decided to make the priory a target. On 29 April 1296, a Scots force, led by Sir John Comyn, had attacked Lanercost and burned some of the buildings and the following year the priory had been ravaged by Wallace. Ten years later, however, the damage was sufficiently repaired for the mortally sick Edward to winter at Lanercost in what we may only suppose was a high degree of fourteenth-century comfort.

Early in March the King's condition did, in fact, appear to improve somewhat and he removed to the priory at Carlisle (doubtless to the relief of Lanercost). Troops were summoned to Carlisle for the pursuit of Bruce; men were recruited from throughout Cumbria, some 2,300 in all. Meantime, the papal legate being in Carlisle, the absent Bruce was solemnly and thunderously excommunicated at a special ceremony held in the cathedral, in the presence of the King.

By June an invasion force of 5,300 men-at-arms was gathered and ready at Carlisle. Edward I, seriously ill again, left Carlisle in his litter on 25 June; his weakened condition made progress slow. His party halted for a few days just outside Carlisle; then once again the litter was borne seawards, towards Edward's intended route, via Holme Cultram, along the coastal road to Skinburness where the royal fleet rode at anchor.

But the King's rapidly worsening condition forced an emergency camp on Brough Marsh and there, two days later, on 5 July, Edward died. A memorial was not erected to mark the spot until 1685; it was replaced by a second stone in 1803.

Edward's reputation as a ferocious man of war was such that it was deemed unpolitical to let his own troops know at this stage that they had lost their leader, or the enemy learn that they no longer had the Hammer of the Scots to reckon with. Edward's body was embalmed and for a while was borne about in the litter as if he were still alive. His viscera, as aforesaid, found their way to Holme Cultram; a king's entrails could not be thrown away as if they came from any common soldier. But at last his death had to be made public; Edward II was proclaimed at Carlisle and Edward I's body was conveyed south for burial at Westminster.

The name of Edward I was destined to become loathed in Scotland down the centuries. His campaigns against that country were not confined to ensuring that England's northern border was secured (a far from unreasonable precaution); they were calculated to humiliate Scots national pride and to leave a totally demoralized population prostrate in the wake of the English armies.

The incident which, above all, ignited undying Scots hatred of the memory of Edward I was his sacking of Berwick-on-Tweed. Seventeen thousand persons, it is said, were put to the sword, irrespective of age or sex; we are told that for two days the city ran with blood. The cliché phrase, "he crushed his enemies" becomes exact terminology when applied to the Hammer of the Scots. It would also be equally exact to say that, from the sacking of Berwick onwards, the Scots considered conflict with the English to be a species of "holy" war.

Bruce certainly viewed his sacking of Lanercost Priory in this light. It was a ceremony, rather than a reprisal; designed to reveal the utmost hatred and contempt for the name of Edward I. Bruce, at the head of a large army, came to Lanercost in August 1311, and stayed there three days, during which visit he flung most of the canons into prison and then desecrated the priory. Thirty years later Lanercost was still a target for the fury of the Scots: King David, in 1346, reduced it "into nothingness". Phoenix-like, Lanercost rose once again from the ashes and rubble, but the process of complete restoration was slow; as late as 1409 many of the buildings were still in a ruinous condition, the lands uncultivated, the canons in great poverty. Recovery and restoration gained ground during the following century, until the Dissolution closed the priory for ever, in 1536.

The site and buildings were then granted by Henry VIII to Sir Thomas Dacre (natural son of Thomas, Baron Dacre of Gilsland), who thereafter founded the family of Dacre of Lanercost. He converted the west range of the monastic buildings into a residence for himself; putting in new sixteenth-century windows and strengthening the prior's pele-tower (at the end of this west range).

The nave of the priory church, St Mary Magdalene, which Bishop Christian of Candida Case (Whithorn) had consecrated in 1166, remained in use as the parish church, following the Dissolution. Thus we find Lanercost still a living presence today.

The lovely position of the priory, lying deep and secluded in the Irthing valley, in itself makes it a place deserving pilgrimage. The first impression received, on arriving at Lanercost, is one of inviolate peace; wholly and astonishingly at variance with so much of the priory's history.

The beautiful thirteenth-century figure of St Mary Magdalene still stands proudly in her niche high in the church's west gable; an adoring Augustinian kneeling, in worship, upon her right. Above her is the blue of heaven; below her is the glory of the church's west façade, with its early Gothic splendour of lancets and arcading and a magnificent and deservedly famous portal. This west façade is the finest of all the fine things at

Lanercost and gives us some idea of what the priory must have been like before the Scots fell upon it.

The church, as with Holme Cultram, is now confined to the nave; though happily the result is not one of painful mutilation, as at Holme Cultram. The ruins of Lanercost stand like visible ghosts and are of such beauty, dignity and tranquillity that, in their serene and lovely decrepitude, they are an embellishment to the living church that still sings and vibrates beside them.

The Dacre and Howard tombs are a memorable feature of Lanercost. The Dacres played a great part in the history of Cumberland. Their chief stronghold was fourteenth-century Dacre castle, on the river Tirrill between Penrith and Pooley Bridge; they had a Border fortress at Naworth, where Ranulph of Dacre received licence to crenellate in 1335 (that is, he received permission to raise battlements). The Dacres subsequently divided into two families; Dacre of Gilsland and Dacre of the North. Naworth passed into the hands of the Howard family when Lord William Howard (Belted "Will") married Anne, daughter and co-heir of Lord Dacre of Gilsland.

The Dacre tombs and memorials at Lanercost include the altar tomb (in the north transept) of Sir Humphrey Dacre, eighth holder of the barony and first Baron Dacre of Gilsland, who died in 1485, and his wife Mabel, born a Parr. In the south chapel stands the altar tomb of their son, Sir Thomas Dacre, who commanded a company of horse at Flodden Field and who died thirteen years later, in 1526. His wife, Elizabeth of Greystoke, lies with him.

Modern beauties of the parish church include two windows by William Morris and Burne-Jones; one commemorating George William Frederick, seventh Earl of Carlisle; the other a memorial to John Addison, yeoman, whose more famous younger brother, the great Thomas Addison, physician and lecturer at Guy's Hospital, lies buried in the churchyard. He died in 1860. Also designed by Burne-Jones are the scenes in relief on the memorial to Charles Howard and his wife. These scenes depict the Nativity, and the Entombment.

The See of Carlisle, like Lanercost Priory, was greatly impoverished by Border warfare, so that the rebuilding of the cathedral following the Great Fire of 1292 was a slow process. The work went on throughout the fourteenth century. The clerestory and the roof were reconstructed, the aisles were extended to the length of the original Early English chancel, new piers were inserted in the choir. A window was placed in the north transept (this was later removed). The great east window was not wholly completed until 1850: the tracery of this window is chiefly 1340–45, but some of the stonework remained unfinished until the mid-nineteenth-century date. The stained glass of this window is by Hardman and dates to 1861; however, at the very top of the window is some of the original fourteenth-century glass, representing Christ in Judgement and, below this, the place of punishment to which the wicked are condemned; a place set apart. This distinction is subtly but unmistakably conveyed to the onlooker by the thickening of the tracery of the top of the circle containing this quatrefoil, giving it a heavily ominous and forbidding aspect.

The sculptured capitals of the piers of the choir are famous; twelve of them comprising a complete and perfectly presented series depicting the twelve months of the year and the activities connected with each month (the carvings also hold theological significance). January is shown as Janus with two heads feasting; February warms himself at a fire; March is digging and ploughing; April is pruning; May proffers a delicious foliaged branch; in June there is hawking; in July the hay is being mowed (northern hay-time!); August works among crops; September reaps corn. October harvests grapes (an unconvincing Cumbrian activity—did the priors somewhere have a vineyard on an exceptionally pleasant hill?). November is sowing. December rounds off the year with the killing of an ox, in readiness for Janus to begin his feasting all over again.

The activities thus depicted, month by month, bear a remarkably close resemblance to those detailed in the eighteenth-century set of dialect verses composed by William Dickinson of Thorncroft, Workington, and published in 1876 as *Cumbriana, or fragments of Cumbrian Life*. Of these the present author has written elsewhere;[1] sufficient to remark here that the fourteenth-century cathedral carvings of rural activities and the versified calendar of eighteenth-century Cumbrian rural life are strikingly akin, save that Dickinson's Cumbrians did not harvest grapes, while the cathedral carvings do not indicate the pre-occupation with sheep and shepherding that we find in *Cumbriana*. When these capitals were made Cumbria's great fell flocks and woollen industry had not yet emerged.

By the year 1400 Carlisle cathedral bore a close resemblance to the building which we see today, except that the Norman nave still extended for its full length. A great deal of further work, particularly to the interior, was carried out during the final century-and-a-half of its history as an

Augustinian priory, especially by William Strickland, who became bishop in 1400. It was he who built the tower as we now see it and who rebuilt the north transept, together with the beautiful Perpendicular so-called "strainer" arch, to the north of the crossing. Also to Strickland's time belong the 46 choir-stalls with their fascinating carved misericords; exceptional in the liveliness of both content and carving. The canopies over the stalls were added after 1430, in Prior Hayworth's time; the niches have lost the figures which originally stood in them.

The choir-screen, too, belongs to this period. The paintings on the backs of the choir-stalls belong to the era of Prior Thomas Gondibour (1484–1507): we must not forget that at this period the whole interior of the cathedral would have glowed with colour, wood and stone alike being painted and gilded. The choir-stall paintings depict the Apostles and incidents taken from the lives of St Anthony, St Augustine and St Cuthbert. As paintings they are poor, if we compare them with the church paintings for that period which we find on the Continent. The interest of these Carlisle paintings lies in the St Cuthbert panels; thirteen of which were copied from a medieval manuscript of Bede's Life of St Cuthbert (now at the British Museum). It is interesting to compare this MS with the Carlisle paintings, which entirely lack the moving poignancy of the originals. Formerly the manuscript belonged to Durham, and it is thought that Richard Bell, Prior of Durham and subsequently Bishop of Carlisle from 1478–95 (and a great collector of manuscripts), lent it to Carlisle in order that the paintings might be copied.

Bishop Bell's impressive memorial brass will be found in the centre of the cathedral choir.

Prior Gondibour was responsible for the exceedingly lovely screen enclosing St Catherine's Chapel (just on the right of the south door as you enter the cathedral). Similar screens enclosed the choir, until they were removed in the mid-eighteenth century. But this cathedral is particularly rich in screens: the fifteenth-century choir-screen is of most sumptuous, yet elegant, beauty, while, in the north aisle, the considerably later Salkeld screen (the gift of Prior Lancelot Salkeld in 1545 after he had become the cathedral's first dean, following the Dissolution) is an exceptionally magnificent and undamaged example of English Early Renaissance work. This screen is of political interest, too, for it is embellished with the Prince of Wales's feathers, the Tudor rose and Tudor beasts, and the initials GSPE (God Save Prince Edward), combined with a large array of other designs and devices of contemporary significance. Clearly, Salkeld was anxious to make the right impression, now that he had ceased to be prior and had instead become dean! This was in May 1541, when the present foundation of the Cathedral Church of the Holy and Undivided Trinity came into being; the priory having been dissolved in 1540.

The cathedral precinct, always known as The Abbey, is entered through Prior Slee's tunnel-vaulted gatehouse, built in 1527 and inscribed for him. This gatehouse has two entrances; one for horses and carriages, the other for pedestrians. The small, pretty building which you see to the right dates to 1699 and was used at one time as the Bishop's Registry. Opposite to it is the Early Georgian No. 2, Canonry. Next to the registry is the deanery, which backs upon the west walls. Before becoming the deanery it was the prior's lodging. It consists today of a pele-tower and a range on either side. The pele is early sixteenth-century and contains a splendid painted ceiling.

Mere traces remain of the priory cloister. South of the south transept of the cathedral you will discover a path with a low wall on the east, a higher one on the west. This path represents the east range of the former cloister; over this range was the dormitory. The thirteenth-century doorway in the east wall led into the former chapter house; the doorway in the west wall was that of the chapter house vestibule.

The fratry (refectory) still survives. It was built in the early fourteenth century and was restored by Prior Gondibour about 1482. The fratry has a splendid first floor hall, 79 feet long by 27 feet wide, with two large late fifteenth-century windows (their tracery is Victorian restoration), and a small two-light window in the west wall; this window is Decorated, and original. In the south wall of the fratry is the reading pulpit, from which lessons were read to the canons during meal-times. In the west wall are two hatches, formerly leading into kitchens in the, now vanished, west range. Today the fratry is used as the cathedral library.

The fratry porch is Victorian. The two beautiful copes displayed therein are both of great age; one, of Lucca silk, dates to 1460, the age of the other, a sumptuous garment of Venetian velvet, is unknown. Part of a Saxon cross is also on view; this was found by workmen when Walter the Norman's church was being built!

Below the fratry is a vast vaulted undercroft; dating in its entirety to the fourteenth century. This should not be missed.

The city tithe barn, standing by the west walls, near the deanery but outside the cathedral precinct, is another beautiful building; the work of Prior Gondibour for the storage of tithes in kind, collected for the church. Recently it has been restored and it is now a community centre.

Opposite the tithe barn, and set in the city wall, are some steps that still go by their old name of Sallyport. These led to a small door at the foot of the wall, used by sortie-parties during times of siege.

Carlisle's longest and most famous siege occurred during the Parliamentary Wars. Carlisle was Royalist, and from October 1644 to June 1645 lay under siege by General Lesley. The garrison lived on horseflesh (keeping the horses alive, until they were required for eating, by feeding them on thatch from the roofs). After there were no more horses left cats, dogs, rats and hempseed were consumed. The cathedral plate was coined; the library disappeared (according to Bishop Nicolson even the very Charter was sold "to make a taylor's measures"). Carlisle finally surrendered on 25 June 1645, following the defeat of Charles I at Naseby on 14 June. Thereafter the fabric of the cathedral suffered severe damage at the hands of Lesley's men; the chapter house was destroyed (hence the reason why, from 1688 onward, the fratry was used as chapter house), and six bays of the cathedral's Norman nave suffered demolition; some of the stones being used to build Parliamentary guardhouses and to repair the city walls (these Norman cathedral stones, it should be recalled, had been Roman stones in the first instance).

Yet it would seem that not all the damage to the cathedral might fairly be attributed to Lesley. The fabric had been much decayed before the Parliamentary Wars; in 1639 Charles I had himself written to the Chapter, warning that the building needed repair, else it were "lyke to fall" into "ruines". The Parliamentary forces simply hastened the process of ruination.

Following the Restoration the damage to Carlisle cathedral was made good; though the nave remained (as Pevsner puts it) "only a stump".

Exploration of Carlisle should include a walk along the west walls, past the tithe barn, south-eastwards to the Citadel, today the Assize Courts, but still standing on the site of Henry VIII's Citadel, which was built by the king in 1541–3 at the time that he had the castle defences strengthened by Stefan von Haschenperg. The Citadel was intended as a second fortification in the event of the castle being taken. The Citadel originally consisted of two towers, with a turret and curtain-wall linking them. At the side of the western tower was placed English Gate (the city, it must be remembered, was entirely enclosed by walls, in which were set gateways; these were barred at dusk, when the curfew sounded. No Scotsman was allowed to move about inside the city, after dark, unless so authorized).

The old Citadel was demolished in 1807 and the present one, incorporating the Assize Courts, was built in 1810 by Sir Robert Smirke. Inside the wall of the eastern tower may still be seen, preserved, part of the wall of the original tower.

From the Citadel the left side of English Street leads to the market square, the site of the Roman forum. Carlisle Cross stands here, with the town hall behind it. This present cross replaced an earlier one in 1682. This is the traditional core of the city; the very heart of Carlisle for almost 2,000 years. Here, since Roman times, all important announcements have been made. Here, on 16 November 1745, the exiled Prince James Edward Stuart, "the Young Pretender", was proclaimed King James III of England and Scotland, following the surrender of Carlisle to his son, Prince Charles Edward Stuart. Here, less romantically, were posted the names of wanted men: murderers, reivers, outlaws. Here too, in times of plague, were displayed lists of names of citizens who had died. Here stood the pillory and the stocks (now in the City Museum at Tullie House). Around the cross, until quite recent times, were held the markets. Even today the annual Carlisle Great Fair is proclaimed from the steps of the cross each 26 August at eight o'clock in the morning; a centuries-old ceremony.

The present town hall was built in 1717 upon, or very close to, the site of the Tudor moot hall, on the roof of which hung the market bell that was also used as the curfew bell. Beside it hung Carlisle's "Muckle Town Bell", dating back to 1400 or thereabouts; the bell that sounded the alarm for many a Border fray. These two bells may both be seen today at Tullie House, which you will find along Castle Street, on the left, a short distance beyond the cathedral.

Tullie House, a fine Jacobean mansion, was built for Chancellor Tullie in 1689. The new buildings annexed to it, their faces to Castle Street, were by Ferguson in 1892–3 and it is interesting to compare them with the true Jacobean of the old house. It is the southern façade of Tullie House which is the best; overlooking the garden at the back. Tullie House Museum, an important one, deserves at least a morning of your time.

So, after Tullie House, to the castle. It is impossible for anyone who knows something of the history of Carlisle Castle to look at its dark cavern of an entrance without a shudder. Through it, in our mind's eye, we see passing an endless procession of prisoners; centuries of prisoners; either on foot, shuffling and lurching forward, bound and tethered with rope or shackled with chains, or else riding on horseback as rode the captured reivers (and Prince Charles Edward's surrendered officers); their arms pinioned behind their backs, feet bound together beneath their horses' bellies. Of all the many, many prisoners who passed under that archway into the castle, scarcely any came out that were not about to face execution. This is a gateway of doom, if ever one were such.

The '45 Rebellion saw the close of Border violence; it was a final act of horror equal to any that had gone before. Following the surrender of the garrison left in Carlisle Castle by Prince Charles Edward when he and the rest of his army withdrew back into Scotland, the officers gave themselves up as prisoners to England's Duke of Cumberland, while their men laid down their arms in the market square and then retired into the cathedral ("So that they defiled the Temple, which used to be the House of Prayer, but was now become a Den of Thieves"—Ray). On 10 February 1746, all the prisoners were sent south; some to be tried and executed there, while the others were brought back to Carlisle for trial. Few were acquitted. Those convicted in the south were hanged on Kennington Common. Those convicted at Carlisle were hanged at Harribee (Carlisle's time-honoured execution place), Brampton and Penrith. Afterwards the heads of the rebels were distributed about the towns and villages of the region, to be displayed as a dreadful warning to the populace. At Carlisle the heads of the executed English rebels were placed on English Gate; Scotch Gate was adorned with the heads of two Highland lairds, Macdonald of Tirnadris and Macdonald of Kinlochmoidart.

The main gate of Carlisle Castle was built in 1378–83. It incorporated a barbican and had a tunnel-vaulted prison and store cellar on the ground floor, with a hall and kitchen above. The actual entry tunnel had holes in its roof (these are still visible) through which boiling oil might be poured upon invaders. A further ditch separated the inner bailey from the outer, where today stand barracks built in 1819 and later. These barracks were, and in spirit still remain, the "home" of the Border Regiment, even since its merger and departure in 1959.

The gatehouse of the inner bailey (known as Captain's Tower) dates from the fourteenth-century, though it underwent considerable alteration in the reign of Henry VIII, when the growing use of artillery brought mounted guns to the castle. The inner bailey is triangular in shape, with the Norman keep in the south-west corner. The Border Regiment's museum was opened here in 1932. A fascinating feature of this keep is the many carvings cut in the walls by prisoners held here over a period extending from the fourteenth-century to the '45 Rebellion.

Carlisle Castle was Mary Queen of Scots' first prison after she had fled from Scotland, to land on English soil near Workington in the summer of 1586. The private apartments that she used in the castle were pulled down in 1835; a beautiful fourteenth-century tower, traditionally known as Queen Mary's Tower, survives, but its real association with the Queen of Scots is uncertain.

Robert Bruce's father was commander of Carlisle Castle from 1295–7. Perhaps this in part accounts for Bruce's subsequent obsessive determination to capture Carlisle. This he swore to do and in 1315, following the Scots victory at Bannockburn, he besieged the city. However, in spite of the determination of his siege he failed to take Carlisle, which was defended with tremendous spirit by the gallant Sir Andrew de Harcla, whom Edward II (to quote the original Charter of Creation) "did for his honourable and good services . . . by the girding of a sword created Earl under the honour and title of Earl of Carleol".

Edward II's weakness as a monarch encouraged Bruce not only to reconquer most of Scotland and to establish himself as King of Scotland, but it further permitted him to ravage the northern counties of England in merciless revenge for all that Scotland had earlier suffered at the hands of the English. At last de Harcla, for the sake of his fellow north-countrymen, was obliged to come to an understanding with the Scots. This showed great wisdom, but at Westminster de Harcla's move was seen as treasonable. He was proclaimed traitor and on 3 March 1325 (according to Thomas Avensbury), "For being degraded he had his spurs cut off with a hatchet, then his sword-belt was taken from him; next his shoes and gloves were pull'd off; after which he was drawn, hang'd, beheaded, and quarter'd." Following which, his various parts were distributed for public display.

So fighting between Scotland and England continued; the Scots attacking Carlisle in 1337, 1345 (when the city was severely damaged by a force commanded by Sir William Douglas), and in 1380. In 1385 a combined force of Scots and French attacked Carlisle, but without success; two years later a similar attack was made, again without success. During the Wars of the Roses the Scots, ostensibly in the Lancastrian interest, once again attacked Carlisle and despoiled the outskirts.

Even after open warfare between Scotland and England had ceased

Border fray kept Carlisle's "muckle bell" tolling and the castle's beacon fires reddening the sky at night. Carlisle Castle became the headquarters of the Warden of the English West March and this, in itself, was sufficient to ensure that Carlisle must be a place of constant alarm and violent excursion, with the hangman busy at Harribee.

7

ARMSTRONG'S LAST GOODNIGHT

Border Marches and Wardens—The Debateable Land—Reiving and Reivers—The Riding Clans—The Armstrongs—A Border Widow—A Famous Rescue—Broken Men—Exploring the Cumbrian Border—Armstrong's Last Goodnight

THE EARLY thirteenth century saw the first serious attempt to define a border line between England and Scotland. Twelve English and twelve Scots knights, under the sheriffs of Northumberland and Berwick respectively, in consultation produced the Laws of the Marches of 1249. Yet despite this, the Border remained a region of unceasing altercation.

From the early fourteenth century until the Union of Crowns in 1603 the Border country was divided, upon each side, into three Marches: an East, a Middle and a West march. Each of these six Marches was in the charge of an officer appointed by the Crown and known as the Warden of the March. In time of war the Warden was empowered to call upon the full force of the wardenry for purposes of invasion and defence; in time of peace his chief duty was to meet and confer with the Warden of the opposite March on appointed days of truce, for the purpose of settling disputes and granting redress for injuries on either side. Six Wardens' jurors for each side were appointed to attend these truce meetings, which assumed the nature and office of courts of arbitration and appeal. The position of Warden became more or less hereditary in certain families: notably the Maxwell, Douglas, Ker and Hume families on the Scots side, and the Forsters, Fenwicks and Dacres upon the English. The Wardenries were themselves supervised by a Lieutenant, who was empowered to act in any circumstance as the king himself.

Roughly speaking the East March ran from the North Sea to the line of Auchope Cairn on Cheviot; the Middle March extended from that point to a line marked by Kershope Burn in the Larriston Fells, and from thence the West March extended to the Solway coast. The name "March" derived from marsh, moss, merse, ultimately related to the old English *mēas* (moss); the East March traditionally being the region of the Merse. The so-called Debateable Land and the Solway region of the West March, alike being places of low-lying dampness, were generally known as Mosses. From this same source derived the appellation of "moss-troopers", bestowed upon the reivers, or reavers (ravagers) of the Border country; who, being mounted men, gained for their lawless activities the brief, all-embracing euphemism of "riding".

The term "Debateable Land" did not apply to the entire Border, as is sometimes supposed. According to a truce in 1449, "The Landez called Batable landez or Thorpe landez, in the West Marchez" included the baronies of Kirkandrews, Bryntallone, Canonbie, and Morton, lying to the north of the Esk[1] between its junction with the Liddel and the Solway. The "debate" originated as a controversy concerning a salmon garth, built by the English. The result was that the Scots living among the upper reaches of the river were deprived of salmon, since these now became trapped in the English garth. In 1494 commissioners met at Lochmarben to decide the question of the bounds and limits of the area involved. The result was inconclusive and the 'Bateable Land remained Debateable: the home of the chief reiving communities and, as time passed, a refuge for the "Broken Men".

It is not altogether without reason that Edward I has been called "The original reiver".[2] Reiving, "the theft of cattle and insight" (goods and gear) was unknown on the Border before the advent of the Hammer of the Scots, who purloined the coronation stone of Scone. The undying hatred for England which Edward engendered in the Scots made (so claims one Scots writer of Border history), "The profession of moss-trooper an honourable one by any standard, and for this reason within a few decades [of the sacking of Berwick] we find the practice widespread among the highest and the lowest along the Border."[3]

The English Borderers, harried and ravaged by the Scots frays, in turn reived from their side of the frontier and saw their activities, too, as "honourable by any standard". Thus the Border obsession with moss-trooping came about.

The one side was as dedicated to raiding and ravishing as the other. A letter from Lord Dacre of Gilsland, Warden of the English Middle March, dated 29 October 1513, reads,

> On Tuewsday at night last past, I send diverse of my tenants of Gillislande to the nombre of LX personnes in Eskdale moor upon the

Middill Merches, and there brynt vll howses, took and brougth away xxxvj head of cattle and much insight. On Weddinsday at thre of the clok efter noon, my broder Sir Christopher assembled diverse of the kings subjects lying under my reull, and roode all night into Scotland, and on Thurisday, in the mornynge, they began upon the said Middill Merches and brynt Stakeheugh, with the hamletts belonging to them, down,—continually birnying from the Breke of day to oone of the clok after noon, and there wan, tooke and brought away CCCC. hede of cattell, CCC. shepe, certaine horses and verey much insight, and slew two men, hurte and wounded diverse other persones and horses, and then entered Ingland ground again at vlj of the clok that night.[4]

The English government complained to Lord Dacre that his raids were not subduing the Scots Borderers to the extent hoped for. Dacre replied, "I assure your lordships for truthe that I have . . . caused to be burnt and destroyed sex times moo townys and howsys within the West and Middill Marches of Scotland, in the same season than is done to us."[5]

In war or fray the Borderer was equipped with an armoured leather jerkin, leg armour, a helmet, "buklairs and sweirds", spears, staves, hagbuts and daggers. In time of war he wore the cross of St Andrew or St George, according to nationality, together with distinguishing arm-band. The fray-parties had battle slogans, or war cries; usually the name of their chief, but sometimes the name of the district from which they came. They carried their riding as far as Biggar in the north, and Richmond (Yorkshire) in the south, for they were superb horsemen. "The very best and hardest light horsemen in Western Europe," one authority has called them (Veitch) and they took enormous pride in the ownership of fine steeds.

Despite the fact that the folk on each side of the Border claimed to be of a different race their genealogy was fundamentally a shared one, as was their environment and way of life. The small communities from which they came were not wealthy, but hardily self-sufficient. Each side was raised upon steel and regarded fighting as a natural occupation. Each side was as tough as the other and it was therefore pure Scots chauvinism that prompted gibes about "the delicat persons of Ingland, whais bodeis are gearin to quytness, rest and delicat feeding, and consequentile desyrous of more sleap and repose in bed. Whereas be the contrare [the Scots are] ordinar nycht-walkers."[6]

In short, the Borderers, from whichever side of the Border they came, were all immensely tough, violently energetic, devil-may-care "nycht-walkers". Hurling insults back and forth across the Border was part of the game.

For, viewed in retrospect, moss-trooping must be seen to have been, fundamentally, a game. The immense importance attached to the "rules"; the scrupulous observance of the truces for the settlement of "bills", or complaints (the day and place of meeting having been proclaimed in all the market towns on either side of the Border); the forswearing of all blood feuds during the truce; the attendance at these meetings of Wardens, jurors, lords, knights, esquires, gentlemen, officers and servants; the giving of persons as "pledges"; the observance of these pledges; the complicated ritual of a tradition such as the famous "Hot Trod";[7] the immensely involved March Law which stipulated how, and by whom, and when the Debateable Land might be crossed; the law which laid down how a felon might be used; the strict rules of pursuit, of complaint and counter-complaint; the very code of loyalty and allegiance among the clansmen of either side; all reveal the extent to which Border fray developed into a game: a desperate game, but a game sure enough, in the strict sense of that word.

A vivid account of a small fray, the capture of a Scots pele-tower, is given in Nicolson and Burns' *History of Westmorland and Cumberland* (vol. 1, p. liii) from a manuscript narrative by Sir Thomas Carleton, who conducted the said fray into Scotland under Lord Wharton, Warden of the English West March:

> It was a fair large tower . . . with a barnekin [bailey], a hall, kitchen, and stables, all within the barnekin, and was but kept by two or three fellows and as many wenches. We thought it might be stolen in a morning at the opening of the tower door. . . . We came in there about an hour before day, and the greater part of us lay without the barnekin; but about a dozen of the men got over the barnekin wall. . . . And at sun rising, two men and a woman being in the tower, one of the men rising in his shirt, and going to the tower head, and seeing nothing astir about, he called on the wench that lay in the tower, and bade her rise and open the tower door. . . . She so doing . . . our men within the barnekin . . . entered. . . . We found the house well purveyed for beef salted, malt big [barley], havermeal [oatmeal], butter, and cheese.

This was an easy capture, described as a mere "practise".

A fray, or foray, offered challenge and excitement. It placed emphasis upon skill and daring; the negotiation of dangerous hill tracks in the darkness, the outwitting of the watchmen in each township with their "slough dogs" (blood hounds), the droving of the stolen stock safely back to some secluded "beef-tub" in the hills; in short, adventures packed with dare-devil bravado and breathless exploit. The bravado, it should be noted, was no insignificant element of moss-trooping; witness that the reivers not infrequently raided in broad daylight, carrying banners.

None the less it was a miserably savage way of life, when it came to the final assessment; with violent death (often on the gallows) as the almost inevitable outcome. Perhaps it did not matter so much that the moss-troopers themselves died violently; that was part of the game and they accepted it in that spirit; but the violence done to innocent people in the course of the raids was frightful and the whole atmosphere of the Border was saturated, literally, with fire and slaughter.

Yet these riders were not fundamentally wicked. It was their misfortune to have been born into a kind of buffer state between two hostile nations. They were also the victims of a peculiar system of land tenure, whereby the overlord within his own territory had powers of pit and gallows over his vassals. These paid no rent but were committed to Border service, which meant military service, for their laird in whatever cause he might choose.

Gradually, over the long decades, Border fray underwent certain significant changes. Despite all the meticulous rules accompanying the truces and the "bills", injustices inevitably arose, neither could malice altogether be excluded from playing a part in the settlements. Out of such incidents as these there arose deadly feuds, involving entire clans, or families, and handed down from one generation to the next. Thus a *vendetta* system (strikingly akin to that of Corsica, for instance) came into existence along the Border. One murder led to reprisal, which in turn led to another. Many a man had to turn "hastelie fugitive" as a result. Many who became fugitive sought refuge in the mosses of the Debateable Land. Such fugitives were virtually outlaws excluded from society. In inevitable *contre-coup* these outlaws hit out at that exclusive society. Society then took further punitive measures, to which the outlaws responded with further violence. Thus, in one way and another, Border fray entered a complex pattern of infinite regress.

Reiving was at its worst in the last quarter of the sixteenth-century. The most notable reiving families on the English side were the Musgraves of the Middle March and the Grahams of the West. On the Scots side were the Scotts of Branxholm, Johnstones of Lochwood, Eliots of Larriston,

Maxwells, Kerrs and Beattisons. The Armstrongs, probably the most notorious clan, or group of families, of them all may properly be labelled as neither Scots nor English. They came from Liddesdale in the Debateable Land and though their original allegiance was to Scotland they, because of their ambiguous geographical position, were to change sides more than once.

Liddisdale today is a deserted area; particularly to the south, where the parish of Castleton lies between Kershope Burn and the Liddel Water. Here is the heart of what was once Armstrong Borderland; adjacent to the Debateable Land and facing towards Bewcastledale, up which rode the English and down which rode the Scots; the ubiquitous Armstrongs riding, as it were, for themselves.

The Armstrongs were at first Maxwell-protected and their well-being depended on the balance of power sustained between the Scott and Maxwell baronies. However, the growing strength of the Armstrongs in time made them a family to be reckoned with on their own account. Increasingly they became allies of the Douglas, Earl of Angus, who, having incurred the wrath of James V of Scotland, had fled to England. The strongest Armstrong of all, John, Laird of Gilnockie,[8] was feared by the English (even the south had heard of him) and esteemed by the Scots. He was treacherously murdered (hanged) together with the rest of his party of 35 persons (not all of them Armstrongs) by James V at a truce meeting called at Carlenrigg in 1530. It is more than probable that Gilnockie's downfall was, in part at least, engineered by Maxwell, who increasingly had seen him as a rival.

Following the hanging of Gilnockie many Armstrongs fled to England and transferred their allegiance to King Henry. Even those who remained living on the Scottish side of the Border claimed allegiance to England and the Debateable Land, as a result, began to be seen virtually as English territory.

As early as 1528 the men of Liddisdale, together with the banished Earl of Douglas, Lord Dacre, and 500 Englishmen of Gillisland and Tynedale, ran a fray into Teviotdale and captured the Lord of Botlough and some of his friends. On 13 March 1536, another John Armstrong, alias "Jony in Gutterholis" (Gutterholes), together with a Christopher Henderson, was "drawn to the gallows and hanged as Traitor" for "treasonably inbringing Englishmen, common Thieves and Traitors, within Scotland" and committing "Hereschip and Stouthreif, Murder and Fire-raising".

The true horror of what it was like to live on the Border at that time in history is perhaps best of all conveyed in the blood-freezing "Lament of the Border Widow". Scott, in his accompanying notes to this ballad, tells us that it relates the execution of Cockburn of Henderland, a free-booter (reiver) who was hanged over the gate of his own tower by James V in the course of the king's memorable "hunting" expedition of 1530 (during which he killed Armstrong of Gilnockie, Scott of Tushielaw, and others). The king surprised Cockburn while he was seated at dinner. His lady fled to a nearby glen down which rushed a noisy burn by which she crouched, in the vain hope that the noise of the water would drown the terrible sounds of her husband's last moments.

My love he built me a bonny bower
And clad it a' wi lilye flower;
A brawer bower ye ne'er did see
Than my true love he built for me.

There came a man by middle day,
He spied his sport and went away;
And brought the King that very night,
Who brake my bower, and slew my knight.

He slew my knight, to me sae dear;
He slew my knight and poin'd his gear;
My servants all for life did flee,
And left me in extremitie.

I sew'd his sheet, making my mane;
I watched the corpse, myself alane;
I watched his body, night and day
No living creature came that way.

I took his body on my back,
And whiles I gaed, and whiles I sat;
And digg'd a grave, and laid him in,
And happed him with the sod sae green.

But think na ye my heart was sair
When I laid the moul' on his yellow hair;

Oh think na ye my heart was wae,
When I turned about, awa' to gae? . . .

Historically, it seems, this ballad is at fault inasmuch as both Cockburn of Henderland and Scott of Tushielaw, accused of "outrages within the realm of Scotland", received benefit of assize in Edinburgh before they were convicted and executed. But who can doubt that the above lament, if not an exact account of Cockburn's death, is based on the brutal facts of an actual Border slaying and a widow's hideous ordeal?

There is evidence that the Armstrongs, during the final decades of the sixteenth century, had some secret understanding with the English government, "for the annoyance of Scotland". Not only the Armstrongs. By the reign of Edward VI virtually the whole of the Western Marches, on each side of the Border, lay in the service of the English king. Such service was far from being rendered through motives of sentiment; pockets were undoubtedly lined with the king's silver. The reivers were beginning to assume their ultimate rôle of mercenaries.

In 1552 the Debateable Land was finally divided. The part which was awarded to Scotland was almost wholly Armstrong country. The Armstrongs were thus obliged to resume their Scots allegiance at a time when any security that they might have enjoyed depended upon their remaining English. They now found themselves without guarantees of protection from either nation and, having no security of tenure, were entirely at the mercy of their neighbouring, powerful, clans.

During the latter part of the sixteenth century the Scots overlords of the Border region struggled ferociously among themselves in their respective bids for power. The lesser riding clans followed opportunist paths; siding first with this protagonist, then with that; their concern in the struggling being confined purely to day-to-day self interest and survival.

Thus Armstrong of Kinmont attached himself to Buccleuch and was rescued from Carlisle in his hour of extremity. Others of the Armstrong clan attached themselves to other houses, and did not fare so well in times of crisis.

Kinmont Willie, as he was popularly known, was a famous reiver who was captured by the English, by trickery, during a truce. He was taken as prisoner to Carlisle Castle. In one of the most daring rescues ever recorded Kinmont Willie was liberated from the Castle under the very nose of Lord Scrope, Warden of the English West March; the rescue party consisting of five Scotts (led by their chieftain, Scott of Buccleuch), four Bells, two Eliots, and no fewer than nineteen Armstrongs. The details of the rescue are too well known to need retelling here, but it is impossible to forgo the pleasure of reminding ourselves how Kinmont Willie, before being borne out of the castle by his rescuers, insisted on saying "good-night" to Lord Scrope,

> Then Red Rowan has hente him up,
> The starkest man in Teviotdale:
> "Abide, abide now, Red Rowan,
> Till of my Lord Scroope I take farewell.
>
> "Farewell, farewell, my gude Lord Scroope!
> My gude Lord Scroope, farewell!" he cried;
> "I'll pay you for my lodging maill,
> When first we meet on the Border side."

Or, as the Newbattle MS. tells us, "The assaulters . . . broght furth thair countreman . . . and convoyit him to the court, whare the lord Scroopes chalmer has a prospect unto, to whom he cryit with a lowd voyce a familiar gude nycht, and another gude nycht to his Constable callit Mr Sawghell."

Meantime all Carlisle was in a growing uproar.

> At the first entre [of the rescue party, and their silencing of] the wacheman, the bell of the castell soundit a fray, fyre was kendlit on the top of the hous, the great bell of the cathedrall kirk was rung. . . . The watche-bell of the mute hall [the "muckle town bell"] was also rung for harmonie; and to conferme the fray the more, the drum of the toun soundit allarum uncessantlie.

Kinmont Willie was lucky; he had solid Buccleuch backing. The Armstrongs of Whithaugh attached themselves to the house of Bothwell, while other Armstrongs were dependent on Maxwell. Buccleugh ousted Bothwell. Lord John Maxwell was executed. The Scots Border became dominated by Buccleuch and Johnstone. These seized the lands of less powerful "riding names" (including the Whithaugh Armstrongs) who, dispossessed and discredited, congregated increasingly in the mosses of the Debateable Land. Thus they became "Broken Men"; virtual outlaws, with nothing left to live by save their skills as fighters and horsemen. The rôle of mercenaries and cattle thieves was all that remained open to them. They rode and reived with anyone who would make it worth their while. Buccleuch, leading in person increasingly violent and daring frays into Tynedale, Gilsland and Bewcastle, could always call on "Broken Men" to ride with him. The violence of this Cumbrian section of the Border became increasingly horrible. In the frays scores upon scores of perfectly innocent and harmless people were put to death by "fire, sword, the pit, drowning and spoiling, sparing neither age nor sex".

The government of each side now began to see the "Broken Men" as a serious threat. Lord Herries, in troubled accents, reported to James VI of Scotland that they numbered some "three to four hundred . . . [all of whom are] well armed, have good horses, and upon a simple shout are ready to join in defence of one another". Distrust of the "Broken Men" as a nucleus of trouble was not misplaced; following the death of Queen Elizabeth they staged an uprising to prevent the uniting of the two kingdoms. Armstrongs, Eliots, Hendersons and Grahams all took part. The uprising (which occurred while James was at Berwick, on his way south to London) was quickly and brutally suppressed. James thereafter passed an Act of Parliament declaring all Borderers riding (moss-trooping) into England guilty of treason. The Border country (now named the Middle Shires) was placed under the jurisdiction of a Royal Commission and was governed as a Crown colony. In 1605 Sir Wilfred Lawson was elected Governor. Many of the "Broken Men" were forcibly enlisted and sent to fight overseas; 114 male Grahams, together with their families and 45 horses, were transported to Ireland.

The Armstrongs, in order to avoid a similar fate, retreated into Tarras Moss. Thus the Debateable Land, even after the union of the crowns, continued to harbour the most desperate of the Border marauders; though over the next 50 years many of them dispersed.

However, following the Parliamentary Wars, the region experienced great hardship and poverty and the old raiding and reiving habits revived. Following his restoration Charles II had to pass an Act "preventing . . . theft and rapine upon the Northern Borders of England", as the activities of "lawless and disorderly persons, commonly called moss-troopers" had "increased since the time of the late unhappy distractions". An officer called the County Keeper was appointed, with twelve men under his command, to hunt moss-troopers and bring them to justice. Gradually "riding" became a thing of the past.

Those who truly fall under the spell of the Border will surely decide, at some point in time, to explore it with a thoroughness beyond the scope of these pages. Scottish and English sides alike are full of beauty and fascination, from wild St Abb's Head in Berwickshire, right across Cheviot to Langholm, and so westward to Canonbie where the Liddel Water flows into the Esk.

For our part, we must content ourselves here and now with exploration of the Cumbrian West and Middle Marches. The West March, as we have learned, was very much Graham territory. Longtown, a small, bleak Border market town, lying just within the English side, after much repeated destruction at the hands of raiders was rebuilt and replanned on a grid system by Robert Graham of Netherby, in the late eighteenth century. Netherby Hall, a Graham property since the sixteenth century, originated as a fifteenth-century pele-tower. Netherby itself is, of course, on the site of an outpost-fort of Hadrian's Wall (above, p. 41).

Two miles from Netherby, right by the river Esk and on the very Border line, stands the splendidly named Liddel Strength; an ancient motte-and-bailey, perched on the top of a steep cliff and commanding an extensive view over the surrounding Debateable Land. At one end of this natural fortress was a look-out point; in the centre are the remains of the foundations of a square tower. On the weakest side are signs of earthworks; with a deep foss. Leland tells us that, "This was the moted place of a gentilman cawled Syr Walter Saleby, the which was kylled there, and the place destroyed yn King Edward the Thyrde time, when the Scottes went to Dyrham." It was stormed and taken by David II of Scotland, who had Sir Walter's two sons strangled before their father's face, after which Sir Walter himself was beheaded. At a later period the Grahams strengthened the place and held it. Another Graham stronghold was Brackenhill Tower; the sixteenth-century fortress of Richard Graham.

Stonehome, on the edge of Kershope Forest, is another ruined pele celebrated in the history of Border fray. Shank Castle, a ruined pele-tower near Stapleton, is yet one more place of bloody memories. So is Sikeside, Kirklinton; though today it is better known for its charming little 1736 Friends' Meeting House. Kirkandrews, a great name in Border history, was a fine Graham lair; here they had an early sixteenth-century pele.

Arthuret deserves a visit because of its famous battle (p. 55); this is historic ground. The church of St Michael, here, dates at least to the thirteenth century, though the church which we see today was built in 1609 to replace the earlier church; this having been completely destroyed by the Scots. The new church was built with money collected through the permission of James I of England and VI of Scotland. In the church is a 1657 monument to Sir George Graham, and another, of 1782, to Dr Robert Graham. A small brass plate in the north wall of the chancel, inscribed with two hands holding a heart, marks a fourteenth or fifteenth-century heart burial.

The stone cross, with a Maltese cross-head, in the graveyard, is Norman.

Bewcastle (for me, at all events, the most fascinating place in the whole English Middle March) we have already visited. While in this Middle March region we should not forget to go to Warwick, celebrated for its little Norman church of St Leonard, anciently known as Warthewick Chapel. Our journey there will take us through Wetheral (Wedderdale, a name that speaks for itself) and though, as we have already learned, nothing remains of its Benedictine priory save the gatehouse, we shall find, in the church of Holy Trinity near that gatehouse, inscriptions for two Wetheral prelates; namely, Prior William Thornton and Prior Richard de Wetheral, respectively. The two somewhat battered early fifteenth-century effigies discoverable on a tomb chest are of Sir Richard Salkeld and his wife Jane. Sir Richard, who was knighted in 1487, was a notable governor of Carlisle. He died in 1500.

Holy Trinity church, today, is best known for its associations with the Howards of Corby Castle, who built a family chapel here in 1791. Chief among the chapel's monuments is a Neo-Classical group by Joseph Nollekens; it is one of his major works and commemorates Lady Maria Howard, who died in 1789 at the age of 23, together with her new-born child. Lady Maria, moribund, with her dead infant reposing in her lap, is supported in a half-raised attitude by Faith, who points upward in the direction of Heaven. In white marble and life-sized it is all too coldly formal to be deeply moving; nonetheless Fuseli was among those who became much excited by it, which must be held in its favour, and Wordsworth drew attention to it in his *Guide*, and wrote two sonnets about it.[9]

Corby was one of the dependent manors of the Gilsland barony and, together with neighbouring Warwick, was given to Odard, first lord of Corby, by Hubert de Vallibus (de Vaux). Corby originated as an eleventh-century pele-tower and became the property of Sir Andrew de Harcla, Earl of Carlisle, but following his tragic attainder and execution for

Rock architecture: chock-stone, Cust's Gully, Great End (Abraham)

Crosthwaite church, *circa* 1890 (Abraham)

Boot, Eskdale, *circa* 1885 (Green)

Road up Borrowdale, *circa* 1870

Picturesque tourists, *circa* 1860–70

Bowder Stone,
Borrowdale, *circa*
1885 (Green)

Grange, Borrowdale, *circa* 1870, but doubtless little changed from the hamlet which Gray saw

Market Square and Moot Hall, Keswick, *circa* 1890 (Courtesy Mayson)

Market Square, Ambleside, *circa* 1890 (Abraham)

"Easter Rush", Wastwater Hotel, *circa* 1895 (Abraham)

The Buttermere Round; descent of Honister Pass into Gatesgarthdale, *circa* 1890 (Abraham)

treason Corby was forfeited to the Crown. It was subsequently granted to the Salkeld family; hence Sir Richard and his lady in Holy Trinity church. At length, in 1624, Corby was sold, by descendants of Sir Richard, to Lord William Howard ("Belted Will"), third son of Thomas, fourth Duke of Norfolk.

The Howards added to Corby in the early seventeenth century, much changing its ancient appearance and the early nineteenth century saw the house further transformed into its present rectangular and stately shape. The grounds and gardens were laid out by Thomas Howard in 1740. They are open to the public (the house is not).

Railway buffs (and dedicated Wordsworthians!) most certainly won't want to leave the Wetheral district without viewing the viaduct of the Carlisle–Newcastle section of the old North-Eastern Railway. This viaduct, built in 1830–34, has five semi-circular arches, each of an 80-foot span, and each 100 feet in height. The total length of the viaduct is over 600 feet. It was built by Francis Giles, who also has another fine viaduct to his credit across nearby Corby Beck valley, as well as the famous skew-arched railway bridge (a very early example) about a mile north-east of Wetheral.

Wordsworth mentioned these viaducts in the final (1835) text of his *Guide*: "The banks of the river Eden, about Corby, are well worthy of notice, both on account of their natural beauty, and the viaducts which have recently been carried over the bed of the river, and over a neighbouring ravine." These viaducts were in the poet's mind when he wrote his (slightly uncharacteristic) sonnet, "Steamboats, Viaducts and Railways"; one of the *Itinerary Poems* of 1823.

Wordsworth as a young man had, of course, attempted to write about the Border, in the shape of a poetic drama, *The Borderers*, which he hoped would prove suitable for Drury Lane. Unfortunately he neglected the blood-and-thunder aspects of his subject and instead made an intellectual study in depth of what we today would call "the psychopathic mind", with the result that the work, though an interesting one to read, is of excessive tedium when performed on the stage. Drury Lane understandably turned it down; it was produced, however, as part of the poet's bi-centenary celebrations in 1970. Watching it was an ordeal which many Wordsworthians, even of the most dedicated vein, recall with a scarcely repressed shudder!

So now to Warthewick Chapel, described by Pevsner as "the most memorable Norman village church in Cumberland". It was given to the

Benedictines of St Mary at York by Ranulph de Meschins in 1088 (note, within this context, the rebus of Prior Thornton of Wetheral on one of the chancel buttresses). After the Dissolution the chapel was granted by Henry VIII to the Dean and Chapter of Carlisle. The chapel suffered much through the centuries of Border unrest. It was repaired on several occasions, and extensively restored in 1870, but miraculously much of the wonderful original fabric survives.

The present church consists of chancel, semicircular apse and nave. The external view of the building carries us at once in imagination to Norman France; the little building's style is totally unexpected in this northern English countryside. The articulation of the apse is unforgettably powerful; square, utterly plain, projecting pilasters creating thirteen narrow, arched recesses; each recess being pierced for light by openings too slender to be termed windows.

Within the church, at its west end, is a splendid Early Norman arch, of about 1130; formerly the chancel, now the tower, arch. Its beautiful scalloped capitals are highly reminiscent of the Norman capitals in Carlisle cathedral. Originally the church had a narthex (an enclosed vestibule or porch at the main entrance); the foundations of this still exist.

For all who admire Norman architecture Warwick is a thrill not to be missed. Nor should be left unvisited the church of Our Lady and St Wilfred at Warwick Bridge. This Roman Catholic church is an outstandingly important example of nineteenth-century Gothic revival, being built by A. W. N. Pugin in 1841.

The eighteenth-century devotees of the Romantic (who played so great a part in shaping today's Lake Country) greatly favoured the English Gothic of the Perpendicular period (*c.* 1360–1530); finding in this their inspiration for much Picturesque building, carried out with a heady disregard for antiquarian authenticity. Romantic Gothic style was in the spirit of Horace Walpole, rather than any genuine attempt at recapturing the medieval; it was Gothick, not Gothic.

Dizzy flights of Gothick Fancy may be found throughout Cumbria; from the ambitious Lyulph's Tower on the shore of Ullswater, to the smaller fantasies of innumerable chapels, vicarages, hotels, lodges, boat houses and glorified garden sheds. But round about 1840 there occurred a momentous change in the approach to Gothic Revival; this was chiefly attributable to Pugin.

It has been said that in Norman building one form was added to another, producing a whole by addition, as in the formation of a honeycomb.

Gothic building was a process of creating a whole, differentiated into parts, like an organism. Certainly Pugin saw Gothic not simply as an architectural style, but as the outward expression of a spiritual way of thinking, feeling and living. In this he was fundamentally correct; Gothic architecture (which, of course, has never at any time had any connection with the Goths) sprang from a period in history when religious worship was of immense significance to Western man; satisfaction was obtained from religious faith to an extent, and in a way, which our day not only no longer comprehends, but sees no point in comprehending. Yet even today many people must surely experience at least a faint echo of awe and excitement when they enter a great Gothic cathedral: however irrational they may consider such sensations to be, such sensations are involuntarily experienced, none the less. Pugin, being an artist and greatly obsessed by the Gothic, took Gothic seriously; so seriously indeed that he became a Roman Catholic, believing this to be a prerequisite for the understanding of the spirit and nature of Gothic, and true understanding to be essential for revival. As a result of his work associational, or Fancy Gothick, was replaced by building of an archaeological authenticity sufficient, if not to deceive the expert, at least to convince the layman that a genuine medieval building stood before his eyes. And even the expert would grant that the new building breathed the spirit of true Gothic. Accuracy was the essential ingredient for the achievement of this end, and it was here, at Warwick Bridge, in the church of Our Lady and St Wilfred that (to quote Pevsner yet again) archaeological accuracy first began in English church design.

It is interesting to think of Pugin and Gothic revival in comparison with the earlier development of the Gothic novel and the revival of serious interest in the traditional Border ballads. It is tempting to compare Sir Walter Scott with Pugin (though whether many would consider it a fruitful exercise is doubtful)! Scott, in his novels, never got away from the Gothick. He knew his Border history, but he always saw it through a veil of Romantic glamour; for this reason his novels never reproduce the Border past with any degree of accuracy. Which was a good thing, doubtless, for his popularity as a novelist; his readers would have turned in horror and disgust from any attempt to produce, say, Jony in Gutterholis as he must have been in real life. But when it came to rescuing and repopularizing the old Border ballads Scott did some serious and important work. He could not wholly resist the temptation to dress them up and "improve" them a little; but with these ballads, working as a dedicated revivalist, he drew nearer to Pugin in the spirit in which he worked.

Scott's revived Border ballads,[10] though not accepted as the real true thing by purist experts, at least do breathe the very essence of their time. They wholly convince the non-expert, while even the expert will find poems like "The Lament of the Border Widow" and "The Ballad of Kinmont Willie" satisfying music as background to his wanderings about the Border.

But when we come to Bewcastledale we are caught up by another strain. Here, in this once notorious reiving, riding territory we catch, on the wind, an echo of a song which Sir Walter did not touch or improve. Plaintive, yet not undaunted, it is the true original voice of one Thomas Armstrong of the Debateable Land, who was hanged on 16 June 1600, for being an accessory to the butchering of Sir John Carmichael, a King's Warden. The night before his execution Thomas Armstrong composed his own brief lament,

> This night is my departing night
>   For here nae longer must I stay;
> There's neither friend nor foe o' mine
>   But wishes me away.
>
> What I have done thro' lack of wit
>   I never, never can recall:
> I hope ye're a' my friends as yet;
>   Good night and joy be with you all!

PART TWO

EASTERN CUMBRIA AND KENTDALE

Oblivion may not cover
All treasures hoarded by the miser, Time.

William Wordsworth, "*On the power of Sound*"

PART TWO

EASTERN CUMBRIA AND KENTDALE

Oblivion may not cover
All treasures hoarded by the miser, Time.

William Wordsworth, "*On the power of Sound*"

8

EASTERN APPROACHES

The Cumbrian Pennines—The Eden Valley—Looking Forward, Looking Back—Patterns in Architecture—Great Families, Great Castles—The Cliffords—Kirkoswald—Penrith—Brougham—Ninekirk—Countess Pillar—Lowther and Lonsdale—Brough Castle—Appleby—Kirkby Stephen

CUMBRIA'S EASTERN BOUNDARY is a region which, even today, remains relatively little known and largely unspoiled. For the tough walking fraternity there is all the magnificent freedom of the Pennines; for the less hardy, there is the Eden Valley to explore; one of the finest valleys in the kingdom, and one most rich in the treasures of Time.

The Cumbrian Pennines are presided over by Cross Fell; just under 3,000 feet in height and a relentless test of merit, as all will agree who have battled over this heathery, solitary, wind-keen, sprawling giant. North of Cross Fell and hard upon the Northumberland county boundary is Alston Moor; a great place for walkers who also cultivate an eye for industrial archaeology. This is an immensely ancient mining area; the Romans mined here and from their time onward there was intermittent mining activity for both lead and silver, until the twelfth century saw the virtual commencement of a fully developing lead-mining industry which thrived until the present century.

South of Cross Fell the Pennine pedestrian enters Westmorland to top Mickle Fell and survey the bleak landscape of Stanemoor; bordering first on County Durham and then Yorkshire. This way came not only the Romans, but all the English armies marching into Scotland; and over Stanemoor centuries later, on a coach, rode William and Dorothy Wordsworth, buttoned together in William's greatcoat to protect them from a wild rainstorm.

The Pennines are not walking country for the tiro; they are solid, exacting, twenty good miles a day stuff. Hostels and hostelries are few and far between and bad weather and mist often prolong the day's walking.

The Helm-wind blows, chill and penetrating, fastening a long pennant of cloud to Cross Fell's brow. In spring the sleet storms march and wheel in grey cohorts, with snow flurries skirmishing suddenly out of hidden folds in the fells. Then come the days of bubbling curlew and mewing buzzards, when the cold clear April sunlight is sliced at intervals with hail which leaves your face seemingly mutilated. In June the daylight goes on for ever, enticing you to walk until late into the evening: the peat is spangled with rosy mosses and the bog smells of nectar, the uplands are delicious as wine, and the midges grow increasingly remorseless as the day advances. During late summer the knee-high heather fights you all the way, yet this dense vegetation has its compensations, for as you wade, rather than walk through it, perspiring and grumbling, your every step is beguiled by clouds of tiny, pale moths that blow out in puffs of languid, slow-motion flight and drift ahead of you; *Les Sylphides.*

This country, of course, is part of the famous Pennine Way. Yet, even if you are not a walker who wants to do the whole Way in one prolonged masochistic orgy, you should sample at least something of the Cumbrian Pennines; that is, if your walking is of a durable, experienced standard and you are sensibly equipped, and enjoy a strong element of the proudly bleak in a landscape, and have a good companion or two for company (this is strictly no part of the world in which to walk alone).

The more gentle reader has doubtless, by this time, decided to eschew the Pennines and instead embrace the manifold charms of the Eden Valley; High Hesket and Kirkoswald, Glassonby and Selkald, Penrith and Brougham, Appleby, Brough and Kirkby Stephen. All this is country of historic event and immeasurable fascination, as well as of infinite beauty; though everyone should make at least one sortie up on to Stanemoor to see the site of the Roman marching-camp and the remains of the ancient and famous Rey Cross, that once marked the boundary between England and Scotland.

The eastern region of Cumbria is famous above all for its castles and the great names that go with them: Clifford, Neville, Dacre, Lowther. The presence that will most accompany us during our exploration here will be that of the redoubtable Lady Anne Clifford, "Countesse Dowager of Pembroke, Dorsett, and Montgomery, sole daughter and heire to the late noble George Clifford, Earle of Cumberland, and by my birth from him Lady of the Honor of Skipton in Craven, Baronesse Clifford, Westmerland, and Vessey, and High Sheriffesse by inheritance of the county of Westmerland", to quote from her will of 1 May 1674. Here was an imperishable aristocrat, with English history, rather than blood, in her veins. Hers is a name that still lingers green in these parts, despite the long passage of years between her day and ours.

The Cliffords, albeit somewhat by conjecture, traced themselves back to the Norman Conquest. They claimed to be descended from a soldier named Richard FitzPune or Payne, or De Pons, a grandson of Richard, Duke of Normandy. Richard FitzPune's son married a bride who inherited the castle and estates of Clifford in Herefordshire; FitzPune then abandoned his Norman patronymic and took the name of De Clifford.

The ensuing importance of the De Cliffords stemmed from the marriage, in 1269, of Roger de Clifford with Isabella de Veteripont (Vipont), one of the two co-heiresses of Robert de Veteripont, who had supported the cause of Simon de Montfort and had married a great heiress, Isabella Fitzpiers, or Fitzgeoffrey. Roger de Clifford also brought the Skipton Castle estates into the family: Henry III granted to him certain valuable possessions in Scotland and Monmouthshire, but these were later exchanged with Edward II (7 September 1311) for the Skipton Castle estates.

The Veteriponts traced themselves back to William de Veteripont who, in the mid-twelfth century married Maud, daughter of Hugh de Moreville, or Morsville, of Kirkoswald. Their son, Robert, married Idonea, daughter and heiress of John de Busley, or Burley. The son and heir of this marriage took for wife Sibilla, daughter of William, Lord Ferrers. Their son, Robert, was the father of the above mentioned Isabella who became the wife of Roger de Clifford. The sisters, Isabella and Idonea, between them owned vast properties, including the castles of Brougham and Appleby. Idonea, who married twice, died without issue and left to Robert, Lord Clifford, grandchild of Isabella and Roger, all her estates. Thus the entire wealth of the Veteriponts passed into the hands of the Cliffords, including the hereditary Sheriffdom of Westmorland and extensive property in Craven, with the result that the Cliffords henceforth held the ancient Honour of Skipton with Skipton Castle and all the estates that went with it.

There is not space in these pages to trace the outstanding military careers of the successive Cliffords and their equally brilliant marriages. Perhaps the most celebrated wedding of all was that of John, the seventh lord (1389–1422), to Elizabeth, daughter of Henry, Lord Percy (usually known as Hotspur), son and heir of Henry Earl of Northumberland and a descendant of Edward III. Their grandson was John, ninth Lord Clifford

(1435?–1461), a figure of great notoriety, known as "The Black-faced Clifford", or, even more succinctly, simply as "The Butcher". Among his evil deeds was the cold-blooded slaying of the young Earl of Rutland, son of Richard, Duke of York, after the Battle of Wakefield; Clifford saying to the youth, when he begged for mercy, "Thy father slew mine, and I will slay thee!" This killing forms a dramatic incident in Shakespeare's *King Henry VI*.

Clifford himself was killed the day after the Battle of Ferrybridge, in 1461, when the Lancastrian cause was defeated decisively and the House of York came into possession of the throne. The Cliffords were attainted; their titles and estates became forfeit. The Yorkists searched for the Clifford children, that they might be destroyed. Henry (1455?–1523), the Clifford heir, was concealed in the fells of Cumberland, living the life of a shepherd's child in Skiddaw Forest. He is said to have been kept in ignorance of his true identity and to have learned neither to read nor write. Late in life he succeeded in learning to read, but he was never able to sign his own name.

He lived a humble shepherd's life for some twenty years, after which time Henry VII succeeded to the throne, uniting the Houses of York and Lancaster. The attainder upon the Cliffords was reversed, Henry, the "Shepherd Lord", was restored to his blood and honours and in 1485 was summoned to Parliament, where he sat until 1497. Lady Anne, writing of him, tells us, "He was a plain man, and lived for the most part a country life, and came seldom to Court, or to London. But when he was called thither to sit in them a peer of the realm . . . he behaved himself wisely and nobly and like a good English Manne." Lady Anne also tells us, "He did exccedingly delight in Astronomy and the contemplation of the Course of the stars, which it is likely he was seasoned in, during the course of his shepherd's life."

The Shepherd Lord married twice, his first wife being Anne, daughter of Sir John St John, a distant cousin of Henry VII, while the second wife was Florence, daughter of Henry Pudsey of Barfoot, Yorkshire. By the first marriage there were several children; by the second there was one child only, a girl, Dorothy, whose first husband was Hugh Lowther of "Lowther in Westmerland" Esquire, son and heir of Sir John Lowther, Knight.

Henry, eleventh Lord Clifford (1493–1542) was created Earl of Cumberland by Henry VIII, having been a close boyhood friend of that monarch, The first Earl of Cumberland married twice, his second wife being Margaret, daughter of Henry Percy, fifth Earl of Northumberland, from which marriage the Clifford estates were further extensively increased. The twelfth Lord Clifford, second Earl of Cumberland (1517–1570) married "Lady Eleanor Brandon, Her Grace", daughter of Charles Brandon, Duke of Suffolk, by Mary, Queen Dowager of France, daughter of Henry VII. The bride's uncle, Henry VIII, attended the excessively magnificent wedding. The one child of this marriage, Margaret, married Henry, Lord Strange, Earl of Derby.

In 1552 or 1553 the second Earl of Cumberland married, in Kirkoswald church, as his second wife, Anne, the daughter of William, Lord Dacre of Gillesland (the second marriage of a Clifford to a Dacre; Thomas, the eighth lord, having also taken a Dacre bride). There were three children of this marriage, two boys and a girl. The elder boy, George (1558–1605), succeeded to the title and was the father of Lady Anne; his brother, Francis (1559–1640), eventually became fourth Earl of Cumberland.

George, the third earl, when aged nineteen, married Margaret, the daughter of his guardian, Francis, second Earl of Bedford. Though the marriage was an arranged one the young couple, who had passed much time together in childhood at Chenies and Woburn, at first found great happiness. Later, however, George Clifford took to extravagant ways, becoming a sea-going adventurer, a gambler, a great dandy and a favourite of Queen Elizabeth. As time went by he saw less and less of his wife, from whom he at last separated. His debts were prodigious and concern for the future of his line doubtless influenced him in making a will which was to give rise to subsequent decades of bitter litigation.

His two sons, Francis and Robert, had both died in infancy; Anne was thus the sole surviving heir. Lord Cumberland knew that his daughter could not succeed to the earldom, but he did not appear to realize, and nor did Lady Anne herself at first, that the barony of Clifford could pass to her and that the family estates were already entailed on her by an entail of Edward II. As Anne was in due course to appreciate, and thereafter endlessly repeat, she was by birthright and as only surviving child of her parents "Baroness Clifford, Westmoreland and Vescy, High Sherifess of that county, Lady of the Honour of Skipton-in-Craven". But her father, in his will, illegally broke the entail and bequeathed his estates and possessions to his brother, Sir Francis Clifford; the Appleby and Brougham property alone continuing in the possession of the Dowager Lady Cumberland, as this formed her jointure.

Lady Anne's explanation of her father's unfortunate will was that it was made through "the love hee bare to his Brother, and the Advancement of the heires male of his howse". The will, however, concluded with the proviso that all the "Castles, Landes and honors" were to return to Anne if Francis, fourth Earl of Cumberland, were to die without male heirs. Lady Anne, writing in her diary about her father's death, at which both she and her mother had been present following a reconciliation between Lord Cumberland and his wife, said, "A little before his death Hee expressed with much affection to my mother and mee. And a great Beliefe that hee had that his Brother's sonne would dye without issue male, and thereby all his Landes would come to bee myne."

This prophecy did indeed prove to be a true one, but much trouble and legal strife occurred during the 38 years which intervened between the death of Lady Anne's father and that of "his Brother's son, Henereye, Earl of Cumberland [who] dyed without Heires male in the Citie of York, the eleventh of December, 1643".

Lady Anne tells us that

> after the death of my Father . . . his widdow my deare mother, out of her affectionate care of my good, caused mee to chuse her my Guardian, and then in my name, shee began to sue out a Liverie in the Court of Wards, for my right to all my Father's Landes . . . which caused great sutes of Law to arise, between her and my said Unckle, which in effect continued for one Cause or another dureing her life. In which she showed a most Brave spirritt, and never yielded to any opposition whatever.

Lady Anne's first marriage took place in 1609, to Richard Sackville, then Lord Buckhurst. Two days after the wedding his father, Robert Sackville, Earl of Dorset, died and the newly-weds became the Earl and Countess of Dorset. Dorset was unwilling from the first to support his wife and her mother in their legal contests. We find him writing to Lady Anne to assure her of his devotion in these revealing words, "I love and hold [you] a sober woman, your land only excepted, which transports you beyond yourself, and makes you devoid of all reason". Dorset's lack of sympathy estranged him from his mother-in-law, who passed acrid comments upon him, but Lady Anne continued to be loyal in her feelings towards her husband, telling her mother, "whatsoever you may think of my Lord, I have found him, do find him, and think I shall find him, the best, and most worthy man that ever breathed".

In 1616 the Dowager Lady Cumberland died and there arose further litigation involving Appleby and Brougham, which property, much to the distress and anger of Lady Anne, was awarded to the fourth earl, her uncle Francis.

During the fifteen years of her marriage she bore her husband five children, the first of whom, Margaret, was born in July 1614. The second, a boy, died at the age of six months; two more infants who succeeded him likewise died in infancy; the fifth child, Isabella, was born in 1622 and grew up to become the first wife of James Compton, third Earl of Northampton. Margaret, in 1629, married John Tufton, second Earl of Thanet. There were twelve children by this marriage.

Dorset died in 1624 at the age of 35, his health undermined by reckless and extravagant living. He and his wife were seeing but little of one another by the end, but Lady Anne was never slow at any time to pay tribute to her husband's "sense of justice", "sweet disposition" and "valiant behaviour". She was ever a woman most generous in her opinion of men.

On 1 June 1630, after six years of widowhood, she became the second wife of Philip, Earl of Pembroke, whom she had known in the old days as Earl of Montgomery. He was a handsome man of 46; an explosive psychopath who owned much of his influence at Court to the fact that, in his youth, he had been a favourite of James I. Lady Anne is said to have been infatuated with him at the time of her marriage to him, but infatuated or not there is little doubt that she saw marriage to this influential man as a kind of protection. By him she had two children, neither of whom survived for more than a few weeks. Lady Anne and her second husband separated after four years and six months; his violent temper was, as she herself described it, a species of "lunatic behaviour" which made life with him impossible.

In 1643 Lady Anne's cousin Henry, fifth Earl of Cumberland, died without male issue and she at long last inherited the Clifford estates. However, due to the unrest, not to say dangers, of the Parliamentary Wars Lady Anne did not travel north to her ancestral lands until the summer of 1649. During these five years her estates were cared for by her cousin, Sir John Lowther, a relation whom she held in warmest esteem. At last, following the marriage of her daughter, Isabella, in July 1649, Lady Anne set out for Skipton, where she arrived on the eighteenth day of that month. On 8 August, travelling via Kirby Lonsdale, she came to Appleby Castle, "The most auntient Seate of mine inheritance, and lay in my owne chamber there, where I used formerly to lye with my deare Mother".

After ten days at Appleby she went on to visit and inspect her castles of Brougham, Brough and Pendragon; finally going to Wharton Hall, which had been the home of her cousin, Lord Wharton. She then returned to Appleby, where she learned the news of her husband's death. Soon after this she returned to Skipton Castle and commenced the repair and restoration of her several "Howses". She was informed that, if she rebuilt her castles, Cromwell would have them destroyed; to this she replied, "Let him destroy them if he will, but he shall surely find that as often as he destroys them I will rebuild them, while he leaves me a shilling in my pocket." Cromwell had the good sense not to put her determination to the test.

Lady Anne was 59 when she came north to settle and to rebuild her ancestral strongholds: Skipton Castle and Bardon Tower in the West Riding of Yorkshire; Pendragon, Appleby, Brougham and Brough castles in Westmorland. Yet these ancient strongholds were strong only in name: Skipton, the chief Clifford seat, was the least damaged; Barden and Pendragon had long been in ruins, Brough had been ruined since 1521, Appleby since 1569, Brougham since the Parliamentary Wars.

Lady Anne's decision to live in the north on her ancestral lands coincided with a big, new domestic building boom in England. The northern counties were rebuilding and modernizing as avidly as the south. All Lady Anne's neighbours were renovating their houses; often rebuilding entirely. The old, Tudor style was out. The classical style was in.

Tudor building was delightfully idiosyncratic. It personified an age which gloried in the Individual Man. A Tudor Englishman's home was his castle and if he wanted his front door squeezed into a corner and every single chimney-pot different in appearance from its fellow chimney-pots, then he would have these things and be damned if his house looked lop-sided and dotty.

The Parliamentary Wars, however, ushered in a new era. Idiosyncrasy and nostalgia were *passé*; harmonious classical design, light, space and all mod. cons. were the rage. No more knobbly, turreted, tunnel-vaulted castles (Cromwell had knocked most of them down, anyway); an Englishman's home was now an elegantly proportioned, well-balanced mansion, full of light, warmth and comfort. Mullioned three-light windows gave way to unmullioned two-light windows; some adventurous folk, by the 'eighties, were even using sash windows. Front doors were centralized; classical pediments, brackets, pilasters and balustrades made homes stately in appearance; handsomely-wrought guttering and drain pipes kept buildings dry; there was a vast improvement in sanitation. Staircases were broad and easy to walk up; smoky inglenooks and dark, winding passages were things of the past. The changes were radical.

Even the statesmen (yeomen farmers) were rebuilding their farmsteads; though still on traditional, basically Scandinavian patterns. Nevertheless these new farmhouses of the mid and late seventeenth century, stone-built, with large spinning-porches (and sometimes spinning galleries), flagged floors and two-light windows must have seemed wonderful improvements upon the previous wooden and wattle-and-daub houses, with their rush-strewn earth floors, smoke-filled interiors and tiny, small-paned windows.

None of the earlier farmhouses have survived into the present century, though many of their large timber beams were re-used in the structure of the "new" buildings. These stone buildings are themselves now three centuries old and throughout Cumbria they rejoice the eye; delightful, two-storeyed, stone farmhouses with big front porches.

Castles lay in ruins and nobody cared. Who wanted castles? Kirkoswald Castle itself was a typical case in point; doomed to neglect and decay, fast falling into hopeless decrepitude. The Dacres removed some of the better fabric from it to Naworth, including a magnificent carved and painted ceiling. The castle today lies forgotten among nettles and matted briars; yet it deserves better remembrance. In its earliest days it was the fortress of Sir Hugh de Morville, one of the four knights who slew Thomas à Becket. The sword used by Sir Hugh for this murdering was long preserved at the castle as a Black Relic. What at last happened to it nobody knows. "Time brings to forgetfulness many memorable things in this world, be they ever so carefully preserved," as Lady Anne herself was to sigh.

When Lady Anne arrived in the north her neighbours must have watched with keen interest to see what kind of fine new residence she would build for herself. Naturally she would not live in any of her castles: none of them could be thought fit to live in and, in any case, who wanted to live in a draughty, out of date castle? But Lady Anne confounded her neighbours. She carefully and lovingly restored her Norman castles in the style and spirit of the past and having restored them she lived in them. They must have been far from truly comfortable, let alone convenient, but they were the homes of her ancestors and she, as befitted a Clifford, lived in them exactly in the manner of her ancestors.

Lady Anne took up residence first at Skipton, remaining in residence there for a year, while she put that castle and Barden Tower in order, before turning her attention to her Westmorland possessions. Yet we learn that sufficient had been done at Appleby by Christmas, 1652, for her to be able to celebrate the festival there with many of her family, including her favourite grandchild, John Tufton: she mentions that it was the first time any of her grandchildren had spent Christmas with her in Westmorland.

In the New Year of 1653 she started to restore the great tower of Appleby Castle, which she was to name "Caesar's Tower"; she laid the foundation stone of this on 21 February and we learn that the work had been completed and the tower fit for residence by July of that year.

Appleby had been a "new town" in its day; admittedly a day now far distant in time. It had been built in the year 1110 by Ranulph de Meschines; one broad street running from the church to the castle. This castle, with its massive twelfth-century keep, had been in disrepair since 1569. Earliest mention of Appleby dates to 1174, when it was a keep besieged by William the Lion of Scotland. It was repaired in 1200, early in the reign of King John, and formed the most important part of the grant by that monarch to Robert de Veteripont "in consideration," says the deed, "of the singular good service done by him to that King and kingdom".

The town of Appleby was sacked by the Scots in 1314; the castle was repaired in 1383 and five years later was again besieged by the Scots. In 1422 John, seventh Lord Clifford, built on to the castle "a strong and fine artificial gatehouse, all arched with stone, and decorated with the arms of the Veteriponts, Cliffords and Percys", to quote the records preserved by Lady Anne. In 1454 Thomas, the eighth lord, who married Joan, daughter of Thomas, Lord Dacre, extended the castle towards the east and repaired the chapel and the great chamber "which were then fallen into great decay". A century later Appleby castle had fallen into decay again and it was further damaged 30 years later during the Rising of the North.

In 1641 Henry, Lord Clifford, fortified the castle for the King, for whom Sir Philip Musgrave held it until after the Battle of Marston Moor. In 1645 it was reoccupied by the Royalists, but three years later, on 16 October 1648, the castle surrendered to the Parliamentary forces under General Ashton, after which it was dismantled.

Lady Anne's repairs must have been very extensive. She came into full residence at Appleby Castle in 1662 and lived there frequently from that date down to the period of her final illness fourteen years later, doing much entertaining there.

Ten miles to the south-east of Appleby stands Brough, more properly known as Brough-under-Stainmoor. Brough Castle was first built in 1095 or thereabouts, by William Rufus, on the northern half of the ruined Roman fort, Verterae, meaning a summit; a splendid name for a fort on this brow of cliff rearing high above Swindale Beck and commanding an excellent view over the surrounding terrain. The function of Verterae was both to police the region to the south and to secure the western end of the Stanemoor Pass. The Roman fort's position was such an undeniably strategic one that William Rufus could not have placed his Norman castle anywhere better.

This castle was badly damaged by William the Lion of Scotland in 1174. Subsequently it was rebuilt and granted to Robert de Vipont and thus passed to the Cliffords.

Almost miraculously parts of the original, 1095, curtain-wall still survive (NNE. of the fourteenth-century gatehouse). The keep, the so-called Roman Tower, was rebuilt after William the Lion's onslaught; it is now much ruined again, but a beautiful two-light Norman window is perched high in its west wall. The window on the north side of the keep dates to Lady Anne's restoration.

The early fourteenth-century round tower, Clifford's Tower, at the south-east corner, was rebuilt too by Lady Anne: note the square mullioned windows, already old-fashioned even in her day. Here it was that she had her own private apartment, in the top of the tower.

Between this tower and the gatehouse stood the fourteenth-century hall range; restored by Lady Anne, complete with tunnel-vaulted undercrofts; all the work of her seventeenth-century masons and replacing earlier undercrofts of which hers were a loyal copy. In front of the hall range she made the innovation of placing new rooms; but we need not doubt that these were decorated and furnished in keeping with her fundamentally archaistic taste. Hers, too, was the great staircase, of which the lowest steps still remain.

Lady Anne first came to Brough in 1649, when, she tells us, "I went into my decayed castle of Brough". The following year she commenced the restoration. "This April, after I had first bin there my selfe to direct the Builting of it, did I cause my old decayed Castle of Brough to be repaired, and also the old Tower, called the Roman Tower in the sayd Castle, and a Court house, for keeping my Courtes in, with some twelve or fourteen rooms to be built in it, upon the old foundation." In 1662 she built a kitchen, bakehouse and brewhouse on the north side, in the castle court, and a stable on the south side. Now the time had at last come when she could take up residence in the place; thus, in September, she removed from Appleby Castle to Brough,

> "Where I now lay for three nights together, one night in the highest room in that half-round tower called Clifford's Tower, and for two other nights in the second room of the great Tower called Roman Tower . . . both which towers and Castle then were newly repaired by me to my exceeding great Cost and charges, after they had layne desolate ever since . . . 1521.

She was mightily proud to think that by sleeping thus at Brough she was doing something which "none of my Auncestors had done in a hundred and forty years before till nowe".

Lady Anne had a passion for towers and whenever possible chose to have her private apartment in the top of one. To reach these lofty chambers she, an old woman, had to toil up steep, spiralling turret stairs; yet this she did, relishing her eyries among the winds and the stars. At Pendragon in Mallerstang, which she started to repair in 1660, she had her private chamber in the top of the west turret, reaching it by going "up staires and . . . through the great chamber". She was first able to stay at Mallerstang in 1661, when, "on the 14th of October . . . I lay there for three nights together, which none of my Auncestors had done since Idonea ye yonger Sister of Isabella de Veteripont lay in it, who dyed the 8th year of Edward III. without issue."

In 1663, to her keen delight, she was able to spend Christmas there. "Soe I now kept Christmas here in this Pendragon Castle this yeare and this was the first time that I ever kept Christmas in it, of any ancestors before me, for three hundred years before or more, and I now lay in it till the 27th day of January." In 1665 she was similarly proud to keep Christmas at Brough, none of her ancestors having done this since 1521.

Yet though it had been Lady Anne's girlhood dream to one day restore Pendragon, there can be no doubt that Appleby and Brougham were her favourite castles; Brougham particularly so, for it was here that her father had been born, and her mother had died. It formed part of the grant of King John to Robert de Veteripont and tradition has it that the outworks of the castle were the work of Robert himself.

The castle was built on part of the site of the Roman fort of Brocavum, on the bank of the Eamont (the fort outline is still clearly discernible today, though somewhat obscured in detail by the castle). The castle was originally built in, or about, 1175, but the fabric that we see today is largely thirteenth and fourteenth century; between 1270 and 1315 a great deal of work was carried out upon it by Roger de Clifford, the first lord, and by Roger the second lord, who built the outer gatehouse. The third lord, also a Roger, also did much building at Brougham; a small stone about fourteen inches square may be seen over the outer gate; this bears the inscription, "Thys Made Roger" and in, or about, 1830 was, it is said, removed from another, unrecorded, part of the castle to be placed here. Also above this outer gatehouse is an inscription telling us that Lady Anne restored the castle in 1651 and 1652, "after it had been ruinous ever since about August 1617". (Lady Anne set inscriptions upon all the buildings which she restored and these further testify to her great feeling for history.)

This outer gatehouse was a massive tunnel-vaulted affair; with a portcullis, a porter's lodge and a garderobe (medieval privy). The smaller gatehouse, also with a portcullis, is earlier in date than the outer gatehouse, being thirteenth century. Between the two gatehouses was a courtyard, and beyond the inner gatehouse lay a second courtyard, L-shaped, with a range of domestic buildings along the west side. In the south-west corner stood a thirteenth-century tower of three storeys, with a fireplace on each floor and garderobes on two. A further, late thirteenth-century range extended along the south side of this courtyard.

The big castle keep is twelfth century in origin, though scarcely anything survives today of this earliest fabric. The keep's main entrance was originally on the second floor, for purposes of defence. The early thirteenth-century great chamber lay on the first floor, to the south of the great hall which was built 100 years later; though this second apartment was in truth not much larger than the old great chamber. The kitchens, somewhat unusually, were also on the first floor. A passage was pierced through the keep about 1300.

The south range was very early thirteenth century and consisted of two separate buildings, between which a chapel was set in the late fourteenth century. Two single-light windows survive here; notice, too, the sidilia and piscina.

It was a Clifford family tradition that much money should be spent upon the repair and maintenance of Brougham. The castle was sacked by the Scots in the early fifteenth century, but was repaired soon afterwards. In the sixteenth century Henry, the second earl, spent so much money upon Brougham that he could not, he said, afford to carry out repairs at Brough. It was at Brougham that James I was entertained in August 1617, for three days, by Francis the fourth Earl of Cumberland (Lady Anne's uncle) when the king was returning from his last visit to Scotland. Charles I stayed at Brougham in 1629.

Lady Anne commenced repairing Brougham immediately upon her return to the north, for she intended to use it as one of her main residences, in spite of the fact that it was "verie ruinous and much out of repair". By 1651–2 it was ready for her to live in. Among the extensive repairs which she had carried out was the building of a new bakehouse and brewhouse, erected within the courtyard walls; the old bakehouse and brewhouse she had taken down and had had the ground levelled; this, she said, made the courtyard larger and handsomer than it had been before and gave a better view of the tower, which here she speaks of as the "Tower of League", though elsewhere she names it the Pagan Tower; perhaps having the Romans in mind, or, possibly, thinking of Brougham's history as a place to which St Ninian had come to convert the pagan British?

The church of St Ninian (Ninekirk) stands above the River Eamont at a point just under two miles distant from Brougham Castle. Lady Anne, finding the church in a parlous state of decay, rebuilt it in its entirety in 1660. The result was a perfectly unpretentious, yet most dignified, place of worship; from an architectural point of view quite out of date at the time of its building, it goes without saying! The church furnishings remain as Lady Anne appointed them: an uncluttered, octagonal font; Jacobean-style screen, benches, family pews and poor box. Everything here is Lady Anne, with the exception of the cupboards in the south wall, which are early nineteenth century and much the same date as the porch of 1841. In the east wall of the church is Lady Anne's dedicatory wreath, with her initials AP (Anne Pembroke) and the date 1660.

The gesture most often cited as wholly expressive of Lady Anne's passion for the backward glance is the so-called Countess Pillar, two miles east of Brougham, set on the side of the road from Penrith to Appleby (A66 T). This is the old Roman road and it runs straight as a die; moreover today it is a big and busy road, thereby making it difficult to inspect this octagonal stone pillar, surmounted by a pyramid roof and a round finial, that stands neglected and sadly in need of rescue and repair by some modern Lady Anne! The monument is about twelve feet high in all and as if to speak of the passing of time are sundials set on the east, west and south faces of the head. On the north face are two heraldic shields, carved in stone work; one is of Clifford impaling Veteripont, the other of Clifford impaling Russell. On the southern face of this cubical head, combined with the sundial, is a copper plate inscribed as follows,

THIS PILLAR WAS ERECTED IN ANNO DOMINI JANUARY, 1654 BY YE RIGHT HONŌBLE ANNE, COUNTESS DOWAGER OF PEMBROKE, ETC. DAUGHTER AND SOLE HEIRE OF YE RIGHT HONŌBLE GEORGE EARL OF CUMBERLAND, ETC. FOR A MEMORIAL OF HER LAST PARTING IN THIS PLACE WITH HER GOOD AND PIOUS MOTHER, YE RIGHT HONŌBLE MARGARET, COUNTESS DOWAGER OF CUMBERLAND, YE 2nd OF APRIL 1616, IN MEMORIAL WHEREOF SHE ALSO LEFT AN ANNUITY OF FOUR POUNDS TO BE DISTRIBUTED TO YE POOR WITHIN THIS PARISH OF BROUGHAM, EVERY 2nd DAY OF APRIL FOR EVER, UPON YE STONE TABLE HERE HARD BY. LAUS DEO.

Lady Anne's journeys from castle to castle were in the nature of ceremonial progresses, being made in great state. She herself travelled in a horse-drawn litter at the head of her retinue; her ladies-in-waiting followed immediately behind in a coach drawn by six horses, behind which rode the gentlemen of her household. Then came her women servants in another coach and her men servants mounted. In addition to these people of her own household Lady Anne, as High Sheriff of the county and Lady of the Manor, would summon her neighbours and tenants to accompany her on these progresses. Sometimes as many as 300 persons would accompany her; she speaks of the neighbouring gentry, of magistrates and of her own relatives riding with her in this manner (Sir Richard Lowther, Sir Philip Musgrave and others are specifically named).

When she arrived at the castle of her destination Lady Anne would take ceremonious leave of her retinue, receiving each person singly, either in the inner courtyard, or in her own private apartments (her relatives, such as the Lowthers or the Whartons, seem always to have been received inside the house, there to be given an affectionate farewell). She gave all "the men her hand, kissed the women", thanked each one for their company, bade them farewell and dismissed them, whereafter they returned home. Having at last taken leave of everyone who had attended upon her, Lady Anne retired to her chamber; as she says of one such arrival at Brough, "I came away into my own chamber in Clifford

Tower", where she rejoiced in solitude at being back. Of her last recorded visit to Pendragon in 1671 she writes,

> I came safe and well into my Castle of Pendragon, haveing bin accompanyed in the way by severall of the Gentry of this Country and of my Neighbours and Tennants, both of Appleby, Kirkby Stephen, and Mallerstang. And my two gentlewomen and my women servants rid in my Coach drawn by six horses, my Men servants on Horseback. But wee had a great storme of Raine and wind during the latter end of this journey. And after the said companie had taken their leaves of mee here at Pendragon Castle, I came up stairs and went through the great chamber into my owne chamber.

These removals from castle to castle necessitated the transportation of bedding from place to place, together with curtains, carpets, chairs and tapestry hangings. In short, Lady Anne kept the medieval way of life of her ancestors in every possible respect. She liked to travel by unfrequented roads, partly because this enabled her to see as much as possible of her estates but also because in this way she was able to confer bounty upon people whom she would not normally have reached. She was immensely generous; her large establishment of servants, who were all devoted to her, felt her kindness equally with her tenants. Yet Lady Anne herself displayed great personal frugality; her own diet was sparing and homely, and she clad herself "more coarsely and cheaply than most of the Servants in her House"; her dress, "not disliked by any, . . . yet imitated by none" was of rough black serge. She who had once been a glittering figure at Court now saved on her own wardrobe in order that she might have the more to give to others.

It was her great delight to have

> her daughters and grand-children often coming to stay with her, and she always set down in her diary the exact time they came, and in what rooms they lay whilst they stayed, and in this settled above, in her ancient houses of her inheritance, she more and more fell in love with the contentments and innocent pleasures of a country life . . . for, said she, "a wise body ought to make their house the place of self-fruition". (Harleian MS.)

Increasingly Brougham came to be her favourite castle. Here, in her final years, she spent longer and longer periods of time; her own room being particularly dear to her for it was, as she never tired of observing, the room in which her noble father was born, and her blessed mother died. And in this room she herself died, aged 86, on Wednesday 22 March 1676, "about 6 o'clock in the afternoon", after four days of pain and sickness; probably, to judge by her own account of her symptoms, a heart attack. She

> endured all her pains with a most Christian fortitude, always answering those that asked her how she did, with, "I thank God I am very well," which were her last words directed to mortals, she, with much cheerfulness, in her own chamber in Brougham Castle, wherein her noble father was born, and her blessed mother died, yielded up her precious soul into the hands of her merciful Redeemer. (Lady Anne's Day Book, this last entry written in another hand.)

Lady Anne bequeathed a life interest in the whole of the Clifford estates to her only surviving child, the widowed Lady Thanet, entailing them thereafter to John Tufton, Lady Thanet's second son and then in succession to his brothers, Richard, Thomas and Sackville, and afterwards to the eldest son, Nicholas, Lord Thanet; naming him last "Not for any want of affection or goodwill . . . but because he is now, by the death of his father, possessed of a great inheritance in the southern parts," as Lady Anne explained in her Will. Lady Thanet survived her mother by only two years; immediately after his mother's death Nicholas, Lord Thanet, took possession of the entire Clifford estates and held them to the exclusion of his brother. However, he died three years later, in 1679, and was then succeeded by his brother, John Tufton, who lived but another year. His brother Richard then succeeded him, to die four years later, when Thomas became sixth Earl of Thanet and eighteenth Baron Clifford. He lived until 1729 and demolished his grandmother's castles of Pendragon, Brough and Brougham so that today we find them lying once again "verie ruinous", as they were when Lady Anne first travelled north to rebuild them in 1649.

Both Margaret, Countess Dowager of Cumberland, and Anne, Countess Dowager of Pembroke, lie buried at Appleby. Here Lady Anne had not only founded and built a hospital, St Anne's, in 1651 (it will be found in the upper part of the town) but she had also done much repair work to the churches of St Michael, and St Lawrence.

St Michael's, Bongate, is mainly fourteenth century (Lady Anne was not adhering strictly to the truth when she claimed, in her inscription, that she had raised it from its ruins). An effigy of a lady lying in a recess in the south wall, and dating to the late fourteenth century, is interesting because it bears the arms of Roos and Vipont. An inscribed tablet in the chancel carries Lady Anne's initials, AP. The north doorway should not be glanced over merely; it is of Saxon origin and its lintel is a Saxon hogback gravestone that has been requisitioned as building material.

For the rest, the north tower is Victorian and so are the transept windows and the east window. The wall-paintings are early twentieth century.

Set in the wall of the former vicarage, opposite the church, are fragments of a tomb canopy, fourteenth century, and bearing the arms of Roos and Vipont; together with other fragments of stone of the same date, from the church. (It might perhaps be noted here that Shap Abbey was the traditional Veteripont burial place).

The church of Sr Lawrence is mainly fourteenth century to early sixteenth century externally and fourteenth century within; although the earliest part of the fabric is Norman. The chancel is part of Lady Anne's restoration work and so, of course, is her family chapel, built in 1654.

The great organ case is famous; it is mainly early sixteenth century and comes from Carlisle Cathedral, where it replaced the old organ case that had been damaged during the siege of that city during the Parliamentary Wars. This organ case was given to Appleby in 1684.

The monument that we see here to Lady Anne's "pious mother", Margaret, Countess Dowager of Cumberland, was erected by her daughter in 1617. It depicts, in black marble and alabaster, the old Countess, an impressively and rather disturbingly realistic corpse, lying with clasped hands, and wrapped in her mantle; the same way in which Queen Elizabeth lies in Westminster Abbey. Lady Anne gave her mother a fine, old-fashioned memorial; nothing new-fangled was allowed to mar the dignity of the dowager here laid to rest. The inscription is marvellous and rings in the ears long after you have left the church: " . . . this monument thou seeist in sight the cover of her earthly part. But passenger know heaven and fame contains the best of her."

The authentic voice of Lady Anne. Yet when she came to design her own monument (and to ensure that it was exactly what she wanted she had it erected during her own lifetime!) she had no effigy of herself, but instead, in a magnificent gesture of nobility, simply placed on record her family tree of 24 shields, displayed in a classical setting. It was typical of her that she, who hitherto had always avoided the contemporary, when the time came to make her last statement, concerning her own demise, should choose a memorial that was not only up-to-date but was so much so that it, in fact, anticipated fashion. It was as if, in dying, she knew that the time had come to face the future.

There remain two more castles for us to visit while we are in this part of Cumbria. The first is Penrith; odd-man-out amongst Cumbrian castles. It was not built, as the others were, on the motte-and-bailey pattern, but it was square, with four ranges round a court-yard, with towers on the eastern and northern sides. Penrith was a Neville property and was not crenellated until the close of the fourteenth-century, when William Strickland, later Bishop of Carlisle and, still later, Archbishop of Canterbury, received licence to fortify the building against danger from Scots armies.

A hundred years later Richard of Gloucester (the future King Richard III) made Penrith his base while he campaigned against Scotland. During his tenure of the castle he greatly enlarged and improved it. In the Parliamentary Wars Penrith was held by the Royalists for a short period in 1648; thereafter it was dismantled by order of the Cromwellian Parliament and much of the stone was carried away to be used for local building purposes. In spite of this sufficient of the castle remains to make it an interesting ruin to visit.

The castle stands at the top of the town, opposite the railway station and adjacent to a pretty recreation ground. The most impressive feature of this gaunt, red sandstone ruin is the south wall; towering massive, blank-faced and impenetrable. One wall of the north-eastern tower still stands and this tower's basement tunnel-vaulting also survives. The main gateway was by this tower; this gateway was strengthened and enlarged with forebuildings during the time that Richard of Gloucester had the castle (we should remind ourselves that, as the young and dashing Duke of Gloucester, he was a highly esteemed and popular figure with a reputation decidedly different from that which he earned as King Richard III).

On the south side of the castle lay the Great Hall and to the east of this extended the solar (upper living-room). Below the solar you can see traces of an oven, together with a smoke-hole. The castle kitchens were in the west range, conveniently adjoining the hall. Other fireplaces, too, are clearly visible in the ruins.

South of the east tower was a second, smaller gateway. The large and rather fine clerestory windows are attributed to Richard, who obviously kept the castle in style; but the windows of the great hall and solar were small and designed with military matters much in mind. We must visualize Penrith castle, all in all, as a grim-looking edifice when in its prime.

Penrith itself is a very typical flourishing North Country market town, with a beautiful red sandstone church, in the churchyard of which the already mentioned Viking monuments (p. 70) never cease to fascinate. The churchyard is surrounded by old and attractive buildings: indeed this part of the town is graced with a gentle and sleepy charm quite lacking from the busy, plain-faced streets and shops of the market area. It should be added that Penrith is a wonderfully good shopping centre where you can buy everything from a bottle of *Arpège* to a coupling-chain for terriers! Which takes some beating.

Energetic folk, who find mere strolling round a town insufficient exercise, should walk up Beacon Hill: the tower on the top marks the spot where the great beacon fire was lit to give warning of raiding Scots.[1] It was last lit in warning when Prince Charles Edward's Highland army advanced into Cumbria.

The second and last castle on our visiting list hereabouts is Lowther; a ghost castle.

The Lowthers trace themselves back to Sir Hugh of that name, who founded the line in the reign of Edward I. Mary, Queen of Scots, at the time of her flight into England in 1568, was received by Sir Richard Lowther, Sheriff of Cumberland and Lord Warden of the English West March. He, together with his brother Gerard, was subsequently involved in attempts to rescue Mary from captivity. Sir Richard's elder son, Christopher, was ancestor of Sir John Lowther (d. 1706) who transformed Whitehaven from a little fishing hamlet into England's third most important coal port (p. 31). Another descendant was John Lowther (1655–1700) who was created Viscount Lonsdale in 1696. Before this creation, however, he had succeeded his grandfather (Lady Anne's cousin, Sir John Lowther, who died in 1675) as baronet. In 1690 he was First Lord of the Treasury and he was Lord Privy Seal from March 1699 until his death in July 1700.

James Lowther, first Earl of Lonsdale (1736–1802), was descended from Sir Christopher Lowther and, through his mother, was a great-grandson of the first Viscount Lonsdale. The first earl, an enormously wealthy man (thanks to West Cumbrian coal) wielded extensive political power in the north of England; he was a Member of Parliament from 1757 to 1784 and at one time controlled as many as nine seats in the House of Commons, where his nominees were known as "Sir James' Ninepins". He was created Earl of Lonsdale in 1784. It was he who had, as his agent, the father of William Wordsworth, and the young orphaned Wordsworths, as is well known, suffered considerably straitened circumstances in their youth because Lord Lonsdale had been in debt to their late father to the tune of several thousand pounds.

The earldom became extinct in 1802, but was revived in 1807 when William Lowther, a cousin of James, was created first earl of the revived earldom. Upon succeeding to the estates he had the Wordsworths paid the money that was owed them: an important event for the four young men and their sister, but perhaps of particular importance for Dorothy and William, for the change in fortune gave Dorothy a welcome sense of secure independence, while William found himself in a position where he might marry and support a wife and children.

It was in 1682 that Sir John Lowther, the future Viscount Lonsdale, purchased an estate at Lowther, in Westmorland, and set about building a splendid seat for himself: Lowther Castle. He also extensively rebuilt the nearby church of St Michael and furthermore he pulled down the old village of Lowther and began building Lowther New Town in its place (not to be confused with Lowther Village, another community built from scratch by the family in the second part of the eighteenth century, the architect being, it is thought, John Adam).

The first Viscount Lonsdale died in 1700. Twenty years later his castle was all but totally destroyed by fire. Plans were made for rebuilding in 1767, to a design by Robert Adam, but the scheme was abandoned and it was not until 1806 that a great Gothick castle, in full Romantic fig, was commenced upon. It took five years to complete. The architect was Robert Smirke (himself to be knighted later); he was 25, just returned from a tour of Italy and Greece, and Lowther was his first commission. He had been recommended by Sir George Beaumont, a prominent patron of the arts; with such a man to vouch for him the youthful Smirke was off to a flying start and Lowther Castle confirmed Sir George's judgement.

It was indeed "a magnificent Pile" (as Wordsworth put it); all turrets, towers, pinnacles, porches and parapets; a Gothick fantasia indeed. Within were enormous and stately rooms; extraordinarily impressive to look upon and surely equally extraordinarily cold and uncomfortable to live in! It was to Lowther Castle that Wordsworth was from time to time an obsequious visitor in his later years; as a youth he would have ridiculed the place.

It is not surprising that the Lowther family ultimately found the castle impossible as residence; they moved to a less grandiose place close by. Lowther Castle is now no more than a shell; yet it is an awe-inspiring shell and we can only repeat in whole-hearted agreement what Pevsner has said, that it is a shell which must be safeguarded because the country can ill afford to lose so spectacular a ruin.

The church of St Michael (already mentioned, p. 72, in the context of Anglo-Viking sculpture, which in itself indicates the early date of the church's first foundation) has a Victorian tower, constructed in 1856; the rest of the exterior is mainly the work of Sir John Lowther in 1686. Inside, much of the medieval church has survived; but this interior is somewhat over busy with Lowther monuments, of which by far the most arresting is that of John, the first viscount. A pleasant effigy, by William Stanton, depicts the first Viscount Lonsdale as a comfortably semi-reclining figure modestly explaining to Someone overhead that he has not lived entirely without merit in this vale of tears and perhaps might now justly anticipate some suitable award in the realm above? There is nothing of pompous self-esteem in his attitude; he is clearly simply making a reasonable statement of fact. After all, had he not been First Lord of the Treasury and Lord Privy Seal? Quite apart from having been Viscount Lonsdale. Would not . . . ? Might not . . . ?

Kirkby Stephen, five miles south of Brough, is a delightful market town with a very fine church, the early thirteenth-century arcades and southern transept arch of which are justly renowned for their outstanding beauty. The lovely trefoil-pointed sedilia and piscina in the chancel were retained and re-used when chancel and chapels were restored in 1847. The mid-Victorian pulpit is a splendidly flamboyant creation in brilliant-hued red and green marble.

The church has a wonderful collection of Saxon and Viking sculptures. In the north aisle, west, is a fine hogbacked gravestone, while beneath the tower arch is assembled a collection of pieces which include the celebrated Bound Devil (p. 65). There is also a detached Norman capital beautifully carved in almost Byzantine mood.

In the north chapel are effigies of the bearded, elderly, tetchy-looking

Thomas, first Lord Wharton, of nearby Wharton Hall. He died in 1568 and lies here between his two wives; the first a plain, middle-aged and rather grumpy matron, the second young and not uncomely. In the south, Musgrave, chapel are believed to rest the dismembered remains of the tragic Sir Andrew de Harcla.

9

A TRADITIONAL GATEWAY

Kirkby Lonsdale—Kentdale—Beetham—Levens Hall—Sizergh Castle—Kendal—Turnpike Roads

KIRKBY LONSDALE STANDS where three counties, Lancashire, Yorkshire and Westmorland meet (we will forget Cumbria for a moment: Westmorland has been a notable county for too long to be dismissed and cast into oblivion at one fell bureaucratic sweep). Kirkby Lonsdale is an English town such as overseas visitors imagine all English towns to be; alas, few are. But Kirkby Lonsdale must delight and satisfy all who see it.

The great place of pilgrimage here is, of course, the church of St Mary: famous for its Early Norman arcades; massive, austere, truly splendid. Pevsner calls it "the most powerful Early Norman display" in Cumbria. The piers of the arcades differ one from the other in appearance; the most beautiful of all being decorated with incised trellis work and in every detail enormously reminiscent of the piers of Durham Cathedral, indeed no doubt directly inspired by Durham. All this dates to about 1150. A south arcade was built later in the twelfth century.

From the churchyard there are marvellous views of the Lune valley: Ruskin (who never could resist handing out awards for scenery) pronounced this "one of the loveliest scenes in England—therefore in the world".

The church lies behind Market Street; a fascinating place along which to wander, with the 1854 Market House, a fine building, set on the corner, and a lovely Georgian building, Fountain House, at the end of the street. There are two irresistible inns here; the Sun, with a seventeenth-century pillared frontage, and the Georgian façaded King's Arms (inside is a handsome seventeenth-century plaster ceiling). The market square rejoices in the eighteenth-century Royal Hotel, several nice shops, an 1840 Savings Bank, and numerous other buildings all of equally pleasing aspect. The present market cross dates no further back than 1905; you will find the earlier, sixteenth-century cross now removed to retirement in a small square off Mill Brow, at the end of Main Street. From here it is only a short walk to the late sixteenth-century manorhouse.

But all of Kirkby Lonsdale should be relished, without rush; from Prospect House in Jingling Lane to the renowned Devil's Bridge, spanning the river with wide, beautifully effortless arches.

Kirkby Lonsdale makes a perfect base from which to explore Kentdale; a district which, throughout its history, has been subject to invasion, due to its proximity with the easily navigable Morecambe Bay, with its three estuaries of rivers Kent, Lune and Leven. For this reason it was a district in which fortified homesteads and pele-towers abounded.

One of the most famous early manorhouses of this region is Levens Hall, now expanded into a huge old house presiding over a garden of fabulous topiary work. Levens Hall in part dates back to 1188, when the Redman family bought the manor of Levens from Ketel, Baron of Kendal, and built a pele-tower (possibly two towers) together with a great hall, kitchens and other domestic offices; a Plantagenet dwelling of substance.

Matthew de Redman in 1305 was summoned, together with one John d'Ewyas, both as elected knights of the county, to serve in Parliament. To the statement of their election both knights affixed their marks, neither of them being able to write. It took six days for them to make the journey between London and Lancaster, and this was excellent going; in snow or foul weather it took from eight to ten days. Expenses might be claimed for the journey.

Once established politically the Redman family carried on the tradition of service to their country, both in civilian and military spheres. Sir Matthew Redman, who died in 1360, sat for Westmorland in Parliaments of 1357 and 1358. His son, also Sir Matthew, served in France and Spain under John of Gaunt, while his son, Sir Richard Redman, became Speaker in the House of Commons.

The Redmans sold Levens to Alan Bellingham of Burneside in 1489. In 1585 Sir James Bellingham followed the fashionable course of rich Tudor gentlemen and set about converting his old Plantagenet house into a fine modern mansion; fortunately, however, part of the pele-tower survived.

A new central tower was built at the front of the house, the former Great Hall and kitchens were replaced by an impressive entrance hall with fine oak and plaster work; a Spanish-leather-covered dining-room named "The Gilt Parlour"; two drawing-rooms, each with a magnificent chimney-piece, and a series of handsome bedrooms. In 1689 another Alan Bellingham sold the house to Colonel Grahme, MP, Privy Purse to James II and later Deputy-Lieutenant for Westmorland. Grahme made several further improvements to Levens Hall; it was he who had the gardens laid out by Beaumont, who had been working on the grounds of Hampton Court Palace for James II. The gardens at Levens today remain virtually as Beaumont designed them.

But Colonel Grahme left no heir to the home of which he was so proud and it passed into the Bagot family. For over two centuries there was no direct male heir to Levens; the result, it was said, of a curse which a beggar woman, refused alms and refreshment, placed on the house, pronouncing that no male heir would be born until the river Kent ran dry and a white stag appeared in the park. In 1896 the river Kent froze solid and an off-white stag was born in the park; in February 1896 a Bagot heir was born. Levens still remains in the Bagot family.

Sizergh Castle, a few miles further along the old road from Levens to Kendal, has been the home of the Strickland family since 1239. The pele-tower, one of the largest in the region, dates to about 1340. Sizergh is above all renowned for its marvellous early Elizabethan woodwork, in particular the chimney-pieces; five in all, of carving of the most outstanding spirit, crispness and beauty. Some of the panelling from Sizergh, together with a bed dated 1568, may now be seen in the Victoria and Albert Museum (it seems sad that panelling and bed cannot be restored to their original place in the castle's marvellous Inlaid Chamber from which they were removed and sold in 1891).

The name, Sizergh, derives from the Scandinavian *Sigaritherge*, or *Sigrittsergh;* the summer pasture of Sigred. The Stricklands came from the manor of Great Strickland, near Appleby. Earlier they were known as "de Castlecarrock" and there is little doubt that they were descended from the Norman family of de Vallibus (de Vaux) and also of Gilles, son of Bueth, the British chieftain of Gilsland; thereby uniting two houses that had been enemies to the death (p. 88).

Sizergh came to the Stricklands by marriage, having been granted, together with other lands, by Henry II in 1170–80 to Gervase Deincourt, whose great-granddaughter and sole heiress, Elizabeth, married Sir William Strickland in 1239.

We find Stricklands serving in Parliament from the first known return of 1258. At the Battle of Agincourt, in 1415, the then Sir Thomas Strickland carried the banner of St George: a signal honour. During the

Wars of the Roses the family was Yorkist; on the accession of Edward IV Walter Strickland, son of the aforesaid Sir Thomas, was awarded a grant of general pardon, indemnifying him for any offences committed by him through his loyalty to the House of York. The Sir Thomas of the following generation married Agnes, daughter of Sir Thomas Parr, the grandfather of Katherine, sixth and last wife of Henry VIII.

During the late sixteenth and early seventeenth centuries the Strickland family fortunes were seriously reduced through fines and sequestrations for recusancy.

Strickland loyalty to the old faith at the time of the Reformation was matched by loyalty to the Royal Family at the time of the Civil Wars. During the reign of Charles II the Sir Thomas Strickland of the day was Keeper of the Privy Purse. His second wife, Winifred Trentham, was a member of the household of Mary of Modena, consort of James II. Following the abdication of James II in 1688, Sir Thomas, his wife and their close relations accompanied the former Royal Family into exile in France at the Court of St Germain. Lady Strickland was governess to the young Prince James Edward Stuart and from this period derives Sizergh's remarkable and fascinating collection of Stuart relics, together with the Hyacinthe Rigaud-y-Ros portraits of the Stuart family in exile.

Particularly poignant is a portrait, by an unknown amateur brush, of little Prince James Edward Stuart, leading by the hand an even smaller Francis Strickland, cousin of Sir Thomas. Both children wear classical costume, but while their dress is decidedly fanciful, their faces bear the very real roguish grins of two mischievous small boys brimming over with bounce and high-spirits.

Prince James, known as the Chevalier St George, grew to regret the ebullience of Francis Strickland. The latter became the boon companion of the Chevalier's son, Bonnie Prince Charlie: a Falstaff to a young Prince Hal, it would seem, to judge by the Chevalier's disapproval of the friendship, on the grounds that Francis led Prince Charles astray. Francis Strickland's last adventure was to accompany Prince Charles to Scotland on the desperate business of the '45 Rebellion. Strickland went with the Prince as far south as Carlisle, where the older man fell gravely ill. He remained in Carlisle while Prince Charles and his troops marched further south to Derby, to return from there to Carlisle, some six weeks later, in retreat. By this time Francis Strickland was dying and he breathed his last as the Highland army recrossed the Border.

Sir Thomas Strickland and his wife died in exile; their son, Walter, was allowed to return to England from France in 1700. Thereafter he lived quietly and frugally at a much impoverished and dilapidated Sizergh. Thomas Peter, his eldest son, revived the Strickland fortunes by marrying heiress Cecilia Towneley. Cecilia was one of those people who are forever seeing "wonderful possibilities" in old buildings. She made ruthless alterations (she, of course, believed them to be improvements) to Sizergh Castle; these, subsequent Strickland generations have lamented.

So, at last, into Kendal, still guarded by its thirteenth-century castle, a stronghold now sadly crumbled yet impressive none the less as it crouches amidst old wind-bent trees atop a round green earthwork on a little hill. This was Katherine Parr's birthplace and girlhood home.

Not only was Kendal protected by its castle; the very town itself was built with an eye for defence, the houses being grouped round yards, or wynds, each yard secured in the old days by a strong gateway. Many of these houses have been rebuilt, but still around the yards; this new building has been carried out with exceptional sensitivity.

Kentdale was granted by William Rufus to his baron, Ivo de Taillebois, in recognition of services rendered. Kendal's civic history is preserved in the famous *Boke of Record of the Burgh of Kirkby Kendal*, dated 1577. In spite of Border turbulence Kendal was from the first a town of steady industry and thriving enterprise: a flourishing market town, and an established weaving and cloth centre from at least the fourteenth century.

Milk-white cloth was a Kendal manufacture in much demand during the fifteenth and sixteenth centuries; even more so was the celebrated "Kendal green" cloth (students of Shakespeare will recall Falstaff's "three misbegotten knaves in Kendal green" who came at him when "it was so dark, Hal, that thou couldst not see thy hand" and Prince Henry's rejoinder, "Why, how couldst thou know these men in Kendal green, when it was so dark thou couldst not see thy hand?").

The town's woollen industry began to decline in the reign of Elizabeth I; the celebrated Kendal cloths started to go out of fashion in London, then gradually elsewhere. Although Kendal still maintains some textile industry it would be true to say that, comparatively speaking, it is nothing now to what it was 300 years ago and more. But if the textile industry has declined, Kendal's other traditional industries have not followed suit. Kendal has been famous since the seventeenth century for the manufacture of snuff, particularly a type known as "Kendal brown". This snuff trade is still going strong, with special triumph for "Kendal brown". The old Kendal boot and shoe industry also flourishes.

Kendal's church of the Holy Trinity was radically restored in 1850–52, so that its appearance today is fundamentally Victorian. However, traces of thirteenth-century structure have survived and a fragment of ninth-century Anglo-Saxon cross-shaft testifies to early foundation.

The church was not immune from Border violence. It is on record that in 1129, during a particularly savage Scots raid, the townspeople fled into the church for refuge, whereat the invaders followed them into the building and massacred them.

There are chapels of the Strickland, Bellingham and Parr families in the church, added in the late fifteenth or early sixteenth centuries. In the Bellingham chapel is an interesting late thirteenth-century coffin lid. Near the chapel hang a sword and helmet, said to have belonged to "Robin the Devil", a member of the Philipson family who formerly owned and lived upon Windermere's Belle Island. During the Parliamentary Wars (always referred to in this part of the world as the Troubles, or the Time of the Troubles) the Philipson brothers took up arms for the King. The elder became a colonel, the younger was a jaunty major whose spirited behaviour earned him the name of "Robin the Devil". One Colonel Briggs, a Kendal magistrate who had joined Cromwell's army, besieged Major Robin Philipson on Windermere for eight months, at the end of which time Colonel Philipson came to his brother's assistance and raised the siege. The following Sunday the Major, accompanied by a small force of mounted supporters, cantered into Kendal and, understanding Briggs to be in church, posted his men round the building while he himself, armed, rode into the church and down the nave, looking for his enemy. One can imagine the effect that this dramatic entry must have had upon the congregation! Colonel Briggs was not in the church after all; an attempt was made to arrest the Major who, attempting to gallop out through a smaller door at the further end of the church, had his helmet knocked from his head by the low archway. Presumably he also let drop his sword.

This tale of sacrilegious disturbance is no mere myth, as some have supposed; we find the incident recorded by Machell.[1] Robert (Robin) Philipson was baptized at Kendal on 11 September 1623; he lived a life of non-stop adventure, including his gallop down the nave of Holy Trinity church, and was "killed at last in the Irish wars at Washford", to quote Machell. In his gentler moments he courted and married Ann Knipe, of Burblethwaite Hall. They had three children.

Among the many memorial tablets in Holy Trinity church is one to the painter George Romney. His first known work is a sign for Kendal post office; a hand posting a letter. Some of his later, and greater, work hangs in the town's Abbot Hall Art Gallery, which was built as a private house by John Carr in 1759.

Kendal also has a renowned library, the Carnegie, in Stricklandgate, and an excellent museum of which the wool and cloth section is particularly interesting. The town itself is full of delightful nooks and crannies to explore, and has a name for antiques and second-hand books.

Invariably nowadays Kendal is referred to as "The Gateway to the Lakes". It first became so, properly speaking, with the advent of turnpike roads.

Following the crushing of the '45 Rebellion the Whig government embarked upon a programme of building roads in the north; principally for military reasons. However, these roads also facilitated and encouraged civilian traffic. From 1750 onwards we find turnpike trusts making their appearance in Cumbria.

A "turnpike trust" was a body of local persons of significance and substance; the trust being established by an Act of Parliament to have control of a specified section of highway, on which were placed toll-bars or gates, in order to collect fees from the road users, thereby financing the upkeep of the road. The first turnpike trust to be established in the Lake Counties was in 1752, for the road running from Kendal through Kirkby Lonsdale to Keighley. In 1761 a turnpike road was extended from Kendal to Keswick; through Ambleside over Dunmail Raise to Keswick, and from thence over the Whinlatter Pass to Cockermouth.

These local turnpikes transformed the way of life of the people of Cumbria. The trains of pack-ponies fast declined, carriers' wagons appeared, post-chaises were introduced, and in 1773 a regular coach service commenced between London and Carlisle. The journey took about 36 hours and the fare was six guineas. The age of tourism had arrived: the age of the Lakers and the Picturesque.

PART THREE

THE LAKE COUNTRY

A LITANY OF LAKES

... and their Early Names

Coniston Water	Thurston Water
Elterwater	
Esthwaite Water	
Windermere	Winandermere
Rydal Water	
Grasmere	
Thirlmere	Wythburn Water and Leathes Water (twin lakes now turned to one)
Derwent Water	Darwent Water (Darrantwater—local)
Bassenthwaite Water	Bass Lake (local name)
Crummock Water	
Buttermere	
Lowes Water	
Ennerdale Water	Ennerdale Broad-water
Wastwater	
Ullswater	Ulswater
Hawes Water	Mardale Water

. . . Many are the notes
Which, in his tuneful course, the wind
draws forth
From rocks, woods, caverns, heaths, and
dashing shores;
And well those lofty brethren bear their
part
In the wild concert—chiefly when the
storm
Rides high; then all the upper air they
fill
With roaring sound, that ceases not to
flow
Like smoke, along the level of the blast,
In mighty current; theirs, too, is the song
Of stream and headlong flood that seldom
fails;
And, in the grim and breathless hour of
noon,
Methinks that I have heard them echo
back
The thunder's greeting. Nor have nature's
laws
Left them ungifted with a power to yield
Music of finer tone; a harmony,
So do I call it, though it be the hand
Of silence, though there be no voice;—
the clouds,
The mist, the shadows, light of golden
suns,
Motions of moonlight, all come thither—
touch,
And have an answer . . .

William Wordsworth, *The Excursion*, II

10

MANY EXQUISITE FEELINGS or THE CREATION OF THE LAKE COUNTRY

THE OPENING UP of a system of turnpike roads in the north-west of England coincided with the growth of the cult of the Picturesque. Hitherto travellers to Cumberland, Westmorland and Furness had been tough, practical men bound for these wild and primitive parts because they were miners, merchants, horse and cattle dealers. Clouds and cataracts, mists and moonlight were of no concern to them; they sought the wilderness simply because the products thereof brought them profit.

The eighteenth-century Romantic School, profoundly influenced as it was by the philosophy of Rousseau, placed great emphasis upon the wild, the primitive, the natural, the unstudied and spontaneous. Rousseau's "noble savage" became the ideal of every sophisticated city dweller in Europe; "*la belle Nature*" was the passion of every elegant stroller in the Faubourg Saint-Honoré, or Pall Mall.

An aesthetic appreciation of natural scenery became of paramount interest and importance within the space of a few decades; it was the hall-mark of a cultivated mind, a rarified taste. The persistent influence of Rousseau ensured that the wild, the primitive, the sublime were the essential ingredients of the kind of scenery, termed Picturesque, which was especially admired.

"Sublime" is not a word that we use much today, though the early tourists to the Lake Country used it all the time. The fashionable source of English thinking on this subject was Edmund Burke's *Philosophical Inquiry into the Origin of our Ideas on the Sublime and Beautiful* (1756). Wordsworth, some 50 years later, was to write an essay of his own upon the sublime in relation to the beautiful within the context of mountainous scenery. In this essay he explained that, "The sublime, to be sublime, must arouse a certain degree of apprehension, or sense of danger . . . But if personal fear be strained beyond a certain point, this sensation is destroyed. . . . Unless the apprehensions aroused terminate in repose, there can be no sublimity."[1]

The scenery of the District of the Lakes of Northern England (as the earliest tourists called it) abounded in the ingredients in which devotees of the Picturesque rejoiced: mountains, torrents, lakes, clouds, cataracts, caverns, ruined castles and abbeys, solitude, sublimity. Visual enchantment was given edge by delicious sensations of foreboding. Suppose a wanderer were to lose himself in the mists among the precipices? Suppose those masses of rock overhanging the road were to fall upon the carriage passing below? Suppose a phantom nun were to glide suddenly from that ivied abbey archway? Suppose. . . ?! It was almost all too sublime for words.

A self-taught artist called Thomas Smith (or "Smith of Derby" as he came to be better known) first drew attention to the Romantic aspect of the Lakes. His engravings of Windermere, Thirlmere and Derwent Water, published in 1761, proved so successful that they were republished in 1767 by John Brydell, together with a fourth view of Ennerdale Broadwater.

In that same year of 1767 there was published a pamphlet, a posthumous work, by a Penrith clergyman, Dr John Brown. It was entitled "A Description of the Lake at Keswick (and the adjacent country) in Cumberland" and had first been penned as a letter to Lord Lyttelton. It proclaimed that "the full beauty of Keswick consists of three circumstances, *beauty*, *horror*, and *immensity* united . . . To give you a complete idea of these three perfections, as they are joined in Keswick, would require the united powers of Claude, Salvator, and Poussin."

Lured thus by Dr Brown there shortly afterwards arrived in Keswick the first poet to be tempted into the mountains of the north: Mr Thomas Gray, best known to posterity for his "Elegy Written in a Country Churchyard". Unfortunately Gray's companion, a Dr Wharton, was taken ill on arrival at Keswick and the tour of the Lakes had to be abandoned; the travellers returned home. In the autumn of 1769 the two friends again set out for the Lakes, but this time Dr Wharton did not even get as far as Keswick; at Brough he was seized by a violent attack of asthma (a modern psychologist would conclude that the doctor was determined *not* to tour the Lakes). Mr Gray, on the other hand, was equally determined to carry on. To console Dr Wharton he promised to keep a record of the journey which would be posted to the doctor in instalments.

Gray was the prototype for all the Picturesque Tourists who were to follow, equipped with notebook and Claude-glass and afire with Romantic ardour. And let us here take a closer look at the Claude-glass, named after Claude Le Lorrain (1600–1682), whose canvases, suffused with delicious light, were so adored by the Romantics, particularly his "Psyche Outside the Palace of Cupid," more popularly known as "The Enchanted Castle" (National Gallery).

This painting tells us volumes about the Romantics. All the ingredients that came to be beloved by the Romantic School are here: a melancholy sea, fantastic rocky cliffs, darkly sad, yet feathery trees, so visibly stirred by an equally sad little breeze; the brooding, gloomy, turreted castle, the glowing evening sky, ethereal and yet mysterious, wholly in mood with the pensive figure seated in the shady foreground, a woman dreaming of—what? Touches of white foam, breaking on the rocks of the bay, are restless like a restless heart, the little white sails speeding to the horizon are elusive as distant thoughts.

And the Claude-glass, of which we were speaking before we succumbed to the potent magic of this picture? The Claude-glass was basically a plano-convex mirror some four inches in diameter (two glasses were, in fact, recommended and indeed usually carried; one dark, on black foil, for use in sunshine, the other backed with silver foil, for dark and gloomy days, or tinted to give the classical "golden glow" effect of Claude's canvases). The glasses were "bound up like a pocket-book" and might "be had of any optician". The person using the glass always stood with his back to the object he was viewing; he suspended the glass by the upper part of its case, holding it a little to the right or left, with his face screened from the sun. The purpose of the glass was not only "to furnish much amusement" but also to heighten appreciation of the scenery; "where the objects are great and near, it removes them to a due distance, and shows them in the soft colours of nature, and in the most regular perspective the eye can perceive, or science demonstrate".[2]

Despite the fact that today we associate the Lakes predominantly with poets, it was the painters, rather than poets, who were attracted to the Lakes during the period of earliest tourism. In 1777 and 1778 Sir George Beaumont (1753–1827), a rich patron of the arts and himself an amateur painter of considerable talent, visited the Lake Country on sketching tours. His companions were Thomas Hearne, the engraver, and Joseph Farington (the latter distinguished as a diarist rather than as an artist, despite the fact that he had been one of Richard Wilson's favourite pupils). Hearne has left us sketches of Sir George and Farington seated among the boulders at the foot of Lodore, at work on sketches of the Falls (in 1803 Sir George visited Coleridge in Keswick and through him presented Wordsworth with two drawings, one of them of Lodore Falls). In 1807 and 1818 Beaumont again visited the Lakes; to this last visit is attributed his delightful painting in oils, "Keswick Lake", now at Leicester Art Gallery.

In the summer of 1783 both Gainsborough and Loutherbourg visited the Lake Country. The two men were friends, but it is not known whether they were together at any point during their respective sketching tours in the Lakes, although it does seem that Gainsborough (a devotee of Gray's "Elegy") may have been stimulated into visiting the Lake Country by Loutherbourg, whose "stile" he greatly admired.

Philip James de Loutherbourg (1740–1812) is not much remembered today, but he was a celebrated man in his own time and his contribution to the popularity of both Romantic scenery and the Lake Country was considerable. A Frenchman, he came to England in 1771 and, during the period 1773–81, was employed as stage-designer at Drury Lane, specializing in Romantic landscape effects. In 1778 he visited Derbyshire to make studies for a pantomime, *The Wonders of Derbyshire*. It was the first time that a production on the English stage had concentrated exclusively on landscape as a form of theatrical representation, the plot being composed purely as a stratagem whereby to introduce numerous changes in scenery.

So great was this pantomime's success that, in 1781, Loutherbourg left Drury Lane to open his own miniature theatre, the Eidophusikon, where he achieved illusionary effects with moving scenery, lights and sound. Among his triumphs were moonlight upon a lake and a storm among mountains. Gainsborough was such an enchanted spectator that he attended night after night.

It was in order to widen his repertoire of scenes for his Eidophusikon that Loutherbourg made his 1783 tour of the Lake Country. As a result of this tour, however, he also produced several paintings unconnected with his theatre, including his "Lake Scene in Cumberland", a somewhat heightened view of Ullswater that is now at the Tate Gallery. There is no doubt that Loutherbourg much advanced the popularity of Picturesque scenery, with particular emphasis upon that of Derbyshire and the Lake Country.

Another popularizing force was William Gilpin, whose *Observations relative chiefly to picturesque beauty made in the year 1772 on several parts of England; particularly the mountains and lakes of Cumberland and Westmorland* appeared in 1786. This book, which became the rage with all persons of sensibility and taste, laid down the most categorical "picturesque rules", the chief of which was that "*roughness* forms the most essential point of difference between the *beautiful*, and the *picturesque*". Nature, as Gilpin himself confessed, did not always conform with the Gilpin taste; nothing dismayed by this, Gilpin, in his sketches, did not hesitate to rectify Nature's errors; "I am so attached to my picturesque rules, that if nature goes wrong, I cannot help putting her right," he confessed.

The adherents of the Picturesque School spent their time viewing, and criticizing, natural landscape as if they were at the Summer Exhibition of the Royal Academy. To visit the Lakes and express opinions upon this view, and this lake, as compared to that and another, quickly became a craze among fashionable people. The drawing-rooms of London and Bath reverberated with this kind of talk. It was a cultivated game which before long quite ran away with itself. It invited what we today would call "back-lash".

James Clark, author of *A Survey of the Lakes of Cumberland, Westmorland and Lancashire together with an account, historical, topographical and descriptive of the adjacent country to which is added a sketch of the Border Laws and Customs*, published in 1789, was among those who roundly condemned

> that cant style of painting which Gilpin and some others have introduced into their writing. Not a tree, a shrub, or an old wall, but these gentlemen take measure of by the painter's scale; a poor harmless cow can hardly go to drink, but they find fault with a want of grace in her attitude; or a horse drive away the flies with his tail, but these critics immediately find fault with too great quickness of his motions.

The first real tourist guide to the Lake Country (as opposed to accounts of personal tours) had appeared as early as 1778: *A Guide to the Lakes: dedicated to the lovers of landscape studies, and to all who have visited, or intend to visit the Lakes in Cumberland, Westmorland and Lancashire.* The writer concealed himself with a modest "by the author of the Antiquities of Furness", but so successful was this guide that its author was soon exposed as Father Thomas West, SJ, of Tytup Hall (the seat of the Jesuit Mission in Furness in penal times, and originally a possession of Furness Abbey).

West died on 10 July 1779, two months before the appearance of the second edition of his *Guide* and therefore he never knew the full extent of the success of the book, which by 1821 had gone into a further nine editions. Part of its success was undoubtedly due to its organization; to facilitate enjoyment of the scenery West collected and itemized all "the select stations and points of view, noticed by those authors who have made the tour". This method of instructing readers of the *Guide* upon what to look at from which particular viewpoint saved tourists a tremendous amount of time and trouble; West's "stations" became a ritualistic progress round the Lake Country and many visitors did not linger to look at anything between these stipulated places.

Even Turner, when he came to the Lake Country, painted a view looking up Derwent Water from the celebrated "station" in Crow Park; the point from which Smith of Derby had made his engraving. Turner's visit to the Lakes took place in 1797 and was productive of some beautiful pictures, including "Buttermere Lake, with Part of Cromackwater, Cumberland, a Shower", and "Morning amongst the Coniston Fells" (both now at the Tate Gallery). These oil paintings were based on watercolour sketches made on the spot.

But Constable was not happy in the Lake Country when he visited there in 1806 and failed to produce any examples of his best work. To quote C. R. Leslie, "He said that the solitude of mountains oppressed his spirits."

By the final decades of the eighteenth century rich Romantic offcomes (an "offcome" is someone not born and bred in the Lake Country) were building themselves handsome villas by the Lakes. Some of these new arrivals also played a not unimportant part in providing entertainments for the tourists.

Mr Joseph Pocklington ("Lord Pocky") was responsible for the annual regattas on Derwent Water. This larger-than-life character bought Vicar's Island on Derwent Water in 1778. He was a man of ebullient fancy; restraint was unknown to him. On his island he built several Picturesque extravaganzas, including a "Druid's Circle". At Borrowdale's Bowder Stone (that enormous fragment of rock which at some time unknown detached itself from the mountainside, to crash with behemoth force to its present resting place) Pocklington erected a small cottage wherein he lodged a resident guide, an old woman. Pocky had a hole cut under the Stone and tourists amused themselves by shaking hands with the old woman, by reaching through this hole.

But above all it was for his regattas that "Lord Pocky" was celebrated. These were tremendously popular with the "Picteresk Toorists", as Coleridge called them. The earliest recorded regatta was held on Bassenthwaite Water, at Ouse Bridge, in 1780, and it set the pattern for all the regattas which were to follow. The most popular features of these festivities were the mock battles, during which lively cannonades took place, stirring salvoes of echoes across the water and among the mountains. Firework displays, equally splendid for rousing echoes, as well as being visually exciting, concluded the celebrations after sundown.

Of course the regattas of the final decades of the eighteenth century were enjoyed by hundreds, rather than today's thousands; but the very fact that such regattas were successfully established by that date two centuries distant from us now in time indicates the rapid rate at which tourist invasion of this region had expanded. In less that 25 years the "Lakes of the North of England", to which Gray had ventured with such trepidation, had become acclaimed as a tourist paradise, the Lake Country.

II

ULLSWATER

Pooley Bridge—Glenridding—Patterdale—Greenside Mine—Helvellyn—Striding Edge—Aira Force—Lyulph's Tower—Gowbarrow—"The Daffodils"—Brothers Water—the Hartsops—High Street—Kirkstone Pass—Howtown

"ULLSWATER," DECLARED ACKERMANN, in his famous *Picturesque Tour of the English Lakes* (1821), "is the noblest of the English lakes." This is both true and untrue.

The lake has three reaches, or basins. The lowest is set in drowsy surroundings; pretty, gentle, but decidedly not noble.

At Pooley Bridge, where the shallows quiver with rushes and minnows, the steamer starts its journey up the lake.

First aquaintance with a lake should always be made by water. Moreover, the boat should follow Wordsworth's precept and travel from the foot of the lake into the gathering and growing mountains, because, as the Master explained, "these Lakes . . . suffer almost as much, at first sight, in being approached from the head as an affecting Story would do, should the Reader begin with the last Chapter & read the whole backwards". True indeed.

Therefore, reader, let us hasten to Pooley Bridge, buy a ticket for Glenridding and board the steamer.

At first we glide along past a landscape that is green and tranquil, with cows in lakeside pastures. Dunmallet, a low wooded hill to the west of Pooley Bridge, is the site of a British hill fort; at sleepy Caerthanock, nearby, is another and on the common of Moor Divock, lying between Pooley Bridge and Bampton, are many ancient borrans, or cairns (according to West there were formerly also stone arches and traces of alignments). Of these things we think as we glide up the lake; this is the land of the ancient British and it was here that the young Patrick came to convert the heathen.

Gradually the hills draw closer to the lake and crane taller. By the time that the steamer has reached, and left, Howtown, to round the big bend in the twisting bay, the fells are growing dramatically in stature, with the grand High Street range overshadowing all.

The third and final reach of Ullswater is a marvellous experience; Ackermann thought it the essence of the "sublime". The steamer advances with Glencoyne Park on the one hand and Silver Point on the other. St Sunday Crag commands the head of the lake, with Place Fell on the left and Stybarrow Crag on the right. The lake surface becomes kaleidoscopic; now crossed with long, gleaming ripples, now dazzling with motes of sun-reflection as if suddenly garbed in a suit of lights, now in reaches solid as pewter, now slapping in small waves against huge, smooth old rocks from which trees grow at unbelievable angles.

So to Glenridding. Here the Picturesque Tourists were diverted by the rousing of echoes. To quote Ackermann again, "Cannon are kept at the inn for the gratification of travellers, the effect of which is very appalling."

At Glenridding we disembark. We must now do a little exploring on foot; wandering up Patterdale, musing as we go upon the missionary from Bewcastle who gave this place its name. About a quarter of a mile from St Patrick's church, with its nearby holy well, is Patterdale Hall, extensively rebuilt now, but with traces of the seventeenth-century building that formerly stood here, upon the site of an even earlier house. There is a doorway marked I and DM 1677. This house was known in the old days as the Palace of Patterdale; for it was here lived the Mounseys, "kings" of Patterdale.

These remote dales were frequently presided over by one particular family which claimed a kind of sovereignty (for example, the famous Holme dynasty of Mardale). The Patterdale Mounseys traced their dale supremacy back to an ancestor who led his fellow dalesmen into battle against a band of marauding Scots and successfully ambushed and repulsed them. This incident in all probability occurred in the late fourteenth or early fifteenth century: we know that the ancient chapel at Gowbarrow was destroyed in a Scots raid at this date. This chapel stood by the lakeside on a site today known as Oldchurch, near Gowbarrow Hall. The Scots are thought to have advanced from here up the lake-shore towards Patterdale; tradition has it that the "battle" itself took place where the lakeside road passes beneath Stybarrow Crag; then a very narrow path between steep fellside and water's edge and an ideal spot for an ambush (this road has subsequently been greatly widened and modernized and no longer bears any resemblance whatever to what it must once have been). The Mounsey dynasty survived until 1824 when John Mounsey sold his house to William Marshall, a rich mill owner from Leeds.

The ancient pedestrian and pony road between Ullswater and Thirlmere is Sticks Pass. This rises steeply by Stanah Gill on the Thirlmere side and, as it descends towards Glenridding, skirts the edge of the reservoir, now drained, that used to collect water for the Greenside Lead mine. This mine first opened in the latter part of the eighteenth-century and was worked extensively until about a decade ago. There is now a Youth Hostel on the site of the miners' huts.

The great expedition from Patterdale is, of course, the ascent of Helvellyn. Although Helvellyn may be climbed from the King's Head, Thirlmere; from Wythburn (pronounced Wyburn); from Grisedale Tarn by Dollywagon Pike, and many ways more, the northern ascent from Patterdale is the best (I do not mean the easiest) by the track from Grassthwaite How, onto Striding Edge. By this route you advance into a magnificent horseshoe of screes and precipices, deep in the heart of which lies Red Tarn. At the centre of the horseshoe rears the head of Helvellyn himself; the two curving arms are Striding Edge and Swirrel Edge, the latter terminating in Catstycam (pronounced Catsteecam).

The fatalities claimed by Helvellyn happen chiefly in the winter and spring when these Edges, or ridges, coated with ice, become lethal. The sweet, green, sheep-filled coves of Helvellyn's summer-time southern face will give no visitors qualms, except as a hard upward slog that, on a warm day, seems to go on for ever. The northern precipices are a different matter and should be treated with respect; avoided in bad weather, never ventured upon when daylight is running out, and left strictly alone during winter and early spring, or whenever conditions are frosty. It should be remembered that Striding Edge does not mean that this is a narrow edge along which you blithely stride, but an edge so narrow that it may be *bestridden*. There are one or two decidedly awkward spots.

Helvellyn had become a "must" for the agile and adventurous by the close of the eighteenth century. A far less strenuous, but in no whit less Picturesque attraction was, and is, Aira Force, a series of waterfalls lying just within the boundary of Gowbarrow Park. Aira Force is not high; a mere 60 feet. Its chief beauty lies in the down-leaping motion of the white water piercing the chasm of green tree-filled gloom; the cascade pouring at last into a deep rocky basin. There is a kind of Romantic perfection about all this which is almost too good to be true.

The Picturesque Tourists, however, not satisfied by the waterfall's visual pleasures alone, were regaled by a story of blighted love, concocted as a treacly backcloth to this delicious place. The palpitating Emma and her wandering Sir Eglantine were scarcely convincing characters; but they were lapped up by crinolined sentimentalists,

> In dreams she threaded her way to the holly bower on Airey stream, where she last parted from her errant lover. One evening, when she had betaken herself thither, her faculties wrapped in sleep, Sir Eglantine unexpectedly approached the castle, and perceived her, to his great astonishment; upon advancing she awoke, and fell with the suddenness of shock, into the stream, from which she was rescued by the knight only in time to hear her dying expression of belief in his constancy. Straightway he built himself a cell in the glen, and spent the remainder of his days as an anchorite.[1]

Ah me!

The suggested site of Sir Eglantine's castle was Lyulph's Tower, an eighteenth-century Gothick "folly", built by one of the dukes of Norfolk; in all probability upon, or very near, the site of an ancient fortress belonging to Lyulph, first Baron Greystoke. From him Ullswater took its name: correctly Lyulph's Water. Lyulph derives from L'Ulf, or Ulf, the Scandinavian for wolf; this *ulf* theme recurs frequently in the name places of the Lake Country. Lyulph's Tower is not open to the public, but this is no deprivation, as its fascination lies purely in its outer appearance and its reputed associations.

The lake shore here is hallowed ground, for it was while they were walking here, on Thursday 15 April 1802, that Dorothy and William Wordsworth saw the daffodils. Dorothy recorded the walk in her *Journal*. Brother and sister were returning on foot from Eusemere to Grasmere. It was a windy day and the lake was rough,

> When we were in the woods beyond Gowbarrow Park we saw a few daffodils close to the water-side . . . as we went along there were more and yet more; and at last, under the boughs of the trees, we saw that there was a long belt of them along the shore . . . I never saw daffodils so beautiful. They grew along the mossy stones about and about them; some rested their heads upon these stones as on a pillow for weariness; and the rest tossed and reeled and danced, and seemed

as if they verily laughed with the wind, that blew upon them over the lake; they looked so gay, ever glancing, ever changing . . .

Later, inspired perhaps as much by Dorothy's description of the scene as by his memory of the flowers themselves, William Wordsworth wrote,

I wandered lonely as a cloud
That floats on high o'er vales and hills,
When all at once I saw a crowd,
A host, of golden daffodils;
Beside the lake, beneath the trees,
Fluttering and dancing in the breeze . . .

The waves beside them danced; but they
Out-did the sparkling waves in glee:
A poet could not but be gay,
In such a jocund company;
I gazed—and gazed—but little thought
What wealth the show to me had brought:

For oft, when on my couch I lie
In vacant or in pensive mood,
They flash upon that inward eye
Which is the bliss of solitude;
And then my heart with pleasure fills,
And dances with the daffodils.

It was on the same journey back to Grasmere from Eusemere that Wordsworth composed another short poem,

The Cock is crowing
The stream is flowing,
The small birds twitter,
The lake doth glitter,
The green field sleeps in the sun;
The oldest and youngest
Are at work with the strongest;
The cattle are grazing,
Their heads never raising;
There are forty feeding like one!

Like an army defeated
The snow hath retreated,
And now doth fare ill
On the top of the bare hill;
The Ploughboy is whooping—anon—anon:
There's joy in the mountains;
There's life in the fountains;
Small clouds are sailing,
Blue sky is prevailing;
The rain is over and gone!

Here is Dorothy writing of the same scene; in her *Grasmere Journal*, as before,

> When we came to the foot of Brothers' Water, I left William sitting on the bridge, and went along the path on the right side of the Lake through the wood . . . When I returned, I found William writing a poem . . . There was the gentle flowing of the stream, the glittering, lively lake, green fields without a living creature to be seen on them, behind us, a flat pasture with 42 cattle feeding; to our left, the road leading to the hamlet . . . The people were at work ploughing, harrowing, and sowing . . . cocks crowing, birds twittering, the snow in patches at the top of the highest hills . . .

The bridge is still there, the lake glitters, Dorothy's path winds away to the right through the trees. Brothers Water (the name a derivation of the ancient Broad Water and in all probability having no connection at all with any brothers who may, or may not, have drowned there) is a small, always brightly shining stretch of water, beloved of water-fowl in the winter. Near it stands sixteenth-century Hartsop Hall (extensively rebuilt and altered), once the home of the de Lancasters, later of Sir John Lowther, first Viscount Lonsdale.

The village of Low Hartsop, Dorothy's "hamlet" that lay "to our left", is quaint in the truest sense of that much abused word; quite lost from the world, with delightful old buildings typical of the region before the late nineteenth century brought modernization. Motorists, however, should be warned that there is no parking space in this tiny village; they must proceed there on foot.

Stout walkers will come this way to take the pedestrian route to Hayes

Water, Kidstye Pike, Hawes Water and Mardale; starting up Hayeswater Gill. Also starting from the mill, forking right, goes the track up Pasture Beck into Threshthwaite Cove. At Threshthwaite Mouth you will meet the extension of the Roman road over High Street. All this is grand walking country.

The Kirkstone Pass, which connects Patterdale with Ambleside, was described thus by Ackermann, "On the sides of the mountain are immense peat mosses where, in the summer season, may be seen small parties of women and children digging and preparing the turf, which in several parts forms the only fuel of the inhabitants. In this occupation, which falls exclusively to the female part of the family, the wives of the dalesmen . . . may be seen labouring with their maids."

These days no women with their maids and children are to be seen cutting turf in the peat mosses. Nothing of any special note is to be seen, in fact; only the long, narrow, winding road. The rock from which the pass takes its name, the Kirkstone, lies to the right of the road, near the summit (as you come up from the Ullswater side). The Kirkstone Inn, at the top of the pass, is one of the highest licensed premises in the country, at 1,468 feet above sea level. It is believed to have been built in 1840 at the instigation of Parson Sewell of Troutbeck, for the refreshment of travellers, including himself.

Sewell was Vicar of Troutbeck for 40 years, dying in 1869 at the age of 88. He was headmaster of Kelsick School, Ambleside, for 58 years. He was a man of pithy common sense, likely to build an inn where one was much needed. It was Parson Sewell who replied, when a parishioner asked him to pray for rain, "It's no use praying for rain while the wind's in this quarter."

Glancing down the road as it winds away from Kirkstone, to Troutbeck and Ambleside, we should visualize for a moment that elderly couple who once went down there arm-in-arm, stoutly stepping out; William Wordsworth and his wife Mary, "Darby-and-Joaning it" as the poet described it in a letter. Their destination was not Dove Cottage, but the home of their final years, Rydal Mount.

But we will not yet go with the Wordsworths down to Windermere; we shall return to Ullswater, to roam and amble just a little longer. There are some lakeside walks which it would be a sin to miss; the best of these being from Sandwick to Patterdale, a heavenly day of some seven miles actual walking, combined with a steamer trip from Glenridding to Howtown. The lake is an enchantment all the way, tempting us to burst into Picturesque ecstasies ourselves: "So sublime . . . with such beautiful colourings of rock, wood and water, backed with so stupendous a disposition of the mountains . . . The sublime and beautiful in nature—all that renders earth 'an Eden scarce defaced'—are here reflected in a mirror more potent than the wizard's glass!"[2]

12

KESWICK AND THE OLD MEN

St Kentigern Country—Crosthwaite—The Old Men—Early Keswick—Mines and Mining—The Radcliffes—The Amazing Amelia

THE ROAD FROM Ullswater to Keswick crosses Matterdale Common to Troutbeck and from thence over Troutbeck and Threlkeld Commons; today peaty, mossy, tummocky, grey, windswept, rain-soaked expanses of beautiful emptiness, where snipe, curlew, sheep and foxes live unobtrusively, small forests have been recently planted (as Coleridge, in 1799, observed should be done) and any attempt at walking is purgatory. Threlkeld Common climbs up to the rough green feet of White Pike; which is the way Coleridge went on his great Helvellyn walk. Threlkeld village lies tucked under the grey and silver coves and ridges of the mountain which the Brigantes called Blencathra and later generations have known as Saddleback.

It was this way that St Kentigern came, on his journey from Mungrisedale to the place that was thereafter to be known as Crosthwaite. The landscape in his day would have been rather different: no open, windy commons, but much thick forest, with scattered British settlements set among tiny fields.

Never at any point in its history more than a mere hamlet, Crosthwaite none the less is "the ancient and original valley of the vale", as Eliza Lynn Linton phrased it; speaking lovingly of her birthplace and childhood home. St Kentigern set up his cross here in the mid-sixth century; Keswick did not come into being until the late seventh century, or thereabouts, having its origin as an Anglian dairy farming settlement; as we learn from its name, *kes*=cheese, *wic*=a village. Crosthwaite today appears to the casual eye to be virtually a part of Keswick itself; though a few decades back you could still walk to it, from Keswick, along a meadow path, as Coleridge and Robert Southey did.

The Church that we see at Crosthwaite is the fourth to have stood upon this time-honoured site. It is one of the most interesting churches in the entire Lake Country and provides, in itself, a synthesis of the history of the district. The first church here, a little wooden chapel, founded in the mid-sixth century by St Kentigern, belonged to the See of Glasgow, of which he was bishop. In the twelfth century this earliest church was replaced by something altogether more splendid; Joscelin of Furness, in 1180, recorded that, "In this very locality [where St Kentigern had planted his cross] a basilica recently erected is dedicated to the name of the blessed Kentigern."

A basilica, in terms of medieval architecture, was an aisled church with a clerestory (viz. the nave walls had an upper storey pierced by windows). This basilica of St Kentigern was endowed by Alice de Romeli, Lady of Allerdale; the great religious benefactress of the district in early Norman times. She made a gift to Fountains Abbey of the rectory at Crosthwaite, together with one of the four islands of Derwent Water; today's Derwent Isle (then known as Vicar's Isle). The patronage of the vicarage, however, was reserved within the See of Carlisle. Fountains Abbey established a grange of monks at Crosthwaite, from which derives today's Monks' Hall.

Of Lady Alice's basilica nothing now remains. Of the fourteenth-century building which succeeded it there survives the north chapel, windows, and the font. This last was presented to the church in the final decade of the fourteenth century by Lady Derwentwater and Lady Maude, wife of the Earl of Northumberland, as a tribute to the vicar, Sir Thomas de Eskhead.

The fourth church was built by Sir John Ratcliff, or Radcliffe, who died in 1527, though the west tower was not completed until a decade or more after his death. The east end of the south aisle is traditionally known as the Derwentwater, or Lord's chapel and also as the Magdalen Chantry: the Derwentwaters being lords of the manor and Mary Magdalene being the patron saint of Keswick. Here, in this chapel, prayers were said daily for the souls of the departed Derwentwaters, through the intercession of "Sancta Maria Magdelena de Keswyke".

The original home of the Derwentwaters was just outside Keswick, at Castlerigg, where they had a fortified manorhouse. The family became amalgamated with the Radcliffes of Dilston, Northumberland, in 1417, when Sir Nicholas Radcliffe married the heiress of John de Derwentwater. Sir John Radcliffe, aforesaid, was buried in an altar tomb in the chancel of Crosthwaite church. He and his wife, Dame Alice, are each depicted in brass thereon; Sir John in his armour. He led a contingent to Flodden

Field, but survived that; dying at last peacefully at home. His widow did not in fact share his Crosthwaite tomb, but was buried in Salisbury cathedral.

The surviving early windows of the church range in date from the fourteenth century to the mid-sixteenth century. On several of them, to the left side of the window, may be discerned a "chrism" or consecration cross. Such crosses are somewhat of a rarity and these should not be missed.

The church's best-known monument is of Robert Southey, one-time Poet Laureate, who was induced to take up residence at Keswick in 1803 by his brother-in-law, Coleridge, and who made Keswick his home for the remaining 40-odd years of his life. The white marble monument, by John G. Lough, shows the poet lying asleep, one hand on his heart, the other holding a book. Cuthbert Southey, the poet's son, called it the truest likeness of his father that he ever saw. The epitaph was composed by Wordsworth, who changed the last two lines after they had been cut in the marble; the erasure is still visible.

More recent memorials than the effigy of Southey are the baptistry, commemorating Canon and Mrs Rawnsley; and the organ, restored tower and west window which together form the 1914–18 War Memorial. Canon Rawnsley was vicar of the parish for 34 years, as well as being one of the chief creators, in 1895, of the National Trust. Many will feel that his best memorial is Friars' Crag, Lord's Island and Great Wood; given to the National Trust as a living monument to him.

There are a number of interesting gravestones and tombs in the churchyard, including, of course, that of Southey, together with members of his family and household from Greta Hall. Indeed, all Keswick lies buried here; farmers and flock masters, waggoners and quarrymen, miners, pencil makers and mill hands, fox hunters, poets and foresters, clergymen and the wildest of their flocks resting together between the mountain and the lake.

Keswick lies at the centre of an ancient and famous mining region. The Cumbrian miners of centuries long gone became known to later generations as the Old Men. The Old Men! They haunt the Lake Country: ghosts of incredible, subterranean toilers, grey with dust, blear-eyed with working in the darkness, their knotted hands grasping ancient mells, picks and shovels. These are the legendary shades that people the fells around Keswick.

The Old Men are not infrequently confused with "the Germans"; but the true Old Men were working the Cumbrian mines long before the Bavarian mining experts arrived in the Lake Country in the reign of Elizabeth I. It is, indeed, impossible to assign any certain date to the first of the Old Men. If we were to include, in the mining history of this region, the axe makers who struggled to dislodge great flints from ages-old repose we could claim, with complete confidence, that mining has been a Cumbrian industry right back to man's earliest presence here. However, during discussion of this fascinating subject with an octogenarian friend, himself once a worker in the Greenside mine, I was firmly dissuaded from pursuit of that idea: "Nay, lass; axemen were quarry lads."

Camden describes "Keswicke" as "many years famous for the copper works, as appears from a charter of King Edward IV". In fact, Keswick had been associated with copper-mining activity since at least the time of Henry III (1207–1272).

Keswick received its market charter from Edward I (Camden tells us that, "The privilege of a Market was procur'd for it of Edward the first by Thomas of Derwentwater, Lord of the place"). A weekly market has been held in the town ever since. Certain other specific fairs were also a regular feature: for the sale of cheese, of cattle, and for the hiring of hands. Keswick's best-known fair was held each year on 2 August: the Morlan Fair, so called, in honour of Mary Magdalene. After the Reformation the celebration continued in secular disguise as a leather fair and, when this was at last discontinued in its turn, Keswick shoemakers still kept 2 August as a day upon which they got gloriously drunk.

Keswickian commemoration of this day throughout the ages gave rise to a local proverb, "Morlan fluid ne'er did guid"; said by some to refer to the violent rain storms which not infrequently explode over the district in July and August, while others maintained that the fluid of the proverb was not rainwater but ale. It is interesting to note, in passing, that today's Keswick Annual Show (a combination of agricultural, horticultural, dog and hound show, together with wrestling contests and gymkhana, not to mention the conviviality of a beer-tent) is held in August, thereby preserving the ancient Morlan note of Keswickian festivity.

Until the first decades of the mid-nineteenth century mining, textile mills and pencil making were the major source of Keswick's prosperity.

> May God Almighty grant his aid
> To Keswick and its woollen trade

ran the old rune, cut into a flagstone further adorned with what seems to have been a bas-relief portrait of the head of an awe-inspiring tup. This flagstone embellished what was then a woollen-textile mill by Greta Bridge (later a pencil-mill and today a youth club).

The Keswick woollen industry, dating back to early medieval times, was at its zenith in the sixteenth and early seventeenth centuries; with spinning, carding and weaving going on all over the adjoining district. The industry slackened during the eighteenth century, though some of the larger mills, notably the blanket mill at Millbeck, Underskiddaw, prospered into the earlier decades of the nineteenth century; but there were relatively few hands employed in Keswick's woollen industry by the late 1770s and the wool-pack trains that had once kept the single main street noisy with the clatter of hooves and the cries of drovers had dwindled into non-existence. Many of the mills that had dealt in woollens had turned to cotton by 1800.

It was as a mining town that Keswick most made history, before tourism took over. In the time of Elizabeth I the countryside about Keswick was the contemporary Yukon and Keswick itself was the Dawson City of the age.

Mining in the Lake Country has always had a somewhat erratic history; periods of strong activity being followed by decades of quiescence. It is not surprising to learn that the mineral wealth of the region aroused intense interest during the enterprising reign of Good Queen Bess. Prospectors appeared to appraise the earlier mines, which, says Fuller in his *Worthies*, "lay long neglected, choaked in their own rubbish, till renewed about the beginning of Queen Elizabeth".

In 1561 the Mines Royal Company was chartered, with the Queen as patron and the Earl of Northumberland and Lord Burghley among the leading shareholders. The actual mining was placed in the hands of Bavarian experts; Bavaria being the most advanced mining area in Europe at the time. Accordingly, indentures were made between Queen Elizabeth and Thomas Thurland, Master of the Savoy, and Daniel Hechstetter of Augsburg, for the discovery and working of minerals. Hechstetter brought a number of Bavarian miners to England to work with him and more, in due course, followed.

The basic principles of mining, even as the industry is carried out today, are now known to have been practised in pre-historic times; indeed, mining techniques seem to have been among the first to be developed to an advanced industrial standard by early man. Modern archaeology has greatly enlarged our knowledge of the extent and expertise of ancient mining activity.

The mines were worked by a series of horizontal tunnels, or levels (as they are usually called), driven along the vein of ore; the ground above and between the levels afterwards being "stoped", or "headed", out. If the ore continued downwards, then a shaft was sunk and levels driven from this shaft.

The heading process, Postlethwaite[1] tells us, took place thus:

> Five or six feet of the vein is cut away from the roof of the level, for three of four fathoms in length, when strong timbers are fixed across, about three or four feet apart, where the roof of the level originally was; over these, longitudinal timbers are placed, and above these a covering of fragments of rock or vein-stone. This structure is called a "Bunyan" or "Bunnin" and is made sufficiently strong to support the debris which accumulates upon it. As the miner cuts the ground away above, he retains sufficient of the debris beneath his feet to raise him up to his work, and throws the surplus down to the level below, whence it is carried out to the surface. In this way he proceeds until he reaches the level above, after which the whole of the debris upon the bunyan . . . is carried out to the dressing floors, where the ore is separated from the vein-stone and other earthy matter, and made fit for the market.

When the early miners encountered loose rock they erected oblong timber frames to support the rubble; the level below the frame would then be cleared, another oblong frame would be erected, the area of the level below that cleared, and so on. Wooden pumps were used to clear the water which collected in the levels. Before metal tramways and wagons were used to fetch the ore from remote parts of the mine wheel-barrows, jackrowls and kibbles were used. The most favoured and easiest method of ventilation of the mines was by having more than one opening to it, or by the sinking of air shafts. Foul air was sometimes overcome by artificial air currents produced by waterfalls; the air current from the water-fall was conveyed to the miners by an ingenious system of wooden tubes.

The ore, in the early days, was washed and dressed by a process of "tubbing". Later a system was introduced whereby the ore was dressed over a grate upon which a stream of water fell; the small dirt filtered through the grate, the remainder was passed on to a table and picked over by hand. This job was usually done by boys.

The water for the mining processes was obtained from specially constructed reservoirs. If you search above an old mine you will usually find either a man-made reservoir or a tarn that has been adapted for the purpose of storing and supplying water. The water was conveyed down to the mine in a wooden open trough, or sometimes wooden pipes. The route over which this aqueduct passed was specially constructed and causeyed to keep it at the correct slope for the water to obey the laws of gravity; where necessary the trough, or pipe, was propped on wooden supports.

Although gunpowder (black powder) may have been discovered as early as the tenth century (possibly even earlier) there is no record of it having been used as a blasting agent until the sixteenth century. Before the use of explosives in mines, rock was split by the process of fire-setting: that is, by building a fire against the face of the rock, which, on cooling, split and flaked off. Later came laborious excavation by hammer and chisel, developed into the "stope-and-feather" method, of which Postlethwaite tells us that the feathers were two thin pieces of iron, about six inches long and half-an-inch broad, flat on one side and round on the other, while the thin, tapering wedge, or "stope", was of the same length and breadth. A hole was bored in the rock and the feathers placed in it, with their flat sides together, parallel with the cleavage of the rock; the point of the stope was then introduced between the feathers and driven in with a hammer until the rock was split. This was a slow, exhausting business; the apertures that the Old Men thus made were therefore kept as small as possible, not larger than was required to admit one man at a time.*

The Germans, when they commenced operating in Cumbria, both opened up the mines of the Old Men and discovered new veins. The great and already ancient copper mine in Newlands (the date of the first working of which is not known) was found to be still immensely rich in ore. Gold and silver, as well as copper, were found in this mine; today known as Goldscope. Queen Elizabeth started a lawsuit against the Earl of Northumberland, making exclusive claim to the richer minerals, saying that the Royal metals belonged to her alone while the baser (by which she meant the copper) belonged to the earl. Of course her majesty won the case.

Teams of pack-ponies transported the ore from Newlands to the western shore of Derwentwater where, from today's Hawes End, it was ferried across the lake to Keswick (Copper Load Bay is said to be named

* Entry and exploration of old mines in this region is HIGHLY DANGEROUS and should never be attempted.

after a cargo that sank to the bottom of the lake at that spot). At Brigham a smelting-works was built beside the Greta. This smelting-works was famous in its day; Camden speaks of the "forcible stream, and other ingenious inventions, [which] serveth them in notable stead for easy bellows-works, hammer-works, forge-works, and sawing of boards, not without admiration of those who behold". Keswick itself, he said, was "at present inhabited by miners".

The local people so greatly resented the presence of these miners in the town that, at one point, the Germans had to be lodged on Derwent Isle for their safety. Gradually, however, they became accepted, many of them marrying local girls (though this again caused resentment). Thus a Bavarian strain was introduced into the Keswick bloodstream, for when their contracts expired many of these miners chose to remain in the district.

According to Robinson's *Natural History of Westmorland and Cumberland* (1704), the Germans opened up and worked eleven veins in Newlands, including several at Dale Head. This Dale Head mine was subsequently worked by the Duke of Somerset, who built bloomeries in the valley bottom. There was also a larger smelting-works in Stonycroft Gill (Smelt Mill Gill).

The Yukon-like element of these mining days in the western fells was heightened by the lone prospectors who came to the district, lured by tales of rich strikes. They paid tribute to the owner of the land which they proposed to mine, then got to work on their own account, usually trying their luck with some mine which had been abandoned. If they found a good deposit of ore they kept the find strictly to themselves. Sometimes one would build up a hidden hoard, then die with his secret intact, until some other man unwittingly followed in his footsteps and stumbled over the hoard. Between the years of 1848 and 1865 two such stores of ore were discovered in the Barrow mine.

The great mining boom lasted for just on a century. The Brigham smelting-works were destroyed by Cromwell's troops. Mining in this district saw a series of sporadic revivals thereafter, but nothing resembling the period of the Mines Royal. A writer of 1749 described Keswick as "much inferior to what it was formerly".

Keswick, by that date, had suffered not only from the Civil Wars but also from the Jacobite Risings. These traumatic episodes together had robbed the town of its major source of prosperity and its much esteemed lords of the manor, the Derwentwater-Radcliffes, who, over the centuries had, through their mining interests in the Alston area, become increasingly rich and powerful.

They had moved their seat from Castle Rigg, above Keswick, to the more splendid Dilston Castle in Northumberland at the time of the marriage of Margaret de Derwentwater to Sir Nicholas Radcliffe, but had built themselves a summer residence on Lord's Island, Derwentwater, using, it is said, the stones from the old mansion at Castle Rigg. Lord's Island was not a natural island, but was made so by cutting through a spit of connecting land at Strandshag. Henceforth the newly created island was connected with the mainland by a drawbridge.

In 1619 Sir Francis Radcliffe was made a baronet and in 1688 the third baronet, also a Sir Francis, was created Viscount Radcliffe and Earl of Derwentwater by James II. His eldest son, Edward, married Lady Mary Tudor, an illegitimate daughter of Charles II. Their eldest son, James, the third earl, was reared in France at the court of the exiled Stuarts, where he grew up in close companionship with Prince James Edward.

In 1710 James Radcliffe was permitted to return to England. He took up residence on his family estates and quickly became a most popular figure with the tenantry. In 1715 he was called upon by Prince James Edward to support his attempt to regain the Throne. James Radcliffe was taken prisoner following the battle of Preston, when the Jacobite armies capitulated. The young earl was carried to London, tried for treason and executed. He died before a large crowd on Tower Hill on 24 February 1716, still proclaiming, from the scaffold, his loyalty to King James III and his adherence to the Roman Catholic faith.

The Aurora Borealis, not infrequently visible in the Lake Country, shone with exceptional brilliancy on the night following the earl's execution and ever since has been known in the district as "Lord Darrantwater's Lights". The name of this tragic young man has lived on in the region to this day (the present author has heard him referred to, locally, as "our earl").

Following his execution his family removed to the Austrian Netherlands. Usually the attainder and execution of a man meant forfeiture to the Crown of his estates; but James Radcliffe had settled the entail on his infant son, John, whose rights of inheritance were upheld in 1719. John Radcliffe died in childhood. His uncle, Charles Radcliffe, claimed the estates and continued to use the title of Earl of Derwentwater, despite the fact that he himself was under attainder for his part in the '15 Uprising. He, like his brother, had fought at Preston and had been taken prisoner, but he had managed to escape from prison and had fled to Rome.

In 1745, together with James Bartholomew, his son and heir, Charles Radcliffe embarked for Scotland, intending, it seems, there to join Prince Charles Edward and to support him in his attempt to regain the Throne for his father. On the way to Scotland Radcliffe's ship was captured by an English vessel and the unlucky man was taken prisoner and beheaded for his former treason. James Bartholomew then claimed the family estates and title, but not unnaturally without success. The estates had passed to the Crown and had been entrusted thereby to Greenwich Hospital (in 1865 they passed to the Commissioners of the Admiralty). James Bartholomew's only son and successor, Anthony James (1757–1814) died without issue, whereat the Derwentwater title became extinct *de facto* as well as *de jure*. Lord Petre subsequently became the Radcliffe family representative and in 1874 the bodies of the first three earls of Derwentwater were reburied together in the family vault of the Petres at Thorndon, in Essex.

Shortly before this ceremony of Derwentwater re-entombment there had been a small spate of spurious claimants to the estates and title.

The first of these was a portly, greying female of decidedly eccentric behaviour who suddenly appeared in the neighbourhood of Dilston in 1868, calling herself Amelia Matilda Mary Tudor Radcliffe, "granddaughter of John Radcliffe", who had not died in 1731, so she declared, but had merely staged an "accident" in order to escape Hanoverian agents who had been plotting his assassination.

Claiming to be the rightful Countess of Derwentwater, this extraordinary person gave a press interview at which she produced her "family tree" and spoke of her collection of Radcliffe family heirlooms. She also referred to her so far fruitless attempts to win her "rights" through litigation.

Whether a genuine Radcliffe or not, one thing was certain; she was not the Countess of Derwentwater, for the title could not be inherited by a female, considerations of attainder apart. Neither did the lady's age tally with her "family tree", which gave her birth as 1830. This would have made Amelia 38 in 1868, yet the *Newcastle Courant* for October of that year described her as "a fine-looking, elderly lady".

Evidence has recently come to light which suggests that the "Countess" had made a preliminary appearance at Crosthwaite, Keswick, nine years earlier. At that time restoration of the church (commenced in 1845) had not long since been completed; work was still in progress on restoration of the Radcliffe tomb, by a craftsman named Martin. Certain members of the Crosthwaite congregation had resented, from the first, the "improvements" that had been carried out. These opponents of Mr Stanger, who had been responsible for the church restoration, of the vicar, the Reverend Henry Gibbs, and of the "fellow Martin", had their objections fanned to fever pitch by an unexpected ally in the shape of a lady, "in the female line of Radcliffe", who appeared in Crosthwaite church, placed seals on the Radcliffe tomb and sat herself down beside it, challenging poor Martin to continue his work upon it.

Although this redoubtable female has not so far been identified by name, she was almost certainly the self-styled Amelia Matilda Mary Tudor Radcliffe, Countess of Derwentwater.

A fascinating account of this episode has survived in the form of a letter jointly to Mr Dover of Millbeck and Mr Leck, churchwardens of Crosthwaite, from persons identifying themselves as "grave Observers" (not, one feels, intended as a pun, though it might be read as such).

The letter, written in exceptionally large handwriting (half-inch letters) on both sides of a sheet of coarse paper, measuring nineteen inches by twelve inches, was discovered recently in the church vestry. Although it touches upon various grievances connected with alterations in the church, its main theme is the Radcliffe tomb and the mysterious female who had suddenly turned up to defend this.

The envelope in which the letter was contained was addressed, in the same hand as that which wrote the letter, to "Mr Dover of Millbeck, Churchwarden, Crosthwaite 1859". The letter itself was headed, "Remarks from grave Observers to Mr Dover, Mr Leck Church-Wardens at Crosthwaite".

> Gentleme, [*sic*]
>
> . . . We have been solicited at a distance, from high Authorities to give our aid and Observation to what is going on at Crosthwaite Church: and we are prepared to act gravely: and trust you will hold yourselves to act like Men in your office.
>
> We give the Rev: Vicar no credit for the way he has meanly Sub let the Church and the Tomb of the Radcliffes to be made Traffick of by a low Fellow, working six Days of the Week on the Tomb.
>
> It is not a little difficult for us to contain ourselves when we hear this Fellow Martin boast how he had insulted the Lady at the Tomb when she went to put on the seals to guard it from his sacrilege:

which have been broaken off four times. We observe, there is a trite Adage, that spite and envy are generally self murderers.

Turn OVER!

We have been informed who this Lady, who sits by the broaken Tomb is a Radcliffe and a Lady born in her own Right, other Sovereigns in Europe have given a deffence to the Female line of Radcliffe which the English Government cannot ignoble, The tragedies of high life, are generally folded in obscurity from the Vulgar. We have no Lady here to compare with her Birth, Talent and Education. And because this Lady has no Relations with her in Keswick, the Vicar has let the Rabble loose on her. The Fellow Martin declares he heard the Vicar tell the Lady herself, he would have the seals taken off the Tomb: and put her and her Seat out: this gave Martin the liberty when the Lady went back to the Tomb: to pull her gloves out of her hand and cast them back in her face.

We blush for the Vicar's priestly Tyranny in this free Parish, and bid him put this Lady or any other quiet Worshiper out of the Church if he dare and

We'll sing the Vicar the Habeas Carpus
It's always sweet to us;
Because it was made on purpose
To keep us free from Brutes.

Oh, it makes us sick to think of such a Vicar, a Man that eats his Bread and his son too off Radcliff Lands; and to behave with such disrespect both to the lonely Lady and the Tomb.

We applaud the Lady for her Radcliffe Politie, when she went the fourth time to put the Seals on the Tomb and found the fellow at work on the Tomb again who was still as voilent as ever to her. She took the keys of the Church to the Police when she found the Vicar had made the Church into a "Den of thieves". The Police refused to take the keys: but the Vicar sent him for them, and when he arrived the Lady was dressed to go to Carlisle to give the keys of Crosthwaite Church to the Bishop.

We remain Gentlemen
your Friends.

P.S. The Lady was told to put the seals on the Tomb and take the Police to guard her Person.

This sounds so completely in the high-handed and astonishing style of Amelia that it would be coincidence of the most extraordinary kind were it any other claimant to the Radcliffe title. The letter itself may well have been written by Amelia; subsequently she was to reveal a talent for composing letters (and in one case a pamphlet) in which she wrote about herself on her own behalf most cogently, in the third person.

A period of nine years elapsed during which Amelia would seem to have been lying low. There is reason to suspect that during this period she attempted to approach persons of rank and influence in order to get "justice" done on her behalf; perhaps, too, she was painting the astounding collection of "Old Masters" that she presently produced, saying that they were Radcliffe family heirlooms. These canvases, allegedly by Titian, Raphel, Reubens and other great names, were undoubtedly her own work.

On 29 September 1868, Amelia surfaced again. Attired in Austrian military uniform, complete with sword, she advanced upon the ruins of Dilston Castle. With her went a small cart carrying articles of a frugal domestic nature; this cart was in the charge of two retainers, one of them the railway porter from Blaydon station.

Upon arrival at the castle Amelia performed the ancient ceremony of taking seisin of her estates; that is to say, she cut a sod and her attendants then reverently placed it in her hands. This done, the "Countess" camped in the castle ruins. The unpleasant and, as it proved, difficult task of removing her fell to Charles Grey, agent of the Admiralty Commissioners. Amelia refused point blank to leave the castle of her own accord and finally had to be carried out, still seated in her chair, brandishing her sword and complaining furiously about her treatment at the hands of this "dingy Grey man".

Evicted thus from what she called her family home, Amelia camped on the roadside near the castle; first under tarpaulin and later, as the winter advanced, in a small temporary hut. The local populace treated her with sympathy and respect and she received a good deal of publicity, mildly cynical, in the local press. Attempts were made to dislodge her from her hut-dwelling; finally Hexham Highway Board fined her ten shillings for obstruction and pulled down the hut.

Some twelve months later the intrepid "Countess" returned to the attack; this time disputing the right of the Admiralty Commissioners to take the rent from her "tenants". She served notice of distraint on several of these and in one case, aided by a local auctioneer named Henry Brown who seems to have been quite captivated by her, she removed some stock. She then presented herself with pomp and ceremony to the public; riding in a hired coach and wearing a velvet gown and huge plumed bonnet, with an escort of local supporters, mostly small tradesmen, who each sported a blue and orange rosette, sash and streamers.

The newspapers began to hint that she must have powerful and sinister supporters behind the scenes. *The Daily Telegraph* itself weighed in, "Something must be done, and that sharply and speedily, with the crazy woman who is going about the North of England . . . calling herself the 'Countess of Derwentwater' . . . We may ask, is there no constabulary in Durham, Westmorland, or Cumberland?"

A writ was served upon Amelia to restrain her from calling herself the "Countess of Derwentwater". Brown received nine months' imprisonment with hard labour and in due course the wretched Amelia herself went to gaol as a bankrupt. She had now become convinced that there was an official plot afoot to murder her. Yet, when she was released from gaol, Amelia proved her customary perverse self and had to be forcibly carried out to freedom. She subsequently faded from sight and died in poverty early in 1880.

Stimulated perhaps by the publicity given to Amelia, two other claimants appeared: a James Scott, who alleged himself to be John Radcliffe's "great-grandson", and a woman named Lovegreen, who said that she was descended from Francis the second earl. They seem to have lacked Amelia's *panache* and made little, if any, impression.

The former Radcliffe estates were placed on the market: Dilston Castle came into the possession of the Beaumont family, while the lands of Castlerigg Manor were purchased by John Marshall.

Of the old Castlerigg Manor no sign now remains. Excavation on Lord's Island has discovered traces of medieval building. Tradition has it that it was from her Lord's Island home that Lady Derwentwater stole, one dark night, to flee up the great cleft in Walla Crag (known to this day as the "Lady's Rake")[2] and from thence to travel at speed by coach to London, in a futile attempt to purchase, with tears and her family jewels, the freedom of her imprisoned and doomed earl.

13

KESWICK AND THE HUNDREDTH SUMMER

Romantic Borrowdale—Greta Hall—Coleridge—Charles Lamb—Caldbeck and John Peel—A Laureate's Household—A Rebel on Chestnut Hill—The Last Romantic—The Museum—The Moot Hall—Jonathan's Up-the-Steps—Tennyson—Dickens on Carrock—Victorian Explosion—The Convention—Keswick's Hundredth Summer

THE TOURIST TRADE, Keswick's major industry today, started inconspicuously, as we have already learned, with the quiet arrival of shy Mr Thomas Gray at the Queen's Head on 2 October 1769; lured there by the rapturous praise lavished upon Derwent Water by Dr Brown.

The Keswick which Gray saw was nothing more than one single, main street, with an old courthouse presiding over the market square at the top end, and a large tithe barn at the lower end. In between lay a huddle of cottages; dilapidated tenements built round cobbled yards off either side of the street; dingy little pot-houses, of which the Queen's Head was one and the George another; water-wheeled mills scattered along the banks of the Greta; and the church of St Kentigern standing in the meadows of Crosthwaite to the north.

Despite the fact that Gray was much fatigued, having paid a rapid visit to Ullswater before coming on to Keswick, he had no sooner dined (immediately upon arrival at the Queen's Head) than he "struggled out alone" to watch the October sun "set in all its glory". Nor did he lie abed long the following morning: "A heavenly day; rose at seven, and walked out under the conduct of my landlord to Borrowdale..." Gray's enthusiasm mounted to excitement as the lakeside track entered the so-called "jaws of Borrowdale" and he saw the "turbulent chaos of mountain behind mountain, rolled in confusion...".

With his guide, Gray continued his way up the dale to Lodore Falls. Here, like so many people, he was disappointed. "The quantity of water is not great." (Charles Lamb was to scramble among the boulders cracking unkind jokes about the reputed Niagara. Another visitor, less illustrious and therefore not known by name to posterity, is reputed to have asked to be directed to the Falls, only to be told that he was sitting on them!) The truth is that Lodore only lives up to its reputation when it is in spate following heavy rain; then, indeed, it is grand and exciting.

It was the road into Borrowdale that produced a thrill amounting to alarm in Gray; a true instance of "sensations of terror introduced into the sublime". Gray, in his journal, may have exaggerated the danger of rock falls on to the roadway, but most certainly these occurred from time to time, his guide no doubt commented upon them and poor Gray became all apprehension as he passed under:

> Gowdar-crag—the rocks at the top deep-cloven perpendicularly, by the rains, hanging loose and nodding forwards, seem just starting from their base in shivers . . . the road on both sides is strewed with piles of the fragments, strangely thrown across each other, and of dreadful bulk; the place reminds me of those passes in the Alps, where the guides tell you to move with speed, and say nothing, lest the agitation of the air should loosen the snows above, and bring down a mass that would overwhelm a caravan. I took their counsel here, and hastened on in silence.

The resultantly speechless poet did not, however, avert his eyes from the mountains crowding upon him. He noted that, "the hills here are clothed all up their steep sides with oak, ash, birch, holly, &c . . . in a place where no soil appears but the staring rock, and where a man could scarce stand upright" (a beautiful feature of Borrowdale to this present day). Alongside, but below, the road ran the Derwent, "clear as glass, and showing under its bridge every trout that passes". Near this bridge (the rare double-spanned bridge into Grange village), Gray and his guide encountered "a civil young farmer . . . who conducted us to a neat white house in the village. . . ." Here Gray and his guide were plied with simple, yet delicious, refreshment and topographical information. They were taken to the door and various landmarks were pointed out to Gray; he was told about Eagle Crag, where the golden eagles nested above Stonethwaite, and how they depleted the local flocks to feed their young; he gazed at Castle Crag, rearing its knotty head behind Grange and apparently barring all further access up Borrowdale and learned how—

By the side of this hill, which almost blocks up the way, the valley turns to the left, and contracts its dimensions till there is hardly any road but the rocky bed of the river . . . The dale opens about four miles higher, till you come to Seathwaite (where lies the way, mounting the hill to the right, that leads to the wad-mines); all further access is here barred to prying mortals, only there is a little path winding over the fells [the Sty] for some weeks in the year passable to the dalesmen; but the mountains know well that these innocent people will not reveal the mysteries of their ancient kingdom, 'the reign of *Chaos* and *Old Night*' only I learned that this dreadful road, divided again, leads one branch to Ravenglass, and the other to Hawkshead. For me, I went no farther than the farmer's. . . .

We returned leisurely home the way we came, but saw a new landscape; the features indeed were the same in part, but many new ones were disclosed by the mid-day sun, and the tints were entirely changed . . . This was the best, or perhaps the only day for going up Skiddaw, but I thought it better employed; it was . . . hot as midsummer.

Next day Gray walked on the shores of Derwent Water, in Crow Park (from which viewpoint Thomas Smith made the sketch for his celebrated print, mused Gray). The poet now had a taste of the vagaries of the Lake Country weather: "A little shower fell, red clouds came marching up the hills from the east, and part of a bright rainbow seemed to rise along the side of Castle Hill." Nothing deterred, Gray returned to the lake shore on the following morning, 5 October; he strolled about, delighting in the view, then visited the stone circle at Castle Rigg. On 6 October he made an excursion by chaise along the east side of Bassenthwaite Water to Ouse Bridge and, after dinner at the public-house there, and some sauntering, he returned to Keswick. "Several little showers today. A man came in who said there was snow on Cross-Fell this morning."

The next day proved damp and cold; in the morning Gray once again strolled in Crow Park; in the evening he walked up the Penrith road. "The clouds came rolling up the mountains all round, very dark, yet the moon shone at intervals." With him we can see the autumn mist and feel the nip in the air. "It was too damp to go towards the lake." He concluded, "Tomorrow I mean to bid farewell to Keswick."

It was "a gloomy morning" when he set off for Ambleside (8 October), but he had scarcely reached Castle Rigg when the sun broke out and discovered such an "enchanting view" of Keswick, its vale, two lakes, and the surrounding mountains, that he was almost of "a mind to have gone back again".[1]

When Coleridge came to live at Keswick in the summer of 1800 he found a town which had already established the pattern that it was to follow for generations to come; crowded for the few brief weeks of the summer-holiday season and sleepily quiet for the rest of the year.

Coleridge, together with his wife, Sara, *née* Fricker, and their little boy, four-year-old Hartley, moved into Greta Hall on 24 July, 1800. S.T.C.'s object was to be the not-too-distant neighbour of William and Dorothy Wordsworth, who were by that time most happily installed at Dove Cottage, Grasmere. Greta Hall was at that date a recently built house, standing on a knoll just outside Keswick and surrounded by market gardens and hop fields. Today it is part of Keswick School and accommodates boarders; understandably it is on view to the public only by request. Few visitors, therefore, penetrate the rooms of this house whose literary associations are so many and so utterly fascinating.

Greta Hall was built by William Jackson, who had become prosperous as a carrier between Whitehaven, Kendal and Lancaster and who, in his mid-40s, decided to retire and spend time among his books, for he was, as Coleridge put it, "a lover of learning". Greta Hall was a large house: Mr Jackson's plan was that he and his housekeeper, Mrs Wilson, should inhabit the northerly part of the house while letting the southerly, rather better half. When the approach was made to him to take Coleridge as tenant Jackson was so delighted at the thought of having the poet-philosopher under his roof that he charged Coleridge (who did not hide the fact that he was poor) a mere half of what had already been offered in rent by a rival prospective tenant and, for the first six months, Coleridge was charged nothing at all.

It was in August 1802 that Charles Lamb and his sister, Mary, came to stay at Greta Hall. Lamb, whose friendship with Coleridge dated back to their schooldays at Christ's Hospital, had already been invited to the Lake Country twice, but on each occasion had refused the invitation. In 1800 Charles Lloyd had attempted to lure him there; Lamb, a dedicated Cockney, had firmly declined. "Hills, woods, lakes and mountains, to the eternal devil . . ." he confided to his friend Manning. "I am not romance-bit about Nature."

In January 1801, a second invitation arrived; this time from Wordsworth. Lamb's reply was wicked; we must imagine with what mischievous, indeed devilish, delight he composed it,

> I ought before this to have replied to your very kind invitation to Cumberland. With you and your sister I could gang anywhere; but I am afraid whether I shall ever be able to afford so desperate a journey. Separate from your company, I don't much care if I never see a mountain in my life. I have passed all my days in London, until I have formed as many and intense local attachments, as any of you mountaineers can have done with dead nature . . . I often shed tears in the motley Strand from fulness of joy at so much life. All these emotions must be strange to you . . . as are your rural emotions to me . . . have I not enough, without your mountains? I do not envy you, I should pity you, did I not know that the mind will make friends with anything . . .

This to the very Bard of mountains, lakes and streams himself!

In August 1802 Coleridge had a try. Lamb succumbed; one suspects because he wished to see Coleridge, rather than Skiddaw. On 24 September Lamb was writing to tell Manning all about the trip,

> Coleridge . . . received us with all the hospitality in the world, and gave up his time to show us all the wonders of the country . . . So we have seen Keswick, Grasmere, Ambleside, Ulswater . . . and a place at the other end of Ulswater, I forget the name, to which we travelled on a very sultry day over the middle of Helvellyn. We have clambered up to the top of Skiddaw, and I have waded up the bed of Lodore. In fine, I have satisfied myself that there is such a thing as that which tourists call *romantic*, which I very much suspected before; they make such a spluttering about it . . .[2]

It was becoming clear to Coleridge, however, that the Lake Country climate disagreed profoundly with him. He concluded that he must go abroad, to see what sunshine would do. After some discussion between himself and his wife it was decided that Robert Southey and *his* wife, Edith (who was Mrs Coleridge's sister) should have it put to them that they might share Greta Hall with Sara, during Coleridge's absence.

The Southeys arrived at Greta Hall a trifle sooner and rather more abruptly and tragically than had been envisaged. The death of their infant daughter, the delightfully-named "Passionate Pearl", brought them hastening to Keswick for solace.

Coleridge endeavoured to raise Southey's spirits by taking him on walks. "I have been round the Lake, and up Skiddaw, and along the river Greta, and to Lodore", Southey was soon able to announce. A project, dear to Coleridge, for a walking tour in the central fells, resembling that which he had made the previous summer (Chapter 14), had to be abandoned; Southey had no heart for it. At least, however, Coleridge got him over Saddleback to Bowscale, Caldbeck and the Howk; places favoured by the Romantics (although it is difficult at this distance in time to determine to what extent Coleridge himself helped to make them popular by his own enthusiastic recommendation of them).

The charm of Bowscale lay in its tarn and the charm of the tarn derived not from its scenic qualities, but from a tradition which said that within these waters lived two immortal giant trout, known to former generations of men as Adam and Eve. What the longevity of a trout may be I do not know; certain it is that, by the time the "Picteresk Toorists" arrived, the fish had not been seen by anyone within living memory; but Mungrisedale and Caldbeck still spoke of them as there and parties of happy tourists went up to peer for them in the tarn's shadowy depths.

At Caldbeck the Romantics exclaimed (as Coleridge never tired of exclaiming) at the terror and splendours of the Howk,[3] a place of Devil's Cauldrons, caverns and waterfalls, literally howked out of the limestone by the River Caldew. It is still worth a visit. The Howk is shaded with trees through which filters a green gloom; there are wooden stiles and winding paths and a bridge. The ruin which visitors today see is that of an early nineteenth-century bobbin-mill, which virtually stood intact until quite recently, when it was set upon and burned by vandals.

Caldbeck is noteworthy not only for its church, its rectory, its Howk and its old mills, but also because the great John Peel lies buried in the churchyard, in a grave marked by an ornate sandstone headstone which cannot be missed; it has been painted an arresting white. Peel died at the age of 78, of pneumonia following a fall in the hunting-field

Coleridge left Keswick for Malta at the close of 1803; thereafter he returned but intermittently. His final visit was in 1812. His wife and children continued to live at Greta Hall with the Southeys. For Southey, almost unintentionally, Keswick became a lifelong home. He and his

Edith produced a brood of seven little Southeys. Mrs (Aunt) Lovell, the eldest Fricker sister, who had been widowed early in married life, came to live with them and two further Fricker sisters not infrequently stayed. Southey, for obvious reasons, nicknamed Greta Hall "the Aunt Hill".

Unlike Southey, Coleridge never witnessed the metamorphosis of Keswick from Hutchinson's "mean village, wholly indebted to the amenity of its situation to the notice of travellers"[4] into the select and fashionable tourist resort of some 30 years later. The story of how Keswick abandoned its somewhat uncouth past, spruced itself up, took tourism to its bosom and finally received the accolade of patronage by royalty, makes fascinating study.

By the close of the first decade of the nineteenth century everyone in the town who could manage it was offering summertime accommodation to ladies and gentlemen. Keswickians began to discover a surprising number of new ways in which to supplement their incomes. Boatmen proliferated upon Derwent Water. Guides and mountain ponies became a feature of a town hitherto associated with drovers and pack-horses. Little shops opened to sell fishing tackle, alpenstocks, sketching materials, toffee, and a multiplicity of souvenirs. Old ladies who, all their lives, had come to Keswick on Saturdays to sell eggs and butter in the market now found, to their astonishment, that in the holiday season they could sell as much moss as they had time to gather (the Pikteresk Toorists had a passion for moss); while here and there an octogenarian of suitably picturesque decrepitude would (his rheumatism permitting) be hired as a "hermit" to embellish the crumbling walls and arches of a newly-built "ruin".

Shepherds and poets were immensely popular with Romantics; Keswick was surrounded by dales abounding in the former, while Robert Southey, the Poet Laureate himself, might be relied upon to appear at Crosthwaite church regularly each Sunday.

Ruskin, on a boyhood visit to Keswick in 1831, made no secret of being one of those who attended divine service at Crosthwaite in order to see the Poet Laureate, rather than from motives of strict piety. Ruskin kept notes of this Keswick holiday, writing them in youthful doggerel in the form of an *Iteriad*. His account of the "Hero Worship" of Southey is both amusing and endearing,

> Now hurried we home, and while taking our tea
> We thought—Mr Southey at church we might see!

Next morning, the church how we wished to be reaching!
I'm afraid 'twas as much for the poet as preaching!

Ruskin and his party had the good fortune to sit "cheek-by-jowl" with Southey, and seem to have done their best to stare him out of countenance,

We looked, and we gazed, and we stared in his face;
Marched out at a slow-stopping, lingering pace;
And as towards Keswick delighted we walked
Of his face, and his form, and his features we talked.

It had not always seemed that Southey would become an honoured Establishment figure. In his youth he had been a loudly avowed atheist and fiery Jacobin, holding republican views of the most extreme nature. No one could have been more determinedly anti-Establishment than he.

In 1811 Southey, then two years distant from the Laureateship but already a distinguished and dignified pillar of the literary world, had the strange, almost eerie, experience of meeting a youth who might have been a reincarnation of his earlier self. This was Shelley, then aged nineteen, who, expelled from Oxford for his tract, "The Necessity of Atheism" had, in September of that year, run away with and married sixteen-year-old Harriet Westbrook. Shelley appeared in Keswick a month later with his wife and his sister-in-law, Eliza. The youth was remarkably like Southey in appearance, and a poet into the bargain, but there the resemblance stopped, so far as Keswickians were concerned, for young Mr Shelley never went to church on Sundays, which Southey never failed to do, and Shelley did chemistry experiments at night in the garden of the lodgings he had taken on Chestnut Hill, whereas "Mr Soothey" never let off fireworks of any description whatever.

Shelley, cut off by his father and penniless, had come to Keswick partly because he was a rabid Romantic, partly because he expected it to be secluded and cheap. In this latter expectation he erred; cheap Keswick no longer was, while seclusion was out of the question for a runaway revolutionary and poet whose temperament precipitated him from one drama to the next in frenetic succession.

At first, to do him justice, Shelley did in fact attempt a reclusive life at Chestnut Hill (the cottage he stayed in is still there). He and his companions kept themselves to themselves, living frugally and quietly. The poet took long, solitary walks, revelling in the scenery, which he found "awfully beautiful". "These gigantic mountains piled on each other," he wrote ecstatically, "these waterfalls, these million-shaped clouds . . . and a lake as smooth and dark as a plain of polished jet—oh, these are sights attunable to the contemplation!" But, in spite of this Romantic ardour for mountains, waterfalls and clouds, Shelley's real interest lay in meeting Robert Southey, for whom he entertained the most profound admiration (Shelley was thinking, of course, of the fiery young pantisocrat of twenty years earlier).

Shelley was introduced to Southey at Windy Brow, the home of William Calvert, just before Christmas. Calvert had met Shelley at the Duke of Norfolk's Greystoke seat a few weeks earlier; the duke being an old friend of Shelley's grandfather. Calvert, though shocked by Shelley's radical views, befriended him, got his rent at Chestnut Hill reduced, and introduced Shelley and his wife to people who might be inclined to help the young couple. Among these were the Southeys who, early in the New Year of 1812, followed up the introduction by calling on the Shelleys at Chestnut Hill and inviting them to Greta Hall.

At first Shelley was much impressed and delighted with Southey, finding him " a great man"; an "advocate of liberty and equality" (Mrs Southey's buttered cake was also highly successful, Shelley declaring that he could eat it "forever"). But Southey's support for the existing Establishment rapidly disillusioned Shelley, who found that the Robert Southey of 1812 was far removed from the Oxford undergraduate of twenty years earlier who had walked out of Balliol with the intention of founding (with Coleridge) a Utopian community across the Atlantic. Southey, of course, immediately recognized in Shelley the rebel that he himself once had been. "There is a man . . . who acts upon me as my own ghost would do. He is just what I was in 1794. His name is Shelley . . ." wrote Southey to his friend, Grosvenor Bedford. "I tell him that all the difference between us is that he is nineteen and I am thirty-seven."

Shelley, however, refused to see this. His enthusiastic admiration for Southey underwent a rapid reversal. Southey, for Shelley, had become a man whose character was "stained and false"; of "gross corruption".

The Calverts and Southeys were not alone in attempting to show Shelley kindness; all Keswick went out of its way to be sociable (and there is no greater place on earth for sociability than Keswick). Shelley, by now engaged in a furious writing stint, became increasingly rude and intolerant. He spurned Keswick's advances with all the impatient disdain of late adolescence.

The locality now revealed a rougher face. A gang of hooligans (whose disturbances were keeping half Keswick sitting up of nights, clutching pokers and rusty guns and listening for footsteps) called at Chestnut Hill on the evening of Sunday, 10 January, and knocked Shelley down when he answered the door.

Shelley, by now totally disenchanted with Keswick, contemplated leaving; his landlord clinched the matter by giving the Shelleys notice to quit, following a particularly alarming experience of experimental chemistry. Shelley, his wife and Eliza Westbrook spent their last week at Keswick as guests at Windy Brow, and in the first week of February 1812, set sail from Whitehaven for Ireland.

It was not until June, 1818, that John Keats came to the Lake Country with his friend Charles Brown. Keats, who at this time had not yet developed pulmonary tuberculosis, was an exceptionally vigorous young man of 23. Keats and Brown approached the Lake Country from Lancaster. Keats' first view of Windermere enchanted him. The travellers dined at Bowness on fresh-caught lake trout (in those days dinner was eaten at three in the afternoon, a much more reasonable and civilized hour than that preferred today) and afterwards they rambled along the lake shore to Ambleside, where they spent the night at the Salutation Inn.

Keats, a great admirer and disciple of Wordsworth, was quite carried away by the Wordsworthian scenes and experiences which now crowded upon him. "I live in the eye; and my imagination, surpassed, is at rest," he wrote. "I shall learn poetry here."

Unfortunately Keats was as rapidly disillusioned by his idol, Wordsworth, as Shelley had been by Southey. Keats called at Rydal Mount to pay his respects to Wordsworth. The size, style and prominence of Rydal Mount shook Keats, who had supposed Wordsworth to be living in the "rustic simplicity and seclusion" of a small cottage. Even more shattering was the discovery that Wordsworth, who was absent from home, had gone to Appleby to support the Tory candidate, Lord Lonsdale, in the imminent General Election!

At Grasmere the sight of Dove Cottage, Wordsworth's earlier home, slightly reassured Keats; here was a genuinely humble cot, even if it had long since been abandoned for more pretentious accommodation. The fact, too, that he was walking through the very heart of the country made famous by Wordsworth in his poems helped to raise Keats' spirits to something nearer the exalted state in which he had journeyed before peering through the Rydalian laurels at Wordsworth's gentlemanly drive and well-kept lawns.

Keats and Brown slogged over Dunmail Raise, glancing up to stare at, "That ancient woman seated on Helm Crag" (purported by some to be milking a cow, by others playing the organ. Viewed by those coming from Cumberland she is transformed into a lion with a lamb). Keats and his companion slept that night at the Nag's Head at Wythburn (left standing, but completely closed, when Manchester turned Wythburn Water and Leathes Water, those lovely, linked lakes, into the vast reservoir of Thirlmere). Next morning Keats and Brown trudged through thick drizzle to Keswick for breakfast, after which they walked the full distance round Derwent Water. To this expedition they added the animated *coda* of a scramble up the bed of Lodore. The Falls were in one of their drier moods. "I had an easy climb among the streams, about the fragments of rocks, and should have got I think to the summit, but unfortunately I was damped by slipping one leg into a squashy hole. There is no great body of water, but the accompaniement is delightful; for it oozes out from a cleft in perpendicular rocks all fledged with ash and other beautiful trees."

The explorers then went back to Keswick and, while dinner was being got ready, they raced up to Castle Rigg stone-circle and down again. All in all, a good 25-mile day at the very least. It was not surprising that they "went to bed rather fatigued".

None the less they rose at four the next morning to climb Skiddaw. "It grew colder and colder as we ascended, and we were glad, at about three parts of the way, to taste a little rum which the guide brought with him, mixed, mind ye, with Mountain water. I took two glasses going, and one returning. We went up with two others, very good sort of fellows. All felt, on arising into the cold air, that same elevation, which a cold bath gives one—I felt as if I were going to a Tournament." The ebullient Keats left Keswick that same day, still on foot and bound for Carlisle. At Ireby, where they slept, he and Brown witnessed a Cumbrian dancing class, at the Sun Inn. The pupils, according to Keats, "kickit and jumpit . . . and whiskit and friskit, and toed it and go'd it, and twirl'd it and whirl'd it, and stamped it, and sweated it, tattoing the floor like mad . . .": a Cumberland three-cornered and eightsome reel. Keats declared that he could only compare "the difference between our country dances and these Scottish figures" with the difference between "stirring a cup o'tea and beating up a batter-pudding".[5]

At Carlisle the enthusiastic tourists succumbed to aching thigh-muscles and blistered feet; they had yet to carry out a projected tour of Scotland and Ireland. They treated themselves to a coach ride across the Border to Dumfries, where Keats exchanged thoughts of Wordsworth for those of Burns. In a Lake Country context Keats might almost be seen as the last of the true Romantic tourists.

As early as 1785 Keswick was providing wet-day entertainment for tourists in the form of a museum, owned and managed by an enterprising local man named Peter Crosthwaite. This museum exhibited natural curiosities, fossils, "Saxon antiquities, Greek and Roman remains, coins, swords, celts, urns, bronze eagles and the like" (Lynn Linton). While some of these objects were without doubt genuine, others, it has been suggested, may have been custom-made for the museum by an enterprising blacksmith.

The museum's *pièce de résistance* was a weird and wonderful musical-instrument made by Crosthwaite himself: "a double octave of musical-stones"; prototype for a succession of bizarre but popular instruments which would seem to have been peculiar to Keswick.

Postlethwaite is highly informative on this odd subject, telling us that the stones selected by Peter Crosthwaite for their musical qualities were a "hard, massive, foliated and sonorous rock . . . called Spotted (or Andalusite) Schist". Crosthwaite's instrument consisted of sixteen stones that had been split and hammered into graduated size and key. It resembled a giant xylophone, the stones uttering chiming notes when struck by wooden mallets. Swiss airs, sentimental songs and popular refrains were performed upon it; the National Anthem was received with rapture.

Musical stones and their nostalgic chimes rang throughout the early years of Keswick tourism as if to provide a substitute for that tolling of cow and goat bells which fills Alpine valleys with day-long tintinnabulation. At Keswick musical stones lifted their voices in support of those guide-book writers who loved to refer to the Lake Country as a "British Switzerland" and Keswick itself as a "little Alpine town".

In 1813 the old court house in the market square was pulled down and a moot hall built instead in distinctly Tyrolean mood; it was to become the town's most famous and best-loved landmark (recent efforts to have it demolished in order to make greater space for parked cars would seem to have been quashed). It is always said that the stones used for the building were brought from the ruins of the Radcliffe house on Lord's Island; which, if true, means, in turn, that at least some of the Moot Hall's fabric must derive from the original fortified manor house of the Derwentwaters of Castle Rigg. Thus the ancient lords of the manor still preside, even today, in the very heart and centre of Keswick.

The clock bell has an almost illegible date on it, given by Mrs Lynn Linton as 1000, but recent authority suggests that it reads 1300, a more likely date. The initials HDRO are also engraved. This bell certainly came from Lord's Island; it is always supposed that the Derwentwater-Radcliffes themselves removed it to the island from Castle Rigg, where it had been the curfew bell.

Here, at the Moot Hall, the annual Court Leet, or Manorial Court, continued to be held every 22 May, as it had formerly been held in the ancient court house. At the Moot Hall, too, were held the weekly Petty Sessions, until a police station with adjoining court house was built in 1902. On market days the ground floor of the building was used for the sale of eggs, poultry, butter, cheese, fruit and flowers; a practice which continued until very recently, when the Tourist Information took over the ground-floor as a centre.

But perhaps, during the nineteenth century, the Moot Hall was best known as the show-place for a giant plaster bas-relief model of the Lake Country, made by Joseph (Josh) Flintoft, a Primitive painter and Keswickian. This model, together with Peter Crosthwaite's musical stones, may be seen by today's visitors at Keswick Museum. Here, too, are geological specimens long ago presented to Peter Crosthwaite's museum by Jonathan Otley, in his day a renowned geologist and naturalist.

Otley, a swill maker of ancient Grasmere stock, came to Keswick in 1791, as a young man of 25. Not only a swill maker but a clock and watch "reightler" too, he was exceptionally clever with his hands and soon earned himself the reputation as a chap who could "fettle up maist anything". In 1797 he moved to King's Head Yard, in the centre of Keswick, where he lived for the remainder of his long life, in a tiny cottage up a flight of steps; "Jonathan's up the steps", his abode was called. Visitors will find these quaint steps and the tiny cottage immediately to their left as they enter the yard from the market square; a commemorative plaque to Otley is on the wall nearby.

Otley was not only a geologist of note; his importance also lies in the role he played in introducing a science-oriented attitude of enquiry towards the Lake Country, as opposed to the Romantic-literary approach.

In Otley's time scientific knowledge was a matter of practical study and not the complex academic discipline that it has become today. Thus through his observations of the mountains around him the self-educated Otley became a geologist, botanist and scientific observer of distinction. Dr Dalton, Professor Sedgwick, Professor Phillips (curator of the York Museum) and Sir George Airy, the Astronomer Royal, were among his friends and colleagues. John Clifton Ward, author of the classic *Geology of the Northern Part of the English Lake District* (1876) never disguised his indebtedness to Otley's *Remarks on the Succession of the Rocks in the District of the Lakes* (1820) with which Otley established his reputation as a geologist. In 1823 Otley went on to consolidate his name with *A Concise Description of the English Lakes and Adjacent Mountains*; he had already, in 1818, produced the first accurate map of the district.

It is said that one of Otley's favourite hobbies was planting flowers and ferns beside the mountain springs. Another of his hobbies was measuring the summer levels of Derwent Water. He first cut a notch-mark in the rocks below Friars' Crag in the dry summer of 1824 and by this preliminary notch he continued to chronicle the levels of the lake. 1826 and 1844 were both seasons with lower levels than 1824; in 1844 by four inches. In 1852 Otley, then 86, cut yet another level. These Otley level-markings with their dates still survive; in 1973 they were all visible.

Otley died in 1856, in his 91st year. Until almost the last he was an active fell walker, making expeditions with his close friend and contemporary, Professor Sedgwick. Otley at last died of a stroke and we are left a touching account of the eminent Sedgwick, himself now a frail and aged man, clambering up the steps in King's Head Yard to weep and pray at the bedside. Otley lies buried in Crosthwaite churchyard.

Keswick Museum, of which Crosthwaite's museum formed the nucleus, will be found in a building (dated 1897) in Fitz Park, near the railway station. This station, itself now a museum piece, houses a fascinating model-railway display.

Southey died on 21 March, 1843, at the age of 69. He was succeeded by Wordsworth as Laureate; but the Master enjoyed this honour for no longer than seven years.

The demise of Wordsworth, in April 1850, was symbolic of the demise of an entire era. The mid-nineteenth century marked, for the Lake Country, not only the close of the first century of tourism; changes of an exceedingly traumatic nature were now taking place in the region. As is invariably the case, these changes first came to public notice in the guise of persons symbolizing the shape of things to come: though, again as is invariably the case, at the time of their actual appearance these symbolic individuals were regarded as impossibly and uniquely eccentric, resembling nobody who had gone before and nobody who would come thereafter (it would be safe to say that Keswick of 1769 had seen Mr Gray as a decidedly unique phenomenon; anyone suggesting that he was the shape of things to come would have been laughed off the street).

Tennyson came to Keswick on a honeymoon visit in the autumn of 1850, a mere few weeks before his nomination as Poet Laureate in succession to Wordsworth. The rumour was flying, it had even reached Keswick, that here was the Laureate-to-be. Keswick, accustomed to Southey and Wordsworth, was deeply shaken by Tennyson. He trailed no clouds of glory, but travelled instead obscured by clouds of dense tobacco smoke. Glimpses of him, obtained through rents in this ungentlemanly fog, revealed an Italianate person of gypsy-complexion; a dramatic swirl of cape, sombrero and flying mane.

It was too much for Keswick. Miss Mary Robson, a milliner with whom the Tennysons took lodgings (in a little cottage then standing beside the Queen's Hotel), undoubtedly voiced the feelings of the majority when she confessed that the poet frightened her. She was relieved when he and his wife (though the latter was sweet and gentle, "easy to get on with") departed to stay at Mirehouse, Bassenthwaite, with the Speddings.

In the late summer of 1857 Dickens burst upon the Lake Country, travelling with Wilkie Collins. "I have arranged with Collins that he and I will start next Monday on a ten or twelve days' expedition to out-of-the-way places," Dickens wrote to his friend, John Forster, in late August of that year. The tour was planned as the subject for an article, in five parts, to appear in *Household Words* during the ensuing October: thus *The Lazy Tour of Two Idle Apprentices* came into being. However, the liveliest accounts of this anything but lazy tour are to be found in the letters from Dickens to Forster: hilarious bulletins. "Our decision is for a foray upon the fells of Cumberland." Most intriguing of all, for Dickens, was Carrock Fell, "a gloomy old mountain" that he decided to climb at all costs.

The true Romantics were too intense to permit themselves much sense of humour among the mountains. Sublimity implied solemnity. Joanna, William Wordsworth's young future sister-in-law, received a famous rebuke (a highly poetical one, but a rebuke none the less) when she laughed at his "dear friendships with the hills and groves", his habit of looking "upon the hills with tenderness",

> I . . . stood
> Tracing the lofty barrier with my eye . . .
> —When I had gazed perhaps two minutes' space,
> Joanna, looking in my eyes, beheld
> That ravishment of mine, and laughed aloud.[6]

Poor Joanna! She was never allowed to forget her lapse. It was fortunate that Wordsworth was not on Carrock Fell when Dickens (CD), Collins (C) and the landlord of the Mill Inn, Mungrisedale, Mr Porter (Mr P) made their ascent on 9 September, 1857. To quote Dickens, recounting the adventure to Forster by letter, next day,

> We came straight to it (Carrock) yesterday. Nobody goes up. Guides have forgotten it. Master of a little inn, excellent north-countryman, volunteered. Went up, in a tremendous rain. . . . Rain terrific, black mists, darkness of night. Mr P. agitated. C.D. confident. C. (a long way down in perspective) submissive. All wet through. . . . Not so much as a walking-stick in the party. Reach the summit at about one in the day. Dead darkness as of night. Mr P. (excellent fellow to the last) uneasy. C.D. produces compass from his pocket. Mr P. reassured. Farm-house where dog-cart was left, N.N.W. Mr P. complimentary. Descent commenced. C.D. with compass triumphant, until compass, with the heat and wet of C.D.'s pocket, breaks. Mr P. . . . inconsolable, confesses he has not been on Carrick Fell for twenty years, and he don't know the way down. Darker and darker. Nobody discernible, two yards off, by the other two. . . . It becomes clear to C.D. and to C. that Mr P. is going round and round the mountain, and never coming down. Mr P. sits on angular granite, and says he is "just fairly doon". C.D. revives Mr P. with laughter, the only restorative in the company. Mr P. again complimentary. Descent tried once more. Mr P. worse and worse. Council of war. Proposals from C.D. to go "slap down". Seconded by C. Mr P. objects, on account of precipice called The

Black Arches. . . . More wandering. Mr P. terror-stricken, but game. Watercourse, thundering and roaring, reached. C.D. suggests that it must run to the river, and had best be followed, subject to all gymnastic hazards. Mr P. opposes, but gives in. Watercourse followed accordingly. Leaps, splashes, and tumbles, for two hours. C. lost. C.D. whoops. Cries for assistance from behind. C.D. returns. C with horribly sprained ankle, lying in rivulet! . . . We got down at last in the wildest place, preposterously out of the course; and, propping up C. against stones, sent Mr P. to the other side of Cumberland for the dog-cart, so got back to his inn, and changed. Shoe or stocking on the bad foot, out of the question. Foot bundled up in a flannel waistcoat. C.D. carrying C. melo-dramatically (Wardour to the life!) everywhere; into and out of carriages; up and down stairs; to bed; every step. And so to Wigton, got doctor, and here we are![7]

Thus did Dickens unabashedly shatter,

> The silence that is in the starry sky,
> The sleep that is among the lonely hills.[8]

(He also presaged the future tide of cheerful city-dwellers whose feckless forays into the hills keep Mountain Rescue so busy today.)

Slater's Royal National Commercial Directory of the Northern Counties (vol. 2), for 1855 tells us that Keswick now had two banks, two booksellers and stationers, eighteen boot and shoe makers, eight butchers, two chemists, four china and glassware dealers, two confectioners, nine insurance agents, two fishing-tackle makers, twenty-seven grocers, nine bakers, two hair cutters, five painters, plumbers and glaziers, two saddlers, seven blacksmiths, seven linen drapers, nine milliners, eleven tailors, two umbrella makers, three watch-and-clock makers (one of whom was also a jeweller), ten public houses, two wine and spirit merchants, five surgeons, two attorneys, two architects and two auctioneers.

There were two museums (Crosthwaite's, now owned by Elizabeth of that family, and a rival establishment belonging to Hannah Hutton), a fancy bazaar, a subscription library, a subscription News Room and, listed among these social amenities, a botanist. Maria Wright.

The town boasted five inns, now on the verge of calling themselves hotels, and 28 lodging-houses. The population was given as 2,618 (in

1851). Industries listed included pencil mills, bobbin mills, corn mills, saw mills, stone masons, slate, quarry and mining companies, nail manufacturers, seven wool manufacturers, millwrights, coopers, swill makers, breweries, and a gas works. Tourism was not yet recognized as an industry.

There were five places of worship (including Crosthwaite church). The nearest railway stations were at Penrith and Cockermouth. There were regular daily mail-coach services and frequent carrier services. The *Directory*, in its general portrait of the town, described it as consisting of "one long street . . . protected from the north winds by the stupendous Skiddaw".

During the following twenty years Keswick's one long street expanded into a highly attractive little town. Neat terraces of apartment-houses appeared like magic, to provide accommodation for the ever-growing annual invasion by visitors. Shops and inns donned fresh façades. The town already had a new church, St John Evangelist, built in 1838 by John Marshall, the Leeds industrialist who, in 1832, had become lord of the manor of Castlerigg. Learning that the original lords of the manor, the Derwentwaters, had enlarged and improved St Kentigern's, Crosthwaite, Mr Marshall had decided that he should emulate their seigniorial generosity: accordingly he gave Keswick its own parish church, designed by Anthony Salvin.

This pretty, modest sandstone building with its graceful spire adds much to the charm of Keswick when seen at a distance (which is not to say that the church is unattractive in itself). Further additions were made to it between 1862–89. If for no other reason it should be visited for its 1888–9 stained glass by Henry Holiday (born 1839), a disciple of Burne-Jones, with much work to his credit in the region; this Keswick glass is always reckoned to be some of his best.

The arrival of the railway in 1865 brought increasing numbers of visitors flocking to the town: in high summer the railway station, smart with flower-beds and green paint, puffed, blew, bustled and whistled in an absolute apogee of holiday spirit. The stretch of line between Penrith and Keswick was one of ever-increasing scenic delight and mounting visual excitement. Today's tourists, obliged to motor in, deserve condolence. Poor souls, they will never know that thrill of the final bend of track when Kewick suddenly opened beyond and below and Catbells and her kindred peaks shot into the sky. And then there were the roses and begonias of the station platform, and the cheerful faces of the station staff, and outside, in the station yard, in our day an array of waiting taxis; the motorized descendants of the assemblage of horse-drawn hotel-omnibuses and carriages which greeted Victorian visitors.

The railway made Keswick immensely more accessible than had hitherto been the case; thereby opening up all manner of developments. Chief of these, undoubtedly, was an annual ten-day Evangelical Convention, held each July from 1875 onwards,[9] its object being "to promote practical holiness". Each day of the ten days a vast marquee, the celebrated Convention Tent, throbbed with prayer and praise, while all Keswick resounded with the message, "Jesus saves!"

Thus, in 1875, the Convention Tent rose for the first time and, after ten days of glory, fell for the first time, collapsing like an exhausted old elephant spreading itself on the ground in baggy grey folds. Hot on the heels of holiness came secular invasion; Keswick's hundredth summer of tourism, or thereabouts. Advertisements (quoted at random from guide-books of the period) speak volumes about the kind of place that "the mean village" had now become (no attempt is here made to reproduce the wonderful diversity in type and ingenuity of lay-out of these excerpts):

Under the patronage of H.R.H. The Prince of Wales. Alfred Pettitt's Fine Art Gallery of the Lake District, and the Derwentwater Portrait & Landscape Photographic Establishment, St John Street . . . Keswick. Open 8–0 A.M. to 10–0 P.M., free. (Established 1854). The Paintings (in Oil and Water Colours) Exhibited for Sale, represent the Mountains, Lakes and Passes of the English Lake District; by Alfred Pettitt, Keswick.

Photographs. Mr Pettitt's series (4) of the English Lake District are the Largest and most complete published, and include views of and from the summit of Scawfell, Scawfell Pike, Great Gable, Helvellyn, Striding Edge, Red Tarn, Wastwater, &c. Catalogue on application . . .

The Derwentwater Portrait Studio (in connection with the Fine Art Gallery) is Open Daily, and Portraits Taken in all the Newest Styles, including the "Rembrandt", "Tourist", &c. &c.

Derwentwater Lake, Keswick.

Wilson's "Royal Oak" Hotel (Patronised by H.R.H. the Prince of Wales, the King of Saxony, and other Distinguished Visitors). The above old established Family Hotel (the oldest in the town) has just been purchased and entered upon by the present proprietor, who has made extensive alterations and improvements . . . no expense having been spared to make it worthy the patronage of Families and Tourists visiting the "English Lakes" . . . New Billiard Room and First-class Table, by Orme and Sons.

A good Dinner Provided on Fair and Market Days.

Established 1805.

Robert Bailey, Machine Printer, Bookbinder, Bookseller, Stationer, News Agent, Pianoforte & Music Dealer, &c., 12, Main Street, Cockermouth, and Market Place, Keswick. Desires gratefully and respectfully to acknowledge the kind patronage accorded him during the number of years he has been in business, and, in soliciting a continuance of those favours so liberally bestowed upon him, pledges himself that no exertion will be wanting on his part to merit the confidence reposed in him . . .

Plain and Fancy Stationery of every description, of the First Quality and Cheapest Rates.

Rimmel's Celebrated Perfumes.

The Weekly and Monthly Periodicals supplied. A Parcel from London every Week . . .

In the Printing Department: Sermons, Pamphlets, Bill-heads, Posters, Circulars, Cards, Catalogues &c . . .

E. Glover, Boot and Shoe Depot, Market Place, Keswick, has the most extensive stock in the Town of ready made Boots and Shoes of every description, for Men, Women and Children. Repairs executed with neatness and despatch. Fishing Tackle in Great Variety.

HORSES—Taylor's Condition Balls
The Field—"Try Taylor's Condition Balls"
Bell's Life—"They possess extraordinary merit"
York Herald—"An invaluable preparation"
Sunday Times—"They are peculiarly efficacious"
John Scott—"They are invaluable"
John Osborne—"They are unequalled"
Samuel Rodgers—"Send me Six dozen packets"
Thomas Dawson—"Send me a good supply"

The celebrated perfumes of Rimmel, however generously lavished upon the person, were quite overpowered by the all-pervading odour of horse wafting from the market square and Main Street. Here, daily throughout the season, all was a freneticism of horses, ostlers, drivers, coaches, carriages, brakes and chays and mountain ponies. Hooves clip-clopping over the cobbles, wheels scraping and grating; eager visitors teeming from every direction, avid to become excursionists; voices of every key and social nuance, speaking every variation of the Queen's English from Cambridge to Camberwell, Cumbrian to Caledonian, together with a fair sprinkling of foreign tongues; a chaos of tweed knickerbockers, serge skirts, panamas, parasols, umbrellas, mackintoshes, alpenstocks, guides, infants, picnic-hampers, ginger-beer and general genteel pandemonium.

The greatest commotion occurred outside Rigg's coach office in Main Street. Rigg's had first started with mail coaches, but rapidly expanded to cover every kind of tourist conveyance as well as carry the mail. Not only did Rigg's advertise "Coaches to Windermere and intermediate places, daily", this firm also ran what was probably the Lake Country's best known and most enthralling circular-tour, the Buttermere Round.

14

THE BUTTERMERE ROUND

Borrowdale—Walla Crag—Barrow—Lodore—The Floating Island—Troutdale—Grange—Bowder Stone—Stonethwaite—Seathwaite—Seatoller—Honister Pass—Slate Quarries—Gatesgarthdale—Buttermere—Crummock Water—Newlands Hause—Nichol End and Portinscale—Scale Hill—Lowes Water—Lake Country Storms—Lorton—Whinlatter—Evening on Derwent Water—Friars' Crag

"Coaches leave Keswick every day throughout the season at 10 a.m. via Borrowdale & Honister Pass, arriving at Buttermere at 1 p.m. & returning by 4 p.m. by the way of Newlands, in connection with the evening trains."

SO READ THE placard outside the coaching office. And each morning at ten o'clock throughout the season, fair weather or foul, the intending passengers appeared, suitably clad in sensible garb with which to greet the capricious moods of August and stoutly shod because, although the expedition was ostensibly a coach tour, none the less much of it would have to be accomplished on foot.

Let us transpose ourselves back a century in time and take places on the coach ourselves; not without some trepidation, let it be added. Mrs Lynn Linton, author of our favourite guide-book, has given us a fairly vivid idea of what to expect, "good broad carriage-roads, severe in their structure certainly, and demanding extra strength of horse-flesh and more stoutness of skid than usual to ordinary highways—but carriage-roads all the same; though not a little frightful to those unaccustomed to them, and absolutely perilous if south-country horses are used, or, indeed, any but those trained in the mountain ways—then they are safe enough, provided the driver is sober and the tackling sound."

We are not accustomed to mountain roads and therefore cannot help feeling just a little apprehensive as we leave our hotel and hurry into the market square. It has been raining hard all night and the morning so far has been a drizzly one, but now the cloud is lifting somewhat, in confirmation of the optimism of those gentlemen in our party who, having strolled down to the lake before breakfast, assure us that the weather will improve as the day goes on. However, the barometer in the hotel entrance hall remains in an unpromising condition, so that we decide to take mackintoshes, in spite of what the men say.

We are much encumbered; the gentlemen all tweed, we ladies in heavy serge walking costumes, our boots hidden by the folds of our long, ample skirts. Our hats and bonnets are tied down to our heads with yards of ribbon and scarves. We all carry, as aforesaid, heavy mackintoshes. The gentlemen have walking-sticks and field-glasses, we females are armed with umbrellas and bulky holiday reticules stuffed with guide-books, sketch-books, handkerchiefs and smelling-salts.

The coach is waiting in the square. It is a vehicle entirely open to the elements; a brake, or waggonette, rather than a coach. The horses stand patiently; we eye them anxiously. They look strong enough. Their tackling, too, which we inspect with even greater anxiety, seems in good condition. When the driver appears we search his cheerful red face for indications of insobriety, but can see no evidence of anything that suggests that he should not be entrusted with our lives. So we clamber aboard the coach and settle ourselves on the long bench seats, each of which has a heavy leather apron suspended from the back of the bench in front of it; these aprons are to protect us if, or more correctly when, rain decides to fall.

By shortly after ten o'clock our full load of passengers is perched aloft and our driver takes his seat, gathers up his reins, cracks his whip, gee-ups, and off we go; smartly up the market square and out by Lake Road, past shops and houses, and then into the Borrowdale Road, leaving the last of Keswick behind us as we bowl along between fields where farmers and their families are still trying to get in the last of the hay crop; always late in this part of the world.

The coach travels this first stretch of Borrowdale Road at a brisk pace. To our right shines Scarf Close Bay (so named after the Scarf Stones lurking under its waters), to our left are Great Wood and Walla Crag. Our driver, obviously a wit, keeps us informed on places of interest as we go along, enlivening his discourse with plenty of anecdotes and asides; unfortunately his dialect is so broad that, so far as most of his passengers are concerned, he might just as well be speaking Double Dutch.

He recounts the story of Lady Radcliffe's escape up Walla Crag by the rake named after her and also tells us how, until a few years back, you could see her white handerkerchief still lying where she dropped it; only nowadays "it's sae lang since it went to laundry, it's become inveesible to t'naked eye". We have read about this handkerchief in the pages of Mrs Lynn Linton,

> In old times . . . a large white stone in among the boulders used to be pointed out as the Lady's Pocket-handkerchief; and it was firmly believed in a certain nursery then filled with rosy-cheeked credulity, that the Lady had dropped her handkerchief in her flight, and that it still hung among the crags, where no one could get at it. It was a sad blow struck at faith when it became known that the handkerchief was a stone to which a certain Crosthwaite and one Atkinson were said to climb every year, and paint with a material paint-brush and white lead.

Walla Crag gives way to Cat Gill and then Falcon Crag is towering high over us. Now we begin to understand something of the fears of Thomas Gray when he strolled along this road with his landlord, for the crags spring up one beside the other like pinnacles and are decidedly awe-inspiring for anyone walking below them, or travelling in an open vehicle. A little beyond is Barrow House, in the grounds of which are the once-celebrated Barrow Cascades; largely the work of Lord Pocky who was not above using gunpowder to blast away rock in order to "make the leap grander than . . . nature had ordained", to quote Mrs Linton.

Lodore Falls, which we soon reach, are a far finer spectacle; at least, they are this morning, after last night's rain. We dismount from the coach and climb up to the Falls which we can hear roaring well before we see them. Here is Lodore (strictly speaking Watendlath Beck), hurling and dashing itself in a wild and magnificent confusion of rocks, trees and boulders; a great chasm of gloom chaotic with a frenzy of plunging white water. On either side of this chasm are famous cliff precipices, Shepherd's Crag and Gowder Crag, each festooned with clambering trees and foliage.

The waters of Lodore flow into the lake, which in this part is rushy and swampy. Here, in hot weather, appears the famed Floating Island which, though a subject for Romantic ardour is, disappointingly, no more than a mass of vegetation from the lake bottom which becomes forced to the surface by marsh gas.

So back to our coach and on to the Borrowdale Hotel and the sweet little valley of Troutdale, thus named because here was once a fish hatchery. A steep pedestrian track takes you up the aptly named Ladder Brow, to High Lodore and some spectacular crag-top viewpoints. All this part of Borrowdale (Bleaberry Fell, Ashness, High Lodore, King's How, Grange Fell and Brund Fell) is delightful territory to explore in a series of walks and strolls that, although in parts steep and strenuous enough, need never be very long. Indeed, thinking of these walks we almost regret our coach, but there will be plenty of other days for walking.

So far we have followed Gray's route. Now we come to the beautiful and unique double-spanned pack-horse bridge across the Derwent; on its other side lies the little village of Grange. Unlike Gray, we don't cross the bridge, but continue up Borrowdale.

Borrowdale, in medieval times, was held by the monks of Furness, while "Watendlath and the fells thereof" belonged to Fountains Abbey. After the Dissolution these possessions of Furness and Fountains were seized by Henry VIII, who granted the former Watendlath lands to Richard Graham of Netherby and his heirs. The Grahams held this grant until 1606, when the clan was deported to Ireland for causing Border disturbances; in 1613 James I granted the manor of Borrowdale (the former Furness possessions, which had remained in the hands of the Crown, as well as the forfeited Graham possessions which had now returned to the Crown) to William Whitmore and Jonas Verdon. They, by a deed dated 24 November 1614 (known thereafter as the Great Deed of Borrowdale), "sold and conveyed to Sir Wilfred Lawson of Isel and thirty others therein named, all the said manor of Borrowdale, with the appurtenances of what nature or kind soever, except all those wadd holes and wadd ... within the commons of Seatoller ... one half of these belonging to Henry Banks, Esq., MP and the other half subdivided in several shares. ..."

Grange, in the days when it belonged to the monks of Furness, was exactly what the name denotes, a grange; where the corn was stored that had been grown in Borrowdale, the valley then being highly productive of crops. Our glimpse of Grange, from the coach, is fleeting. On we go, past the roadside fountain, past Quay Foot slate quarry, through the gorge of the Jaws of Borrowdale, where the road, poised on the very brink of the river, bends and slants as if it wished to tumble us all off the coach into the water.

Now comes a brief halt for us to alight and inspect the Bowder Stone.

There is no longer any old woman underneath it, waiting to shake hands; for tourist amusement there is instead a railed ladder to the top of the Stone. Up this we climb, to perch on the Stone's head. Nobody knows when this vast block tore itself away from the heights above; our guide-books tell us only that it is 30 feet high, 60 feet long, and has a computed weight of 1,900 tons. We gape, wonder and chatter, turn dizzy with looking down and have a horrid time descending the ladder; without the help of the gentlemen we should surely be stranded on the Stone's top for the rest of our holiday. Down at last, we all sign our names in the visitors' book and troop back to the carriage.

And now the gorge of crowding rocks and hanging terraces of trees gives way to the green heart of Borrowdale, where once waved acres of monastic corn. Today the dale is patterned with small, stone-walled fields, many at this season studded with rows of haycocks. We bowl along the flat valley bottom while our driver indicates with his whip various landmarks. Here, now, is Rosthwaite village and beyond it rises Glaramara; the pinnacled head of a horseshoe formed by the ridges of Chapel Fell and Thornythwaite Fell respectively. In the hollow of the horseshoe lies Comb Gill. To the left of Chapel Fell winds the deep and narrow valley of Stonethwaite with the hamlet of that name. A mile beyond the hamlet Stonethwaite Beck divides at the foot of Eagle Crag; the left fork of the beck becomes Greenup Gill and leads to Greenup Edge; this pass leads over Greenup down into Far Easedale and thus to Grasmere. The right fork of Stonethwaite Beck becomes the Langstrath and a lang and desolate strath it is, though beautiful in its desolation. This is the way to the Stake Pass and the Langdales.

Our coach-driver tells us these things, and about the deep pots, or pools, in the Langstrath Beck in which, throughout the ages, the unwary have drowned; and of travellers over the Stake getting lost in mist and snow, and dying, benighted; and then he points out the chapel, yonder, and the tiny school, yonder, and then he points again and says, in the same voice and manner, "It's raining yonder, seesta," and we look where he points and there is a large grey cloud sweeping down Glaramara, straight towards us, with rain streaming from it in long slanting spouts; an astounding sight. We don't need the driver to tell us that it will be pouring over us in no time at all. There is a great upheaval as we struggle into macs, and unhook the leather aprons and pull them over ourselves, each apron buttoning at either corner on to the seat-back facing the seat-back from which the apron is suspended; an ingenious arrangement.

Umbrellas are raised, likewise; so that the general effect is one of battened-down hatches and the hoisting of domed black lids.

Our driver merely turns up his coat collar, pulls his hat well over his ears and hunches his shoulders. He continues to be as cheery and full of information as ever. He points to a deep, narrow valley opening up on our left, impenetrable with rain and cloud. "Sea'waite, wettest place in England," says he, with a kind of pride. "Average annual rainfall one hundred and twenty-five inches."

"Whatever happens to the people who live there!" exclaims a lady passenger.

"Drink themselves to death, ma'am," replies the driver, straight-faced.

We are now at Seatoller, a small huddle of cottages and farms at the foot of Honister Pass. Here we have to start to walk, for the pass is very steep. The long pull uphill seems to last for hours; the rain, however, gradually stops, the air for a while becoming full of glittering, flying silver needles, or so it appears, as the sun comes out and shines upon us through the shower. Then the rain ceases entirely, the sun grows strong. We close our umbrellas and take off our mackintoshes. On and up we toil, the road growing steeper and stonier at every bend; we are soon uncomfortably hot.

At last, after what seems an eternity of painful climbing, we reach the final struggle of Honister Hause: a *hause*, or *hawse*, being a neck (what the Swiss call a *col*) linking two mountain ridges. In the Lake Country a *hause* further means that there is a road, or track, crossing the *col*, thereby giving access from one valley to the next. Honister Hause is therefore a *col* linking Dale Head, to our right, and Gray Knotts, to our left; it is also the road over the pass between Borrowdale and Buttermere.

And now we are standing on the summit of the Hause, but we barely notice our triumph, for we are entirely taken up by the wholly unexpected and dramatic sight that greets us. The road falls away at our feet into a deep, narrow cleft between two vast fellsides of shattered slate, topped, far above, by cliffs of broken crag; so high that their tops are lost in the mist. In these crags gape the dark mouths of man-made caverns and there, too, we see tiny stone huts perched, like sea birds roosting on stacks. The whole scene is one of wilderness shattered and honeycombed by generations of quarrymen; all brooded over by Honister Crag itself, an immense black prow.

Our driver tells us that the men live up here during the week and return to their wives and families "for Satada' nights and Sundays". We are further told that from Yew Crag, the quarry high above us to our right, came the slate that took first prize at the Great Exhibition of 1851. However, it is in the quarry to the left of us, gnawed and carved into the very heart of Fleetwith itself, that the main activity now takes place and it is from here that crashing of stones and shouting comes. We stand staring up at this vast quarry face and there, toiling upward, are several men, carrying on their backs small, empty wooden sleds. Mrs Lynn Linton's description of them is right; they exactly resemble "some strange sort of beetle or fly". These men, having accomplished their descents down the face with laden sleds, are now climbing up again for fresh loads.

Mrs Linton cannot be bettered for an account of the famous Honister sled-gait runs,

> It is simply appalling to see that small moving speck on the high crag, passing noiselessly along a narrow grey line that looks like a mere thread, and to know that it is a man with the chances of his life dangling in his hand. As we look the speck moves; he first crosses the straight gallery leading out from the dark cavern where he emerged, and then he sets himself against the perpendicular descent, and comes down the face of the crag, carrying something behind him—at first slowly, and, as it were, cautiously; then with a swifter step, but still evidently holding back; but at the last with a wild haste that seems as if he must be overtaken, and crushed to pieces by the heavy sled grinding behind him. The long swift steps seem almost to fly; the noise of the crashing slate comes nearer; now we see the man's eager face; and now he draws up by the road-side . . . It is a terrible trade—and the men employed in it look wan and worn . . . The average daily task is seven or eight of these journeys, carrying about a quarter of a ton of slate each time; the downward run occupying only a few minutes, the return climb—by another path not quite so perpendicular . . . half an hour. Great things used to be done in former times, and the quarrymen still talk of Samuel Trimmer, who once made fifteen journeys in one day, for the reward of a small percentage on the hurdle and a bottle of rum; and of Joseph Clark, a Stonethwaite man, who brought down forty-two and a half loads, or ten thousand eight hundred and eighty pounds of slate, in seventeen journeys . . . These are almost legendary days, though, in the Honister world . . . Twelve journeys a day rank now as a feat scarcely to be compassed; for no man of modern slate-

quarrying powers can do anything near to these giants of the elder time.

Our driver now intimates that it is time to begin our own desperate descent—of the pass, which certainly looks alarming enough from where we stand; a narrow, rough road, tipping away beneath us in a series of treacherous bends. In fact, this part of the road is too dangerous for a loaded coach, so down we walk for a goodish part of the way, until the coach draws up on a small area of level ground and we are informed that it's "a'reet" for us to resume our seats. This we do, but not without qualms, for the road still appears frighteningly steep as it zig-zags down into the valley. The driver urges the horses forward, reigning their heads up hard as they go. They brace themselves fiercely against the weight of the coach, the muscles of their straining haunches standing out in ridges and they descend with jerks, rather than steps.

Over all this killing stretch of so-called road hangs Honister Crag, rising above us in a succession of sinister walls and buttresses. The mountain on the opposite side of the road is scarcely less oppressive. Honister Beck, pale and thick from the slate which is washed in it, runs beside the road, the verges of which are littered with huge boulders that, some time or the other, have fallen from above. It is a most grim place and it is impossible not to think of brigands and ambushes and massacres. To add to our depression the rain comes on again. The driver observes that it's "a droppy kind of day"; an understatement indeed for such an inky, gloomy, glowering experience, with the rain visible as heavy curtains that some giant hand draws, sweepingly, across the crag faces; while the clouds roll in cascades of mist down the gullies, to curl and wreathe and wander over and among the rocks.

The road at last bends less precipitously, the water of the beck becomes clearer, the valley itself broadens out a little. The scene is still desolate, but less desperate. New mountains rise into view ahead of us as we gather speed along the flattening road. This part of the valley is known as Gatesgarthdale and now we reach the very foot of the pass and see farm buildings and a house; Gatesgarth itself, one of the largest and most famous sheep farms in the entire region.

Buttermere, when we arrive beside it, is grey and wild, slapping ceaselessly on the shore with angry waves that are almost midget breakers. It is hard to believe that this blea mere, enclosed by dour fells each with its head hidden from view in heavy cloud, is famous for its tranquil reflections; we are not going to see these today, nor are we going to see the tops of High (or Black, or Raven) Crag, High Stile and Red Pike which, from left to right, form the tall ridge facing us across the mere.

Our driver introduces us to the various mountains and landmarks as if to an assembly of living friends. The mist-filled hanging valley between High Stile and High Crag is Birkness[1] Combe; the deep corrie scooped in the mountains behind Gatesgarth is Warnscale Bottom. The sharp peak with its razor-edge ridge dividing Warnscale Bottom from Gatesgarthdale is Fleetwith Pike; Honister Crag juts from its side. Facing Fleetwith Pike across Warnscale Bottom are Haystacks; most aptly named. Beyond Fleetwith we see a huge, dark, forbidding upland mass, so immersed in cloud that it is difficult to distinguish between earth and sky. "Yonder," says our driver, "is three-legged Brandreth" and he goes on to explain that a *brandreth* is Cumbrian for an iron tripod that you place over fire, seesta, for supporting kettle, or pot, and Brandreth yonder is so "verra like" that, it got its name for that reason; only, mind you, it's a brandreth lying on its back with its three legs in the air. He adds that it needs a fine day to appreciate it, and that on a clear day, moreover, we would see Great Gable himself looming beyond Brandreth.

Between Haystacks and High Crag is Scarth Gap; the track zig-zagging up it is the old pony road going over to Ennerdale and thence, from Ennerdale, by Black Sail and Mosedale to Wastdale Head. To our right, gaping immediately above us now, is the chasm of Gate Gill, "a smittle spot for foxes". Buttermere and Crummock, our informant adds, are both grand lakes for char. Then comes a vivid account of char fishing and by the close of this we are dropping down into the tiny village of Buttermere; a midget church, an even smaller school, three farms, a tiny cluster of cottages and two hotels; the Victoria[2] Hotel (converted from a cornmill) and the Fish Inn; to the latter we repair for lunch.

The Fish (in this year of Grace 1879) is owned and run by Mrs Clark, who has recently enlarged and modernized what was formerly, according to West, nothing more than a "humble little pot house". The Fish was renowned among Romantics as the home of Mary Robinson, the "Beauty of Buttermere"; the innkeeper's pretty daughter whose rustic charms first received acclaim in 1792, from the pen of Captain Budworth. Poor Mary, then a mere fourteen years of age, became a Picturesque tourist attraction. In the summer of 1802 she was ardently courted by a handsome tourist who said he was Colonel the Honourable Alexander Hope, MP for Linlithgowshire and brother of the third Earl of Hopetoun. The colonel, who was staying at Keswick, constantly rode over to Buttermere to fish for char and to court Mary, with whom he went through a marriage ceremony at Lowes Water on 2 October.

The honeymoon was interrupted by exposure of "Colonel Hope" as plain John Hadfield, already a married man and, what was worse, a convicted swindler and confidence trickster, now wanted on a charge of forgery (at that time a crime which carried the death penalty). Hadfield managed to evade the police and remained at large for the best part of two months. Caught at last, he was tried at Carlisle Assizes, found guilty and hanged. The case was written up by Coleridge in three articles for the *Morning Post*, as the account of *A Romantic Marriage*.

Mary gave birth to a still-born child in the July following her "wedding". She remained at Buttermere, an unhappy object of idle curiosity, until a second suitor, a Caldbeck farmer named Richard Harrison, made her his wife and carried her off to his own home "back o' Skidda". Mary presented him with seven children, five of whom survived to adulthood. She handed down her beauty to her daughters who, according to Mrs Lynn Linton, were "the loveliest young women in the district". A contemporary sketch of Mary still hangs at the Fish; at this we look as we enter to have our lunch. The proprietress of the Fish, Mrs Clark, is decidedly obliging; she advertises luncheon served "from 1 till 5 o'clock" and offers "Private dinners at any hour".

Our lunch includes fresh-caught trout and we are tempted to linger over it, but the desire to get a glimpse of Crummock Water forces us away from Mrs Clark's hospitable premises. We saunter across some fields, gazing about us as we go and exclaiming over Sour Milk Gill, a broad white ribbon of water plunging down from a corrie between High Stile and Red Pike. The source of Sour Milk Gill, as we earlier learned from our driver, is Bleaberry Tarn; impossible to glimpse from the valley, but tempting to think about as it lies far above us in Brigante-mysterious mist.

Crummock Water, its waves even wilder than those of Buttermere, adds to our illusion that Brigantes are near at hand. The very name, Crummock, is derived from the Gaelic, *cromach*, a crook; and crook-shaped this lake is.

We stare across it towards Melbreak; a great green whale of a fell (from this angle), and we peer into misty Mosedale, where Scale Beck flows through bog into the lake, after having had its giddy moment plunging 125 feet as Scale Force; the highest single drop of any waterfall in the Lake Country and worth seeing. However, it is a six-mile walk, all told, to make from Buttermere, as well as a very boggy one: we haven't the time for it, nor are our ladies all wearing suitable boots for ankle-deep peat mire. So we plan a picnic expedition for another day, to see this waterfall which West called "a most astonishing phenomenon" and which all the Picturesque Tourists went to see (often, however, being rowed across Crummock Water by boat, to spare them the long and sloppy walk).

We stroll back to Buttermere and peep in the tiny church, one of the smallest in England; indeed, before it was enlarged and restored in 1841 it was the smallest. West, writing of Buttermere at the close of the eighteenth century, not only made this claim for the church but added, of the valley in general, "The life of the inhabitants is purely pastoral. A few hands are employed in the slate quarries; the women spin woollen yarn, and drink tea. . . ."

Our driver now appears, if possible, even more cheerful than he was earlier in the day. He tells us that it is time to set off up Newlands Hause for Keswick. The coach goes ahead and we trudge behind, past the church on its rocky perch and up the narrow white road climbing across the flank of Buttermere Moss, topped by the great brow of Robinson. The road is so steep that our party stops frequently "to admire the view"; the best of all being that which we have left behind us; Buttermere village reposing in the green cup of the Dubs, with a glimpse of lake, and the white streak of Sour Milk Gill forever falling down the dark mountain.

Immediately below us to our left a dizzy slope swoops to Sail Beck, with Blake Rigg (*blake* is Cumbrian for yellow); Whiteless (properly, Whitelees) Pike and Wandhope (locally always pronounced Wandup) rising in a rampart beyond.

At the top of Newlands Hause (all too often mistakenly called Buttermere Hause, which in fact is in quite a different place) we stop to peer down Keskadale; treeless, mist-enshrouded. Our driver tells us that the rather straggly waterfall on our right is called Bear Force because of a great rock bear climbing up the middle of it; but stare as we may we can distinguish nothing resembling a bear. It is difficult not to wonder if the name "Bear Force" didn't really start with Coleridge; who came here when the water was in full, furious spate and, in his poet's fancy, spied polar bears frenziedly spinning in it. The more usual names for the waterfall are Robinson Force, Hause Force, and Moss Spout. You will hear it called, locally, by any of these. The last is the oldest name.

And now, as we mount the coach, the rain comes on again; not wildly, but with a kind of melancholy resignation. "Setting in for the night, I doubt," says our driver (when a Cumbrian tells you that he doubts something it means, by ancient turn of speech, that he is certain of it). So to the sharp, hair-raising bends of the Devil's Elbow at Ill Gill; this gill clad with scrubby, ancient oakwood, "Kesk'd'le yaks"; and on past small farmsteads and green fields all the way down gentle Newlands to Stair, with its mills, and then to Portinscale. Mrs Lynn Linton waxes eloquent here; writing of this "delicious bit of road, dark with wood, and fragrant as no other road in the world—turning aside to the old landing place of Nichol Ending by the lake", where, in her childhood, was always to be found a "deformed, half-idiot lad . . . hammering at his boat . . . who had but two loves in the world, of which his boat was one, and the Portinscale cockatoo the other". The poor idiot lad passed from the scene, but the white cockatoo, of greater longevity, "still flies among the trees, and speaks to the passers-by," Mrs Linton reported in 1863.

So back to Keswick, over ancient Derwent Bridge, under which the river nurses "those mysterious and fatal 'cradles' always causing the death of drunken men and unwary children" (and visitors, too, from time to time) and past Crosthwaite and High Hill. The Moot Hall appears; the coach slows, stops. The driver helps us climb down to the cobblestones and receives our thanks, and tips, graciously; and that is the Buttermere Round.

Another excursion popular with the Romantics and their Victorian successors was a coach trip to Scale Hill, near Lowes Water. The route taken was over Whinlatter, the old turnpike road from Keswick to Cockermouth (which all good Wordsworthians must visit, to see the Poet's birthplace).

The modern motorist may incorporate Lowes Water in his own, extended Buttermere Round. Instead of stopping in Buttermere (as we have just done in our imaginary coach-tour) he will continue along the road over the bridge by the Bridge Hotel (the old Victoria) and thus proceed to Crummock Water, where today's road follows the lake verge under Rannerdale Knotts, to round a rocky headland jutting into the water; *this* is Hause Point and the rock has been blasted away to make the present road. The old road traversed the side of Rannerdale Knotts at a much higher, steadily rising, level than the modern road, until at last it climbed up and over the rocky headland. *This* was Buttermere Hause, hence the name, Hause Point; the old road may still be traced from Buttermere to the top of the Hause, though the blasting of the new road virtually obliterated the descent of the old road down to the low ground beyond the Point.

Grasmoor now soars into the sky on the right; here the swine used to be put to graze on the vast, grassy table of common land that is this mountain's head. At Grasmoor's feet lies Cinderdale Common, so named after the smelting that once went on here; while further on lies Lanthwaite Green, where the Early British had a large settlement: but few traces of it now remain, for all this area of flat land lying at the feet of these fells and extending down to the lake and even away to the plain of the Cocker itself was laid waste by a disaster which occurred in 1760. On 9 September of that year a terrible storm burst over the Coledale Fells. An enormous deluge of water tore its way down Gasket Gill, between Grasmoor and Whiteside, to explode over Lanthwaite Green. "It laid devastate ten acres with stones." Brackenthwaite, the hamlet of Scale Hill, escaped only by what at the time seemed a miracle. The avalanche of water, mud and stone, wrenched from the sides of the mountains as the flood rushed down the funnel-like gill, accumulated material as it travelled; every wall and building was destroyed, boulders were uprooted, each swollen beck added to the tide, which at last poured into the River Cocker. This, in turn, burst its banks, to become a vast, stagnant inundation. West, describing the affected area 30 years later, spoke of the "great ruin" still visible.

Fearful storms and deluges occur from time to time in the Lake Country, usually in late summer. The last was in 1966, when devastation was caused in Borrowdale on such a scale that it was suggested that it should be designated a "disaster area". Today, evidence of the havoc may still be seen at Stonethwaite and Rosthwaite, while the appearance of Seathwaite, the lower slopes of the Sty, and the area above Burnthwaite, at Wastdale Head, is entirely altered. Visitors who were staying in Borrowdale at the time returned home with goggle-eyed tales of cars caught in the tops of trees and furniture afloat in hotel lounges and bar parlours. Fortunately the storm broke in the late afternoon, before campers were in their tents, therefore no human lives were lost, but Seathwaite poultry drowned in multitudes and sheep by the score.

Here is David Wright, one of the Lake Country poets of today, telling how it happened,

That Saturday evening I was at the pub
When it began—an exhilaration of lightning
As floury water like meal from a split sack
Stammered and slatted on slate roofs in our valley.
Other phenomena played up—thunder sledded
From rock to rock, hurrahing, grumbling with solid

Devotion to the increment of hubbub
While wind helped water to flog the trees again.
Every ditch and gutter aroar, each conduit choked,
The most alterable of elements at play
Footballing with boulders, boxing caryatid
Mountains until their entablature tottered.

Water fell like a wall or the blows of a club.
Whatever it was you could not call it rain.
I left my beer in a hurry and waded back
To see if the house where I lived were tight and dry
As overhead the elements shook and glittered
Underfoot my road already was a river.

Yet I didn't expect the animal under our bridge
Familiar with the conversation of our stream
Below the garden wall, or sometimes, when in spate,
Its rougher habit, burlier and free,
I did not recognise the livid rapid
That lipped the bank and, reared on hind legs, battered

The stone arch, hurtling missiles—e.g. a tree-stub,
A concrete slab, and, once, a huge black oil-drum
Aimed slap at the bridge, travelling like a rocket.
The beck had its dander up, and wonderfully.
Three hours it went on. The village shop got flooded,
But the bridge held till the rain at last abated.

The catchment saved us and there was no landslip.
Nonetheless we agreed it had been a near thing—
What fool called out the fire-brigade, in that wet?

Still, they had it worse than us up the next valley:
Breached walls and broken bridges, rivers gutted,
No lives lost though, just a farm or two bankrupted.

Today the light syllables at our doorstep
Recreate their bucolic, but I am not won,
Having seen the rocks gouged from a mountain slope
Witness that language, what it means to say,
And by what sufferance I have inhabited
These aspects, neither loved by them nor hated.[3]

Lowes Water is an enchanting little lake; drowsily idyllic for picnics, and so peaceful that it seems utterly to belie all talk and thoughts of storm. It is reached via Scale Hill, where there is now a hotel; in West's day a lowly little inn that must have been much astonished by the early Picturesque Tourist invasion.

The return to Keswick is by Lorton; a village in two parts, Low and High. The church is dedicated to St Cuthbert; though the building which we see today is early nineteenth century. The saint's body was brought to Lorton during the course of the long, long journey to Durham, and was given brief sanctuary at Lorton Hall: at that date (the year 850 or thereabouts) a two-towered pele. We are told that St Cuthbert's coffin lay "next to the little tower" (that is, the smaller of the two towers). Over the spot where the saint reposed a chapel was subsequently built, dedicated to St Cuthbert and Our Lady.

Of the two pele-towers of Lorton Hall only one survives today. It is tunnel-vaulted at ground level and traces have been discovered (though not yet exposed) of the ramp up which the cattle were driven, into the pele, during times of alarm. The interior of the tower has undergone extensive alteration. Attached to it is a fine range dating to 1663, with seven bays of mullioned windows with interesting early pediments above the upper windows and one above the large central window on the ground floor. A further range dates from 1880.

The house has a fascinating history. Malcolm III and Queen Margaret of Scotland are said to have visited here in 1089 (this region was then, of course, part of their kingdom). Over the ensuing centuries Lorton Hall remained a loyal stronghold and following the Reformation became a noted house of recusancy. It contains several concealed apertures and narrow tunnels that are thought to have been priest-holes, and escape routes for fugitives. The Hall is also said to be haunted.

The Whinlatter Pass leads from Lorton back to Keswick; a drive between magnificent heather slopes and shadow-filled pine forests. An even greater feast greets the eye, on the last lap of the descent; a view over Keswick Vale, Bassenthwaite Water and Skiddaw that will keep you on the car-park terrace of this famous viewpoint, gazing and gazing as you have rarely gazed before.

The roads of the Buttermere Round were adapted to the requirements of motorists (and thereby rendered wholly unsuited to horses) during the third decade of the twentieth century. Until then a horse coach continued to make the Buttermere Round and I myself recall, as a child, watching this nostalgic vehicle perilously (or so it looked) traversing the mountain-side, over Newlands Hause.

There it goes, that coach, to pass into the long, long gallery of Lake Country memories; ours, and those of the generations that have gone before us. My coach joins Mrs Lynn Linton's pathetic idiot boy and the talkative white cockatoo, and boy and bird in their day moved among people one or two of whom could remember, doubtless, a funny owd body called Mr Gray, from Cambridge, seesta, that the landlord of Queen's Head took walking up Borrowdale.

The memories which best stick in the mind are of small incidents and odd characters; history that is handed down by word-of-mouth has an idiosyncratic quality that never finds its way into official records. Old John Rigg, who joined Keswick's railway-station staff when the horse-drawn coaches vanished from the scene (and who himself has now vanished in his turn), would describe in graphic detail to my children how he, as a boy of nine, rode on the back of the coach on the Buttermere Round, with a senior Rigg driving. On one occasion that he had never forgotten he fell off the back of the coach and had to be carried, half-conscious, into Newlands Hotel at Rigg Beck[4] where he was given brandy by Miss Gibson, the proprietress, "It was first time in my life I had supped brandy."

For the Victorians, as with the Picturesque Tourists, no Keswick holiday was complete without an evening of boating on Derwent Water. After a day of perilous travel over Honister and Newlands, not to mention the long trudges up hill and all the excitements of spectacle and vista, it was wonderfully soothing to glide serenely in and out between the islands, Derwent Isle, Lord's Island, St Herbert's Island and little Rampsholme (so-named after the ramp, or wild garlic, that once abounded there); to gaze up a lake silver and pewter with reflected sky and mountains, to see Castle Crag and the Jaws of Borrowdale sinking into the obscurity of twilight, while owls began to call from Brandelhowe Woods where the "Will Watches", or moonshiners, used to live.

Keswick boating station, even today, has miraculously preserved much of its Victorian aspect and atmosphere, so that it is not difficult to visualize these family parties of a century ago. Their voices echo to us over the water; we hear their laughter and the splashing of their oars.

The little motor launches of a few decades later have somehow survived to carry us round the lake in the wake of our ancestors. It is all enchantingly old fashioned; almost a total escape into the past. We take the last of the evening's trips right round the lake and find ourselves sighing and exclaiming with all the Romantic ardour of good Dr Brown.

Afterwards we will walk to Friars' Crag for one last look at that famous view; one of the very finest in Europe, said Ruskin. By rising moonlight it is all subdued and, as it were, frosted, even on a warm summer's evening. The Victorians, who loved this place, did not associate it so exclusively with Ruskin as we ourselves perforce must do: the Ruskin Memorial now stands near the promontory's tip and tells us, in words which we may read aloud if there remains light enough to decipher them, "The first thing which I remember as an event in life was being taken by my nurse to the brow of Friar's Crag on Derwent water."[5]

The memorial is a pity in a way, for it prevents us from thinking of the Lindisfarne pilgrims, or of old Jonathan Otley, or the Radcliffes, or the Coleridge and Southey children, or Squirrel Nutkin, but instead fixes us with the image of that precocious infant Ruskin, staring down at the twisted tree roots and forming indelible impressions of aesthetic significance. But for me the infant Ruskin has been displaced on Friars' Crag by another child; a very tired and cross six year old, worn out by an afternoon's Christmas shopping in Keswick and now hauled by his silly mother to take a look at the lake from Friars' Crag in the winter twilight. "Come along darling; you'll find it so beautiful, you'll never forget it." And as I tug him along (my younger son of twenty years ago) I tell him all about the infant Ruskin and how he was taken to Friars' Crag by his nurse. . . . My son grumbles and kicks the tree roots and hangs back and says he doesn't like Friars' Crag and I tell him he has never looked at it *properly* and it is important to learn how to look at things *properly*, and so on and so forth, in an elevated and encouraging strain. We reach the Memorial; my son refuses to give it a glance. Worn out, I stagger to a seat overlooking the lake, flop into it and try to revive myself with the view; a tapestry of grey waters, misted mountains and russet winter woods. I steal a glance at my son to see how he is responding to this incredible beauty (for truly it is beautiful in spite of all the words that have been written, enough to endanger any place). My son is seated with his back ostentatiously turned on the lake; he is staring point-blank at a litter basket. "Oh darling, do look now you're here! It's worth looking at . . . You'll never forget it . . ." He continues to stare fixedly at the basket. "Darling, don't you want to be like the infant Ruskin and see something you'll remember the rest of your life?"

My son possesses by nature a determination, not to say obstinacy, that is not out of place in an adoptive Cumbrian, and he has already spent enough time in Cumberland to have picked up certain mannerisms of local speech. Without stirring or glancing round he says, "Bugger the infant Ruskin."

It is time for us to leave.

15

CENTRAL MASSIF

The Sty—Burnthwaite—Wasdale Head—Wastwater and the Screes—Coleridge in Wasdale—Scafell—Hollow Stones—Mickledore—Scafell Pike—Pillar Rock—Wilson and Ritson—The Great Climbing Epoch—Wastwater Hotel—Owd Joe—Scafell Chimney—Esk Hause—the Gables—Upper Eskdale

Skiddaw, Lanvellin, and Casticand
Are the highest hills in all England.

SO RAN THE ancient adage, believed to be hard fact and quoted as such even by Camden. Indeed the statement went unchallenged until Samuel Taylor Coleridge came to live in the Lake Country and commenced his brief, but brilliant, career of pioneer fell walking and mountaineering. His insatiably enquiring mind prompted him to buttress his exploration of the fells by gathering all the information that he could from the dalesmen whom he met on his various expeditions. "The summit of Sca' Fell," he wrote to a friend in 1802, "[is] believed by the Shepherds here to be higher than either Helvellyn or Skiddaw."[1]

Like all right-minded addicts of the Lake Country STC was always trying to persuade his friends to buy property therein, so that a variety of congenial base camps might be at his disposal. In July 1802, when he was brooding over a scheme to climb Scafell, he did his best to persuade his farmer friend, Tom Hutchinson, to rent a farm in Wasdale Head. STC wrote to Sara, Tom Hutchinson's sister, drawing her attention to a notice in the Whitehaven newspaper announcing that several Lowther-owned farms were to let, in lots. Lot Two particularly excited STC: "Wastdale Head[2] & Foot with Demings [Demesnes] and extensive Sheep Heaths". Exclaimed STC to Miss Hutchinson,

O would that Lot II were as good for FARMER Tom, as it would be for FRIEND TOM. I know it well—the situation is fine beyond description, eleven miles from Keswick, thro' Borrowdale! . . . I have no doubt the Farm would answer capitally, but for one Thing—the People of England, 'od rabbit 'em! are not Stone-eaters—if they were, I don't know a Place in which there is a greater Plenty & variety of that solid & substantial Food. What soft washy pap-like Stuff is a piece of Beef compared with a stout Flint! . . . But there is no persuading people to their own good.[3]

Wasdale, as STC so truly said, is a place of stones. It is reached from Keswick by Borrowdale and the Sty: this famous pass being, like all the best routes in this region, strictly for pedestrians only. The Sty is the way that Gray did *not* take; the "little path winding over the fells" through "that ancient kingdom, 'the reign of *Chaos* and *Old* Night' ": though, in fact, the Sty in Gray's time was no "little path", but a well constructed and metalled causeway, carefully kept in repair by the townships of Borrowdale at the one end and of Wasdale Head at the other. The Sty today is in a wretched state of disintegration, but traces of the old causeway may still be detected.

Wasdale Head lies deep in the heart of the hub of the Great Wheel of the Lake Country. "The mountains of Wastdale," to quote Coleridge once more, "are the Monsters of the Country, bare bleak Heads, evermore doing Deeds of Darkness, weather-plots, & storm-conspiracies in the clouds."[4]

Many a humble fell walker has felt exactly this as he has plodded up the dale head, from Seathwaite in Borrowdale to Stockley Bridge, at the foot of the Sty: further and further into the heartland of the black giants brooding in thick and secretive mist. What horrors of deluge and windblast do they hold in store? What desperate adventures await the pygmy pedestrian, marching with ever-growing apprehension towards this lowering brotherhood of monsters?

The ascent of the Sty is a steep and lengthy pull, whether you make it from Seathwaite on the Borrowdale side, or from Burnthwaite in Wasdale Head. Sty Head Tarn lies just below the col at the top of the pass; this dour little stretch of water has, in recent years, become popular with gulls, whose white flutterings and sharp, shrill cries seem strangely out of place here. On the col itself is a Mountain Rescue Kit box; there was once a shelter here for the pack-train drovers, but it fell into ruin many decades ago. From this col the Sty continues southward, dropping down to Wasdale Head, while eastward the Band leads up to Sprinkling

Tarn and Esk Hause. This is one of the oldest cross-roads in the kingdom.

The tiny hamlet of Wasdale Head is a chapelry within the parish of Eskdale. The population of Wasdale Head is said at no time to have exceeded 50 persons; in 1910, when the place was, strictly speaking, at the height of its fame and popularity as the centre of British rock-climbing, the resident population of Wasdale Head was 33. Yet the history of this dalehead as a place of habitation reaches back to the twelfth century; perhaps earlier than that.

Almost certainly the herd-wyck of Burnthwaite must have been one of the first places of settlement here. Burnthwaite is one of the largest and most ancient of all the sheep farms in the region; for most of its history having been two farms, High Burnthwaite, and Low. The very name, Burnthwaite (the clearing of, or among, borrans), is suggestive of the Norse origin of the settlement, and of the settlers who, in order to create safe home pastures for their sheep and small fields in which to grow crops, had first of all to clear the valley bottom of stones, piling these up in heaps; the borrans aforesaid.

These enormous quantities of stones explain the Wasdale Head characteristic of small, walled intakes, each intake leading into the next; an incredible sequence, or network, of little, green, walled enclosures which must at least in part be accounted for by the sheer necessity of keeping the ground clear of stones. The famous walls of Wasdale Head today are not what they were even 30 years ago; some have fallen and have not been rebuilt, while others have been removed to facilitate the passage of modern farm vehicles and motor-cars along the narrow roads; but in their heyday these walls were remarkably tall and stout, as if the men who built them had gone on adding stone upon stone because they had so many surplus stones at their disposal that they scarcely knew what to do with them and so found building them into a wall an excellent solution to the problem!

As well as being a sheep farm Burnthwaite must always have played an important social rôle, as a result of its situation at the foot of the Sty. By virtue of this very position Burnthwaite, like Seathwaite, would have been called upon to provide some kind of shelter and stabling accommodation for travellers, and the great kitchen would have been a spontaneous centre for the exchange and dissemination of news.

The hamlet of Wasdale Head lies about half a mile from Burnthwaite. Hamlet is perhaps too grandiose a word; it is a cluster, or more correctly a row, of small toftsteads, huddled together at the foot of Kirk Fell. This cluster of ancient habitations rejoices in a most precise topography: Row Head, Middle Row, and Row Foot. There are no shops; not even a post office. But there is the famous Wastwater Hotel, at Row Foot, and near the midget-sized village green stands the equally tiny (now disused) school; built in 1888, optimistically to accommodate twenty children, though the average attendance was six! The school-mistress was appropriately named Miss Light. Near the school stands the former vicarage; a biggish, square box of a house of much the same date as the school. It has not been in use as a vicarage for many years now, but as a private house.

Between Burnthwaite and Row Foot stands the little church, or chapel. The site is ancient, though the present building does not pre-date the early eighteenth century. There are no old graves in the minute churchyard because, until the nineteenth century, there were no burials here; the dead of the township of Wasdale Head were conveyed across Burn Moor to Eskdale for burial (p. 80). Today's churchyard is a place of pilgrimage for climbers; here is the last resting place of some of the pioneers who lost their lives attempting to conquer the neighbouring crags.

Wasdale Head was the centre of the climbing world during the last decades of the nineteenth century. Before this the dalehead had been exclusively a place of sheep and subsistence agriculture; with social diversions such as weddings, christenings, wakes, courtships, card parties, toffee pulls, sales, fairs, shepherds' meets, cock fights and fox hunts to keep life wagging along. People were not so cut off from other communities as we might suppose; folk walked great distances in those days without thinking anything of it, while longer journeys were made on horseback. It was merely a four-mile step over the Sty to Borrowdale; over Burn Moor to Eskdale was but little more; and six or seven miles by Esk Hause and Rossett Gill saw you down into Langdale. Moreover Wasdale lay open to Gosforth and the busy West Cumberland coast, with its flourishing towns like Millom and Whitehaven. Above all, the Sty brought pack-trains, and all those itinerant travelling folk whom we meet in the pages of Dorothy Wordsworth's *Journals*, including those old men who supplemented their begging by performing the function of a kind of peripatetic news service: "As I was going out in the morning I met a half crazy old man. He shewed me a pincushion and begged a pin, afterwards a halfpenny. He began in a kind of indistinct voice in this manner: 'Matthew Jobson's lost a cow. Tom Nichol has two good horses strayed. Jim Jones's cow's brokken her horn, etc. etc.'"[5]

Tailors, tutors, dancing masters, tinkers, salvers, coopers, wainwrights, fiddlers, herbal doctors and stone masons were among those tradesfolk, or semi-professionals, who travelled from farmhouse to farmhouse, or community to community, to stay in each awhile, making new clothes for the whole family, or teaching all the valley children to dance, or mending everybody's pots and pans, or whatever else the specialist function might be. STC has left us a portrait, for instance, of the "alehouse without a sign" at Nether Wasdale where he stopped for refreshment on his way up to Wasdale Head in August 1802, on his famous Scafell expedition. Gone to this inn for a "dish of tea" STC found that, "In the house there are only an old feeble Woman, and a 'Tallyeur' lad upon the Table—all the rest of the Wastdale World is a haymaking."[6]

We can conjure that scene: the hot, sunny day outside, the quiet, shady, flag-stoned house-place (front-kitchen-cum-living-room), the tailor lad seated cross-legged on the big kitchen-table by the window, sewing away, and the feeble drowsy old woman in her rocking-chair in the vast ingle-nook, with a small-glowing peat fire and a couple of cats and perhaps a pensioned-off sheep dog, as rheumaticky, deaf, feeble and failing as the old woman who snoozed in the rocking-chair, behind which the dog lay curled up and dozing on the floor.

Coleridge's Scafell expedition was a solo one. It was part of a week's pedestrian tour of the central hub of the Lake Country wheel. STC set out on 1 August; going from Keswick over Newlands Hause to Buttermere, from thence by Floutern to Ennerdale, from Ennerdale via Egremont to Wastdale Foot and from there up to Wasdale Head. Here he climbed Scafell; dropping down into Upper Eskdale, after which he crossed the Ulpha Fells to Duddon, went from Duddon to Coniston, from Coniston to Ambleside and so back to Keswick by Grasmere and Dunmail Raise. He prepared himself for this tour by making notes from Hutchinson's *History of the County of Cumberland*, published in 1794; he copied the map which Hutchinson included in his book—a virtually useless map by today's standards.

STC arrived at Nether Wasdale in the early afternoon of 4 August and after refreshing himself at the inn he trudged on up the valley; past Wastwater and the Screes, to Wasdale Head.

In a letter to Sara Hutchinson he described the Screes; that vast cascade of stones that pours down the north-western face of Illgill Head and Whin

Rigg; as if a sheet of falling water has become metamorphosed. STC found the lake still as a mirror:

> & conceive what the reflections must have been, of this huge facing of rock more than half a mile of direct (perpendicular) height, with deep perpendicular Ravines, from the Top two thirds down / other Ravines slanting athwart down them / the whole wrinkled & torrent-worn and barely patched with Moss—and all this reflected, turned in Pillars & a whole new-world of Images, in the water /. [He continued] At the top of the Lake two huge Fells face each other, Scafell on the right, Yeabarrow [Yewbarrow] on the left—and between these Great Gavel intervenes, the head & Centre-point of the Vale.[7]

STC spent the night of 4 August with Thomas Tyson of Row Head Farm (where he and Wordsworth had slept three years previously, on the Pikteresk Toor). Next morning STC set off after breakfast to climb Scafell; following the pony-track up on to Burn Moor and from there striking left-handed up Green How, "by the side of a torrent" (Hardrigg Gill), and so "climbed & rested, rested & climbed, 'till I gained the very summit of Sca' Fell".[8]

This Green How route up Scafell's backside, as it were, was the one which came to be popular with the Victorians. Today it is out of favour; the modern approach being by Brown Tongue to Hollow Stones and from there up the Lord's Rake to the summit: a strenuous route, involving some scrambling on the Rake, particularly so if Deep Gill West Wall Traverse is taken as an exit route from out of the Rake. Unfortunately over the past decade the Lord's Rake and the West Wall Traverse have become increasingly eroded by "pollution by feet", until they are now definitely dangerous, and becoming more so every year. Green How, therefore, is likely to come into its own again as the preferred route up Scafell in the not too distant future. It is certainly the best and quickest way *down* from Scafell and though, as a route up it is a long and tedious pull, at least it does have the enormous advantage of ensuring that you arrive at the top of Scafell undamaged; which is no longer the case with the Lord's Rake and the West Wall Traverse.

So we will follow STC up Green How to Black Crag and at last on to the summit of Scafell. Here STC stood glorying in a view which extended from the Irish Sea to the Pennines. At last he moved forward until he stood on top of Scafell Crag, with Deep Gill below him, and the giant rock masses of Pinnacle and Pisgah (names not yet invented in his day) looming immediately before him. He was on a "great mountain of stones"; stones everywhere, from gigantic turrets to mere boulders; and these but a lesser feature of a landscape of "enormous & more than perpendicular Precipices & Bull's Brows".[9]

At last he moved slowly right-handed, clambering over a multitude of further stones "from a pound to 20 Ton embedded in woolly Moss". He found a small sheltered depression high above the vast rock face which today we call Central Buttress. He sat down and re-commenced writing to Sara Hutchinson,

> here I am *lounded* [Cumbrian dialect for sheltered] so fully lounded—that tho' the wind is strong, & the Clouds are hast'ning hither from the Sea—and the whole air sea-ward has a lurid look—and we shall certainly have Thunder . . . yet here (but that I am hunger'd and provisionless) *here* I could lie warm, and wait methinks for tomorrow's Sun / and on a nice Stone Table am I now at this moment writing to you . . . surely the first Letter ever written from the Top of Sca' Fell! But O! what a look down just under my Feet! The frightfullest Cove that might ever be seen / huge perpendicular Precipices . . . Tyson told me of this place, and called it Hollow Stones . . . I have no shadow of hesitation in saying that the Coves & Precipices of Helvellyn are nothing to these! . . . I see directly thro' Borrowdale, the Castle Crag, the whole of Derwent Water, & but for the haziness of the Air I should see my own House.[10]

While STC is seated, lounded, and writing his letter, we will seize the opportunity ourselves to take a good look round this tremendous cove!

The Hollow Stones lie between Lingmell and the Red Screes that once rattled down from Mickledore, but by now have been scattered far and wide by enthusiastic hikers. (So worn have these screes become that they must be treated with great caution, especially when descending. There have been several accidents on them recently.)

Standing at the foot of these screes, in the little cove of Hollow Stones, that on most days smells of wet rock, you will find yourself staring upwards into great raggy canopies of whitish-grey mist; clouds, in actual fact, but too close to seem anything but dense vapour. Sometimes you will suppose that vast banners are blowing up there; on other days the dark oppression of mysterious movement overhead is such that you feel that Midgardsworm himself is coiling and uncoiling above the invisible crags. Eight visits out of ten you will see nothing but mist. You will hear nothing but a thin wind keening behind a rock; a stone rattle; an unseen sheep bleat. Perhaps a human voice somewhere utters a muffled call; whereat you are thrown into a fearful state of indecision: have you just heard the cry of a fellow-being trying to summon help, or is it some lusty climber bawling an uninhibited shout of satisfaction at having opened a bottle of beer with his teeth? Or perhaps, after all, it was just another sheep? How can you be certain of anything in this featureless world; of anything, save that you are a lunatic to have half killed yourself sweating up here to see *nothing*, nothing except the grass and stones within a yard or two of where you are standing.

But, if you go up to Hollow Stones often enough (or if you are exceptionally lucky first time) the day will come when you reach that famous cove and find yourself confronted by bastions and pillars and pinnacles of rock so magnificent that the Roman might of the Wall, the Norman splendours of Carlisle and the austere Cistercian beauties of Holme Cultram pale in comparison. This rock architecture of Scafell Crag is wholly superb; it defies description. Its sole demerit is that it cannot be seen except by those who clamber on foot up to Hollow Stones (but perhaps this is a virtue; the best things in life are never free, albeit they are paid for in sweat and aching muscles rather than with filthy lucre).

The gap, or col, of Mickledore connects Scafell with Scafell Pike, England's highest peak (though merely some 50 feet higher than Scafell). Of Scafell Pike little may be seen from Hollow Stones; chiefly you see the gully-scarred face of Pike's Crag. But in any case it is impossible to look for long in this direction, because all the time Scafell Crag itself is demanding wonder and admiration; a miraculous rock face that cannot be much more than 700 feet high and yet which, in certain lights, can look at least twice as high again.

The best detailed view of Scafell Crag is obtained from Pulpit Rock, on Pike's Crag. This is gained by Red Screes and Mickledore; a shocking pull up. None the less, to Pike's Crag and Pulpit Rock let us go, to scrutinize the vast triangular rock face of Scafell Crag. This is traversed, at its base, by two rakes. The first, the Rake's Progress, begins just where Mickledore's col abuts against the crags; the first few yards of this rake are in an upward direction, after which it inclines steeply, then runs a somewhat switch-back course to end at the foot of the Lord's Rake. The

Progress is never more than a narrow traversing ledge from which start most of the serious climbs. It is best left alone by walkers.

The Lord's Rake is a deep couloir, slanting up right-handed, on the western side of Scafell Crag.

The central face of the Crag is scored by three great fissures, or chimneys: from right to left as you face them, Deep, Steep and Moss Gills; though "gill" seems too gentle a word for these fierce rents. East of Moss Gill is the famous Central Buttress; familiarly known to the climbing fraternity as CB. Scafell Crag is crowned by the mightily serrated Pinnacle, jutting up to the east of Deep Gill, with Pisgah facing the Pinnacle across Jordan Gap. These are all names bestowed by the Victorian climbers of the knickerbocker and glory school.

But to return to Samuel Taylor Coleridge; the founding father of modern rock climbing. The threatening thunderstorm at last forced him to abandon his letter-writing and to look around for a way down to Upper Eskdale (his goal was Tawes House, near Brotherilkeld). So he "skirted the Precipices" and then came face to face with an obstacle which has confronted and confounded many a fell-walker since:

> I . . . found myself cut off from a most sublime Crag-summit [Scafell Pike] that seemed to rival Sca' Fell Man in height, & to outdo it in fierceness. A ridge of Hill [Mickledore] lay low down & divided this crag [Scafell Pike] & Broad-crag [early name for Scafell Crag] even as the Hyphen divides the words broad & crag. I determined to go thither.[11]

What STC did next was something that Wordsworth, rightly, would never have done. The essential difference between the two men was that Wordsworth was a native of Cumbria, who had been reared from boyhood to regard the mountains with a certain degree of circumspection; while STC was an "offcome" who bounced over the tops with a zesty bliss born of ignorance. To be honest he was much of the sort who, today, keeps Mountain Rescue busy. His reaction to the problem now facing him is given in this confession to Sara Hutchinson,

> There is one sort of Gambling, to which I am much addicted; and that is not the least criminal kind for a man who has children & a Concern.— It is this. When I find it convenient to descend from a mountain, I am

too confident & too indolent to look round about & wind about till I find a track or other symptom of safety; but I wander on, & where it is first *possible* to descend, there I go—relying upon fortune for how far down this possibility will continue. [He went on] So it was yesterday afternoon . . . the first place I came to, that was not direct Rock, I slipped down, & went on for a while with tolerable ease—but now I came (it was midway down) to a smooth perpendicular Rock about 7 feet high—this was nothing—I put my hands on the Ledge; & dropped down / in a few yards came just another / I *dropped* that too / and yet another, seemed not higher,—I would not stand for a trifle / so I dropped that too / but the stretching of the muscle of my hands & arms, & the jolt of the Fall on my Feet, put my whole Limbs in a *Tremble*, and I paused, & looking down, saw that I had little else to encounter but a succession of these little Precipices. . . . So I began to suspect, that I ought not to go on / but then unfortunately tho' I could with ease drop down a smooth Rock 7 feet high, I could not *climb* it / so go on I must / and on I went / the next 3 drops were not half a Foot, at least not a foot more than my own height / but every Drop increased the Palsy of my Limbs—I shook all over, Heaven knows without the least influence of Fear / and now I had only two more to drop down / to return was impossible—but of these two the first was tremendous / it was twice my own height, & the Ledge at the bottom was exceedingly narrow, that if I dropt down upon it I must have of necessity have fallen backwards & of course killed myself. My limbs were all in a tremble—I lay upon my Back to rest myself . . . I arose, & looking down saw at the bottom a heap of Stones—which . . . rendered the narrow ledge on which they had been piled, doubly dangerous / at the bottom of the third Rock that I dropt from, I met a dead Sheep quite rotten—This heap of Stones, I guessed, & have since found that I guessed aright, had been piled up by the Shepherd to enable him to climb up & free the poor creature whom he had observed to be crag-fast—but seeing nothing but rock over rock, he had desisted & gone for help—& in the mean time the poor creature had fallen down & killed itself.—As I was looking at these I glanced my eye to my left, & observed that the Rock was rent from top to bottom—I measured the Breadth of the Rent, and found there was no danger of my being *wedged* in / so I put my Knap-sack round to my side, & slipped down as between two walls, without any danger of difficulty—the next Drop brought me down on the Ridge . . .[12]

This descent by STC is usually regarded as the first recorded descent from Scafell by Broad Stand. Whether he did in fact come down the Broad Stand route, or by Scafell Chimney, is a nice question which we will discuss a little later. But of one thing we may be quite certain: STC had come down from Scafell by a precipitous route that involved some quite tricky rock climbing. It is a place upon which many an unwary walker has become crag-fast since STC's day; and has had to be rescued. STC was something more than a mere walker; he was a born climber and mountaineer. Faced with the problem of becoming crag-fast (and, it should be added, with no prospect whatever of being rescued in that eventuality) he coolly thought out and solved his problem and completed his climb. It was indeed a pioneer achievement.

High on the northern face of Pillar Fell, overhanging Ennerdale, is another mighty mass of natural Gothic architecture. The fell's face is grandly ridged, with sweet green coves reposing between the ridges and in one of these coves stands Pillar Rock; soaring up almost vertically for seven hundred feet on its north side. Wordsworth has described it in "The Brothers":

> You see yon precipice; it wears the shape
> Of a vast building made of many crags,
> And in the midst is one particular rock
> That rises like a column from the vale,
> Whence by our shepherds it is called the Pillar.

Pillar Rock is reached by the High Level Route from Looking Stead. The Rock consists of two towers, as it were, fused together; the one higher than the other. They are named High Man and Low Man. The rock which joins, or appears to join, High Man to Pillar Mountain is called Shamrock, or the Sham Rock, and an eastern gully, Walker's Gully, separates Sham Rock and High Man. Westwards, to the left of High Man, lies the Jordan Gap and to the left of Jordan Gap is Pisgah (names evocative of Scafell).

It was Pillar Rock, rather than Scafell Crag, which first seized the imagination of the embryonic British rock-climbing school. The first recorded climb of the Rock (then known as Pillar Stone), was by a native of Ennerdale named John Atkinson, who climbed it from the west side in

1826. In that same year a party of local shepherd lads followed his example. The next recorded ascent was not until 22 years later, when Lieut. Wilson of the Royal Navy enlivened a shore leave by climbing the Rock (his route is unrecorded). From then until 1860 no real climbing of the Rock is known to have taken place.

Thanks to Coleridge, Scafell Pike had now become widely recognized as the highest of English mountains and more and more people ascended it. Scafell remained neglected; during the opening decades of the nineteenth century nobody showed the slightest desire to emulate STC's exploits upon Scafell Crag. Even the celebrated Professor Wilson seems not to have tried rock climbing; though he sampled almost everything else that sport might offer.

John Wilson (1785–1854), better known to posterity as Christopher North of *Blackwood's Magazine*, was a rich young man who fell in love with Windermere, as a youth, and bought a cottage, Elleray, at Orrest Head. Later he built himself a small mansion there. Wilson enjoyed close friendship with Sir Walter Scott and, being an admirer of Wordsworth as a poet, he became acquainted with the Bard in person and so entered the Wordsworth circle.

Wilson rejoiced not only in belonging to the Lake Country intelligentsia of Wordsworth, Professor Sedgwick, Gough, De Quincey and the rest; he was also a redoubtable athlete. An exuberant giant of a man who never tired, he devoted himself fanatically to fell running, riding, wrestling, sailing, cock fighting and fox hunting. This introduced him into company rather different from that of the Wordsworth Circle.

There lived and farmed at Row Foot, Wasdale Head, one Will Ritson who, born in 1808, grew up to be an ardent wrestler and fox hunter. At an early age he became huntsman to Mr Rawson of Wasdale Hall; then to Mr Huddleston of Gosforth. Later Ritson was able to form and maintain a small pack of his own. His love of local sports brought him into contact with Wilson. In addition to being a sportsman and athlete Wilson possessed tearing high spirits coupled with a boisterous sense of fun. Ritson, for his part, was a great wit and raconteur in true Cumbrian style. Wilson introduced Ritson to his literary friends; they found Ritson delightful. Ritson, courteously, expressed himself equally charmed with the company of Wordsworth, Professor Sedgwick and their milieu. As a result, Wilson took a party of high intellectual calibre camping in Wasdale Head (admittedly it was a camp of considerable luxury and the party was attended by numerous servants). In this way the ensuing intellectual and university attachment to Wasdale Head first became established.

It may, or may not have been during this camping holiday that Wilson made his mark at a shepherds' "murry neet"; described vividly by Ritson,

> Aa remember, theer was a murry neet at Wasd'le Head that verra time, an' Wilson an' t'aad Parson was theer amang t' rest. When they'd gitten a bit on, Wilson mead a sang aboot t' parson. He mead it reet off t' stick end. He began wi't' parson fust, then he got to t' Pope, an' then he turn'd it to th' divil, an' sic like, till he hed 'em fallin' off theer cheers wi' fun. Parson was quite stunn'd an' rayder vex't like an a', but at last he burst oot laughin' wi' t' rest.

The literary and academic gentlemen flocked increasingly to Wasdale Head for a crack with Ritson; by 1856 he was receiving so many visitors at his little farmhouse that he decided to exploit the situation, so he obtained a licence and renamed his ancient home the Huntsman Inn. Hospitality was simple, but the host's personality ensured success. His gift of repartee alone was worth its weight in gold. The story is still told of the visitor from London who was unwise enough to remark, "Fancy living here all your life! Why don't you come to London, Mr Ritson, and see some of the sights?"

"Ah m'lad," replied Ritson, "theer's nea 'cashion for us t' cum up t' Lunnon t' see t' seets, 'cos sum o' t' seets cums doon here t' see us."

When Ritson was a young man rock climbing was still unknown as a sport; by the time he was old, people were coming to Wasdale Head to climb crags, rather than to walk upon the fells. In 1786 Mont Blanc was first ascended by Dr Paccard and a chamois hunter named Jacques Balmat; largely because the scientist, De Saussure, had offered a reward to anyone who succeeded in first scaling the mountain. He himself climbed the mountain the following year, and an Englishman followed suit a week later. It was the English, chiefly, who subsequently developed the Alps as a climbing ground.

1882 is the year usually seen as marking a watershed in British climbing; it saw a systematic attack on the crags and buttresses of the Lake Country by most of the expert climbers of the day. The conquest of almost all the major peaks in the Alps meant that the climbing fraternity turned increasingly to rock climbing, as opposed to pure and simple mountaineering: viz, the ascent of mountains. (It is perfectly possible, strictly speaking, for a mountaineer not to be a climber, and for a climber not to be a mountaineer; bewildering as this may seem to ordinary fell walkers! The definition of a walk, as opposed to a climb, is that in walking you do not use your hands.)

Rock climbing on the crags was already becoming popular in the Lake Country by mid-nineteenth century. This thoroughly puzzled Ritson, who sardonically asked the climbers if the fells weren't high enough for them?

Guides, of course, had been flourishing in the Lake Country ever since the Picturesque Tourist invasion of the final decades of the eighteenth century; they were guides for walking expeditions, rather than climbs. Ritson himself guided many visitors up Great Gable and the Scafells. Not all of his clients were to his liking and there is an account of one occasion when a particularly annoying bishop was taken to the summit of Scafell Pike and deposited by the final cairn with the Ritson observation, "Well, here y'are, Mister Bishop; as near Heaven as ye'll ever be."

Another guide with a reputation for pithy Cumbrian wit was Matthew Barnes of Keswick. He, however, was a pioneer of real climbs and in 1860 he opened up a north-eastern route on Pillar Rock; his companion on this climb being one Mr Graves (better known in the Lake Country as the Chairman of the Manchester Corporation Water Board).

In 1863 a party of Cambridge men, led by Messrs Conybeare and Butler, discovered an eastern route up Pillar Rock. This route, with typical climbing understatement, became known as the "Easy Way". The Cambridge party was quickly followed to the top of Pillar by C. A. O. Baumgartner and in 1865 Sir Leslie Stephen climbed it.

In 1857 the Alpine Club had been formed; in 1856, as we have seen, Ritson opened his inn and among his patrons were many of the earliest Alpine Club members. The "tigers" of those pioneer days included Alfred Wills, the Rev. Charles Hudson, Charles Carrington, E. S. Kennedy, Frederick Morshead, C. A. O. Baumgartner, Dr Richard Pendlebury and, as aforesaid, Leslie Stephen. Women were not yet appearing on the crags; the first female triumph over Pillar Rock was that of Miss A. Barker, who climbed it in 1870.

On to the scene now marches a most remarkable figure: the Rev. "Steeple" Jackson, so called because he once climbed his own church spire to repair the weathercock; the professional local steeplejacks having refused the job. Jackson was a great one for writing short commemorative verses about himself and on this occasion produced:

Who has not heard of Steeple Jack
That lion-hearted Saxon?
Though I'm not he, he was my sire
For I am Steeple Jackson.

The Rev. James Jackson (to give him his correct name), of Sandwith, did not start his career as a fell walker until between the age of 50 and 60 (hope for you, reader!) when, to quote his own words, he began "to knock about amang t' fells until I may say I knew ivery crag". When, in his 80th year, he heard that women were now climbing Pillar Rock he could not restrain himself and on 31 May 1875, together with a companion of somewhat more youthful years, he climbed the Rock. On the summit he deposited a bottle with this message in it:

If this in your mind you will fix
When I make the Pillar my toy,
I was born in 1, 7, 9, 6,
And you'll think me a nimble old boy.

Self-styling himself as Patriarch of the Pillarites, Jackson, in the following year, made a solo ascent of the Rock. He now regarded himself as the "Mountain Monarch"; although in fact he was a fell walker and scrambler rather than a climber. None the less this did not prevent him from adopting a condescending attitude towards the genuine "tigers": for instance, he called Dr Pendlebury, who was a Senior Wrangler, the "Senior Scrambler".

Jackson died alone on the fells in 1878, during the course of a winter day's walk over Pillar Mountain, in snow. He was found lying dead in Great Doup Cove; it is thought that he had slipped in the snow and fallen down the precipices above the Cove. A memorial was placed close to where he was found: at first this was a cairn surmounted by a simple iron cross, but several years later this was augmented by a cross, with the initials JJ on either side, carved on a rock face close to the earlier cairn.

Wasdale Head must have been a refreshingly simple place to stay in during those years of the Huntsman Inn. During the week the visitors climbed with dedication; on Sunday they went to church, if there happened to be a service at Wasdale Head. The clergyman, in those days, was the Rev. George Pigott who, when sober, used to preach in red stockings and clogs. It is recorded that he was seldom heard to preach; but old Dame Tyson, of Row Head, used to regale the visitors, mostly university men, not only with "wonderful puddings and pasties" but with "much useful advice, scriptural and otherwise".

The postman, who like the parson at times drank a little too much, would, in his tipsier moments, dance for the amusement of those present. Visitors' books preserved by the descendants of Ritson refer to "the mercurial postman, the picturesque priest, and the hospitable host".

The Ritsons retired from the Huntsman Inn in 1879 and the Tysons took over; the Huntsman becoming renamed the Wastwater Hotel. The present hotel building was erected a few years later; the original inn remaining as an annexe. The celebrated Whitings, relatives of the Ritsons, ran the hotel after the Tysons retired; upon the retirement of Mr Whiting the hotel was run by Mr and Mrs Wilson Pharaoh, descendants of the Ritsons. Following the death of Wilson Pharaoh the hotel remained in the family; it changed hands in 1974.

Ritson himself died at Strands in 1890, at the age of 83; talking almost to the very last, it is said, of the local hunt. To commemorate him Baddeley named a small waterfall not far from the hotel "Ritson Force" and as such it now appears on the map.

No organized records were kept of the Cumbrian climbs until 1880, when a Climbers' Book was presented to the Wastwater Hotel; in this first and second ascents and notes of special interest were recorded.

The great classical era of British climbing had begun. Increasingly exacting climbs were opened up on Scafell, Great Gable and Pillar Rock. The two outstanding cragsmen of the final decades of the nineteenth century were W. P. Haskett-Smith and Owen Glynne Jones (whose ice axe, until a few years back, hung in the vestibule of the Wastwater Hotel). O. G. Jones was reckoned, by all who knew him, as the most brilliant rock-climber of his day. He was stimulated to climb in the Lake Country by Haskett-Smith's first ascent of Napes Needle on Great Gable in 1886. Haskett-Smith also made the first ascent of the ferocious north face of Pillar Rock in 1891, with Slingsby and Hastings. In 1892 G. A. Solly led a party up the Eagle's Nest Ridge, on the Gable. Scafell Pinnacle was first climbed in 1888; Moss Gill was not climbed direct until 1896, when it was done by a party led by Joseph Collier. Gable's Kern Knotts Chimney was climbed in 1893 and the celebrated Kern Knotts Crack was first climbed by Jones in 1896. George Abraham made further history with his New

Direct Route up the west face of Pillar Rock in 1901. F. W. Botteril led a party up the north-west side of the Rock in 1906.

But it was Jones who was the star of British climbing and it was in partnership with the Abraham Brothers of Keswick, George and Ashley, that some of the most dazzling climbing of the great epoch was performed. This partnership was a brief one, none the less; from 1895 to 1899; in that year Jones was killed on the Dent Blanche, together with three Swiss guides, as the result of a fatal slip by the leading guide.

In the Lake Country remarkably few fatalities occurred among the climbers, though Scafell Pinnacle claimed several lives; in an attempt to climb it direct a party of four died in 1903. Bearing in mind that the technique of roping-up and belaying was but imperfectly practised in that period, it is surprising that not more climbers lost their lives. As techniques improved, so did fatal accidents diminish; when George Abraham wrote, "The numbers of accidents amongst real climbers, as distinguished from ordinary tourists, shows a tendency to decrease,"[13] he was reflecting the steady and marked advancement of climbing expertise.

Of course, when one bears in mind the vast increases in the numbers of people rock climbing today, Abraham's remark still holds true. The people who keep Mountain Rescue so busy are ordinary walkers and tourists; not the rock-climbing fraternity, though the newspapers insist upon calling anyone who meets with an accident upon the fells a "climber."

Abraham also said that, "The Cumbrian crags and cliffs have inspired the enthusiasm and in some degree perfected the craft of many of the greatest modern mountaineers."[14] This was true; but the popularity of the British climbing grounds, and especially of Wasdale Head, during the final years of the nineteenth century and the first decade of the twentieth was in no small measure due to Jones's book, *Rock-Climbing in the English Lake District*, published in 1897.

The Wastwater Hotel was at the height of its fame during this time, and Easter was the climax of the climbing season. Accommodation then was quite inadequate for the numbers of cragsmen wishing to stay. In the evenings, and the early mornings, the "historic entrance hall" of the hotel was crammed and jammed with ice axes, ropes, rucksacks, and a chaos of boots. The owners of this equipment included men famous in almost every profession: doctors, lawyers, clergymen, dons, journalists, military men. Everyone dressed most informally; in fact it was the done thing to resemble a tramp as much as possible, albeit a tramp who favoured old Norfolk jackets. A big chest was kept full of discarded or lost clothing; if one arrived without a second pullover, say, or a spare pair of socks one went to this chest and rummaged in it to find a replacement. At the end of the stay the borrowed article was returned to the treasure chest.

Another agreeable custom (common also to Burnthwaite Farm, where an overflow of climbers stayed) was that climbers at the end of the day tossed their wet clothes in a large heap on the landing outside the bedrooms. In the morning everyone rushed from their rooms to retrieve the dried clothes which had now materialized.

Here is George Abraham reminiscing upon this very subject,

> It is the custom to place all the clothes that have been drying overnight along the upper part of the stair-rail on the lower landing, and the search for one's under-garments amongst such a vast collection is a trying ordeal. Fortunately, lady-climbers are not usually in evidence during the "Easter rush" at Wastdale, but if they are the clothes-hunting operation is a nerve-shaking affair. A thin bed-sheet or table-cloth as an improvised dressing-gown scarcely meets the demands of respectability, and the opening of a door along the corridor usually results in a mad stampede to any available cover.[15]

Breakfast was generally a go-as-you-please meal, continuing for several hours indefinitely; but on fine mornings the hotel was usually empty by ten o'clock and the enthusiasts were tramping up the fellsides, each "rope" to the climb of its choice. Evenings found some of the luckier guests cramming in to "first dinner", while others were upstairs "waiting patiently for a share in the bath". Meantime a climbing chorus resounded from distant rooms, where "another thirty or more hungry cragsmen", awaiting their turn for dinner, allayed their mountain appetites with a little community singing.

The food was plentiful, satisfying and simple, according to George Abraham (but someone else once described it as an unvaried menu of "stewed frayed rope and rice pudding"). Everyone, or almost everyone, knew everyone else and the "loud and jovial conversation dealt almost solely with climbs and climbing". A strong smell of drying climbing clothes pervaded the entire establishment, together with "the strange open-air smell that comes from contact with damp volcanic rocks and rank vegetation, which might aptly be called the 'scent of the gulley'".[16]

After dinner came the famous Wastwater Hotel gymnastics: the billiard-table hand-traverse and the barn-door traverse. There was also the wild, rowdy and dangerous game of "billiard fives". High jinks in the billiard-room came to a close at midnight; the billiard table (an ancient and solid piece of furniture) was required as a bed for some of the guests. Others slept in the hay in the barn. Not infrequently someone slept in the bath. Late to bed and early to rise was the motto at the Wastwater Hotel: six o'clock of a grey cold dawn was considered a good hour for rising, though not all the guests got up so early as others; it rather depended upon where you slept. We are told that the man in the bath was invariably the last to get to sleep, and, understandably, was first to rise!

One of the personalities most affectionately handed down to us from these days was Owd Joe, a Wasdale Head shepherd. He was the delight of all who went to Wasdale and many were the stories told about him (indeed, he is still spoken of). One of the most famous anecdotes tells of the time when Joe, excited by strong drink, burst into a strange tongue, which was identified by some academic visitor as Icelandic. Joe had never spoken Icelandic in his life before, nor was he to do so again (I have always rather thought that Joe, when among the visitors, normally toned down his dialect speech in order to make himself understood by the "foreigners", but on this occasion forgot so to do and simply talked as he normally talked when with his fellow Cumbrians. Good, true, unadulterated Cumbrian sounds extraordinarily Icelandic!).

Another Joe story relates how he accidentally won a first prize for "gurning". Gurning, which means face pulling or, literally, grinning, is a popular item on the programme at shepherds' meets and fairs; the prize going to the man who can pull the worst faces. Joe, it is claimed, won first prize; only for it to be discovered that he had not in fact been taking part in the contest but had simply been following the proceedings with "sympathy and interest" as an onlooker.

There are scores of such Owd Joe stories. I would much like to hear some of Joe's stories about the visitors!

"Owd Joe!" became a traditional toast at the Alpine Club dinners. It is doubtful if Joe himself ever appreciated how famous he had become.

On non-climbing occasions, when, for reasons of bad weather or slight injury it was felt that an "off-day" might be expedient, a walk would be taken; the Mosedale Horseshoe being, we are told, a popular round. This embraces the Yewbarrow, Red Pike, Scoatfell, Steeple, Windy Gap and

Pillar ridges which enclose the head of Mosedale; it is a marvellous day's walking, though if it can be managed in clear weather it is preferable, inasmuch as it includes some utterly breathtaking views. I have done it several times; only once on a fine day! I well remember one occasion when I marched a flagging party round the circuit, attempting to keep their spirits up by gesturing frequently into the mist and announcing, "Now, if it were clear, you would have a magnificent view of . . ." such and such, and so and so. They were surprisingly kind, and refrained from pushing me over the edge of Pillar, to end up with "Steeple Jackson" in Great Doup Cove.

Before the publication of the Coleridge letters and notebooks, whereby his descent from Scafell became known to the world, it was accepted that Broad Stand was first officially climbed by Baumgartner in 1850. When STC's account of his descent from Scafell was published, the first climbing of Broad Stand was attributed to him.

However, the route which we know as Broad Stand, today, did not in fact exist in 1802. Dr Richard Pendlebury (a man whose word is scarcely to be dismissed lightly) has told us that the subsequently popular climbers' route of Broad Stand (known to climbers as a "quick" and relatively easy way up to the top of Scafell) came to be preferred to its neighbouring fissure of Scafell Chimney only in "recent years" (Pendlebury was writing at the close of the nineteenth century). The Broad Stand, explained Pendlebury, was "somewhat difficult" in the old days, in its lower part, until some overhanging rock was removed by artificial means. "It is feared that some minor blasting operations were resorted to."[17]

For those not yet acquainted with Scafell, it should be explained that Broad Stand is situated on the Eskdale side of the Mickledore col, some 22 yards down the screes from the top of the col. Here will be seen, in the dark and frowning rock face, a deep cleft, or split; so narrow that Pendlebury named it Fat Man's Gully (hyperbolized by later climbers into Fat Man's Agony). As Wainright observes, "This cleft is a tight squeeze, well named . . . and ladies, too, whose statistics are too vital, will have an uncomfortable time in it."[18]

A few yards further down the screes from the Agony is a second, less dramatic-looking cleft: Scafell Chimney. This, like Broad Stand, is a proper rock-climb, wholly unsuited to walkers, and like Broad Stand it has changed considerably since STC's day; being now much more

The Nab, Rydal Water, *circa* 1880 (Green)

Ann Tyson's Cottage, Hawkshead, *circa* 1890 (Abraham)

Row Foot,
Wasdale Head,
circa 1890
(Abraham)

Coniston Old Hall,
circa 1885 (Green)

above: St Bees Head,
circa 1880–90 (Green)

Spinning Gallery,
Low Hartsop
(Abraham)

Spinning Porch,
Hawkshead,
circa 1870–80

Great Langdale,
circa 1885 (Green)

below: Keswick, high
summer, *circa* 1885

Furness Abbey, *circa* 1860

difficult than was formerly the case, according to George Abraham, who goes on to explain that this is due to rock-fall.

George Abraham confessed that Broad Stand was "deceptively dangerous and treacherous" (this, after the resort to blasting in order to improve the route!). Broad Stand, deceptively easy as it seems at first glance from below, is even more deceptive when approached from above. Its ascent is made by squeezing through the Agony to reach a broad platform; the Broad Stand. Most walkers, as opposed to climbers, then take one look at the rock face above them and decide that they will do it "next time". Wainright tells us, engagingly, that he has been intending to climb Broad Stand "next time" ever since 1930, but that his "continuing disappointment is amply compensated by the pleasures of going on living".[19]

The hardened climber leaves the platform by a "tricky" corner on the left, over a pitch of "well-scratched indefinite rocks" (George Abraham's description). Above these "indefinite rocks" are two steep "rock steps"; each one, in fact, a nasty little precipice tilted at a most unpleasant angle over a by no means inconsiderable drop. Above these steps come easy rock terraces leading to a delightful grass and rock amphitheatre.

Coming on this, from above, as did STC, a descent appears to be not only possible, but simplicity itself. So down go the unwary, to find themselves crag-fast. Some end up stuck and shouting for help at the top of the pitch of "indefinite rocks"; others make the mistake (to quote George Abraham again) of "getting to the right-hand side at the top of Scafell Chimney . . . the wanderer quickly arrives above precipitous rocks where the danger is aggressively obvious".

STC's account of his descent fits this. At no point did he encounter any overhang; as he would have done in 1802. He continued to drop down ledges until he had only two more to go, but of these "the first was tremendous".[20] His danger, in short, became aggressively obvious! From this point of crag-fast desperation the immediate rent to his left, which caught his eye, would have been Scafell Chimney: the fact that he had no apparent difficulty in reaching it from where he stood goes to confirm this. His account of the last part of his descent states that, having noticed this cleft, he had merely to slip down it. Which altogether sounds much more like the Chimney, in pre-rock-fall days, than Broad Stand with overhang.

In sum, if we accept Pendlebury's word that Broad Stand, in 1802, would have had overhanging rock and, furthermore, if we accept the accuracy of STC's account of his route, we must conclude that STC descended from Scafell not by Broad Stand, but by Scafell Chimney.

Walkers who wish to descend to Mickledore from Scafell must either use the Lord's Rake and Red Screes or, preferably, should take the backside route; down a steep scree slope to Fox's Tarn and from there left-handed down a steep, boulder-filled gully into Cam Spout Gully. Up this they then toil, to reach Mickledore; obtaining as they go an impressive view of Scafell's massive East Buttress and, just below the col's edge, Scafell Chimney and Fat Man's Agony. And, if you are wearing a hat, you will surely take it off to Samuel Taylor Coleridge when you see the place that he came down!

The popular route up Scafell Pike is from Esk Hause; that awe-inspiring highway that runs under the gloomy bastions of Great End and past the sweet shoreline of Sprinkling Tarn (which the Picturesque Tourists preferred to call Sparkling Tarn). Great Gable rivals Scafell Pike as a summit to be conquered; his gable, more correctly *gavel*, is his western face merely; from every other view his is a huge domed bald head. Behind him, overlooking Ennerdale, lies little Green Gable. Kirk Fell, Great Gable's westerly neighbour, is an enormous Greenland whale of a mountain, with a plateau summit as featureless and discouraging as a lunar landscape.

In walking this magnificent and rugged country of the central massif Upper Eskdale should not be neglected. You will get your first view of this as you look down Cam Spout Gully: "The wild *savage*, *savage* Head of Eskdale", as STC called it. The infant Esk squirms and glitters along the bottom of this stone-littered, rock-girt, shadowed, roadless wilderness; desolate and inimitably beautiful.

It is strenuous walking in Upper Eskdale; long days of steady going over rough steep ground, with no possible place to park a car in an attempt to save your legs. Esk Pike, Ure (Ore) Gap, Bowfell, Crinkle Crags, Adam-a-Cove, Stonesty Pike: a twelve-mile day here is worth a 30-mile trek on the flat. Places of solitude and magic; Dow Crag, Little Narrowcove (venture here and you will learn all you ever wish to know about stones!), Cockly Pike, Coldkeld Knotts, Hanging Knotts, Pike de Bield, Yeastyrigg Crags and the so-called Churns of Bowfell; Hart How, Green Hole, Churn How, Long Top, Planet Knott, Swinsty Gill. Upper Eskdale is heaven for a strong and agile walker who would rather explore a small area and get to know it reasonably intimately, than tour a whole district superficially.

And when we have finished wandering over this great central massif we shall find that we have still not had enough and we shall tear ourselves away exclaiming with STC, "O how I wished . . . that I might wander about for a Month together, in the stormiest month of the year, among these Places, so lonely & savage & full of sounds!"[21] Long after he had left these great tops he continued to roam over them in his imagination. "Of all earthly things which I have beheld, the view of Scafell and from Scafell . . . is the most heart-exciting."[22]

16

"ALL WHICH WE THEN WERE"

Grasmere—The Wordsworths at Dove Cottage—Silver How—Greenhead Ghyll—Easedale—Stickle Tarn—Dungeon Gyhll—Great Langdale—Mickleden—Oxendale—Blea Tarn—Little Langdale—Elterwater—Loughrigg Tarn—Skelwyth—Clappersgate—White Moss Common—Old Roads—Loughrigg Terrace—Nab Scar—The Road to Rydal Mount

. . . what we have loved
Others will love, and we will teach them how . . .
William Wordsworth, *The Prelude*, xiv

The bosom of the mountains, spreading here into a broad bason, discover in the midst Grasmere-water; its margin is hollowed into small bays with iminences; some of rock, some of soft turf, that half conceal and vary the figure of the little lake they command: from the shore, a low promontory pushes itself far into the water, and on it stands a white village, with a parish church rising in the midst of it: hanging inclosures, corn fields, and meadows, green as an emerald, with their trees, and hedges, and cattle, fill up the whole space from the edge of the water: and just opposite to you is a large farm-house, at the bottom of a steep smooth lawn, embosomed in old woods, which climb half way up the mountains' sides, and discover above, a broken line of crags, that crown the scene . . . a little unsuspected *Paradise.*

Thus wrote Gray of the Grasmere that he saw when he descended Dunmail Raise to Town Head. It was a Grasmere that differed little, if at all, from the Grasmere to which the Wordsworths came to live some 30 years later. The village was to see many changes during their lifetime (in no small measure due to the publicity which Wordsworth himself attracted to the "little unsuspected Paradise"); it has seen many more changes since, yet, even so, considering its fame and popularity Grasmere has succeeded in remaining surprisingly unspoilt.

William Wordsworth first fell in love with Grasmere while he was a Hawkshead schoolboy and thereafter he nursed a conviction that one day this beautiful spot "Must be his home, this valley be his world . . ."[1]

In the autumn of 1799, while on his walking tour with Coleridge, Wordsworth found a cottage vacant at Town End, Grasmere. He at once had the idea that this might be the Picturesque cottage which he and his sister Dorothy had for so long dreamed of sharing. Such proved to be the case. By the end of December of that same year brother and sister were installed in Dove Cottage.

The cottage, during the first months of their residence, was damp and cold and draughty. It was decidedly more primitive then than the cottage which we see today; being very much one of the little native dwellings of which Wordsworth wrote that they "remind the contemplative spectator of a production of Nature, and may . . . rather be said to have grown than to have been erected;—to have risen, by an instinct of their own, out of the native rock—so little is there in them of formality, such is their wildness and beauty".[2]

William and Dorothy both caught bad colds. To add to her discomfort Dorothy developed raging toothache, from walking in the bitter wind. She was obliged to stay indoors, cosseting herself and busy with her needle: she sat sewing for hours on end, "absolutely buried" by a mound of stuff with which she was making curtains and bed-hangings (some of these may still be seen at the cottage). Old Molly Fisher, who had been engaged to help Dorothy with household chores, provided entertainment in the way of gossip about the neighbours and the daily life of Grasmere. From her Dorothy learned much about the unworldly vale which she and William were already thinking and speaking of as "home".

In the spring their merchant-sailor brother John came to stay. He did many practical odd jobs about the cottage and helped to plant the garden. Here, in due course, the Wordsworths were to build themselves "a little Indian shed" and, on the small rocky eminence at the back of the tiny orchard, Coleridge was to help them construct a seat of which Dorothy would never weary.

Wordsworth has left us a delightful glimpse of this

. . . little Nook of mountain-ground
Thou rocky corner in the lowest stair

Of that magnificent temple which doth bound
One side of our whole vale with grandeur rare;
Sweet garden-orchard, eminently fair,
The loveliest spot that man hath ever found.[3]

Dorothy's Grasmere *Journal* opens with an account of the days in early May 1800, which she spent alone while her brothers were absent from home. The woods were full of flowers and birds; the late northern spring burgeoned into beauty and strength all around her.

Dorothy and old Molly were endlessly busy; not only with common chores such as cleaning, laundering and weeding, but with "improvements" such as binding and fitting new carpets and putting up valances. In the evenings Dorothy refreshed herself with walking; frequently to Ambleside, to post, or collect, letters. When she did not walk to Ambleside Dorothy roamed round Grasmere and Rydal Water. The local people were not used to ladies who went for long evening walks by themselves. Indeed, on one occasion Mrs Nicolson, the Ambleside postmistress, insisted upon accompanying Dorothy on her return walk as far as Rydal. "This was very kind, but God be thanked, I want not society by a moonlight lake" wrote Dorothy afterwards, in her *Journal* for Monday, 2 June.

There was plenty of society, albeit of a simple sort, when Dorothy wished for it. Her neighbours, John and Aggie Fisher (Molly's brother and sister-in-law), who lived at Sykeside, a cottage just across the road from Dove Cottage, helped with some of the gardening in neighbourly fashion, and sometimes Dorothy would assist them with theirs. In the evening she would perhaps drink tea with the Simpsons (the Rev. Joseph Simpson, vicar of Wythburn, and his daughter Peggy, who lived at Broadrain, near the Grasmere foot of the Raise). Tea was also taken with other friendly neighbours. Evening was the usual time for a tea ceremony in those days (contrary to what we are sometimes told, the *Journals* reveal that the Wordsworths were virtually nightly tea drinkers).

William and John soon returned to Dove Cottage and there ensued a most joyful summer; long hot days spent fishing, sailing on the lake in William's boat, gardening, walking, or simply lazing, and nights when the silvery northern gloaming slipped into dawn almost without intervening darkness,

The sun has long been set,
  The stars are out by twos and threes,
The little birds are piping yet
  Among the bushes and the trees;
There's a cuckoo, and one or two thrushes,
And a far-off wind that rushes,
And a sound of water that gushes,
And the cuckoo's sovereign cry
Fills all the hollow of the sky.
  Who would go "parading"
In London, and "masquerading",
On such a night of June
With that beautiful soft half-moon,
And all these innocent blisses?
On such a night as this is![4]

In mid-June Coleridge, together with his wife and little son, Hartley, took up residence at Greta Hall. During the rest of that summer and the following autumn there was constant toing and froing between Grasmere and Keswick. Yet though Dorothy in her *Journals* gives an impression that it was a period mainly of pleasurable relaxation and revelling in the scenery, there was some very hard work done by the two poets, who were preparing a second edition of their joint work, *Lyrical Ballads*. Coleridge was also in the throes of composing the second part of *Christabel*.

Life at Dove Cottage was perhaps more truly Romantic and blissful during these months than it would ever be again. The *Journal* radiates the joy of those early days at "the dear, dear cottage" and the delight that Dorothy and her beloved companions felt in the Lake Country. Thanks to her *Journal* we accompany Dorothy, day by day, through this period of perfect happiness.

July 31st. Thursday. All the morning I was busy, copying poems . . . in the afternoon Coleridge came, very hot . . . The men went to bathe, and we afterwards sailed down to Loughrigg. Read poems on the water, and let the boat take its own course. . . . The moon just setting as we returned home.

August 1st, Friday . . . we all went together to Mary Point, where we sate in the breeze and the shade, and read Wm.'s poems . . . [Mary

Point was one of the twin heath-clad rocks in Bainriggs wood; the Wordsworths had named them after Sara and Mary Hutchinson; Mary being the future Mrs Wordsworth].

[*August*] *2nd, Saturday* . . . Wm. and Coleridge went to Keswick. John went with them to Wytheburn, and staid all day fishing, and brought home 2 small pikes at night . . . A grey evening. About 8 o'clock it gathered for a shower, but afterwards the lake became of a glassy calmness, and all was still . . .

[*August*] *3rd, Sunday*. I made pies and stuffed the pike—baked a loaf. Headache after dinner—I lay down. A letter from Wm. roused me, desiring us to go to Keswick. After writing to Wm. we walked as far as Mr Simpson's and ate black cherries. A Heavenly warm evening, with scattered clouds upon the hills . . .

[*August*] *4th, Monday*. Rain in the night. I tied up Scarlet beans, nailed the honeysuckles, etc. etc. John was prepared to walk to Keswick all the morning. He seized a returned chaise and went after dinner. A very cold evening . . .

William returned home the following night, Wednesday 5 August. He got back at eleven o'clock; "a very fine night". Next day Dorothy made gooseberry preserve. On the Friday she and William were prevented by "the excessive heat" from walking to Keswick before the evening. "Nailed up Scarlet beans in the morning. Drank tea at Mr Simpson's and walked over the mountains by Watendlath . . . A most enchanting walk. Watendlath a heavenly scene. Coleridge's at eleven o'clock."

The Wordsworths stayed at Greta Hall for eight days; the weather remained very hot. When they were not at work upon *Lyrical Ballads* the poets and Dorothy walked in Windy Brow woods and made a seat there; they sailed on Derwent Water, and feasted on gooseberries at Silver Hill. The visit ended on Sunday, 17 August.

Coleridge, during this August and early September, was doing much strenuous solo fell walking; over Skiddaw, Saddleback, the Dash Country and Skiddaw Forest, the Borrowdale Fells, the Newlands Fells. The weather held good. At Grasmere the Wordsworths revelled in their lakes. To quote Dorothy again, for Wednesday, 30 August, "The Evening excessively beautiful—a rich reflection of the moon, the moonlight clouds and the hills, and from the Rays [Raise] gap a huge rainbow pillar. We sailed upon the lake till it was 10 o'clock."

On Sunday, 31 August, Coleridge made his famous walk over Helvellyn (carrying a draft of *Christabel*, Part II, in his pocket). He started out via Threlkeld, across Threlkeld Common to White Pike and hence over Calfhow Pike, Great Dodd, Watson's Dodd and Stybarrow Dodd (he had no map and did not know the names of any of the tops that he was treading). He had not started until late, so that he reached the summit of Helvellyn in the moonlight and gazed about him in an excess of sublimity, "No words can convey any idea of this prodigious wildness!" He descended by Dollywaggon Pike and Nethermost Pike and then "climbed stone after stone down a half dry Torrent" to come out at Raise Gap, "and O / my God! how *did* that opposite percipice [*sic*] look—in the moonshine—its name Stile Crags".[5]

From Raise Gap he jogged down the road to Grasmere (the old road which Coleridge and the Wordsworths knew may be traced on the left-hand side of today's road for the greater part of the way). Dorothy tells us how Coleridge at length arrived at Dove Cottage,

> . . . At 11 o'clock Coleridge came, when I was walking in the still clear moonshine in the garden. He came over Helvellyn. Wm. was gone to bed, and John also. We sate and chatted till ½-past three. W. in his dressing gown. Coleridge read us a part of *Christabel*. Talked much about the mountains, etc. etc . . .
>
> [Her *Journal* continues:]
>
> *September 1st, Monday Morning*. We walked in the wood by the Lake. W. read *Joanna*, and the *Firgrove*, to Coleridge. They bathed. The morning was delightful, with something of an autumnal freshness. After dinner, Coleridge discovered a rock-seat in the orchard. Cleared away the brambles. Coleridge obliged to go to bed after tea. [While he was in bed the Wordsworths walked to Mr Simpson's to borrow some bottles for bottling rum.] The evening somewhat frosty and grey, but very pleasant. I broiled Coleridge a mutton chop, which he ate in bed. William was gone to bed. I chatted with John and Coleridge till near 12.
>
> [*September*] *2nd, Tuesday*. In the morning they all went to Stickel Tarn. A very fine, warm, sunny, beautiful morning. I baked a pie etc. for dinner—. . . The fair-day. . . . My Brothers came home to dinner at

6 o'clock. We drank tea immediately after by candlelight. It was a lovely moonlight night. We talked much about a house on Helvellyn. The moonlight shone only upon the village. It did not eclipse the village lights, and the sound of dancing and merriment came along the still air. I walked with Coleridge and Wm. up the Lane and by the Church, and then lingered with Coleridge in the garden. John and Wm. were both gone to bed, and all the lights out.

On 14 September Coleridge's son, Derwent, was born, at Greta Hall, at half past ten at night. That day, at Grasmere, had passed peacefully and uneventfully, "A lovely day. Read Boswell . . . under the bright yellow leaves of the orchard. The pear trees a bright yellow. The apple trees green still. A sweet lovely afternoon." Thus Dorothy.

From 19 September to 26 September William's former walking companion, the Rev. Robert Jones, came to stay at Grasmere. "We had much rainy weather," noted Dorothy. At Keswick, Coleridge was kept indoors; he had work to catch up with for the *Morning Post* and the new baby was dangerously ill with a chill. The weather suited the situation. Coleridge noted, "After the so unusual continuance of fine weather the rain seems to have come at last." He spent much time at his study window, staring at the ever-changing scene; jotting in his notebook a running-commentary on the fascinations of Lake Country weather,

> . . . ever and anon the Sun is on the Hills and Mounts, the universal mist not *dissipated* but *attenuated*—& sometimes the mist will dissolve wholly from some field or eminence, that stands out from the rest of the Landscape, bright & newbathed—Now the Hills are all in mist but the Vale all bathed and clean, one column of watry Sunshine falls upon the Grange—To the inverted arch in Newlands clear; at the Arch a wall of impenetrable Darkness.—A pelting shower.—Clear—& a road of silver brightness from the woods over the lake to the other side of the Island.—Vanishes—beautiful appearance of moving mist, over Newlands—in long dividuous flakes the interspaces filled up by a thinner mist—all in sunlight.[6]

After John Wordsworth had left at the end of September to join his ship, the *Abergavenny*, the Wordsworths saw a good deal of Charles Lloyd; an old friend who had come with his wife and family to live at Old Brathay, Clappersgate. The Wordsworths went walking much with the

Lloyds; often in Easedale, which the Wordsworths at that time invariably referred to as "the Black Quarter".

> *October 2nd, Thursday.* A very rainy morning. We walked after dinner to observe the torrents. I followed Wm. to Rydale, he afterwards went to Butterlip How. I came home to receive the Lloyds. They walked with us to see Churnmilk force [the main waterfall of Sour Milk Gill, Easedale] and the Black quarter. The Black quarter looked marshy, and the general prospect was cold, but the Force was very grand. . . . After the Lloyds were gone we walked—a showery evening. The moonlight lay upon the hills like snow.
>
> [On 10 October the snow was real:]
>
> In the morning when I arose the mists were hanging over the opposite hills, and the tops of the highest hills were covered with snow. There was a most lovely combination at the head of the vale of the yellow autumnal hills wrapped in sunshine, and over-hung with partial mists, the green and yellow trees, and the distant snow-topped mountains. It was a most heavenly morning . . .

Dove Cottage today, fascinating as it is to visit (together with the neighbouring museum) none the less has become rather too much of a shrine to be greatly redolent of the Wordsworths themselves. We shall more truly encounter Dorothy and William Wordsworth in spirit when we retrace their walks around and about Grasmere.

No guide-book as such is required, other then Dorothy's Grasmere *Journal*. A map is the second essential. Armed thus, we may wander at will with the Wordsworths.

Such expeditions are manifold. A particularly important walk for Wordsworthians is up Greenhead Gill, where once stood Michael's sheepfold. No trace now remains of this; nor is it possible to suggest where it might have been, save that it was somewhere in this gill. Even when Dorothy and William went there together on 11 October 1800, the sheepfold was already "falling-away". The ruin now discoverable in the gill-bottom is that of a small bloomery; post-*Michael* in date. Coleridge's description[5] of the view seen from the sheepfold suggests that it lay not in the gill bottom but up the fellside.

However, apart from the fact that there is no longer any trace of sheep-fold to be seen, the scenery here remains exactly as William described it in the opening lines of *Michael*,

> If from the public way you turn your steps
> Up the tumultuous brook of Green-head Ghyll,
> You will suppose that with an upright path
> Your feet must struggle; in such bold ascent
> The pastoral mountains front you, face to face.
> But, courage! for around that boisterous brook
> The mountains have all opened out themselves,
> And made a hidden valley of their own.
> No habitation can be seen; but they
> Who journey thither find themselves alone
> With a few sheep, with rocks and stones, and kites
> That overhead are sailing in the sky.
> It is in truth an utter solitude . . .

You should extend your walk either by climbing out right-handed on to Heron Pike, to descend by the splendid ridge of Lord Crag and Nab Scar; or left-handed, on to Stone Arthur.

Easedale, the "Black Quarter", is today rather over-popular in summer-time to be an "utter solitude", yet it is too lovely, and too much a part of the Wordsworths to be missed. The road leads out from Grasmere village to Goody Bridge; you must go on foot for there is nowhere to park near the bridge. At the bridge two routes divide; that on the right takes you, via Easedale Hause, into Far Easedale. This is the old pack-road, travelling up the long and desolate Far Easedale and over Greenup, along Greenup Edge and down Greenup Gill to Stonethwaite in Borrowdale; ten wet, wild, lonely miles; one of the most ancient stees in the Lake Country, but strictly for strong walkers who love a wilderness.

Far Easedale is separated from Easedale proper by a tongue of fell protruding above Stythwaite Steps (Stythwaite, the thwaite of the stee, being the old name for lower Far Easedale). To reach Easedale you take the left-hand pony-track at Goody Bridge, crossing the (now much battered) remains of an interesting and ancient stone causeway across low-lying and often flooded pastures. To your left you will notice some farm buildings tucked away at the foot of Blindtarn Gill; here lived the Greene family, whose tale, told by Dorothy Wordsworth and De Quincey respectively, still has a touching ring.

Mr and Mrs Greene, simple and frugal members of the time-honoured statesmen class, died in a snow storm while crossing the ridge between Langdale and Easedale one winter's afternoon, when they were returning from a sale. For 72 hours the storm raged; during that time little Sally Greene, herself only a child, took care of her young brothers and sisters, all tiny, and tended the kitchen fire, milked the cow, and in short kept the farmstead going until at length, the storm having abated, she made her way through the snowdrifts to a neighbour's house where she asked if she could borrow a good shawl, that she might "lait her parents". At once the alarm was raised and a searchparty set out; the Greenes were found dead on the ridge above Blindtarn Moss.

Dorothy Wordsworth was one of a group of Grasmere ladies who formed a committee to help the orphaned children; all of whom were found good homes in the neighbourhood. Sally herself joined the Wordsworth household.

All this was once lively Easedale concern: we think of it as we follow the pony-track up beside Sour Milk Gill, to Churnforce; a foaming tumble of white water. On we clamber; past the remains of the stone hut that used to be a tourist "refuge", and along the shore of Easedale Tarn; a haunting stretch of water.

Some will turn back here. Strong walkers will want to go on, up to stone-girt Codale Tarn and the ridge of Low White Stones, with Sergeant Man to the right. A track to the left leads along Castle Rigg, under Blea Crags; we take a track which leads *down* from Low White Stones, bearing leftward in its descent to Stickle Tarn; one of the Lake Country's most dramatic small waters, lying under the fierce wall of Pavey Ark, with Harrison Stickle, the noblest of the Langdale Pikes, boldly piercing the sky.

From Stickle Tarn the (now over-worn and very rough) track takes yo down by Mill Gill; keep to your right where the track diverges after about half a mile; this right-hand track will bring you to Dungeon Ghyll, a place revered by the Picturesque Tourists. Wordsworth has given us an almost photographic glimpse of it in his pastoral poem of 1800, "The Idle-Shepherd Boys". It is, he says,

> . . . a spot which you may see
> If ever you to Langdale go;

Into a chasm a mighty block
Hath fallen, and made a bridge of rock:
The gulf is deep below;
And, in a basin black and small,
Receives a lofty waterfall.

The poem tells how a young lamb had fallen into this pool and was on the point of drowning when it was rescued by the Poet himself, who handed it to the two young shepherd boys with a gentle chiding, because they had been playing together in the fine spring sunshine instead of minding their sheep.

For those who feel that the walk from Easedale to Dungeon Ghyll is somewhat over much, the charms of Silver How might be sampled instead; one of Dorothy's favourite walks. It is made by starting out from Allan Bank, Grasmere; in this house the Wordsworths lived for a few years after leaving Dove Cottage. You take the track up to two little farm houses at Score Crag and then continue, quite easily, to the top of the fell (it is wise to remember that, as the views are the heart of this excursion, an ascent of Silver How on a misty day is a decidedly pointless exercise).

From the summit of Silver How (1,300 feet), marked by a cairn, you get a marvellous view; embracing Grasmere, Rydal Water, Windermere, Elterwater, and Loughrigg Tarn in Little Langdale. A glint of Coniston Water may just be seen to the left of the Old Man and his brethren. The Langdale Pikes are tremendously exciting from here. Scafell Pike is hidden from you by Bowfell; but Bowfell looks so grandly that he may be forgiven this obliteration.

You will get another lovely view of Elterwater if, before you leave the top, you walk right-handed (your right as you face Grasmere) until you are looking down Meg's Gill; a particularly Wordsworthian vista.

To return to Grasmere you retrace your steps a little from Meg's Gill and take the right-hand track past the old rifle-butts; this will bring you down to Grasmere village. The point to remember when doing this walk is that Grasmere *must* be on your right all the way from Meg's Gill.

Those who go down into Great Langdale from Dungeon Ghyll will discover that the dalehead divides itself into two lesser valleys; Mickleden and Oxendale, separated by Stool End. The old pack-road up Mickleden leads you to a sheepfold where there is a divergence of ways; both important mountain highways in the past. The track to the right goes up Langdale Combe and over the Stake Pass, down the Langstrath and thus to Stonethwaite in Borrowdale. The other, left-hand track, takes you up by Rossett Gill and Hanging Knott to Angle Tarn, on Esk Hause, which will lead you to Sty Head.

From Oxendale you may ascend Bowfell by the Band, or, by taking the track up Hell Gill to Three Tarns, swing left from there for Crinkle Crags. And behold, there below you, to the west, lies the wild heaven of Upper Eskdale.

From Great Langdale over to Little Langdale you travel by Blea Tarn, taking the road past Wall End, at the foot of Oxendale. Below Blea Tarn you will find Little Langdale Tarn, shining in the dale bottom. The Wordsworths occasionally stayed at Hackett, a cottage overlooking Little Langdale. In 1818 Wordsworth was a co-purchaser of Iving How, near Colwith Force.

Little Langdale is a place of dreamlike beauty. You may drive up it, or down it, if you have no real interest in the Lake Country, but to *see* Little Langdale properly you must walk. Elterwater makes a good base.

Elterwater lies at the point where Great and Little Langdales divide; Elterwater village lying about half a mile beyond the mere itself, on the road to Chapel Stile. The river Brathay flows out of Elterwater. Skelwyth Force, just above Skelwyth Bridge, is a most romantic place, with its foaming waters, waving woods and green glades and bowers. From Skelwyth you should take the walk to Loughrigg Tarn (where Sir George Beaumont once nearly built himself a handsome house, but luckily never actually got around to it) and from the tarn continue over Loughrigg Fell down to Rydal Water, finishing with the beautiful Loughrigg Terrace Walk along the fellside above the little lake; a way which the Wordsworths dearly loved.

From Skelwyth too runs the road to Clappersgate, where the Charles Lloyds lived. Across the river from Clappersgate is Brathay Hall; home of the Harden family from 1804–34, after which they moved to Field Hall, Hawkshead. The Hardens became neighbourly with the Wordsworths during the Bard's middle and later years. They at all times contributed much to the life of the Ambleside district and John Harden's wittily observant sketches have survived to tell us much about Lake Country society of that period.

The Wordsworths, when they walked from Dove Cottage to Clappersgate to visit the Lloyds, would have taken the old Grasmere-Ambleside road as far as Cote Howe (Pelter Bridge) where they would have crossed the Rothay, to follow what was then a bridle path to Clappersgate.

Modern Wordsworthians who trace the route will find it quite a walk; ours is a weak era!

The road that the Wordsworths trod from Grasmere to Ambleside, usually to post or collect letters, was, needless to say, not today's motor-road. The old road left Grasmere by Town End (past Dove Cottage) and crossed White Moss Common, dropping down to join the line of the present main road at a point just before Dunney Beck (this section of old road can still be traced by enthusiastic Wordsworthians who, it follows, must also be enthusiastic walkers!). From Dunney Beck to Ambleside the old road ran a course much the same as that which the main road takes today. The lakeside stretch of road between Dunney Beck and Grasmere was constructed in Wordsworth's lifetime and met with his strong disapproval: he lamented to recall the lake, "As it once was . . . fringed with wood, instead of the breastwork of bare wall that now confines it."[7]

Dorothy has left us a touching account of walking the old road over White Moss Common, on the way to collect letters from Ambleside,

> *February 8th, 1802, Monday* . . . After dinner (i.e. we set off at about ½ past 4) we went towards Rydale for letters . . . The Rain had been so cold that it hardly melted the snow. We stopped at Park's to get some straw in William's shoes. . . . We walked on very wet through the clashy cold roads in bad spirits at the idea of having to go as far as Rydale, but before we had come again to the shore of the Lake, we met our patient bow-bent Friend, with his little wooden box at his Back. "Where are you going?" said he. "To Rydale for letters." "I have two for you in my Box." We lifted up the lid, and there they lay . . . We were very thankful that we had not to go on, for we should have been sadly tired . . . The night was wild. There was a strange mountain lightness, when we were at the top of White Moss. I have often observed it there in the evenings, being between the two valleys. There is more of the sky there than any other place . . .

An alternative route that was popular with the Wordsworths was the "foot-road" (as opposed to the road for horses and wheeled vehicles) which diverges from the old White Moss highway just before Dunney Beck is reached on White Moss Common. The "foot-road" runs under Nab Scar and behind Rydal Mount; a route, said Wordsworth, affording "very favourable views of the Lake and the Vale, looking . . . towards Ambleside".[8]

The Wordsworths came that way with Coleridge on a lovely spring morning; Friday, 23 April 1802; as Dorothy tells us,

> It being a beautiful morning we set off at 11 o'clock. . . . We went towards Rydale, and . . . determined to go under Nab Scar. Thither we went. The sun shone and we were lazy. Coleridge pitched upon several places to sit down upon, but we could not be all of one mind respecting sun and shade, so we pushed on to the Foot of the Scar. It was very grand when we looked up, very stony, here and there a budding tree . . . Coleridge and I pushed on before. We left William sitting on the stones, feasting on silence; and C. and I sat down upon a rocky seat . . . [William] was below us, and we could see him. He came to us, and repeated his poems while we sate beside him upon the ground . . . we . . . lingered long, looking into the vales,—Ambleside vale, with the copses, the village under the hill, and the green fields—Rydale, with a lake all alive and glittering, yet but little stirred by Breezes, and our own dear Grasmere. . . . Above rose the Coniston Fells, in their own shape and colour—not Man's hills, but all for themselves, the sky and the clouds, and a few wild creatures. C. went to search for something new. We saw him climbing up towards a Rock. He called us, and we found him in a Bower—the sweetest that was ever seen . . . Above, at the top of the Rock, there is another spot—it is scarce a Bower, a little parlour only . . . It had a sweet moss carpet. We resolved to go and plant flowers in both these places tomorrow . . .

17

RYDALIAN LAURELS

Wordsworth's Marriage—Grasmere Gingerbread—Allan Bank—Rydal—Windermere—Wray Castle—Belle Island—Bowness—Ambleside—Troutbeck—Rydal Mount in later Years—The Nab—Hartley Coleridge—A Visit from Branwell Brontë—Grasmere Churchyard

Adieu, Rydalian laurels! that have grown
And spread as if ye knew that days might come
When ye would shelter in a happy home,
On this fair mount, a poet of your own . . .[1]

William Wordsworth was married to Mary Hutchinson on 4 October 1802, at Brompton, Yorkshire. Dorothy, in her *Journal*, describes the home-coming of bride, bridegroom and herself to Dove Cottage at six in the evening of October 6; two days after the wedding, "Molly was overjoyed to see us,—for my part I cannot describe what I felt, and our dear Mary's feelings would I dare say not be easy to speak of. We went by candle light into the garden, and we were astonished by the growth of of Brooms, Portugal Laurels, etc."

All in all, Dorothy and William had been absent from Dove cottage for three months. Before going to Yorkshire they had journeyed to Calais; there to see William's illegitimate ten-year-old daughter, Caroline, and her mother, Marie Anne (Annette) Vallon.

Back at last at Dove Cottage Dorothy attempted to resume the old way of life as though virtually nothing had been changed by William's marriage. But her *Journal* went limpingly now; indication itself of fundamental change. Finally, after many lapses and gaps, and fruitless resolutions on Dorothy's part that she would "for the future write regularly", the *Journal* faded out. The final entry was for Sunday, 16 January 1803. William "had a fancy for some gingerbread". Dorothy walked into Grasmere village to buy some. "I went into the house. The Blind Man and his Wife and Sister were sitting by the fire, all dressed very clean in their Sunday clothes, the sister reading. They took their little stock of gingerbread out of the cupboard, and I bought 6 pennyworth."

Grasmere gingerbread is a speciality of the place: it is a gingery short-cake, rather than a spongy gingerbread. It is quite delicious, and is still sold in the same tiny house (next to the church lych-gate) that Dorothy went to on that cold Sunday afternoon. Here, in the little lamplit half shop, half parlour (so perfect a period piece that you feel convinced you have somehow escaped from the clutches of time) you may buy not only the celebrated gingerbread, but all manner of old-world sweetmeats and goodies.

In 1808 the Wordsworths, due to their growing family, left Dove Cottage for Allan Bank. They had now three children: John, aged five, Dora, four, and Thomas, two. Three months after the removal to Allan Bank another daughter, Catherine, was born and eighteen months later there arrived a fifth child, William. Dove Cottage was let to De Quincey, who distressed and disgusted Dorothy by ruthlessly pruning the fruit trees in her beloved little orchard.

Coleridge came to Allan Bank to live, intermittently, with the Wordsworths for two years. During this time he produced his periodical, *The Friend.* At Allan Bank William wrote most of *The Excursion.* In October, 1810, the friendship of the Wordsworths and Coleridge came to a traumatic finish: an estrangement principally due to Coleridge's impossible morphine addiction. The quarrel was ultimately papered over, rather than patched up, but the old trust and love between the two poets had been lost for ever.

In April 1811 the Wordsworths, unable to rent Allan Bank any longer, moved to the old rectory (now pulled down) that stood opposite the church. It was a miserably damp, cold house, built in a bog, and in it two of the Wordsworth children died: little Catherine on 12 June 1812, and Thomas the following December.

The Wordsworths, even before Tom's death, were thinking of moving to Rydal Mount, which was now to let; however it could not be leased for more than a year at a time, which did not suit the Wordsworths. Meanwhile William, during that year of 1812, was seeking "an office of emolument", through the influence of Lord Lonsdale. The poet could not earn a living with his pen and his small private income was not sufficient to keep himself and his family.

The Romantic, unworldly Dove Cottage way of life was rapidly receding into the far distance. Wordsworth was now becoming a man of consequence, although not of wealth, and he and his wife as a result found themselves increasingly involved in the social life of the county. Mary Wordsworth's chatty sister, Sara Hutchinson, described how,

> William and Mary did not return from Keswick till Tuesday last—They had had a very pleasant visit—parties for ever visiting all the gentry round—so Mary's dress clothes would come into play. And William had a very agreeable visit at Lowther—My Lord mighty kind & disposed to do all in his power to serve him.[2]

This was in November, 1812. The following March, thanks to Lord Lonsdale, Wordsworth was appointed "Stamp Distributer for Westmorland". On 1 May the family moved to Rydal Mount.

This house had been known to Wordsworth since boyhood; both from hearsay and by sight. In the mid-eighteenth-century the house, not then known as Rydal Mount, had belonged to Michael Knott, agent to the le Flemings of Rydal Hall. The le Flemings were an exceedingly ancient family, tracing themselves back to Reiner le Fleming, Seneschal of William de Meschines, first Lord of Egremont. The chief le Fleming seat was at Coniston and it was from the Coniston copper-mines that the family drew its wealth. Through marriage with an heiress of Sir John de Lancaster, Rydal came into ownership of the le Flemings and, following the Civil Wars, Sir Daniel le Fleming, much impoverished and penalized for his support of the Royalist cause, removed to Rydal from Coniston. Following the Restoration the le Fleming fortunes revived. The formerly modest Rydal Hall was rebuilt as a mansion (this late seventeenth-century house lies concealed from view today behind an early Victorian southern frontage).

Michael Knott, as agent to Rydal Hall, was entitled to customary holdings on the estate and he was permitted to burn timber from these holdings to make charcoal to his own profit. Thus, in due course, he was able to enlarge and improve his simple statesman's tofthouse; adding to it a sizeable left wing and transforming the place into a "gentleman's cottage", Rydal Mount.

In 1772 Michael Knott's son, George, married young Miss Caroline Ford, heiress to a large estate at Coniston Waterhead and the lion's share of the capital of Newland Co., one of the Furness iron industry's most prosperous firms. George Knott lived but little, if at all, in the Rydal house; he leased it to "off-come" tenants. In 1778, following George's death, his son Michael sold Rydal Mount to Lord North of Liverpool, for £2,500; an indication of the desirability of the property. In 1812, following disputes with the le Flemings, North sold the house to them; they advertised it to let and in 1813 Wordsworth at last decided to live in it.

In so doing he must have experienced a certain element of amusement, if not excitement. The old "household dame", Mrs Ann Tyson, with whom Wordsworth had lodged in his Hawkshead schoolboy days, had been in service at Rydal Mount before her marriage; her employer being Mrs Susannah Knott, *née* Fleming. The young Wordsworth thus had heard many Tyson reminiscences about this house at Rydal. His old Dame's anecdotes about the elegancies of Rydal Mount might well in some measure have acted as rootspring for Wordsworth's own "humour", when he moved there himself, to make his new abode smart. Childhood impressions linger long in the heart and prompt many an unexpected, and apparently uncharacteristic, adult decision.

Therefore we find Sara Hutchinson writing to her cousin, Thomas Monkhouse, in London, on 16 May 1813, to seek his help and advice with furnishings for Rydal Mount,

> Our Distributer (this is the *official* mode of spelling the word, therefore you must not question my orthography) . . . is now returned . . .and it is determined that a Turkey carpet must be had for the dining-room—the dimensions of which are 19 F. 4 by 13.4. The proper measurement for the Study Carpet, which room is to serve also for drawing-room, you will find on the other side. This *you say* must be Brussels—we should be very well contented with the old-fashioned Wilton, if it is to be had at a cheaper rate—only we must confine you to colour and pattern—the pattern to be as *small as possible* without regarding the fashion; and the colour to be of drabs, and a light yellow; which last is the colour of the window hangings . . . I have forgotten part of my commission which was that you would be so good as to get William 2 pair of Pantaloons, of the knit kind—such as you got him before when he was in Town—one grey & the other drab . . . William sets off tomorrow to Appleby to take upon him his new office—The income of it we expect will be about 500£ per an:—and the duty very easy. He will keep a Clerk therefore we hope it will not very much interfere with his other pursuits.

The carpets duly arrived; Brussels for the study, not Wilton. Everyone was delighted with the results. William himself was to declare that the carpets were "as beautiful articles as ever came into a house". Miss Hutchinson wrote to tell Thomas Monkhouse that Rydal Mount was now,

> the admiration of everybody—the *crack* spot, and the envy, of the whole neighbourhood . . . We have an abundance of . . . visitors; I think we have scarcely been one day unengaged for the past month—You who are fond of visiting and parties should always come into this neighbourhood in June, or July, or August—and then you would think that we live *in* the world . . . Our study is beautiful—I wish you could see it—and the dining-room looks so comfortable, warm & *genteel* you would be delighted with it . . . Our neighbours the Ladies [Fleming] are very fond of us . . . We have unrestrained right to walk in the grounds as if they were our own—& Lady Di pops in and takes a friendly cup with great pleasure . . . We rue sadly that we did not buy it [Rydal Mount] as we find it would have been quite as agreeable to them & more convenient.[3]

Dorothy, to do her credit, experienced qualms; revealed in this letter to her friend Mrs Clarkson,

> You stare, and the simplicity of dear Dove Cottage comes before your eyes, and you are tempted to say, "Are they changed? Are they setting up for fine folks?" for making parties, for giving Dinners . . . You want explanation. I will give it to you. The truth is that we bought these carpets as an economy, for in fact the most expensive articles are always the cheapest in the end. I confess that Mary and I inclined to something cheaper at the start; we were rather ashamed of our proposed finery and felt a cheaper carpet would look less ambitious and less like setting up on the model of our neighbours the Ambleside gentry, but our Master was all for Brussels, and to him we yielded—a humour took him to make his Room smart.[4]

The shores of Windermere had for long been growing increasingly adorned by impressive residences (today these are hotels) of the "Ambleside gentry". Old guide-books listed these fine houses; naming their owners, and even some of the guests who were entertained therein.

Windermere (more correctly Winandermere, as it was always called until well into the nineteenth century) fortunately is not a lake that can easily be spoiled. It is ten and a half miles long and never more than one and a half miles at its greatest breadth, so that (as Picturesque critics never tired of remarking) it bears a greater resemblance to a river rather than to any popular idea of a lake. It winds and bends in silver flashes between gentle hills; its head made glorious by dramatic views of Langdale Pikes, the Coniston Fells and the mountains of the central massif.

The lake is principally fed by the rivers Rothay and Brathay; the former flowing from Grasmere and Rydal Water and the latter, as aforesaid, from out of Elterwater. The two rivers join at the western corner of the head of Windermere, below Clappersgate; from here they run together in a single flood into the lake at a spot traditionally known as the "Three-foot-brander" (deriving from *brandreth*; p. 227). The Roman site, Borrans Field, will be found at the head of the lake.

One of the finest of fine houses overlooking the waters of Winandermere was Storrs Hall (subsequently the Grand Hotel); the building of which had been commenced by the close of the eighteenth century. Storrs Hall, the work of Sir John Legard, was set on a "noble promontory in the midst of ornamental groves".[5] At the promontory point an artificial causeway was built, leading to an octagonal observatory, known as the Temple; erected by Sir John in 1804 in honour of Admirals Howe, St Vincent and Duncan, and Nelson.

Storrs became the property of Colonel John Bolton, who commissioned Gandy to complete the house with a splendid classical frontage. Bolton was a friend of George Canning, the Prime Minister, who often came to stay at Storrs, "to recreate both body and mind, after the harassing occupations of a parliamentary session".[6]

The great Gothic extravaganza of Windermere is Wray Castle, built by Dr James Dawson, a Liverpool surgeon, in 1840–7 to designs by H. P. Horner. Further to heighten the Gothic effect some "picturesque ruins", also designed by Horner, were placed facing the entrance.

The castle caused immense excitement at the time of its construction. It stirred the Muse in James Gibson, a boatman on Windermere, who "evinced his taste for the beautiful and romantic" by bursting forth,

'Midst woods and waters all sublime
'Midst hills that mock the wreck of time,
'Midst verdant fields and flowery plains,
Where nature decked in beauty reigns;

Amid thy splendours, Windermere,
A castle does its turrets rear.[7]

Dr Dawson also built the church of St Margaret at Wray. Here the famous Canon H. D. Rawnsley of Crosthwaite was pastor before he received the Crosthwaite living.

In 1920 Wray Castle was given to the National Trust and in 1959 it became a training school for Merchant Navy radio-officer cadets. Its chief interest for us nowadays lies in its associations with Beatrix Potter. When she was a girl in her early teens her father was in the habit of renting Wray Castle for summer holidays. Here young Miss Potter learned to love and know the Lake Country and here, too, she met Rawnsley, who was already crusading for the formation of a National Trust, which would purchase and preserve for the nation places of beauty or historic interest. This ambition Canon Rawnsley achieved in 1895, with Miss Octavia Hill and Sir Robert Hunter. Beatrix Potter, too, was fired with enthusiasm for the Trust and in her later years, when Peter Rabbit and his kindred had brought her a wealth in royalties, Miss Potter subscribed generously to it; donating not only money but much property which she purchased with the sole intention of bequeathing it to the Trust.

The most renowned of all Windermere residences was Belle Island. This island, originally known as Langholme, had been, as aforementioned, the property and seat of the Philipsons. After they had forfeited Langholme in retribution for their support of the Royalist cause during the Parliamentary Wars the island changed owners several times until, in 1774, it was bought by Thomas English, a rich merchant, who pulled down the old house, cut down the trees and planted a formal garden in Italianate style. These improvements were loudly condemned by the Picturesque school.

English went on to build a "classical mansion"; a large cylindrical structure which was even more heartily condemned by the tasteful, and which he never completed. English also built a dower house at Sandbeds, on the western shore of the lake. This became known as Belle Grange. In 1779 English went bankrupt and in 1781 his Windermere estates (including Belle Grange) were put up for sale. They were bought by Isabella Curwen of Workington Hall, the heiress of Henry Curwen. In 1782, at the age of seventeen, Miss Curwen became the second wife of her first cousin, John Christian, whose mother had been Jane, sister of Henry Curwen (subsequently, in 1790, John Christian took the name of John Christian

Curwen and assumed the arms of Curwen of Workington Hall).

In 1783 he and his Isabella engaged Thomas White, the landscape architect, to make lavish improvements to Belle Isle and Workington Hall. Picturesque sensibilities continued to be outraged by Belle Isle. The formal Italianate gardens were demolished and the whole island was laid out afresh by White. The Wordsworths were among those who considered the results to be wholly lacking in sensibility. "They have made no natural glades," commented Dorothy. "It is neither one thing or another —neither *natural*, nor wholly cultivated and artificial, which it was before."[8] William disapproved especially of what he called "the paring of the shores": White's idea of a raised gravel walk running right round the island at the water's edge. The Curwens, in short, were as much criticized for their improvements and innovations as English had been for his, but they remained unrepentant, lavishing more and more money upon Belle Isle, which they used as their summer home.

It was not long before the Curwens had become the leaders of Windermere's fashionable high-season society. Curwen was one of the foremost organizers of the Windermere regattas. These regattas followed much the same pattern as those of Derwent Water; with canons firing to rouse the echoes, and processions of decorated and illuminated boats, graced by "regatta queens" who were elected much in the style of modern beauty queens.

The Windermere regattas began and ended at the Ferry, which Curwen had acquired (together with Great Boat, the ferry inn) round about 1788. The most celebrated of all these regattas was held in 1825 in honour of the 54th birthday of Sir Walter Scott. By this date in time the regattas were being organized by Professor Wilson of Elleray, who had by now built his new house at Orrest Head (a famous viewpoint not to be missed; to reach it you take the signposted footpath next to the Windermere Hotel, opposite the railway station). Wilson loved nothing better than organizing lavish entertainments and this Scott birthday celebration was a *tour de force*.

Sir Walter was invited to stay at Storrs Hall as guest of Colonel Bolton. Fellow guests included Canning, Southey and Wordsworth, together with "other illustrious names . . . and beautiful and accomplished women to adorn and enjoy this circle". We are told that,

> The weather was as Elysian as the scenery. There were brilliant cavalcades through the woods in the mornings, and delicious boatings on

> the lake by moonlight; and the last day, Professor Wilson (the 'Admiral of the Lake' as Canning called him), presided over one of the most splendid regattas that ever enlivened Windermere. Perhaps there were no fewer than fifty barges following in the Professor's radiant procession when it paused at the point of Storrs to admit into the place of honour the vessel that carried kind and happy Mr Bolton and his guests. The three bards of the lakes led the cheers that hailed Scott and Canning; and music, and sunshine, flags, streamers, and gay dresses, the merry hum of voices, and the rapid splashing of innumerable oars, made up a dazzling mixture of sensations as the flotilla wound its way among the richly-foliaged islands, and along bays and promontories peopled with enthusiastic spectators.[9]

The little towns of Windermere, Bowness and Ambleside that we know today are largely of mid- and late-Victorian construction. Windermere is graced by the railway station that Wordsworth fought so heatedly

> Is there no nook of English ground secure
> From rash assault? . . .[10]

There is not.

In 1847 the railway arrived at Windermere; until that point in time always known as Birthwaite and no more than a few cottages perched above Bowness. A steamer service opened up on Windermere that same year. While these developments filled Wordsworth with a sense approaching doom they met with the approval of "progressives" like Miss Harriet Martineau; a high-minded, teetotal, outspoken spinster who proclaimed from her genteel farm in Ambleside that,

> We [meaning herself] have no fear of injury, moral and economical, from the great recent change—the introduction of railways. The morals of rural districts are usually such as cannot well be made worse by any change . . . Mental stimulus and improved education are above everything wanted . . . the widest possible intercourse with classes which, parallel in social rank, are more intelligent and better informed than themselves.

Miss Martineau, in fact, disapproved strongly of the dalesfolk of whom

Wordsworth entertained such a high opinion. Miss Martineau maintained that Wordsworth, "a dear, good old man," did not know half of what went on among the dalesfolk. Their drinking habits alone were sufficient to condemn them. "The capacity of the dalesmen . . . in the quantity of strong liquor they can carry—is remarkable; and they have only too good a training. Spirits are introduced on all occasions. It is common to swallow the strong liquor undiluted, in considerable quantity . . ."

Consequently Miss Martineau pinned her faith on the railways. These, she hoped, would introduce new blood into Cumbria, until the "primitive population . . . shall have given place to a new set of inhabitants . . . in every way more up to the times".[11] Poor Miss Martineau! We are not exactly surprised when we find Mrs Lynn Linton referring to her as a "credulous spinster".

Railway, steamers, more and more tourists ever increasingly drawn from "the artisan class": Windermere and Bowness expanded rapidly until they formed two parts of what was virtually one town, Bowness being the old, lakeside quarter.

Here, today, you will find the famous Promenade, steamer piers, tennis courts, putting greens and, in the Glebe, a miniature golf course. In high summer this is a lively spot indeed. Whether Miss Martineau would approve, were she to return, is another matter.

A hundred yards or so distant from all this lively noise and holiday bustle stands the parish church of St Martin; built in 1483 on the site of an even earlier church that had been destroyed by fire. In 1869–73 the fifteenth-century fabric was extensively restored. The invaluable Pevsner tells us that the clerestory seems to be sixteenth century. Over the arches of the nave a number of texts were discovered, under the plaster, in 1870; these, too, date to the sixteenth century. The carved heads on the octagonal font are twelfth century.

The fine carved group of St Martin and the Beggar is thought to be foreign, and probably seventeenth century; it was much restored in the mid-nineteenth century. At the east end of the south aisle is a memorial slab, by Flaxman, to Bishop Richard Watson of Llandaff, who lived at Calgarth Hall (now a hotel) and who died in 1816. In the north aisle is a memorial bust to Fletcher Raincock, QC, who died in 1809; west of this is a window in which, tradition says, there is a piece of glass on which is painted the trademark of the pack-carrier who transported the roof-lead for the fifteenth-century church to Bowness from Whitehaven, over Wrynose Pass.

The presence of the Philipsons is felt in this church: to the right of a small door near Bishop Watson's memorial is a wall-tablet to Robert Philipson (1631), father of "Robin the Devil"; this tablet has an epitaph composed by the deceased himself "in the tyme of his sickness". On the underside of the arch opposite this same door is a plaque, put there by Christopher Philipson, in 1629, to commemorate the failure of the Gunpowder Plot (24 years after the event).

A further curiosity of this most interesting church is the 1822 memorial to Rasselas Belfield, the slave. This is discoverable outside the church, at the east end,

> A Slave by birth: I left my native Land,
> And found my freedom on Britania's Strand.
> Blest Isle! Thou Glory of the Wise and Free!
> Thy Touch alone unbinds the Chains of Slavery.

But the great glory of this church is the late fifteenth-century east window, showing the crucifixion with attendant figures. This glass came from Cartmel Priory (pp. 326–28). Even more marvellous is the central panel containing the Virgin and Child, dating from the thirteenth, or perhaps early fourteenth century, and almost certainly from Furness Abbey. This is some of the most unique stained glass in Europe.

Ambleside today is utterly changed from the Ambleside to which Dorothy and William used to walk to post their letters. It was then a cluster of old-fashioned houses set round a cobbled market square with an early market cross at its centre. The Salutation Inn, which overlooked this square, remains; but changed out of all recognition from the hostelry of which Thomas Gray has left us such a succinct account, "On looking into the best bed-chamber, dark and damp as a cellar, grew delicate, gave up Windermere in despair, and resolved I would go to Kendal directly."

Our knowledge of old Ambleside is drawn largely from the extensive sketches which William Green[12] made in the early years of the nineteenth century.

The parish church of St Mary, built in 1850–54 by George Gilbert Scott, following in Pugin's footsteps of authentic Gothic revival, is in Decorated, or Mid Gothic, style. There are some good windows by Holiday and a 1944 mural by Gordon Ransom, depicting the traditional rush-bearing ceremony which is held here every July (this mural was painted during the time that the Royal College of Art was evacuated to Ambleside, during World War Two).

Rush-bearing originated as a ceremony when new rushes were brought to the church to be strewn upon the floor and the rush-bearers, in those days adults, were blessed by the priest before going on to secular, and less edifying, celebrations. By 1830 the festival had already assumed the features of a tourist attraction; the adults having been replaced by children and the simple rushes by a variety of pretty nosegays, wreaths and other floral devices. The "ale bestowed on ye rush-bearers" had been replaced by "gingerbread". The rush-bearing is, none the less, a quaint and interesting ceremony to attend; it is also celebrated at Grasmere, on the Saturday nearest 5 August.

A mere handful of truly old buildings survive in modern Ambleside. The most famous must be the minute and altogether extraordinary bridgehouse down in the town. Another is the ancient manorhouse on the Kirkstone Road. Visitors who wish to see what one of the old homesteads was like, both without and within, should visit Town End, Troutbeck; this house still contains the original furniture of the Browne family, whose home this was for over 300 years.

At Troutbeck, too, is the lovely Jesus Chapel; of seventeenth and early eighteenth century, much restored in the nineteenth century. The panelling of the stalls came from old Calgarth Hall and is Jacobean. The glass of the east window is by Morris and Co. (Burne-Jones, William Morris and F. M. Brown) and is a particularly beautiful example of their work.

However, when all is said and done, the major visual draw in the Ambleside district today, as of yesterday, is Stockgill Force; surprisingly sylvan and unspoilt, considering that for the past two centuries crowds of people have visited it. The wheel of the old mill in Stock Gill now turns by electricity, as a tourist attraction merely; the beautiful, solemn sound of a mill wheel treading water and cascading as it revolves is no longer to be heard here, but the wheel at least survives, and revolves, albeit in eerie silence. The mill itself is today a pottery, and interesting to visit.

Rydal may be reached on foot from Ambleside by a pretty public footpath through Rydal Park. This footpath brings us out close to Rydal Mount and we must imagine the Fleming ladies walking up this little stretch of hilly road to visit the Wordsworths at Rydal Mount and drink tea with them.

Rydal Mount, open to the public, is a deeply interesting house to see, with a beautiful garden. Here is the terrace up and down which Wordsworth used to walk, composing aloud. And here is the laurelled drive, up which the disgruntled Keats peered! And here is the knoll which the poetess Mrs Hemans (now wholly forgotten) described with rapture when she came to stay in the summer of 1830. Rydal Mount she found a "lovely cottage-like building, almost hidden by a profusion of roses and ivy, with a grassy knoll in front, commanding a view always so rich, and sometimes so brightly solemn, that one can well imagine its influence traceable in many of the poet's writings".[13]

Mrs Hemans would surely have been much disconcerted had she read what Sara Hutchinson had to say of the visit,

> For one *long* fortnight we had Mrs Hemans & one of her boys—he was a sweet interesting creature—but she tho' a good-natured person is so spoilt by the adulation of "*the world*" that her affectation is perfectly unendurable—. . . Mr W. *pretends* to like her very much—but I believe it is only because we do not—for she is the very opposite, her good-nature excepted, of anything he ever admired before either in *theory or practice*—I wish you had been here—I am sure you would have been amused at least—[14]

At Rydal Mount Wordsworth gradually grew into a pillar of the Establishment; assuming so much weighty dignity, at least by reputation, that the day finally arrived when one Grasmere lady, invited to meet and dine with the Bard at the home of a mutual friend, exclaimed, "What, dine with Wordsworth! I should as soon think of dining in York Minster!"

Each summer saw more and more visitors flocking to Rydal Mount: some were personal friends, or at least known acquaintances of the Wordsworths; others came bearing letters of introduction, or introduced themselves on the strength of mutual acquaintance, while others were simply inquisitive strangers, drawn to the gates of Rydal Mount openly to stare at the poet and his family. At times there would be quite a little crowd at the gate, peering, in the manner of Keats, through chinks in the thick shrubbery.

One diversion for these onlookers, we are told, was the appearance of a crazy Miss Dorothy Wordsworth, being given an airing in her wheeled chair, or her small pony carriage. For, tragically, in the early 1830s Dorothy had succumbed to serious chronic illness which had proved to be a prelude to premature senile dementia. The remaining twenty years of her life were spent under eclipse. It was often unbearably sad and difficult for her devoted family circle to bear with her demented incapacities and tantrums. The interminable loving patience shown by the Wordsworths in the face of this long and painful trial was nothing short of saintly. It is possible that Dorothy's condition had been precipitated by the shattering blow, in June 1835, of the death of Sara Hutchinson, from rheumatic fever.

By the lakeside road, below Nab Scar, stands an old, low-built house, Nab Cottage; chiefly known to posterity as the place where Hartley Coleridge lodged in the final years of his life and where he died. The Nab, as it was usually called (today a guest house), was for generations the home of the Parks, a family of yeomen farmers. The last male Park was William, who died there in 1825 at the age of 84. His only son being an imbecile, who died young, William Park was succeeded by his daughter Mary and her husband John Simpson, whose daughter Margaret, or Peggy as she was usually known, married De Quincey in 1816.

The Parks had impoverished themselves with fruitless, if spirited, litigation over manorial wood rights, with the result that De Quincey in due course found himself saddled with the financial burdens of the Nab. These proved too much for him and in 1833 the Nab was put up for sale and the long Park association with the place came to an end.

In spring, 1840, new occupants moved in; a young farmer named William Richardson, together with his wife Eleanor and their lodger, Hartley Coleridge. Hartley's life had been a strange and tragic one; following a brilliant career as an undergraduate at Merton College, Oxford, he had been awarded a probationary Fellowship at Oriel College. But drink was his undoing, and the Fellowship was withdrawn from him. Thereafter he lived a shiftless existence; first in London, then in the Lake Country. He received a small allowance from his family, eking this out with a little authorship and schoolmastering. From time to time he would vanish on drinking sprees and wanderings about the district. Yet he was beloved by all who knew him, for he combined the spellbinding conversational powers of his father with a childlike innocence and simplicity of nature and an irresistible sense of fun. L'al Hartley, as the local people always called him, was very small, with hair that was almost white before he was middle-aged. He was once described as a being "whose head was midwinter, while his heart was green as May".[15] He loved little children, with whom he could be touchingly tender and playful, while they doted on him. Nor was he without brilliance as a scholar and genius as a poet; his sonnets are major achievements.

The ghost of l'al Hartley is one that gently haunts these Rydal fells; he is felt, rather than seen, shambling along, "His trowsers . . . generally too long, doubled half-way up his leg, unbrushed, and often splashed; his hat brushed the wrong way, for he never used an umbrella; and his look wild, unshaven, weather-beaten."[16] Yet he was by no means ostracized by the local gentry and would turn up to evening parties most immaculately, almost elegantly, groomed; his manner old fashioned but perfect, his personality eccentric, but delightful.

There have been many strange encounters between remarkable men, in the Lake Country (indeed it is for ever the realm of the unexpected, the wholly astonishing). One of the most extraordinary meetings ever to have taken place there must have been on that day in the late spring of 1840 when Branwell Brontë arrived in Ambleside to spend a day with Hartley Coleridge. Hartley was then in his 44th year and a poet of not inconsiderable repute; Branwell was 23 and struggling to get a foothold on the bottom rung of literature's perilous ladder. Three years earlier he had sent a letter, together with a long poem, to William Wordsworth, "Sir—I most earnestly entreat you to read and pass your judgement upon what I have sent you . . ." Wordsworth had vouchsafed no reply.

Early in 1840 Branwell, who had always nursed a deep longing to visit the Lake Country, took the post of tutor in a family named Postlethwaite, of Broughton-in-Furness. In April Branwell plucked up the courage to send a poem of his own and two translated Odes from Horace to Hartley Coleridge, asking for an opinion of these. Hartley replied and, sometime in late May or early June, Branwell journeyed to Ambleside, to meet Hartley. No record remains of this meeting, save for a brief comment written by Branwell to Hartley on 27 June of that same year, reminding the poet of the delightful day that Branwell had had "the honour of spending" with him at Ambleside.

We must imagine these two strange spirits together on the shores of Rydal Water. Branwell himself was "almost insignificantly small", wearing his mass of bright red hair brushed high off his brow to counteract his lack of inches. He had a big, bumpy, intellectual forehead, nearly half the size of his facial contour, a prominent Roman nose and a weak mouth and chin. The eyes behind the steel-rimmed spectacles were, we are told, "small, ferrety and deep sunk" and he never looked anyone, or anything, straight in the face; he kept his glance downwards, except for rapid momentary glances at long intervals. He was afflicted by a stammer. Sexually he was somewhat ambiguous.

Hartley had inherited his father's gift of profound psychological insight: we do not know what he made of this, at least superficially, unattractive visitor, at whom he looked with his own soft, brilliant, beautiful and direct gaze; his eyes "remarkably responsive to the movements of his mind, flashing with a light from within", as his brother once wrote. We do know that Hartley was kind to Branwell, and encouraged him to try his hand at further translations: in the aforementioned letter of 27 June Branwell mentions that he has sent Hartley "the first book of a translation of Horace".

Did Hartley take Branwell to the Nab, there to enjoy a dish of bannocks, with which Mrs Richardson customarily regaled visitors? This is an afternoon's encounter which must for ever tease the mind. "You will, perhaps, have forgotten me, but it will be long before I forget my first conversation with a man of real intellect, in my first visit to the classic lakes of Westmorland."[17] Thus Branwell to Hartley.

Branwell never visited the Lakes again. He died four years later, on 24 September, 1848, the victim of pulmonary tuberculosis. Less than four months after that Hartley was dead too; killed by pneumonia, "attributable to his imprudently having been late out twice within the last 3 weeks —leaving his friends' several houses when they ought either to have detained him all night, or seen him home"[18] as Mrs Wordsworth wrote, to Hartley's sister, Sara, in London. Derwent Coleridge had already rushed from London to Grasmere, to be at his brother's bedside.

The Wordsworths, who loved Hartley like a son, called regularly at the Nab throughout Hartley's illness and Derwent has left us a deeply touching account of these visits. "Mr Wordsworth read prayers himself from the Prayerbook, as I have never heard them read before nor (I confidently expect) ever shall again. . . . The old man knelt before the window and read without spectacles."

Dora Quillinan, the Wordsworths' only, beloved, daughter had died a mere eighteen months earlier; Wordsworth was still mourning her passing. After Hartley had passed away Wordsworth accompanied Derwent to Grasmere churchyard to discuss with the sexton where Hartley should be buried. Wordsworth pointed to a place next to Dora's grave and said, "Keep the ground for us—we are old people, and it cannot be for long . . . Let him lie as near us as possible . . . It would have been his wish."[19]

Thus, today, we see all the graves set close together in Grasmere churchyard, together with a graveless memorial stone to John Wordsworth, the first of the circle to die. Here are little Catherine and Thomas Wordsworth, lost in infancy; Sara Hutchinson, Hartley Coleridge, Dora Wordsworth Quillinan, and her husband Edward. Here lies William Wordsworth, who died in 1850, and Dorothy, who followed him in 1855, and Mary Wordsworth, who outlived them all; a blind and serene presence alone at Rydal Mount with her memories. She died in 1859.

These graves are today visited by constant processions of people; some merely out of curiosity, but others in sincere homage. The river Rothay sings close at hand, as it sang to this family in life.

PART FOUR

FURNESS

18

"ALL THAT HAD BEEN LOVED BEFORE"

Windermere Ferry—Furness—High Furness Industries—Grizedale Forest—Claife Heights—Far and Near Sawrey—Hill Top Farm—Esthwaite Water—Waterside Hauntings—Wordsworth's Schooldays—Hawkshead—Colthouse—Nanny's Stone—Hawkshead Church

WORDSWORTH, IN THE Lake Country, is never dead. We have no sooner left his grave in Grasmere churchyard than he is miraculously restored to us; a Cambridge undergraduate now, enjoying his first Long Vacation by returning to Hawkshead, the scene of his schooldays. Here he comes, on the last lap of this holiday journey into the happy past: we both see him and hear him, bounding

> . . . down the hill shouting amain
> For the old Ferryman . . .[1]

There has been a ferry since time immemorial across this narrowest part of Windermere, between Ferry Nab, Bowness, and Ferry House Point opposite. This ferry is associated with a famous phenomenon known as "The Crier of Claife". The Crier is traditionally said to have been heard first in the sixteenth century, before the Reformation. A party of travellers were making merry one evening at the small tavern that then stood on Ferry House point, when a call for the boat was heard from the Nab. The boatman obeyed the call, though the night was a wild one. After a while, anticipating that he should be returning, the tavern revellers went down to the shore, to see whom the boatman would bring. He returned alone, ghastly in the face and speechless with horror. Next morning he was in a high fever, and in a few days he died, without having been prevailed upon to say what he had seen at the Nab. For weeks after there were shouts, yells and howlings on the Nab, on every stormy night; and no boatman would attend to any call after dark. A priest was summoned to exorcize the Nab and services were performed which were designed to confine the disturbing spirit to the quarry in the wood behind the Ferry. This quarry, henceforth known as "The Crier of Claife", continued, down the centuries, to be regarded as a badly haunted spot, from which, at irregular intervals, but always on stormy nights, strange and terrible sounds ensued. Nobody would go there at night and the foxhounds, in full cry, were said always to come to a full stop when they reached that place. Even as late as the nineteenth century it was still difficult to get a ferryman to turn out after dark. Of the Crier of Claife Miss Martineau wrote, "Whatever may be said about the repute of ghosts in our day, it is certain that this particular story is not dead."[2]

The Windermere ferry of today, with its cables, its mechanized and effortless precision and its high-season queues of tourist-packed motorcars is scarcely to be connected with a wild phantom! But a ferry crossing in the old days of an open rowing boat, lighted by a single storm-lantern and with the night howling a gale, must have been a very different experience.

The Ferry Nab shelter was anciently a smithy and even in Wordsworth's boyhood the ruins of this building were still used as a shelter, albeit a somewhat wretched one, by persons waiting for the ferry. Better provision for travellers was made upon the opposite shore.

The Trustees of the old Market Shambles at Hawkshead were responsible for maintaining a cote-house (shelter) on the Claife side of the ferry. We know that such a cote-house (a term which in due course came to be written as colt-house) stood there from at least the late sixteenth century. In the eighteenth century a ferry inn, known as Great Boat, was built; this was acquired, together with the ferry itself, in 1788 or thereabouts by John Christian (Curwen). Yet we also learn that, in spite of the erection of this new ferry-house inn, the old cote-house was enlarged and repaired. Later Curwen enlarged the inn too. Inn and cote-house stood together until both were pulled down in 1879 and a hotel built instead (now Ferry House, used by the Freshwater Biological Association).

Windermere Ferry had many celebrated ferryman, but the most famous of all was George Robinson, who was ferryman from 1786 to at least 1794. It was he whom the undergraduate Wordsworth hailed as he bounded down the hill. In addition to being ferryman George was also innkeeper of Great Boat. In his youth he had lost an eye "from a potatoe wantonly thrown at him" and in his old age he lost the other eye while following his part-time trade as a wood-turner. The Rev. Reginald Braithwaite of

Hawkshead procured a pension of ten pounds per annum for George, who, though now totally blind, remained at Great Boat, his son-in-law acting for him as ferryman. George continued to hire out boats, and became somewhat of a Picturesque Tourist attraction himself. Joseph Budworth has described the still strong and active, blind George, being guided by two little grand-children, like a patriarch led by two cherubs in Heaven.[3]

So let us follow the bounding, shouting Wordsworth down to the ferry and across Windermere, to disembark at Ferry House Point. We are now in that part of Cumbria which, historically, is Lancashire-North-of-the-Sands, or, even more historically, Furness; divided into High Furness and Low.

The traditional industries of Furness have been wool, mining, slate quarrying, charcoal burning and smelting. The famous mines here are the Coniston copper mines. Grizedale Forest is the great wooded area which has a history of being used by man since before the twelfth century, when Norse-speaking settlers grazed their swine here.

Despite some fringe settlement by the Norse, no very great changes occurred here until the monks of Furness arrived in 1127. Furness Abbey, which in wealth and importance was to rank second only to Fountains, was founded by Stephen, Count of Mortain (later King of England) who, in 1123, granted a site at Tulketh, near Preston, to monks of the Order of Savigny. In 1127 they moved to Low Furness, where they built in a desolate little valley with a stream: Bekangesgill, the Vale of the Deadly Nightshade. The house became Cistercian in 1147, when the Orders of Savigny and Citeaux amalgamated.

Stephen endowed the abbey with much land in Low Furness, to which further extensive property was in due course added. In 1163 Henry II confirmed the abbey's possession of the whole of the eastern part of today's Furness Fells, including all the land between Windermere and the Brathay on one hand and Coniston Water and Yewdale Beck on the other. This terrain took in Hawkshead, Satterthwaite and Colton. Furness acquired Borrowdale in 1209 (with the exception of Watendlath, which belonged to Fountains) and in 1242 David de Mulcaster of Butterilkelt in Eskdale granted Furness much of Upper Eskdale. Here, at Throstlegarth, the monks had a summer shieling. *Circa* 1290 Furness received permission to enclose the pastures of Butterilkelt and Lincove. This land adjoined the deer forest of the Lord of Egremont; the original turf bank of the deer fence may still be traced under Cam Spout Crag.

As Cistercians the monks of Furness engaged in sheep farming and wool merchandizing upon a most extensive scale. They enclosed more and more land of the High Furness Fells to accommodate more and more sheep farms; this practice of enclosure continued until the Dissolution, and it is thought that, by this date, most of the walling of the small dalehead intakes had been accomplished.

Besides sheep farms Furness also owned granges, fisheries, forests, deer parks, orchards, coney warrens, quarries and bloomeries (bloomsmithies). The monks, by the thirteenth century, had established highly-organized and flourishing woodland industries; initiating a system of exploitation of the woods for charcoal production (enclosed coppice worked on a fourteen-year rotation). This charcoal was used for smelting iron ore. Following the Dissolution these coppice woods passed into private hands.

The Furness charcoal industry (which continued to thrive until well into the first two decades of the present century) went hand-in-hand with the district's iron-ore industry. Iron was being made in primitive bloomeries (hand-powered hearths) from as early as pre-Roman times (a pre-Roman bloomery was recently discovered near Broughton Mills). These hand-powered hearths were functioning as late as the mid-seventeenth century, when water-powered bloomsmithies came into employ. These produced a high quality malleable iron (though only in small quantities at a time).

In 1711 the Lake Country's first blast furnace came into operation at Buckbarrow. The following year the Cunsey furnace started up; in 1715 the Leighton furnace was in operation. These pioneer furnaces were followed by many more. Fuelled by charcoal they produced immeasurably larger quantities of iron than had the former bloomsmithies (Buckbarrow furnace could produce six tons of iron a day). The only disadvantage was that the iron produced was cast iron: it had too much carbon in it to be malleable. In order to produce malleable iron the metal had to be "reduced"; requiring further processing in, first a finery, then a chafery forge. From 1718 until *circa* 1822 the major finery and chafery forge in Furness was at Stony Hazel, Rusland, which served Buckbarrow, Cunsey and Duddon Furnaces, among others.

Buckbarrow is famous in industrial history because of its association with John Wilkinson of Ironbridge (at Coalbrookdale, Shropshire).

Isaac Wilkinson, John's father, was a Cumbrian farmer who, in 1738, moved to Buckbarrow and involved himself in the development of the iron industry. In 1749, after Buckbarrow Company had been reorganized, Isaac Wilkinson joined his son, John, who had started a furnace at Bilston, Staffordshire. Subsequently father and son had their main works at Broseley, Coalbrookdale, and it was here, in 1799, that John Wilkinson cast the parts for his celebrated bridge over Coalbrookdale gorge; the first iron bridge in history. The Wilkinsons, however, remained Furness men at heart. At Lindale, in the Cartmel fells, you will find Wilkinson House, built in 1748 in conjunction with a furnace. Later, at Lindale, they built themselves "a beautiful modern seat", Castlehead (now St Mary's College). Industrial historians and archaeologists will wish to go to Lindale to see the cast-iron obelisk to John Wilkinson, who died in 1808. It stands in Lindale churchyard (St Paul's), having been removed there from Castlehead. It is strikingly mid-twentieth century in appearance (though 150 years earlier in actual date!).

Since the demise of the time-honoured iron-ore and charcoal industries of High Furness the woodlands of the district have grown wild again. Wolves and boars have gone for ever, but deer, both red and roe, are rife and there are abundant squirrels, badgers, foxes, and birds of many woodland species. The charming pinemartin, too, lives here; after having almost become extinct in the Lake Country. However, he is far from yet being a common animal.

Today the Grizedale Forest is a wildlife centre, where you will find displays and dioramas depicting various aspects of the life of the Forest, together with much fascinating information about the birds and animals that live there, especially the deer. There is a nature trail, with wildlife observation hides, and bothies may be rented by student parties.

A venture of a different kind is the delightful Theatre-in-the-Forest; an intimate theatre in the deepest of glades, where plays, concerts and experimental audio-visual entertainments are put on in this quite unique setting.

The first place that we come to, after crossing Windermere, is Claife Heights, whose enchanting appearance is in great measure due to two men—John Christian Curwen and the Rev. William Braithwaite—each of whom did much extensive and imaginative planting here. In 1809 Curwen was awarded a gold medal by the Society of Arts for "having planted in a single year over a million larches and other forest trees".

However, he was but carrying on the work of a far less flamboyant but none the less remarkable individual, the Rev. Braithwaite of Satterhow, Far Sawrey.

Braithwaite, who was born in 1753, was the great-grandson of William Braithwaite of Satterhow, who had accumulated considerable wealth through the bloomsmithy industry. In 1707 he had purchased the right of ferriage across Windermere, together with the property that went with the ferry rights, and the two ferry boats then in use. His rather unworldly grandson, and namesake, William, went to Hawkshead Grammar School and afterwards to St John's College, Cambridge, where he graduated in 1776. He then took Holy Orders, but he was not offered a living until several years later. He therefore took refuge as a near-recluse at Satterhow and remained there, lonely and embittered, until at last, in 1787, he became vicar of Burton Pedwardine in Lincolnshire, and of Riseley, Bedfordshire. Yet even with these livings to occupy him, he continued to spend much of his time at Satterthwaite. During the 1790s he built a Gothick summer house on the rocky hill above the Ferry Inn, overlooking Windermere.

This hillock had been made famous by Thomas West, who, in his *Guide*, had selected it as his first picturesque station (or view-point) from which to enjoy the raptures of Windermere. Green, in his *Guide to the Lakes* of 1819 described the summer house, or station house as he called it, as being "two stories high; the lower story consists of dining and other rooms, but the upper is a tasteful drawing-room; from this drawing-room there are two fine views of the lake". The windows of this room were partly of stained glass of different colours, in order "to give a good representation of the manner in which the landscape would be affected in different seasons".[4] In Curwen's time an "aged female" was housed nearby in a picturesque cottage; her duties being to act as caretaker and conduct parties of tourists round the summer house.

In addition to building the summer house the Rev. Braithwaite altered the direction of the road which "was rugged and unsafe" (says West) and carried it nearer the margin of the lake. Most important of all, Braithwaite planted the entire rocky hill with upwards of 40,000 young trees and "a great many acorns".

The summer house still stands, though badly dilapidated now, and with all its stained glass long since gone; it is worth a visit none the less, as this involves a trip on the ferry and a pretty stroll. Upon reaching the western shore of the ferry, walk past the Ferry House until you reach a fork in the road. Ignoring the right-hand fork, continue up the Far Sawrey road for a short distance; a track leading off on your right (signposted Claife Heights) will lead you past the summer house and the once celebrated Belle Vue. From here you may continue up on to the Heights, or, turning right at a stile which you will find about half a mile beyond the summer house, follow a downhill track to a road which will lead you back to the ferry.

But though the gentle, mopey, Romantic shade of the Rev. William Braithwaite should not be forgotten, the name of Sawrey today stands, above all, for Beatrix Potter. At Near Sawrey (lying beyond Far Sawrey as we approach from the ferry, the farness, or nearness, of the Sawreys being gauged by their distance from Hawkshead, not from Windermere) we find Miss Potter's house, Hill Top Farm, where lived Mrs Tabitha Twitchett, Tom Kitten, Samuel Whiskers and his wife, and Jemima Puddleduck, while, in the countryside around, Mr Tod, Tommy Brock and Peter Rabbit and his innumerable relatives had their homes.

The little winding roads here once saw the Fairy Caravan rolling along them; the tilt-cart of this tale was based on a reality, as indeed were all of Miss Potter's characters and incidents. In the case of the Fairy Caravan Miss Potter was almost certainly thinking of Hawkshead's once celebrated itinerant conjuror and magician, Bartholomew, or Barty, Purcel, "a gay good hand at pattering," who travelled in a tilt-cart to all the fairs of the region. His assistant was a small boy who, concealed beneath the ample cloth of a table with trap doors in its surface, would hand Barty rabbits and pigeons which the man of magic then plucked "miraculously" out of thin air, to the gaping wonderment of his audience.

Below Near Sawrey the road drops down to Esthwaite Water; a most tranquil little mere, fringed with rushes and willows and green pastures. Here, in hot summer, parties of cows wade through shallows to reach small islets of grass and the scent of hay makes the air thick with sweetness. It is difficult to believe that this bucolic place was formerly notoriously haunted and that, furthermore, it is associated in the minds of thousands with a particularly vivid and horrible account of a drowning.

As we travel along the eastern shore of Esthwaite Water, from Near Sawrey towards Hawkshead, we pass Waterside Cottage (formerly the Claife Poorhouse). The quarter mile or so of road between Near Sawrey and Waterside was famed for being much frequented by a boggle; a white something variously described as resembling a calf, large fox, or dog, or an odd beast which was neither calf nor donkey, but somewhat akin to both. This Waterside Boggle was in the habit of appearing suddenly, to startle night pedestrians. As they drew nearer to it (if they possessed the nerve to do so) the thing vanished as suddenly and disconcertingly as it had appeared; following which there would be a sound resembling a cartload of stones emptied into the lake, or sometimes onto the road. Many believed this particular apparition to be a barghest, rather than mere boggle. As barghest it was much to be feared, for the sight of it portended a death.

Two other spectres are described as having been seen at Waterside; the first, a man garbed in light blue (of whom no further details are given, save that his appearance was not infrequent) and the second an old woman in a wide-brimmed bonnet. Among those who saw her was the Rev. George Park the younger, Vicar of Hawkshead from 1834 to 1865. According to his own testimony, he was walking home to Hawkshead from Sawrey one snowy moonlit night when, at Waterside, he suddenly saw a woman in an old-fashioned wide-brimmed bonnet ahead of him. He caught her up and, as he overtook her, he bade her "good night", certain that she would be one of his parishioners. As she made no reply he turned round to see whom the unsociable old thing might be and perceived under the wide brim of her bonnet a death-like face with goggle eyes, which "gleamed like the red bull's eye at the back of a carriage-lamp".[5] Then, as the vicar stared in horror, she vanished; apparently through a gap in a wall a yard or two distant. The vicar bravely went to this gap and stared through it, but there was no one in sight. He then observed that there were no footsteps in the snow beyond this gap, neither were there any on the road except his own.

It was shortly after William Wordsworth's arrival at Hawkshead as a nine-year-old grammar-school entrant at Whitsuntide, 1779 that, on 18 June, James Jackson, the young school-master of Sawrey, was drowned while bathing in Esthwaite Water. Wordsworth, in Book Five of *The Prelude* describes how, during a twilight ramble, he noticed a small pile of clothes lying on the lakeshore and surmised, rightly, that they belonged to a bather. Next day the clothes were still there, so the lake was searched with grappling-irons and the unfortunate school-master's body was recovered, watched by a small crowd, including little William Wordsworth, upon whom the incident made an indelible impression,

> At last, the dead man, 'mid that beauteous scene
> Of trees and hills and water, bolt upright
> Rose, with his ghastly face, a spectre shape . . .[6]

Poor James Jackson, himself but 21 years of age, was buried next day in Hawkshead churchyard, as the parish register for 1779 tells us.

At the head of Esthwaite Water is a pool known as Priest Pot; perhaps from some Furness ecclesiastic having been drowned in it. This place, too, held shuddersome associations for the schoolboy Wordsworth. As he tells us, here formerly stood a gibbet, "upon which the body of some atrocious criminal had been hung in chains near the spot where his crime had been committed. Part of the Irons & some of the wood work remained in my memory. Think of a human figure tossing about in the air in one of these sweet Valleys. 'Tis an object sufficiently fearful & repulsive upon Hounslow heath . . ."[7] Wordsworth went on to add that at that time the marshy ground at the head of this lake "used to resound with the doleful cry of the Bittern, which, by the bye, has never been heard in its ancient haunts since the great frost in 1740".

Hard winters such as that of 1740 are rare in the Lake Country. Such another came in 1785, when Esthwaite Water was thick with ice. The Hawkshead saddler George Park (one of the Parks of Rydal Nab) supplied the Hawkshead schoolboys with skates. George's son, Tom, a school friend of Wordsworth and his senior by one year, was an outstandingly good skater and in 1785 was the most brilliant of all the youths who

> . . . shod with steel
> . . . hissed along the polished ice

playing games of hare and hounds; imitating the sounds of the horn and the chiming chorus of the hounds. Wordsworth was never to forget how

> through the darkness and the cold we flew
> And not a voice was idle . . .
> . . . while the stars
> Eastward were sparkling clear, and in the west
> The orange sky of evening died away.[8]

To this winter Wordsworth owed his lifelong passion for skating, in which he indulged whenever the opportunity presented itself. For instance, during the first winter at Dove Cottage, Wordsworth was writing to tell Coleridge that he was going to skate on Rydal Water; "not however without reasonable caution".[9] This was on 14 December 1799; Wordsworth was no doubt thinking of the companion of his schooldays,

Tom Park, who had been drowned three years previously while skating on Esthwaite Water when the ice had given way.

Hawkshead, in Wordsworth's boyhood, was still an important woollen-industry and market town. When we walk round the town today we should notice how particularly rich it is in spinning architecture; roomy spinners' porches and galleries, designed to accommodate spinning-wheels and weaving-frames and to provide natural light, together with shelter, for the women busy with this home industry. It is not difficult to imagine what a hive of female activity must have flourished here in the old days! And what a hotbed of gossip! Every porch and gallery would have had its spinners and weavers, and the chatter to go with them.

Hawkshead market was at its height in the second half of the eighteenth century and first decade of the nineteenth. Woollen yarn was the chief commodity ("garn", as it was called locally) and it was brought to Hawkshead from places as far distant as "t'other side o' t'Raise". In 1785, when there were heavy falls of snow, the garn was transported from Hawkshead on sleds, hand-drawn as was the Cumbrian custom. The wool buyers, or middlemen between the farmers and the weavers, or manufacturers, were called "wool-badgers". The Kendal mills procured the bulk of their wool from Hawkshead market.

Towards the close of the eighteenth century Hawkshead also became a leading leather market; saddlers and shoe-makers coming to it from as far afield as Cockermouth. Hawkshead was particularly noted for its "clog-whangs" and "shoe-whangs"; these being leather laces, or thongs (*whang*, like *thong*, derives from the Old English *thwang*, in Cumberland always pronounced as *twang*—an angry Cumbrian father, threatening to strap, or thrash, his son will still bellow, "Do that agin an' I'll twang ye!").

By Wordsworth's day the industry of charcoal burning (which had brought many Irishmen to the district) was at the commencement of its long and gradual decline. Slate-quarrying, on the other hand, was on the increase. There were a fair number of farriers, tanners and curriers in the Hawkshead district and boot and straw-hat making were flourishing minor industries.

Hawkshead was not only famous for its market; its other claim to renown was its Free Grammar School, founded in 1585 by Edwin Sandys, Archbishop of York. The school was rebuilt in 1675 (and repaired and modernized in 1891). It was a free school insofar as actual education was concerned; entrance fees, boarding and certain other expenses had to be paid, including charges, little more than nominal, for tuition in hand-writing, which was not considered a grammar-school subject. A number of boys, however, did receive their schooling entirely free of cost; these were the Sandys Charity boys, so named after the Rev. Thomas Sandys, curate of St-Martin-in-the-Fields, Lecturer of St James, Westminster, and absentee rector of Tunstall-in-Holderness and of Wighton, Yorkshire, who in 1717 established by bequest a charity for boarding, clothing and providing with school books, as well as educating, poor boys at the Grammar School.

John Wordsworth of Cockermouth, attorney-at-law and law-agent to Sir James Lowther (later first Earl of Lonsdale) sent his sons, Richard and William, to Hawkshead school at Whitsuntide, 1779. Mrs Cookson, their maternal grandmother, paid the entrance fees. At their time of going to school Richard was eleven and William nine. Three years later their brother John joined them and in 1785 Christopher, then aged eleven and the youngest of the Wordsworth boys, also came to the school: thus, for a few months, all four brothers were at the school together. Richard left in December, 1785 to become articled to his cousin Richard Wordsworth, a Whitehaven attorney. William left to go to Cambridge in October 1787, and at the end of that same autumn term John, aged fifteen, left school to join the East India Company as a merchant sailor.

The seventeenth-century schoolhouse that visitors flock to see nowadays went out of use in 1909. In this room William Wordsworth (known to his schoolfellows as Bill) received his grounding in the strictly classical education of his day. His name is to be seen, carved in full, allegedly by his own hand, on one of the desks. Perhaps it is genuine; perhaps not. Around it are the names of generations of other, less renowned boys and these incisions, being without doubt authentic, move and interest us more than the slightly dubious WILLIAM WORDSWORTH.

Boarders at the Grammar School were lodged with various motherly Hawkshead dames. The Wordsworth boys lodged with Ann and Hugh Tyson; a childless couple who obviously regarded their young boarders as a happy substitute for the brood that they themselves had never managed to produce.

Hugh Tyson was a master joiner; Ann, as we have already learned, had been in domestic service before her marriage. At the time of her wedding she was 36; Hugh was one year her junior. Both were Hawkshead people. Some ten years after their wedding Ann opened a village shop (in her front parlour). This shop she kept for the next twenty years or so, selling almost everything from groceries to drapery. Her chief sale, however, was of tea, the favourite luxury of Lake Country women of that day.

Hugh's account book (which Ann also used) has survived to tell us a great deal about the couple, their gainful occupations, and their boarders.

When the Wordsworth boys first went to lodge with the Tysons, in 1779, they lived in Hawkshead Town, in the cottage now known as Ann Tyson's Cottage. The room in which William Wordsworth probably slept is on the right as you face the house (the window of this room is not so tall as its fellow). William carved his name on the window seat in 1781, as did his schoolfriend and companion, Philip Braithwaite (later the school-master of Sawrey). This window seat has unfortunately been destroyed.

In 1782 John Wordsworth, as aforesaid, joined his brothers at Hawkshead and in the autumn of 1783 the Tysons, together with the three young Wordsworths, moved from Hawkshead Town to Beckside, Colthouse; about half a mile from Hawkshead centre, and a short distance beyond Town End, below Colthouse Heights (which are an extension of Claife Heights). The exact identity of the house which the Tysons took at Beckside has always been a bit of an open question; it seems that it was the house known as Greenend Cottage, but it could have been Greenend House, on the opposite side of the entrance to Scarhouse Lane. Certainly it was one or the other of these two houses.

Colthouse is but little changed today. Near Greenend (not open to the public, though serious Wordsworthians may view it on application to the National Trust) you will find the 1688 Friends' Meeting House. Wordsworth, in his maturity, was to write elegiacally of this Meeting House. He pointed out how, behind it

> runs a streamlet which is occasionally diverted into a resevoir wherein Adults are dipped, some coming from a considerable distance for this purpose. A little detached from the building lies also a small Cemetery, with one low headstone in the centre . . . This obscure burial place is of a character peculiarly melancholy . . . But among this little company of graves, how much mortal weariness is laid at rest, how many anxieties are stilled, what tender scruples & fearful apprehensions removed for ever![10]

On 1 March 1784 Hugh Tyson died of an "inflammation of the chest";

he was 70. His widow continued to take boarders until 1789; at one time she had as many as eight together. Among them were cousins of the Wordsworth brothers: in 1787 there arrived ten-year-old Richard Wordsworth, son of Uncle Richard to whom William's eldest brother, Richard, was articled. In 1789, during her final year as "Household Dame", Ann Tyson received yet another Wordsworth as boarder: Robinson Wordsworth, youngest son of yet another Richard, a Collector of Customs at Whitehaven.

Ann Tyson's fee for boarding a scholar was at first five guineas for each half-yearly school term of about 21 weeks, with washing as an extra. But during the 1780s the cost of living rose steadily and she increased her fee at first to six guineas and then to six and a half, with fuel (charcoal and peat) and lighting (candles) as extras. Washing was now included in her general fee.

Wordsworth, in *The Prelude* (II, 79–82, 1805 version), was to recall the "frugal, sabine fare" of his schooldays; in fact Ann Tyson's accounts reveal that she fed her young lodgers well, with plentiful provision of meat. However, there were long gaps between meals. School started at 6.30 am (at six in May and June) and dinner was not eaten until early noon (but an old woman kept a food stall on a convenient boulder at the higher end of the market square and there the boys might buy mid-morning snacks). Tea-supper was at 5.30 pm; but, again, extra things to eat, such as cakes, might be obtained from good Ann Tyson and put down on account.

In 1789 it was decided to demolish the old Market Shambles and to build a new, much larger market house (today's town hall) with a yarn market as well as shambles on the ground floor, and a Great, or Court Room (subsequently known as the Assembly Room) on the floor above, with lodging suites at either end. To make room for this new building it was necessary to remove the great stone ("t' Rocking Staen") that stood in the market square: the stone which, down the centuries, had served as a market stall and which, for the final 60 years of its existence had, as aforementioned, been used by

> . . . that old Dame
> From whom the stone was nam'd who there had sate
> And watch'd her Table with its huckster's wares.[11]

This old dame was called Ann (popularly Nanny) Holme and thus "t' Rocking Staen", also known as "Nanny Staen". Nanny was born in Hawkshead in 1711 and she had married John Holme, a tailor of Far Sawrey, by whom she had had one son and four daughters. None of these girls ever married, but remained at home, baking the parkins, gingerbreads, little cakes, pies and biscuits that their mother sold on her "stall".

When Nanny learned that her stone was to be broken up to make way for the new market house she made a spirited protest, declaring that the living of herself and her family depended upon the stone. Thomas Rigge (the celebrated Owd Slaty's son and partner), who was one of the new market house trustees, asked Nanny how much the stone was worth to her and she replied sixpence a week. As she was aged, Rigge offered to give her that sum for the rest of her life, but Nanny was a "canny owd body" and at once retorted, "Aye, but what about my daughters?" Rigge replied that the offer was for her lifetime only; he could not be responsible for the daughters. At length Nanny accepted his offer; but the laugh, as they say, was on her; for she survived to the age of 94 or 95, outliving Thomas Rigge by nearly ten years, but continuing, until her death, in 1805, to be paid twenty shillings a year out of his estate. It was fortunate that Rigge's offer had not been extended to the daughters, for all four survived to a good age and all remained together, as spinsters, at Far Sawrey!

The Hawkshead of Wordsworth's boyhood was full of such eccentric characters. Many of them were numbered among the village elders who assembled at Churchend on fine, warm evenings. Churchend was (and still is) the stone bench running the breadth of the eastern outer wall of the church:

> A place of resort for the old people of the Town, for the sickly, & those who have leisure to look about them. Here sitting in the shade or in the sun, they talk over their concerns, & a few years back were amused by the gambols, & exercises of more than a 100 Schoolboys, some playing soberly on the hill top near them, while others were intent upon more boisterous diversions in the fields beneath.[12]

Thus reminisced Wordsworth.

One particularly noteworthy elder of Churchend was John Hodgson, the Parish Clerk, a shoemaker by trade. Wordsworth loved to watch this old man, during Sunday service, giving the psalm singers their keynote on his pitch-pipe: this Hodgson did with a tremendous air and a flourish. He became Parish Clerk in 1744 and held the office until his death in 1785, at the age of 76; his successor, George Pennington, was also a shoemaker. The famous pitch-pipe may still be seen preserved in Hawkshead church; it bears the date of 1764 and the churchwardens' accounts for that year (which are in John Hodgson's handwriting) show that the pipe was supplied by Isaac Holme, a Hawkshead carpenter. This pitch-pipe remained in regular use until 1828, when an organ was installed in the church.

Another noteworthy parish officer was John "Pharaoh" Pepper, the Dog Whipper, who took over this traditional office in 1772 for a period of ten years at five shillings a year; his task being to ensure that there were on dogs in church during the hours of worship and to remove any that had slipped in unobserved (it should be remembered that most male members of the congregation would be owners of a working dog, the habit of such a dog being to stick to his master's heels with the inevitability of a shadow). The churchwardens provided the Dog Whipper with a dog whip; a new one had been bought in 1769 at the cost of 2s 3d. In Wordsworth's day the grammar-school boys used to amuse themselves (and relieve the tedium of Sunday service) by smuggling dogs into church; much to Pharaoh Pepper's agitation. In the end he reported the matter to the master of the school, with the result that the "young gentlemen" offenders made amends to Pharaoh by leaving the price of a quart of ale for him at his favourite inn.

Hawkshead church, described by Wordsworth as sitting like "a thronèd Lady"[13] upon a small hill, or large knoll, behind the school, remains seated thus today. This mound in itself is an indication that this is an immensely ancient religious site. The date of the earliest Christian church here is unknown; but in 1200, when Hawkshead was placed among the possessions of Furness Abbey, the foundation was referred to as being already an old one. Furness rebuilt the church, but of this Norman church little remains today. Pevsner suggests that the jambs of the north doorway could be thirteenth century. One south aisle window is fifteenth century. Otherwise the church that we see today is sixteenth and seventeenth century. The south aisle bears a date, 1587; on the north the clerestory bears the date of 1633.

In 1792, when a vestry was added, the font and reading desk were removed to new positions and the pulpit was transferred to its original (and present) position against the second pillar of the north arcade and furnished with a sounding-board.

The painted texts which, thanks to Wordsworth, are such a well-known feature of the church, are of 1711. Among the monuments in the church the altar tomb to William and Margaret Sandys, parents of Archbishop Sandys, is the most important.

Ann Tyson retired from her happy occupation as Household Dame to Hawkshead schoolboys in 1789; the year after Wordsworth's Long Vacation visit, when he had stayed with her at Hawkshead and she had paraded him round the town, showing him off to her neighbours, who, of course, all knew him well, but not in his new guise of a Cambridge undergraduate and a bit of a dandy!

Dame Tyson lived on for another eight years, dying in 1796 at the age of 83. She was buried in Hawkshead churchyard. Her grave bears no stone by which it may be identified; it was not the custom, in this region, at that time, to mark graves with headstones. But Ann Tyson has her epitaph written elsewhere, immortally,

> The thoughts of gratitude shall fall like dew
> Upon thy grave, good creature! While my heart
> Can beat never will I forget thy name.
> Heaven's blessing be upon thee where thou liest . . .[14]

When Wordsworth brought Coleridge to Hawkshead during the course of their 1799 walking tour, Ann Tyson had been three years in the grave. Wordsworth, showing Coleridge round Hawkshead vale and town, perhaps took him to the resting place of the simple old woman whom he, together with his brothers and cousins, had "honoured with little less than filial love". The schoolboy of twenty years earlier now regretfully commented that Hawkshead and the manners of the people thereof were "sadly altered".[15]

19

CONISTON COUNTRY, LOW FURNESS AND THE ABBEY

Hawkshead Old Hall—Tarn Hows—Coniston Copper Mines—Green Slate—Coniston Water—Brantwood and its Residents—the Lintons—Ruskin—A Linen Industry—Low Furness—Furness Abbey—Dalton-in-Furness

JUST OUTSIDE HAWKSHEAD stood the Old Hall and Court House. Of the original manorhouse nothing remains but the fifteenth-century gatehouse; a delightful building with stepped gables. It now stands alone, though originally it was part of the manorhouse. To the south of the gatehouse lay the great hall and solar; the sixteenth-century range of the original building is incorporated today in a roomy (private) house that you will see standing behind the gatehouse. The latter is open to the public; it contains an excellent little museum of rural life.

However, the chief fascination of the place lies in the building's Cistercian associations. The manor of Hawkshead was, of course, a Furness possession and the large upper room of the gatehouse was used as a courtroom by the abbots of Furness when they were on circuit. Here, in this big chamber with its handsome dog-tooth moulded red-sandstone fireplace (thought to have come from Furness Abbey itself) were held the manorial Courts of Rights, with the abbot presiding as Lord of the Manor.

A little over a mile to the north-west of the Old Hall lies Tarn Hows; probably the Lake Country's most celebrated beauty spot. Tarn Hows was formed artificially in the nineteenth century from three small tarns under Tom Heights, Monk Coniston. A dam was built across the beck flowing from the lowest of the three tarns, thereby raising the water level in the upland depression where the three tarns lay. The surrounding landscape was planted with patches of woodland. The happy result has enchanted thousands.

Yewdale, down which the road goes to Coniston, is gloomy with wild masses of crag suspended among clouds. Yewdale Beck, that keeps the road company for much of the way, flows into Coniston Water. Behind the nearby village rise the Coniston Fells, with the Old Man and Wetherlam brooding hugely over the ancient and famous copper mines. These have a history reaching as far back into the unfathomed mists of time as that of Goldscope, in Newlands.

The oldest working at Coniston is Paddy End, below Levers Water. On the other side of the ridge, facing the Duddon, lie the Seathwaite workings and below Wetherlam, on his Tilberthwaite flank, are the Greenburn workings. These mines, together with the Coniston Copper Works, comprised the four major workings of the Coniston copper mines complex. All are now disused (and highly dangerous to explore).

The Coniston mines reached the peak of output and prosperity in the early nineteenth century. We are told by Postlethwaite that several hundred men and boys were employed there and that the mine returns were from £30,000 to £36,000 a year. The mines began to decline in prosperity after 1874; partly because their great depth now made them difficult and expensive to work, and partly because the introduction of iron ships to replace the former copper-bottomed wooden ones resulted in a drastic decline in the demand for copper. During the years 1877 to 1889 fewer and fewer hands were employed in the copper mines until at last scarcely a dozen men remained at the Coniston workings; the mine which remained open longest.

The mines are said to be haunted. It has been claimed that Paddy End is disturbed by the shade of Simon of the famous Simon Nick. Tradition has it that Simon discovered a rich strike of copper ore where none but he had seen signs of a vein. His mates were deeply envious and to them Simon at last confided that he had been guided to his vein of ore by the fairies. Alas, his secret divulged, the vein of ore vanished without more ado. Simon, despondent and furious with himself for opening his mouth, became careless over his dangerous work and while in the process of making a gunpowder "nick" he blew himself up.

In pack-horse times the copper ore from Greenburn was transported to the Cumbrian coast over Wrynose and Hardknott; from Seathwaite working it went over Troutal Fell to Dunnerdale, and from Paddy End and Coniston the ore travelled along the Walna Scar Road to Long House. Here the Walna Scar road was joined by the Seathwaite pack-route. The way now crossed the Duddon by the ford below Gill Spout and from there went by the old Norse settlement of Grassgaards, over Birker Moor green-road to the (old) Woolpack Inn at Penny Hill, Eskdale, and from thence down Eskdale to the coast. But by the close of the eighteenth century the ore from the Coniston workings (by now the most productive of the mines) was being transported down the lake, to Nibthwaite.

Coniston Water (known in the old days as Thurston Water, a name derived from the Old Norse Thurstainwater) was an important fishery for the Furness monks, who had the right to keep a boat and twenty nets on the Water. Today the lake is chiefly associated with the names of Sir Malcolm Campbell and his son Donald, who set up their world water speed records here. Donald, who met his death on Coniston Water, still lies in the depths of the lake where he and Bluebird plunged in 1967.

Coniston, throughout the centuries, has been almost as famous for slate as for copper. Coniston green slates, the hardest and most expensive of all roofing slates, were quarried mainly from Coniston Old Man and Tilberthwaite. The leading quarrying firm was William Rigge & Son, of Hawkshead (the celebrated "Slaty"). Owd Slaty remained head of his firm until his death, at the age of 84 or thereabouts, in 1791, after which his son carried on the business.

The dressed slate was carted from the quarries to Kirkby Quay at the head of Coniston Water, from whence it was conveyed, like the later copper ore, by a small fleet of sailing boats down to Nibthwaite Wharf. From here it was carted either to Penny Bridge or to Greenodd, where it was loaded on to coastal craft.

On the western shore of Coniston Water the scenery is tall with mountains. Here stands Coniston Old Hall (today a farm), the ancient seat of the le Flemings. The eastern shore is mainly composed of what was formerly deer park. Close to the lake, below Monk Coniston Moor, lies Brantwood, famous as the final home of Ruskin; though in truth its previous occupants were more interesting than the aged and ailing Ruskin that Brantwood knew.

Ruskin purchased Brantwood in 1867 from William James Linton, a distinguished artist and wood-engraver who was furthermore a dedicated republican and fiery political writer. Linton's work as an engraver is today receiving revived and merited recognition: his political career has been all but forgotten.

Born in 1812, W. J. Linton was apprenticed at sixteen to W. G. Bonner. Specimens of Linton's earliest work are to be found in Martin and Westall's *Pictorial Illustration of the Bible* (1833). Thereafter he rapidly became a foremost wood-engraver of his day.

He also became a zealous Chartist. He married the sister of Thomas

Wade, editor of *Bell's New Weekly Messenger*: a semi-radical London paper. In 1840 Linton wrote a *Life of Thomas Paine*. Four years later he became a friend and follower of Mazzini and resultantly found himself becoming involved in European radical politics. In 1848 he was deputed to bear a congratulatory address from English workers to the French Provisional Government.

Linton now moved to Ravenglass in Cumberland, where he edited a twopenny weekly paper, *The Cause of the People*, published in the Isle of Man. When this failed he wrote for the *Red Republican*. In 1852 he removed himself and his family to Brantwood where, with three fellow craftsmen and republicans, he established a "community"; one of the "Republican Associations for the teaching of Republican principles" which he and fellow enthusiasts were trying to start in various parts of the country. From Brantwood Linton published a monthly paper of his own, *The English Republic*. This organ, yellow-coloured and slender, emerged from a printing press in an outbuilding and after four lean years it folded.

W. E. Adams (later editor of the *Newcastle Chronicle*), who joined the community in 1854, has left posterity a succinct account of life there.

> The family at Brantwood in 1854 consisted of Mr and Mrs Linton and their six children—three boys and three girls—the youngest mere babies . . . All the children were charming romps—The life at Brantwood was very secluded . . . Mr Linton . . . was regarded [by the locals] as a considerable mystery . . . we were all viewed with suspicion . . .
>
> Only an enthusiast would have thought of setting up a printing office in a remote quarter of the Lake District, miles away from the nearest railway station. Paper and other materials had all to be carted over the Fells, from Windermere to Brantwood, and the printed magazines had all to be carted over the Fells from Brantwood to Windermere back again . . .[1]

A mutual friend introduced the Lintons to Miss Eliza Lynn; daughter of the rector of Crosthwaite, Keswick, and a young woman of radical views. She came to visit at Brantwood and quickly became friendly with this eccentric family. She was to recall:

> I felt as if I had got into a new world . . . Playing in the neglected, untrimmed garden . . . was a troop of little children, none of whom

was more beautiful than another. They were all dressed exactly alike—in long blouses . . . of coarse blue flannel . . . and all had precisely the same kind of hats—the girls distinguished from the boys only by a somewhat broader band of faded ribbon . . . even to the eldest boy of fourteen, they wore their hair . . . in long loose locks to their shoulders. It was difficult to distinguish the sex in this queer epicene costume, which left it doubtful whether they were girls bloomerised or boys in feminine dress; for the only differences were—cloth trousers for the boys, cotton for the girls, and the respective width of the hat-ribbon aforesaid. But they were lovely as angels . . . a family consecrated to the regeneration of society. The boys were to be great artists or divine poets. The girls were to be preachers or prophetesses . . .[2]

Mrs Linton and Eliza Lynn became close friends and when Mrs Linton died three years later she, on her deathbed, bequeathed her family to Miss Lynn. In less than two years she and Linton were married. Fond as they were of one another they were basically incompatible. He was a true artist, bohemian and radical; she was an intellectual middle-class blue-stocking liberal. She thought that she might "remould" Linton and his children. These were dressed in ordinary clothes; the boys were sent to boarding school and the girls had a governess. The family removed to London. The children adored their step-mother and she returned their love, but the entire experiment was a failure in every other respect.

In 1863 the family returned to Brantwood, and that summer was spent by W. J. Linton and Eliza in working upon *The Lake Country*, which she wrote and he illustrated. They rambled about the district together and were happy. However, in the spring of 1864 Linton remained with his children at Brantwood when Eliza Lynn Linton returned south to follow her successful career as writer and journalist in London. She joined the family at Brantwood during holidays.

Miss Gedge, Eliza Lynn Linton's niece, was to remember that life at Coniston seemed wholly remote from reality. Particularly she recalled the boat trips to church on Sundays, to avoid walking three miles of road, and "the exceedingly incompetent gardener, chosen by Mr Linton because he had beautiful blue eyes".[3]

In 1867 Mr Linton suddenly resolved to go to America. He first went out alone, leaving the children at boarding schools and under his wife's care. By the following year he had found them all a home at New Haven. The children joined him there, but Mrs Linton remained in

England. Both she and her husband survived for another 30 years and remained regular and friendly correspondents, but they never met one another again; not even when Linton came to England to do research at the British Museum. It was a mutual decision of husband and wife that they should not meet. Linton wrote to Eliza, "It is a happiness that only good thoughts exist between us, that we are, and shall be always, good friends."

He returned to his artist's workshop on the other side of the Atlantic; Eliza, in London, became a celebrated literary figure. She was famous for her journalism on the "woman question". She was herself one of the advanced guard; a pioneer woman journalist and one of the first of her sex to break away from the restrictions of the Victorian family. She summed up her aims and attitudes thus: "That women should have an education as good in its own way, but not identical with, that of men; that they ought to hold their own property free from their husband's control without the need of trustees, but subject to the joint expenditure of the family; that motherhood should be made legally equal with paternity."[4] She lived to see all these aims virtually achieved.

It is ironical that her most successful journalism was that of her middle-age when she castigated the New Woman, "The Girl of the Period". The Girl of the Period had gone a little *too* far. She was not sufficiently high-minded about Women's Aims and in her habits of life, social manners and behaviour had taken a turning that was "brash" and "raucous". *Plus ça change.*

Ruskin was in many respects well-suited to follow the Lintons at Brantwood; though he found the "unworldly" house too damp, draughty and primitive for him, subject to chills and delicate health as he considered himself to be. He did a tremendous amount of rebuilding and improving; changing the place almost beyond recognition. His old age at Brantwood was made distressing by bouts of acute depression, amounting to insanity, but during his happier periods Ruskin pursued his penetrative interest in the arts and social problems, and it was from Brantwood that he encouraged and assisted the incredible Miss Marion Twelves to develop the Ruskin Linen Industry, to which he gave his name and patronage; an enterprise which would have won the whole-hearted approval of W. J. Linton.

Ruskin was deeply aware of the problems of a fast developing age of mass industrialism and being a rich man he embarked upon the project of forming a charitable organization, The Guild of St George (of which he was Master), to encourage the revival of handicrafts and cottage industries, thereby "restoring to village homes some of those necessary arts of life which bring both help and comfort, and that joy in work from which modern life is so largely disinheriting us".[5]

There came to Coniston, in the early 1880s, a formidable spinster named Miss Twelves, already an ardent disciple of Ruskin although she had not as yet actually met him. Miss Twelves became interested in the by now forgotten art of spinning, mastered it herself and began instructing those daleswomen, with the time to spare, in an occupation which had been second nature to their grandmothers. In 1884 Miss Twelves met Ruskin and literally cast herself at his feet. He blessed her revival and development of a "cottage spinning and weaving industry" and, thus encouraged, Miss Twelves resumed her activity with almost frightening dedication and fervour. She gathered round her a group of "spinsters" to whom she preached her ardent gospel, "You come forward to be givers, not receivers in this human world—you are to *give* your time, your thoughts, your labour, and the reward of your labour as far as you can spare it, for the help of the poor and needy."[6]

But the Coniston womenfolk seem to have been too down-to-earth in their approach to the spinning-wheel and so, in 1889, Miss Twelves removed herself to Keswick, in the hope that there she might find people who cared "*not* how many yards of linen may be made and sold, but how what *is* done may influence and help the doers".[7]

This was the great period of the revival of arts and crafts in England; thanks to the influence of men like William Morris and Ruskin, Keswick became a not uninfluential centre of an art and craft industry in the north-west. Mrs Rawnsley, wife of Canon Rawnsley, had started evening classes in craftwork for Keswickians and Miss Twelves, working in conjunction with the Rawnsleys, taught handspinning and weaving. A special spinning and weaving department of the Keswick School of Industrial Arts was opened; this venture flourished and Ruskin allowed his name to be given to the Linen Industry.

By 1894 the Keswick School of Industrial Arts was housed in a handsome purpose-built centre (today the home of Keswick Industrial Arts). But Miss Twelves felt that once more her "methods were called in question"; she broke away from the Keswick School of Industrial Arts and, with the help of Ruskin, the Ruskin Linen Industry, with Miss Marion Twelves as Director, moved to Porch Cottage, High Hill, Keswick, and here, for the next 30 years, Miss Twelves guided and developed the Ruskin Linen Industry until it had become world famous.

When Ruskin died in 1900 the "spinsters" made his exceedingly beautiful pall; still to be seen in the Ruskin Museum, Coniston (the "spinsters", in 1892, within the space of three days and nights had made the pall which had draped the coffin of Alfred, Lord Tennyson, at his funeral in Westminster Abbey).

Following Ruskin's death the Linen Industry was renamed "The Ruskin Linen Industrial and Memorial School". Miss Twelves retired at last in 1917. The Industry attempted to continue without her, but its decline was steady. Miss Twelves died in 1929 at the age of 86. The Linen Industry as such had become defunct, but the arts which she taught, particularly that of making Greek lace, still linger in the Lake Country and today are reviving yet once again.

The Ruskin Museum at Coniston should be visited, if only to see the celebrated pall. The collection includes drawings and sketches by Ruskin; representing his development as an artist at all stages of his life, from boyhood to old age at Brantwood. There are also Ruskin manuscripts, together with his notes on architecture, clouds and mountains. All in all it is a fascinating place in which to spend an hour or two.

Brantwood today is a centre for the Council of Nature. The grounds, however, are open to the public and so is part of the house. It contains pictures by Ruskin and his contemporaries, together with part of his library, and many of his personal possessions.

Attached to the grounds is a nature trail. As you wander here listen for the sound of the voices and laughter, and perhaps a miraculous glimpse, of a troop of little children with flowing locks, all strangely attired in blue; boys indistinguishable from girls, all "lovely as angels". This vision of joy, innocence and uni-sex flashes upon the inner eye of the visitor to Brantwood and remains a haunting memory for long afterwards.

The heart of this country of Furness, both High and Low, is of course the great abbey itself. This, although the heart, lies near the southern tip of the tongue of land between the estuaries of the Leven and the Duddon.

From Coniston the road to Furness Abbey runs through Torver to Ulverston. This had always been an important regional market town, but in the final decade of the eighteenth century Ulverston became a port for the Furness iron industry, when a canal was built (by Rennie) connecting the town with the sea. During the next half century Ulverston throve exceedingly; by 1840 it had a population of over 5,000. But the see-saw progression of industrial development was about to witness the spectacular development of a rival port and the consequent decline of Ulverston's canal traffic.

In 1840 the little village of Barrow, at the very tip of the Furness peninsula, had no more than some 300 inhabitants. Six years later the Furness Railway arrived, to open up the district. Hitherto Barrow had been served only by a small cluster of jetties built at Barrowhead to ship away ore; jetties eclipsed in purpose by the Ulverston canal. The advent of the railway, coupled with the discovery, in 1850, of the famous Park deposit of iron ore, exploded Barrow into giant growth. By 1876 the Barrow steelworks were the largest in the world. A great iron shipbuilding industry had been born there in 1869; the company, in 1897, becoming Vickers. In the decade between 1871–81 Barrow's population expanded from 19,000 to 47,000. By 1921 it had reached 74,000; since when the figures have declined considerably, together with Barrow's industry.

Visitors to Barrow will find it an attractive town; it was planned and built in the mid-nineteenth century and much of its Victorian centre survives, with broad tree-lined streets, spacious, prosperous squares and weighty, worthy public buildings.

But our purpose now is to lose ourselves in time; to move back to the days when the blast furnaces and shipyards and wealth and energy of Barrow lay centuries ahead and the might and power of the region was centred in the small, cup-shaped hollow of Bekangesgill. From here the abbots of Furness ruled with feudal powers; a virtual omnipotence.

The abbey lies just outside and to the north of Barrow and is reached via Dalton-in-Furness (which purists will explore *after* having visited the abbey, for reasons to be explained). The abbey church of St Mary stands surrounded by chapter house, frater, dormitories, quarters for monks, novices and lay brothers, book closets, monks' parlour, warming-room, latrines, infirmaries, offices, kitchens, butteries, abbot's lodging, cemetery, stables, guest house, school, great gates and exterior chapel.

At this point, dear reader, it is necessary to become strictly Wordsworthian. The approach to Furness Abbey *must* be made on foot, if the fullest impact is to be experienced of this altogether wonderful place. Your car, therefore, should be parked a quarter of a mile or so before you come to the abbey; partly to induce a sense of medieval pilgrimage, but chiefly because the humble pedestrian, approaching along the road, receives an overwhelming impression of strength and solemn grandeur as he rounds the bend and sees the great red-sandstone buildings glowing below him. The incredible beauty of the place unfolds itself before you as you walk down to it, as medieval men walked down; wondering and marvelling more and more with every step.

The old Furness railway goes slap bang through the place. But a miracle is attached to this. You think that you will find the abbey desecrated as a result. The strange thing is that once you have made a mental note of the railway buildings you do not notice them any more. It is as though the Holy Ghost has waved a wand and the railway has disappeared. Wordsworth wrote a sonnet about the railway and the abbey. It is worth quoting because it conveys so well the remarkable effect which Furness Abbey has upon everyone who visits it:

> Well have yon Railway Labourers to THIS ground
> Withdrawn for noontide rest. They sit, they walk
> Among the Ruins, but no idle talk
> Is heard; to grave demeanour all are bound;
> And from one voice a Hymn with tuneful sound
> Hallows once more the long-deserted Quire
> And thrills the old sepulchral earth, around.
> Others look up, and with fixed eyes admire
> That wide-spanned arch, wondering how it was raised,
> To keep, so high in air, its strength and grace:
> All seem to feel the spirit of the place,
> And by the general reverence God is praised:
> Profane Despoilers, stand ye not reproved,
> While thus these simple-hearted men are moved?[8]

At Furness Abbey one breaks a time barrier. The past has somehow survived not only in the tangibility of the actual ruins, but in an extraordinary quality of atmosphere; a sense of living past reaching to embrace our present selves. Somehow or other, in spite of Henry VIII and the passing of centuries, the Cistercians have never left Furness Abbey.

So, reader, down you foot-slog into Bekangesgill; feeling more and more of a medieval pilgrim every moment and finding yourself, with each step you take, increasingly and strangely fascinated by the buildings growing ever taller as you near them. Wordsworthian and poetical now in your purpose, medieval in spirit, you approach the outer gate of the abbey; a large and smaller arch, both reconstructed from old materials, a ghost gateway as it were. Here you pause for a moment, more than half surprised that you do not have to tug at a bell, or knock, for admittance. But the massive metal-studded oak doors have long since vanished, though you can see their hinge-sockets in the stone gateposts. No Cistercian lay brother appears, to enquire the purpose of your visit. Nobody comes at all. Yet you, at every moment, expect them.

Adjoining this outer gate stands the gatehouse chapel; the *capella extra portas*, built in the thirteenth century for the use of persons (including all females) not admissible to the abbey. This chapel is excellently preserved; the roof alone is missing. Inside may still be seen the altar steps, three sedilia (seats for the priests) and the piscina (basin, provided with a drain, for washing the sacred vessels).

South of the outer gate and the *capella extra portas* are the foundations of the great twelfth-century gatehouse itself; destroyed, following the Dissolution, to provide secular building material. The foundations indicate the impressive size of this gatehouse, which was designed with defensive purposes in mind, with tunnel-vaulted entry passage and porters' lodges which could also have been manned by guards.

Behind the *capella extra portas* lie the remains of a guest house (where, as a pilgrim, you would have stayed) and behind, south of this again, the stables, where you would have taken your horse or mule, were you of the station of life to travel mounted. Foundations of a probable school have also been traced in this complex of outer buildings (which are reached only by entering the main enclosure, past the custodian's hut). Notice, on the threshold of the guest house, a recently uncovered "board" for the game of Nine Men's Morris; this is thought to date to the thirteenth century.

Now to the abbey church. This is magnificent, even in decrepitude. In sheer dimensions alone it still catches the breath: a total length of 290 feet (eleven feet longer than Holme Cultram); the width of the nave, with aisles, 70 feet; the transept, 130 feet, the chancel 25 feet. The lack of roof together with the now paneless and untraceried windows imparts a sense of soaring unity with the sky, as if Heaven and abbey church were in direct contact.

The plan of the church is unusual; inasmuch as the original intention to build a crossing tower was abandoned in favour of a mighty west tower, partly set into the west bay of the nave. The massive buttresses of the exterior walls of this tower are relieved in their almost military severity by niches in which originally stood sacred images. We must visualize these watchful saints gazing down at us as we pass underneath in a spirit of contrition and modest hope, to enter the church by the main, late-Norman portal in the north transept.

From the north transept we turn right into the north aisle of the nave and look towards the west tower. This rejoiced in a huge window, its great arch echoed by a passionately lofty arch to the nave; as though a succession of shouts of allelujah were offered up in stone, transformed by builders' genius into an expression of worship.

The nave was originally ten bays long and must have been sublime in the truest sense of that word. In the thirteenth century it was divided by a stone screen (the beauty of which we may only guess at) erected after the seventh (now sixth) bay from the west. Floor-marks of this screen are still discoverable. The choir stalls have gone, but joyously are not lost; you will find them in the church of St Mary, Lancaster. They are early fourteenth century and among the most famous in Europe, having canopies of a most fantastically intricate and luxuriant beauty; tall, pointed gables, exquisitely delicate traceries, the arms of the seats embellished with ornate carved heads. The misericords are, in contrast, almost plain. These choir stalls, though no longer within their true context, should not be missed for they convey, better than almost any other surviving feature, the splendour of Furness at its zenith; a splendour which, in itself, indicated the extent, too, of the departure of the Cistercians from the early Cistercian ideals of stark and utter simplicity in all things.

The chancel, like all Cistercian chancels, is straight-ended, with north and south transepts each of which had an east aisle divided into three small chapels. The north transept retains these three chapels. The overwhelming feature of this transept must have been the great 30-foot high window above the main portal.

Note that not only the vault of the east aisle of this transept is still discernible, but that the gallery above it has survived too (the only part of the church gallery remaining). The south transept differs from the north in that the north bay, or chapel, of the east aisle was converted into part of the sacristry. In the south wall of this south transept the night-stair to the monks' dormitory is clearly recognizable.

The east window of the chancel was nearly 50 feet in height and, again, must have been magnificent (outside this window, you will discover two heads, thought to represent Stephen, the founder of the abbey, and Maud, his wife). The greatest surviving glory of the chancel is the splendid group of four (Perpendicular) sedilia together with piscina and aumbries (recesses in which the sacred vessels were stored). All these stand flanked together, under tall, intricately carved and decorated canopies; "one of the best *ensembles* of sedilia and piscina anywhere in England", says Pevsner.

The monastic quarters are reached by an arched doorway connecting the south transept with the south aisle of the nave; a sharp left turn through another round doorway leads into the cloister. However, before leaving the church, do not overlook the round-headed upper doorway set aloft in the west end of the wall of the south aisle of the nave; this stood at the top of the now vanished night-stairway that led into the lay brothers' dormitory in the upper storey of the west range of the cloister (the monks' dormitory was, of course, in the upper storey of the eastern range).

Upon entering the cloister your attention will at once be caught by five marvellous early thirteenth-century round-headed arched openings; the first and third of which are deep tunnel-vaulted library rooms. Between them is the entrance to the chapter house; a most lovely building. The rib-vaulted roof has long since fallen in, but the arcading and windows remain excellently preserved and the design of the interior still survives as an integral whole. All this is finest Early English.

Following this divine beauty we become immersed for a while in domestic details. Next to the second library room is the archway to the walled-off north bay of the monks' dormitory undercroft; this walled-off bay was their parlour. The next archway led to the slype and the fifth, and final, archway leads into the dormitory undercroft, 200 feet long and originally of fourteen bays, and projecting by seven bays beyond the south range of cloister buildings. East of this east dormitory range were other rooms and here, too, we find the stream which was so instrumental in choice of this valley as site for a monastery. Above and over the stream is the late twelfth-century reredorter, or lavatories. Further east, built into rock, is the abbot's lodging; smallish, but lavishly equipped with a handsome hall and a most noble fireplace. This lodging (thought to have originated as a mid-thirteenth-century infirmary and to have been converted into the abbott's lodging later) is served by a branch of the main stream and has a private sluice of its own.

The south range of the cloister garth consisted of a warming-house, west of and adjoining the monks' dormitory undercroft. Next to the warming-house was the frater, or refectory, built at right angles to the cloister walk. The west range consisted of the lay brothers' dormitory, with its ground floor divided into parlours and entrance passage. West of this range are the lay brothers' lavatories; again above a stream, which then runs south-east under the thirteenth-century infirmaries. The foundations only are traceable of the lay brothers' infirmary, but the main infirmary buildings are fascinating. At the west end of this main infirmary building were the lavatories; then came a large hall with a chapel at the eastern end, together with a buttery connected by a passage with the octagonal infirmary kitchen.

In the infirmary chapel you will encounter two recumbent knights, carved in Caen stone with such immense artistry that they almost convince the onlooker that here are two dead warriors, carried into this chapel from the battlefield and laid, not irreverently, on simple makeshift biers upon the floor. They are in armour; their square helmets being of a very early kind. Their shields have been placed over their bodies and their mantles wrapped about them; their legs have been carefully crossed. They date probably to the twelfth century and are the only effigies of this early Norman date in England. They are unique, also, in the total realism with which they have been handled by the artist who carved them: these are not stone effigies of dead knights, but dead knights transposed into stone.

Two other, later, knights and a poker-rigid deacon clasping a book come as an anti-climax after this pair of masterpieces. There is, however, a delightfully gracious and totally unexpected early fourteenth century, unidentified, lady, whose presence in this strictly masculine preserve comes as a distinct shock.

A winding, bosky path along the little cliff above the abbot's lodging leads to an official view-point from where the abbey is seen spread out in clear perspective: but this is rather too objective a way in which to survey so emotive a place and the view-point should therefore be abandoned for a contemplative stroll in the little cemetery; a gentle plot of ground.

Beyond the abbey precincts proper lies the monastery demesne; a large walled area formerly enclosing home-farm and pastures, kitchen gardens, rickyards, granaries, wood stores, orchards, apiaries, fish ponds, and all other appurtenances of flourishing husbandry. Mills were built along the stream. A fine example of a very early stone pack-bridge, parapetless and primitive, still spans the mill stream. You may wander here for as much time as you have at your disposal. Greater tranquillity than this it is impossible to imagine.

Leave time on your journey back to stop at Dalton. Abbot Roger Pile accepted the living here following the dissolution of his abbey.

This most attractive little market town has a bustling market place and a castle which originated as a fourteenth-century pele-tower. The painter, Romney, was born here and a monument to him stands in the churchyard of the parish church of St Mary, which perches on a knoll behind the castle (another probable example of a church built upon an ancient, pre-Christian sacred site). The church that Roger Pile knew has gone; instead we have the 1882–5 building of Paley & Austin; one of their finest, with bold external friezing of red and white chequer that arrests the attention without jarring the sensibilities. The fifteenth-century fragments of stained glass in the north porch are said to have come from Furness Abbey.

20

ENVOI

Swarthmoor—The Sands—Cartmel—Greylags and Canada Geese

THE LAKE COUNTIES, as we have seen, were among the most loyal to the old faith. The post-Reformation period found the people here either adhering doggedly to the Roman church, or, uneasily, adjusting to a kind of twilit territory of God. This uneasy Protestantism made Cumbria, and particularly south Westmorland and Furness, ripe for conversion by the Quakers.

Swarthmoor, just over a mile north-east of Dalton, is an important place within the context of the Society of Friends. The Friends' Meeting House here dates to 1688. It has strong associations with nearby Swarthmoor Hall; for many years the centre of the Quaker movement in the north-west. Indeed, between 1652 and 1654 Swarthmoor Hall was the base from which George Fox conducted his activities. Swarthmoor Hall was the home of Puritan Thomas Fell and Fox first visited there as a guest in 1652. He soon gained Fell's support for the Society of Friends and the Great Hall at Swarthmoor became the Sunday meeting place for Friends in that region, until the Meeting House was built.

Within the sympathetic environment of Swarthmoor, Fox accomplished most of his important thinking and writing. In 1954 Swarthmoor Hall was acquired by the Society of Friends and it has now been opened to the public.

But we are now moving into Cartmel, and in Cartmel it is difficult to remain post-Reformation in mood for long. We are now in that land which King Ecgfrith of Northumbria gave to St Cuthbert, Bishop of Lindisfarne, together with "All the Britons in it".

Cartmel, from earliest days, was easily accessible; the historic route from Lancaster being by the Sands. The district of Cartmel extends as a small peninsula between the rivers Leven and Kent; each river having a broad estuary which may be crossed at low tide. These sandy estuaries were always famed for their treachery; throughout history travellers who attempted to cross without guides, or who made the crossing under unsuitable conditions, lost their lives when caught by the rapid Solway tides. It might be wondered why such hazardous routes were preferred to a safe inland alternative, but in the days before motorized travel the time saved by crossing the Sands greatly outweighed the risks.

The Augustinian establishment of Cartmel Priory was responsible for providing a guide across Lancaster Sands, from the Lancaster side of the then-named Ean, or River of the Sands, to Cartmel. This guide, mounted on horseback, was officially known as the Carter. The priory received a Crown grant for provision of the Carter; the fee paid was £16 a year. Following the Dissolution the office of provision of guides across the Sands passed to the Duchy of Lancaster.

Conishead Priory received a similar grant, in pre-Reformation times, for providing guides across Cartmel Sands to Ulverston. Again, the Duchy of Lancaster provided these guides following the Dissolution.

"Crossing the Sands" was a popular route with early tourists to the Lake Country (and indeed remained a well used passage until the mid-nineteenth century). We find West assuring his readers that, "With the proper guides, crossing of the sands in summer is thought a journey of little more danger than any other". He added, encouragingly, "On a fine day there is not a more pleasant sea-ride in the kingdom".

Turner has left us two water-colours of crossing the sands. Both are painted with that relish for humorous comment that characterizes much of his less formal work. One painting shows us a coachload of travellers setting off across the sands on a truly awful day: rain and mist sweep over the estuary; visibility is down to a few yards merely. The coachman sits slightly sideways to the blast, his top hat tilted forward to meet the wind; resignation is in every line of his body as he cracks his whip and gee-ups the horses. Resigned too are the miserable outside passengers, sitting mutely bowed and huddled together. The horses, equally, are hating every minute of it; yet the journey has only just begun! Oh, the agony of being unable to afford a seat *inside* the coach, or perhaps having applied too late for a place! But the mist and flying rain are already swallowing the coach from view; away it splashes and trundles, into a blotted horizon of saturating wet. Why did we ever think of coming to the Lake Country?[1]

The second painting shows a party of travellers straining every muscle to beat the incoming tide. They are almost at their journey's end; relief is mingled with desperate shortness of breath. The poor horses are tugging at the well-laden coach, and a party of foot people stagger along beside the coach, almost on their knees with breathlessness. Among them is an enormously fat mother, clasping to her heaving bosom personal gear of all kinds (including a babby) while to her skirts cling a troop of little children. Their eyes bulge, their tongues are literally hanging out: Mother, poor soul, is almost done for. They are going to be safe, but it will be many a long day before this particular party will forget crossing the Sands![2]

Of Cartmel Priory, founded in 1188 by William Mareschal, Earl of Pembroke, for Augustinian canons, nothing remains today except the gatehouse, and the priory church. This latter survived because it was spared, at the pleas of the local population, as parish church at the time of the Dissolution.

The church fabric suffered much in the late sixteenth century when the roof of the nave collapsed because the parishioners were too poor to maintain the building. For 80 years this part of the church was open to the skies (look, and you will notice the weathered appearance of the pews which stood so long exposed). During this period the south aisle of the choir was used as the parish church. The roof was at last repaired and the building generally restored by George Preston of Holker Hall, in 1618–23.

Externally this is a somewhat exceptional building inasmuch as the top storey of the central tower is set diagonally, which results in the church presenting to the eye a most interesting conflict of shapes: planes and angles, turrets and buttresses, arches and parapets seemingly at cross purposes and yet resolving into harmony.

Of the late twelfth-century fabric the magnificent south doorway is undoubtedly the most dramatic survival, together with the splendid arcades of the main choir. The beautiful south chapel is fourteenth century, including some of the glass. It was built by the first Lord Harrington, who died in 1347 and who lies here in the famous Harrington tomb; one of the finest of its date in England. The tomb, when opened during the last century, was found to contain the remains of a man and a bird; very possibly his lordship's favourite falcon.

The monument has at some time been moved from its original position; it seems clearly to have been designed to be viewed in the round, rather than in its present decidedly cramped quarter.

The recumbent effigies of the deceased lie under a handsome and ornate

Gothic canopy, decidedly reminiscent of a four-poster bed. This canopy has graceful ogee arches and a wooden painted fourteenth-century ceiling (the painting probably pre-dating the tomb itself). The effigies, offering up their hearts between clasped hands, are surrounded by small, mourning figures; too much out of scale to be anything but symbols of grief, yet too sincerely and profoundly grief-stricken in their attitudes to be dismissed as mere formal figments of funeral ornamentation. They are genuinely emotive. So too are the similarly tiny, yet immensely touching bedesmen squatting in groups below the broad and formally ornate main frieze; these little figures, huddled over heavy, opened books, reading or reciting prayers for the departed, seem to embody the very essence of the spirit of medievalism.

The carving of the misericords of the fifteenth-century choir stalls is also fine. The handsome west screen and the stall backs were given by George Preston when he restored the church.

Finally, there is the marvellous east window. During the Parliamentary Wars the fifteenth-century glass was removed from here in an effort to save it from the Cromwellian troops who arrived in 1643, but too late to damage the glass. Some of it has been replaced in this window; some of it we have already seen at St Martin's, Bowness. More of it remains to be marvelled at in Cartmel Fell church.

The fourteenth-century priory gatehouse stands east of the priory, in today's Cavendish Street. From 1247 to 1790 the upper storey was used as a school; subsequently it became a court room. The little town, indeed, is beautiful in its entirety.

Cartmel Fell lies some three miles eastward of Cartmel itself. Here stands the church of St Anthony. The present building dates to 1505; it stands on the site of a much earlier chapel. Of this original building there has survived a thirteenth-century wooden figure of Christ, traditionally said to be preserved from the rood-beam. It is one of the only two known pre-Reformation crucifixion figures surviving in England.

In the east window you will find the stained glass that was rescued from the priory church to foil the Cromwellians. The Seven Sacraments depicted herein are thought to be copied from the Roger van der Weyden triptych at Antwerp. But the figure of Christ in the Garden is probably thirteenth century and, like the carved figure, comes from the early chapel. To the left of the window stands St Anthony; to whom this church is dedicated. He is the patron saint of basket makers, charcoal burners, swineherds and hermits. The church has several interesting pews, dating from the early sixteenth and seventeenth centuries; the fine three-decker pulpit is of 1698.

From Cartmel Fell we travel through the tranquil green countryside of Winster; a countryside of orchards and time-honoured family homesteads, among them Witherslack Hall, the seat of the Harringtons. They forfeited it in 1485 following the defeat of Richard III (to whom they had been loyal) at the Battle of Bosworth. The Hall's next owner, Sir Thomas Broughton, was unwise enough to back Lambert Simnel's rebellion in 1486; for this he, in turn, was forced to forfeit the Hall. He hid for safety in a cave in Witherslack Woods and here he continued to live for several years, his faithful former tenants supplying him with necessities. When at last he died they buried him in the woods and the site of his unmarked grave was pointed out by members of one generation to the next for over 300 years, until memories at last grew vague and finally faded altogether; Sir Thomas Broughton's grave in Witherslack Woods is now lost. "Time brings to forgetfulness many memorable things in this world, be they ever so carefully preserved."

So, our last evening in Cumbria has arrived; we stand by the estuary Sands and stare across Morecambe Bay. It is time to say good-bye (even if with strong hopes of returning) to this wonderful country, so infinitely more than a mere county, where past and present can never for an instant be isolated one from the other. Today's Cumbria, historically an industrial region, moves eagerly forward to embrace the industries of the future, while its most vital industry of all, tourism, continues to explode almost too fast to be controlled. Yet in the midst of all this forward movement the traditional loyalty to old truths and ancient ways of life still persists and all the time a battle is going on to preserve the centre of the region, the Lake Country, as little changed as is humanly possible; not because, as some folk claim, the desire is to have the place as a kind of museum, but because it is a core of a unique beauty, which it would be as great a sin to destroy as to slash the Mona Lisa, or knock down the Parthenon. And, looking at it pragmatically, in any case is this not the goose that lays the golden eggs?

Thinking thus, not altogether idly, as we loiter by the Sands in the last of the sunset light, with everything about us utterly still and quiet, we suddenly hear a strangely wild and distant sound which grows louder every moment; the honking of an echelon of greylag geese, heading over the estuary, flying with rapid wing strokes high above us, a sight which lifts the heart: a sight that would have rejoiced Wordsworth, yet was one he never saw on an evening in summer, such as this. For in his day the geese did not live in Cumbria as full-time residents; they came here only in the winter.

Once upon a time (until some 200 years ago, in fact) the greylag goose, the great grey goose of nursery rhyme and folk legend from whose pinions were made the flights for the arrows of Agincourt and the quills which wrote *Magna Carta* and *The Canterbury Tales*, lived in Cumbria all the year round as proper Cumbrians live; the only wild goose resident in England. Annually these birds were caught, wing-tipped and herded to market, being first shod by driving them through pitch or mud, which caked hard on their feet. They were sold for eating, or keeping as barn-yard fowls; their feathers were arrowed or quilled as aforesaid, their down filled lavish beds. They were wild geese which laid golden eggs, but at length they abandoned nesting in a country which exploited them so wantonly; they bred henceforth only in the remotenesses of Scotland, Scandinavia, the Faroes, Iceland.

Nevertheless, though they no longer bred in the Lake Country, the greylag still came annually in winter in their thousands to the marshes of the Morecambe area, the Duddon estuary and especially to Rockcliffe Marsh in the upper Solway. Here, after a journey of some 30 hours upon the wing, the birds would establish themselves for wintering; feeding by day on the estuary pastures and marshland sea-washed turf and roosting by night in the shelter of the dunes.

Other geese, too, wintered in the marshes; the beautiful black and white barnacles, the little brents, bean geese, white-fronted geese and the ubiquitous pink-feet. Over the inter-war decades, however, significant changes took place in the region's goose populations and their movements. The brent goose, whose numbers have dwindled alarmingly since the last century, developed a preference for the Scottish shores of the Solway Firth; it is believed because of the decline of its staple food plant, *zostera*, on the English side. The numbers of bean geese coming to England dwindled too, though the bird does well in Scotland. The bulk of the world's population of pink-feet winter in Britain and a steadily increasing proportion of these birds, over a long period, have shown a preference for Rockcliffe Marsh. As a result of this invasion by pink-feet, the Solway greylags, and to a lesser extent the barnacles, retreated to the Duddon estuary and the Morecambe marshes.

During World War Two the RAF used the Duddon estuary as a bombing range and understandably the geese disliked this and left the area. During the immediate post-war years the estuary was overshot by trigger-happy individuals who, in this region, are called marsh cowboys. These destroyed stretches of the marsh edge to make hides and, using rifles, shot at every bird on the marsh.

In 1952 the South Cumberland Wildfowlers' Association was formed; a supporting organization of WAGBI (the Wildfowlers' Association of Great Britain and Ireland). The South Cumberland Wildfowlers obtained full shooting rights for the Duddon marshes. The marsh cowboys went into retreat. But the damage to the greylag population had been done; whereas, before 1939, there would be a wintering flock of several hundred greylag in the Duddon area (including in-coming and out-going variations in numbers sometimes meaning that there would be as many as 2,000 geese in the marsh) by 1958 only a few odd birds were noticed annually.

The wildfowling associations decided to make part of the marsh a reserve with a total ban on shooting. The South Cumberland Wildfowlers, in close conjunction with WAGBI, formed a team to conduct a pilot scheme to re-establish the greylag in the Lake Country.

The next essential was a centre from which the pilot scheme might be run and to this end a small marshland reserve in the Duddon estuary was rented. This reserve (not open to the public) was not a reserve in the sense, say, of the Wildfowl Trust reserve at Slimbridge, Gloucestershire; the Duddon reserve might in fact better be termed an out-door workshop, a launching-place for an experimental scheme covering a very wide surrounding area.

A permit was obtained from the Nature Conservancy to bring greylag goslings down to this Duddon reserve from a loch in Scotland where wild greylag bred. Twenty-six goslings were caught and brought down to Cumbria, where eighteen were allocated for the Duddon reserve, while the rest were divided between Derwent Water and the Kendal area. These goslings were not pinioned (the scheme was to introduce *wild* geese) and greylags being homeloving creatures the goslings, when once they became adult, all flew back to Scotland! The WAGBI team, the following season, returned to the loch and attempted to catch more goslings, but the old geese on the loch obviously remembered the events of the previous year and, upon this second occasion, goslings, thanks to the wariness of the parent birds, proved virtually impossible to catch.

Peter Scott now came forward with an offer of wild geese from Slimbridge, but this was not accepted because wild geese will not breed for sixteen or seventeen years after being captured and wing-tipped and the WAGBI people did not feel that they could afford to wait that long for results. Experiments were now tried with goose eggs, rather than goslings; but the eggs would not travel, because the yolks were too heavy to stand vibration. At last partly incubated eggs were brought down from Scotland (the Nature Conservancy having provided licences) and these, in the season of 1962, were hatched and reared at the Duddon reserve by broodies; mainly jungle-fowl with a few domestic-type hens.

When the goslings had grown their wing feathers they were released at certain selected sites throughout the Lake Country and, because goslings attach themselves to the place where they are hatched, these young greylags at summer's end returned not to Scotland but to the Duddon reserve. There they wintered, feeding at the reserve by day, sleeping out on the marsh by night. In spring they returned to the places to which they had been introduced upon their initial release.

A greylag, in theory, matures in three seasons, but in fact second season birds have been known to rear young. In their first year the birds frequently pair and select a nesting site but do not produce a family; a species of trial run, as it were. The following season they usually return to the site and produce a brood.

The earliest results of the Duddon scheme were seen on Coniston Water, where, in their second season, the first pair of greylags to nest in England for 200 years produced eggs; which were at once stolen by a local bird-nester. The next season the same pair of geese again nested on the same site and this time were successful in rearing a brood unmolested. The parent geese brought the goslings back to the Duddon reserve to winter and in the spring the young birds followed their parents back to Coniston. A full cycle had been established. From thenceforth the scheme prospered; greylags spreading to the lakes and tarns throughout the region and breeding thereon.

Today the resident greylags are a common sight in the Lake Country and few visitors appreciate that the birds have not always nested and raised families here, without a long break in their story. Canada geese, too, are becoming prolific; these are not an indigenous species, but off-comes have have always been drawn to Cumbria. One of them, dear reader, has written this book.

NOTES

BIBLIOGRAPHY

INDEX

NOTES

Introduction Roll the Great Wheel

1. Henry Vaughan (1622–1695), a Welsh poet.
2. Wordsworth, William, *Guide to the Lakes.* Wordsworth's *Guide to the Lakes* first appeared in 1810 as an anonymous introduction to a folio volume, *Select Views in Cumberland, Westmorland, and Lancashire*, by the Rev. Joseph Wilkinson (pub. R. Ackermann, London). Ten years later Wordsworth's text was published separately (by Longman and associates) as *A Topographical Description of the Country of the Lakes*, annexed to the Duddon Sonnets and other poems by the poet. Two years later, in 1822, this topographical essay appeared independently (from the same publishers) as *A Description of the Scenery of the Lakes in the North of England* and a further edition followed in 1823 (this time published by Spottiswoode). In 1835 appeared Wordsworth's final text: *A Guide Through the District of the Lakes in the North of England*, published by Hudson and Nicholson in Kendal, and by Longman & Co., Moxon, and Whittaker & Co., in London. Since then the book has been re-published on several occasions; notably in 1842, with additional matter incorporated, as a *Guide to the Lakes*, issued by Hudson and Nicholson of Kendal. This Guide reached a sixth edition in 1864. It has also found its place in at least three collected prose works of Wordsworth; the most recent being the three volume collection edited by W. J. B. Owen and Jane Worthington Smyser (Clarendon Press, Oxford, 1974).

   1906 saw De Selincourt's famous edition of the *Guide*; an exact reprint of the 1835 edition, with added appendices. This reprint was reprinted in 1930 and in 1970, when four additional illustrations and an index were added. The 1970 edition was reprinted in 1973.
3. Wordsworth, William, "To The Clouds".
4. Wordsworth, William, "There is an Eminence . . ." *Poems on the Naming of Places, III.*
5. Wordsworth, William, *Unpublished Tour of the Lakes*, Clarendon Press, Oxford, 1974.
6. *ibid.* Early version, in WW's hand, of a footnote, p. 341.
7. *Guide to the Lakes.*
8. *ibid.*
9. Wordsworth, William, "Resolution and Independence". (*The Leech Gatherer.*)

1 An Axe Age

1. Pevsner, Nikolaus, *The Buildings of England: Cumberland and Westmorland*, Penguin, Harmondsworth, 1967.
2. West, Thomas, SJ, *A Guide to the Lakes*, Pennington, Kendal, 1778.

3 *A Wind Age, a Wolf Age*

1. *Rune-song of Odin.*
2. The manuscript written by St Asaph subsequently became lost, but certain portions of it had been copied out and these were included in the life of St Kentigern by the scholar Joscelin of Furness, in or about 1180.
3. The island where "Herebert, Priest and Confessor" went into retreat in the latter half of the seventh century is today thickly wooded. Among the trees are some half-obscured ruins; not of the saint's original cell, all traces of which vanished long since, but of an early nineteenth-century "Gothic cell", built to gratify the imagination of Romantics. Mrs Lynn Linton tells us that "everyone lands . . . [there], and wanders through the close-grown paths to the summerhouse, where picnic parties, needing a roof over their heads, spread their table-cloths and bring out their veal pies and cold chickens". Eliza Lynn Linton: *The Lake Country*, London, 1864.
4. This pilgrimage has its delightful echoes in Beatrix Potter's *The Tale of Squirrel Nutkin.*
5. The major kingdoms of Anglo-Saxon England were Northumbria; Mercia (the present day Midlands); Lindsey (today's Lincolnshire and East Anglia); Essex, Kent, Middlesex, Sussex and Wessex.
6. This chalice was found in 1104 when St Cuthbert's tomb at Durham Cathedral was opened: one of several openings during the Middle Ages. The chalice has since disappeared; possibly stolen when the saint's shrine was pillaged at the time of the Reformation.
7. At Brigham, near Cockermouth, there is at the church of St Bridget another cross-socket, on which may be discerned what appears to be the carving of a huge entwined monster. The Midgardsworm, coiled round the base of the World Axis?
8. *The Sculptured Cross at Gosforth, West Cumberland.* Rev. W. S. Calverley, Vicar of Dearham; C. A. Parker, with engravings by Prof. Magnus Petersen of Copenhagen (CWAAS Trans. O.S.; VI, xxxviii).
9. At the bottom of the churchyard, in the right hand corner as you walk down from the church (almost in a line with the Cross) is a splendid cork-tree, protected by an iron-railing.

4 *An Essay in Essence*

1. Baddeley, M. J. B., *The Lake District*, Ward, Lock & Co. Ltd, London. Wainwright, A., *A Pictorial Guide to the Lakeland Fells* (7 vols), Westmorland Gazette, Kendal. Symonds, W. H., *Walking in the Lake District*, Chambers.
2. The five famous packs of fox hounds (all hunted on foot) in the central Lake Country are the Blencathra, the Coniston, the Eskdale and Ennerdale, the Melbreak, and the Ullswater.
3. *Cumberland Heritage*, Gollancz, London, 1970.
4. I am indebted to Dr Frances Taylor for this reminiscence. If any readers have further information about gheist-doors, or similar traditional Cumbrian beliefs, I shall be most grateful to hear from them, care of my publisher.
5. Coleridge, Samuel Taylor, "The Destiny of Nations".
6. William Nicolson, Bishop of Carlisle 1702–1718; a dedicated antiquary.

5 *Norman Landscape*

1. Traditional Border ballad. Corbies=crows. Hause bane=collar-bone.
2. Bolton is five miles north-west of Appleby. This carved relief is a rarity; only three or four such contemporary scenes of battling knights are known in the entire country.
3. William Camden (1551–1623), a renowned historian and antiquary, who travelled through the region in 1582, researching material for his major work, *Britannia*. Quoted here, 1610 ed., trans. P. Holland.
4. The church of St Mary at Kirkby Lonsdale is famous for its magnificent Early Norman arcades.
5. In England, Gothic architecture is divided into three periods; Early English, Decorated and Perpendicular. In the last quarter of the twelfth century, partly through Cistercian and partly through French influence (viz. the early Gothic parts of Canterbury cathedral) pointed arches and other ideas of the so-called Gothic style became more and more frequently used, so that by the close of that century the transitional period was virtually over and the architecture of England had become Gothic throughout. It is this earliest, late twelfth-century Gothic which, in England, is known as Early English. Decorated usually covers the first three-quarters of the fourteenth century. Perpendicular is late English Gothic. It first appeared in Gloucester cathedral about 1360; the style thereafter spread rapidly, persisting until well into the seventeenth century.
6. See note 5 (above). The simple, practical building style of the Cistercians was developed using somewhat rudimentary heavy vaulting with pointed arches, which has since become known as "half Gothic". This special type of building design was favoured by St Bernard and thus became obligatory for Cistercians. The Order was more than reluctant to accept full Gothic style, however; its richness of detail was antipathetic to Cistercian ascetism. None the less, as we shall discover when we visit Furness, such detail did creep into Cistercian abbeys.
7. Holme Cultram Festival of the Arts: enquiries and reservations: Festival Office, Abbey Town, Carlisle, Cumbria. Tel. Abbey Town 654. Enquiries about Arts Centre to Information Centre, Abbey Town.

   Holme Cultram Abbey may of course be visited daily, throughout the year. There is an Information Centre by the Abbey, and a gift shop. For times of church services, apply Information Centre.

6 *Carlisle*

1. *Cumberland Heritage*, Gollancz, London, 1970.

7 *Armstrong's Last Goodnight*

1. This river Esk should not be confused with that of the same name in south-west Cumberland.
2. Armstrong, W. A., *The Armstrong Border*, McQueen & Son Ltd., Galashiels, 1960.
3. *ibid.*

4. Maxwell, *History of Dumfries and Galloway.*
5. *ibid.*
6. Newbattle MS.
7. A person whose cattle had been stolen might cross the Border in their pursuit, without hindrance, up to six days after the theft, in an attempt to recover his property; but he had to carry a burning peat at his lance-tip as intimation of his purpose of mission and his right of travel. Any owner of any goods stolen and carried over the Border might claim them back, but he had to be able to identify them and to be prepared to assert his right by combat on the March itself; either combat in person or by representative. No man might be impeached except on the March.
8. Gilnockie's "keep" was Hollows Tower on the west bank of the Esk about three miles south of Langholm on the road to Canonbie. Scott published the famous ballad, "Johnie Armstrang" (describing Gilnockie's murder) in his *Minstrelsy of the Scottish Border.* 2 vols, Kelso, 1802.
9. "Monument of Mrs Howard (by Nollekens) in Wetheral Church, near Corby, on the Banks of the Eden", and, "Suggested by the foregoing". (*Poems composed or suggested during a Tour, in the Summer of 1833.*)
10. Sir Walter Scott, *op. cit.*

8 Eastern Approaches

1. The other beacon stations in Cumbria were Black Combe, Bootle, Muncaster Fell, St Bees Head, Workington Hill, Moothay, Skiddaw, Sandal Top, Carlisle Castle, Lingy Close Head, Dale Raughton, Brampton Mote, Spade Adam Top, Stanemoor Top, Orton Scar, Farleton Knott, Whinfell, and Hard Knott.

9 A Traditional Gateway

1. The Rev. Thomas Machell, chaplain to Charles II and an antiquarian.

10 Many Exquisite Feelings

1. *Prose Works*, II.
2. West, *Guide to the Lakes.*

11 Ullswater

1. Linton, Lynn E., *The Lake Country.*
2. *The British Switzerland: or Picturesque Rambles Amongst The Lake and Mountain Scenery of Westmorland, Cumberland, Durham and Northumberland.* From Drawings on the Spot by Thomas Allom. With Descriptions by Thomas Rose. Fisher, Son, & Co., Caxton Press, London, 1847.

12 Keswick and the Old Men

1. Postlethwaite, John, *Mines and Mining in the English Lake District*, Whitehaven, 1877.
2. Rake: a narrow, slanting trod, or sheep walk; the Icelandic *rachan.*

13 *Keswick and the Hundredth Summer*

1. Gray's *Journal;* West's *Guide to the Lakes*, 1799 ed.
2. Lamb's *Letters* (ed. E. V. Lucas), Vol. I. 3 vols, London, 1935.
3. *Howk:* to dig out with a pick or spade (Cumb. dialect).
4. Hutchinson, W., *Excursion to the Lakes in Westmorland and Cumberland*, 1773.
5. Quotations from *The Letters of John Keats*, ed. Sidney Colvin, Macmillan, London, 1891.
6. "To Joanna" (*Poems on the Naming of Places*).
7. Forster, J., *The Life of Charles Dickens*, Chapman & Hall Ltd., and Humphrey Milford, London.
8. Wordsworth, William, "Song at the Feast of Brougham Castle".
9. 1975 saw the centenary of Keswick Convention. In July a Convention Tent was hoisted for the hundredth time and Keswick resounded with a crescendo of evangelical rejoicing. As climax to the celebrations, Dr Billy Graham preached at Crow Park to 20,000 people.

14 *The Buttermere Round*

1. The traditional local name. Modern maps call it Burtness.
2. Today the Bridge Hotel.
3. "Storm".
4. Not named after Rigg's Coaches! A *rigg* is a bridge, either man made or a natural causeway.
5. "The first thing I remember, as an event in life, was being taken by my nurse to the brow of Friar's Crag on Derwentwater; the intense joy, mingled with awe, that I had in looking through the mossy roots, over the crag, into the dark lake, has associated itself more or less with all twining roots of trees ever since." *Modern Painters*, iv, xvii, 13.

15 *Central Massif*

1. Coleridge, Samuel Taylor, *Collected Letters* (CL), ed. Griggs, Clarendon Press, Oxford. Quotation from CL 453.
2. It can be spelled either Wastdale (silent t) or Wasdale; the latter is the more usual nowadays. The lake is *always* Wastwater, pronounced Wostwater (local, Wust-wutter).
3. CL 448.
4. CL 450.
5. Grasmere *Journal*: 16 May 1800.
6. CL 453.
7. *ibid.*
8. *ibid.*
9. *ibid.*
10. *ibid.*
11. *ibid.*

12. *ibid.*
13. Abraham, George D. *The Complete Mountaineer*, Methuen, London, 1907.
14. *ibid.*
15. *ibid.*
16. *ibid.*
17. *ibid.*
18. Wainwright, A., *Pictorial Guide* (4).
19. *ibid.*
20. CL 453.
21. *ibid.*
22. CL 452.

16 *"All which We then Were"*

1. *The Recluse.*
2. *Guide to the Lakes.*
3. "A Farewell".
4. *Evening Voluntaries*, viii.
5. Notebooks, 798. 5½.42.
6. Notebooks 1782 16.168.
7. *Guide to the Lakes.*
8. *ibid.*

17 *The Rydalian Laurels*

1. Wordsworth, William, *Poems: Tour of 1833.*
2. Hutchinson, Sara, *Collected Letters* 19 November 1812.
3. *ibid.*, 23 June 1813.
4. *Wordsworth Letters: The Middle Years.*
5. Black's *Romantic Guide.*
6. *The British Switzerland.*
7. *ibid.*
8. Grasmere *Journal*, 8 June 1802.
9. Lockart, J. G., *Life of Scott*, 7 vols.
10. "Sonnet on the Projected Kendal and Windermere Railway" (1844).
11. Martineau, Harriet, *The English Lakes*, Simpkin, Marshall, & Co., London, 1858.
12. *The Tourist's New Guide, Containing a Description of the Lakes, Mountains, and Scenery in Cumberland, Westmorland, and Lancashire*, 2 vols, Kendal, 1819. *Guide: Seventy-eight studies from Nature*, London and Ambleside, 1809. *A Description of Sixty Studies from Nature . . . Comprising a General Guide to the Beauties of the North of England*, London, 1810.
13. Black's *Romantic Guide.*
14. Hutchinson, Sara, *Collected Letters*, 19 July 1830.
15. Coleridge, Derwent, *Memoirs: Poems by Hartley Coleridge* (2nd ed.), Moxon, London, 1851.
16. *Letters of Hartley Coleridge*, ed. G. E. and E. L. Griggs, Oxford, 1936.
17. Du Maurier, Daphne, *The Infernal World of Branwell Brontë*, Gollancz, London, 1960.

18. Griggs, E. L., *Coleridge Fille: A Biography of Sara Coleridge*, Oxford, 1940.
19. Coleridge, Derwent, *op. cit.*

18 "All That Had Been Loved Before"

1. *Prelude*, IV, 12–13.
2. Martineau, Harriet, *The English Lakes.*
3. Budworth, Joseph (Palmer), *A Fortnight's ramble to the Lakes*, Hookham and Carpenter, 1792.
4. Otley, Jonathan, *Concise Description of the English Lakes, and adjacent Mountains*, Keswick, 1823.
5. Cowper, H. S., *Hawkshead*, London and Derby, 1899.
6. *Prelude*, V, 448–51.
7. Wordsworth, William, *Unpublished Tour.*
8. *Prelude*, I, 433–46.
9. *Wordsworth Letters: The Early Years.*
10. *Unpublished Tour.*
11. *Prelude*, II, 34–36.
12. *Unpublished Tour.*
13. *Prelude*, V, 400.
14. *ibid.*, IV, 30–3.
15. CL 299.

19 Coniston Country

1. Kitten, F. G., "William James Linton, Engraver, Poet, and Political Writer", *English Illus. Mag.*, April 1891.
2. Layard, George Somes, *Mrs Lynn Linton*, Methuen, London, 1901.
3. *ibid.*
4. *ibid.*
5. Benjamin, Frederick A., *The Ruskin Linen Industry of Keswick*, Michael Moon, Beckermet, 1974.
6. *ibid.*
7. *ibid.*
8. *Miscellaneous Sonnets*, XLVIII.

20 Envoi

1. *Lancaster Sands* (*c.* 1818), Birmingham City Museum and Art Gallery.
2. *Lancaster Sands—Lancashire* (c. 1826), B.M. (1910–2–12–279). Engraved R. Brandard, 1828, for *Picturesque Views in England and Wales*, Part V, No. 3.

BIBLIOGRAPHY

Abraham, George D., *The Complete Mountaineer*, Methuen, London, 1907.
Armitt, M. L., *Rydal*, Kendal, 1916.
Armstrong, William, *The Armstrong Borderland*, McQueen and Son, Galashiels, 1960.
Benjamin, Frederick A., *The Ruskin Linen Industry of Keswick*, Michael Moon, Beckermet, 1974.
Bruce, J. C., *Handbook to the Roman Wall*, revised I. A. Richmond 12 ed., Newcastle, 1967.
Calverley, Rev. W. S., *Notes on Early Sculptures*, ed. W. G. Collingwood, Kendal, 1899.
Camden, William, *Britannia*, 1610 ed., trans. P. Holland.
Coleridge, Derwent, *Memoir of the Life of Hartley Coleridge*, Moxon, London, 1851.
Coleridge, Samuel Taylor, *Collected Letters* (CL), ed. E. L. Griggs, 6 vols., Oxford: 1956–72.
—— *Notebooks* (NB), ed. K. Coburn, Routledge: 1957–62.
—— *Poetical Works*, ed. E. H. Coleridge, Oxford, 1904.
Collingwood, R. G., *Archaeology of Roman Britain*, revised I. A. Richmond, London, 1969.
Cowper, Henry Swainson, *Hawkshead*, London and Derby, 1899.
Cumberland and Westmorland Antiquarian and Archaeological Society's Transactions, Old Series (CW) and New Series (CW2).
Curwen, John F., *Kirkbie Kendall*, Kendal, 1900.
Du Maurier, Daphne, *The Infernal World of Branwell Brontë*, Gollancz, London, 1960.
Fell, Alfred, *The Early Iron Industry of Furness and District*, Ulverston, 1908.
Fell, Clare, *Early Settlement in the Lake Counties*, Dalesman Press, 1972.
Grainger, F. and Collingwood, W. G., *Register and Records of Holm Cultram*, Kendal, 1929.
Hughes, Edward, *North Country Life in the Eighteenth Century* (2), London, 1965.
Hutchinson, Sara, *Collected Letters*, ed. K. Coburn, Oxford, 1954.
Hutchinson, W., *History of the County of Cumberland and some Places Adjacent*, 2 vols, Carlisle, 1794.
Kitten, F. G., "William James Linton, Engraver, Poet, and Political Writer", *English Illustrated Magazine*, April 1891.
Layard, George Somes, *Mrs Lynn Linton*, Methuen, London, 1901.
Lees, Rev. Thomas, "St Kentigern and his Dedications in Cumberland", *CWAAS Transactions*, O.S., VI, xxxl.
Lynn Linton, E., *The Lake Country*, illus. W. J. Linton, Smith Elder & Co., London, 1864.
Moorman, Mary, *William Wordsworth, a Biography*, 2 vols, Oxford, 1957–65.
Nicholson, Norman, *The Lakers: The Adventures of the First Tourists*, Hale, London, 1955.
Nicolson, J. and Burn, R., *The History and Antiquities of Westmorland and Cumberland*, 2 vols, London, 1777.
Parker, C. A. and Collingwood, W. G., "A Reconsideration of Gosforth Cross", 1917, *CWAAS Trans.* N.S., XVI.

Parsons, W. and White, W., *History, Directory and Gazetteer of the Counties of Cumberland and Westmorland with that Part of the Lake District in Lancashire, etc.*, Leeds, 1829.
Pearsall, W. H. and Pennington, W., *The Lake District: A Landscape History*, Collins, London, 1973.
Pevsner, Nikolaus, *The Buildings of England: Cumberland and Westmorland*, Penguin, Harmondsworth, 1967.
Postlethwaite, John, *Mines and Mining in the English Lake District*, Whitehaven, 1877.
Rawnsley, Rev. H. D., *Five Addresses on the Lives and Work of St. Kentigern and St. Herbert*, Carlisle and London, 1888.
—— *Literary Associations of the English Lakes*, 2 vols, James MacLehose & Sons, Galashiels, 1894.
Richmond, I. A., *Roman Britain*, Penguin, Harmondsworth, 1955.
Salway, P., *The Frontier People of Roman Britain*, Cambridge, 1965.
Thompson, T. W., *Wordsworth's Hawkshead*, ed. R. Woof, Oxford, 1970.
Tough, D. L. W., *The Last Years of a Frontier*, Oxford, 1928.
West, T., *A Guide to the Lakes*, incl. the *Journal* of Thomas Gray, 1799 ed., London.
—— *The Antiquities of Furness*, London, 1774.
Williamson, G. C., *Lady Anne Clifford*, Wilson & Son, Kendal, 1922.
Wordsworth, Dorothy, *Journals*, ed. M. Moorman, Oxford, 1971.
Wordsworth, John, *Letters*, ed. C. H. Ketchum, Cornell, 1969.
Wordsworth, William and Dorothy, *Letters: Early Years*, 1787–1805, ed. de Selincourt, rev. C. L. Shaver. *Middle Years*, 1806–1811, ed. de Selincourt, rev. M. Moorman. *Later Years*, 1811–1820, ed. de Selincourt, Oxford, 1937–1970.
Wordsworth, William, *A Guide to the Lakes*, 5th ed. 1835, ed. de Selincourt, Oxford, 1970.
—— *Unpublished Tour of the Lakes: The Prose Works of William Wordsworth*, vol. 2., ed. W. J. B. Owen and J. W. Smyser, Clarendon Press, Oxford, 1974.
—— *Poetical Works*, ed. T. Hutchinson, rev. de Selincourt, Oxford, 1905.

INDEX